THE McGRAW-HILL
36-HOUR
ACCOUNTING
COURSE

Other Books in the McGraw-Hill 36-Hour Course Series

THE McGRAW-HILL 36-HOUR ACCOUNTING COURSE

Third Edition

ROBERT L. DIXON

Professor Emeritus of Accounting
School of Business Administration
University of Michigan

HAROLD E. ARNETT

Professor of Accounting
School of Business Administration
University of Michigan

McGraw-Hill, Inc.
New York   San Francisco   Washington, D.C.   Auckland
Bogotá   Caracas   Lisbon   London   Madrid   Mexico City
Milan   Montreal   New Delhi   San Juan   Singapore
Sydney   Tokyo   Toronto

Library of Congress Cataloging-in-Publication Data

Dixon, Robert L.
    The McGraw-Hill 36-hour accounting course / Robert L. Dixon,
Harold E. Arnett. — 3rd ed.
        p.   cm.
    Includes index.
    ISBN 0-07-017093-2 — ISBN 0-07-017094-0 (pbk.)
    1. Accounting.   I. Arnett, Harold E.   II. Title.   III. Title:
McGraw-Hill thirty-six hour accounting course.
HF5635.D63   1993
657—dc20   92-37850
                                                                   CIP

1 2 3 4 5 6 7 8 9 0   DOC/DOC   9 8 7 6 5 4 3 2

ISBN   0-07-017093-2   {HC}
ISBN   0-07-017094-0   {PBK}

*The sponsoring editor for this book was Caroline Carney, the editing supervisor
was Joseph Bertuna, and the production supervisor was Suzanne W. Babeuf. It
was set in Melior by ComCom.*

Printed and bound by R. R. Donnelley & Sons Company.

Contents

6 The Funds Statement—Working Capital Flows   82

7 The Funds Statement—Cash Flows   96

8 Inventories   110

9 Fixed Assets and Depreciation   126

10 Corporation Accounts   141

Preface

For Whom Is This Book?

This book is designed for the person who has had little or no formal training or experience in accounting, or who had only a course or two some time ago and has forgotten most of it, and whose current or possible future occupation calls for a breadth of understanding of the internal or financial affairs of a business enterprise. This definition would appear to fit the person who now carries executive responsibilities or who believes that an opportunity for promotion to executive levels would be enhanced by some familiarity with the inner workings and concepts of accounting. Another class of people who are prospective users of this book are members of the legal profession who have had scant training in accounting but who undertake to prepare tax returns or, particularly, become involved in litigation which is concerned with such matters as business profit determinations, rates of return, taxes, and financial damages. To those groups we must add several others: financial analysts, stockbrokers, engineers, and, in fact, all who do some investing and want a better understanding of financial statements.

What Does It Offer?

The big problems in gaining an understanding of accounting are, first, getting over the threshold with minimum pain; second, choosing, with a certain amount of discrimination and sophistication, specific areas of the field for study; and, third, examining those areas enough not only to feel at home with them but, more importantly, to develop an ability to discuss them and other areas with accountants, financial personnel, and lawyers.

In seeking to surmount the threshold, this book starts with the known and proceeds, at a modest pace, into the unknown. The first four chapters are intended to parade the vocabulary and principal accounting reports and to develop a minimum understanding of the debit-credit structure—or, we may call it, "the accounting method." Then the remaining sixteen chapters apply accounting method to the analysis of certain prominent areas of accounting in the belief that one need not suffer through the whole accounting spectrum to achieve only an understanding rather than a pick-and-shovel knowledge of accounting. The third goal comes from achieving the first two. If you "know" some accounting and have exercised your mind a bit in tussling with some of its favorite problems, you should then be capable of (1) understanding the meaning and significance of the data that come across your path, (2) recognizing your own needs for accounting data as related to the evaluations and decisions you are called upon to make, and (3) formulating quite explicitly your requests to the accounting staff for special reports or accounting schedules. This book is definitely not designed to teach you how to be a bookkeeper or to become a CPA, and it does not undertake to present the ever-evolving views, rules, and regulations of the Securities and Exchange Commission, the Financial Accounting Standards Board, Committees of the American Institute of Certified Public Accountants, or other accounting authorities. However, it should help you very much to understand and communicate with accountants and financial personnel—in short, to be a better manager or executive. It should also help you in your investment decisions.

How Should You Read It?

For a person to become a qualified professional accountant requires depth of study and accounting experience. This book is fairly short; in fact, a fast reader probably could "read" the entire thing in a day or less. Don't! A good deal of the book is devoted to topics that the best accountants in the world find troublesome in spite of their years of exposure to accounting. So please be fair with this book; it is intended for *study* rather than bedtime reading. Some chapters are quite short, and you might do a whole chapter in a single sitting; some chapters are quite long, and you certainly should divide them into two or more reading periods. As a rule of thumb, be satisfied to read no more than about eight to ten pages at one time. Study the illustrative examples very carefully, and, by all means, do the short tests that appear at the end of most chapters.

Certain chapters, especially Chapters 16 through 18, are somewhat specialized and can be read in any order, or skipped entirely if you wish, but you should be sure to include Chapter 19 in your itinerary. When you have finished this book, if you feel interested in pursuing accounting further, you should find little difficulty in reading any of the widely used textbooks leading into advanced accounting, and you should enjoy reading some of the accounting and finance periodicals such as *The Journal of Accountancy, The Financial Executive,* and *The Wall Street Journal,* Barrons, Forbes, and Money.

We wish to express our special thanks to Caroline Carney, who was most helpful and instrumental in bringing about the publication of this book by the McGraw-Hill Book Company. At the same time it should be recognized that the authors, and not McGraw-Hill Book Company, are fully responsible for all opinions expressed in the book.

Robert L. Dixon
Harold E. Arnett

Instructions and Study Plan

This is a concentrated self-instruction course that can be completed at your own pace in time segments as short as 10 minutes or as long as your schedule allows. It is designed for the intelligent person who, as an *executive,* must be able to communicate with, and understand, accountants; for the *lawyer* who is faced with client problems that are interlaced with accounting; for *engineers* who must deal with business matters and who wish to be better qualified for executive positions; for financial analysts and stockbrokers who will be far better qualified to interpret financial statements for their clients; and, of course, for the "ordinary" *investor* who wants to understand accounting statements. The course assumes the reader to have a layman's acquaintance with such terms as *accounts receivable* and *common stock,* but it also assumes zero knowledge of the accounting process at the outset.

Made up of only 36 hours of assignments, the course quickly and effectively "paints the big picture" and leaves the many small details to be filled in from daily experience and from a continuing habit of regular study which it can instill. It does not aim to qualify you either as an accountant or as a bookkeeper; perhaps its most important aim is to develop your ability to read accounting literature and to listen to and converse with the professional accountant. Then you will be able to understand what the accountant is up to and to communicate your needs.

YOUR STUDY PLAN

The serious student of this course should bear the following points in mind:

1. Be prepared to concentrate. If accounting were easy, the world would be flooded with accountants and this study would have little value.
2. Time spent on the course must be taken from other activities in your day. Sacrifice is involved (though the tuition is low!).
3. *Continuity* is very much to be desired. Study sessions should be scheduled from the beginning to the end of the course. This will require real determination, but a steady rate of progress through the course will repay you. If steady progress is not made, you are almost sure to lose interest and drop the course.
4. Best results are obtained if a definite hour, or other time period, is set for study sessions—the optimum, probably, is two separate sessions per week, for example, Tuesday and Thursday, 8:00 to 9:30 P.M.
5. Accounting, like law, medicine, or any other profession, is loaded with controversy. Accountants love to argue with each other. You may well find, in talking with accountants about the materials you are covering in this course, that the practitioners have contrary views. If so, listen politely but don't be persuaded that the book is dead wrong—at least not until you have finished the course. Then you should be able to size up the elements of any controversy and reach your own rational conclusion.
6. Toward the back of the book you will find a set of supplementary problems; there are two or three problems for nearly every chapter. It is not mandatory that you work these problems, and they are not included in the overall allowance of 36 hours. But if you want a deeper and more lasting comprehension of the field of accounting, it will be worth your while to work as many supplementary problems as your ambition dictates.

PROGRAM OF STUDY SESSIONS
(Average one hour each)

LESSON 1   Read Chapter 1; work the test problem. You should have no trouble reading this chapter in an hour, but you should use most, if not all, of the hour anyway. Each of the first six sections is headed by a question (e.g., What Is a Balance Sheet?). After you have read through the chapter once, go back to these introductory sections and test yourself by seeing if you can answer each of the questions. Then, by all means, work the test problem. (Note that the author's solution to each problem appears in the appendix.)

LESSON 2   Read Chapter 2 and work the test problem. This chapter follows a format much like that of Chapter 1. You should be able to absorb its content in one session and work the test problem too. Possibly the most important principle of accounting is found under the heading The Accrual Concept. You should really concentrate on this section and, as before, be sure you have found the answers to the questions posed at the beginning of a number of the other sections.

LESSON 3   Read Chapter 3 to the middle of page 36. The chapter contains the internal organs of bookkeeping. Boring as it may be, most accounting language is related to the process of properly analyzing and recording business transactions, and you shouldn't leave this chapter until you feel quite familiar with it.

LESSON 4   Finish Chapter 3 and work the test problem. We'll make considerable use of the material in this chapter throughout the rest of the book, and the use of debit and credit sides of an account will become very familiar to you.

LESSON 5   Read Chapter 4. This chapter pulls it all together for you. The work sheet is a most useful tool for providing interim, as well as end-of-year, statements. Work the test problem in Chapter 4.

LESSON 6   Study Chapter 5. We've finished the survey of the bookkeeping framework of accounting, and now we begin study of specific areas of general interest. You'll find a large number of journal-entry illustrations of a variety of transactions. Please be sure to study the explanations that follow the transactions, and be sure you understand the logic of the debit and credit entries that have been made in each case.

LESSON 7   Work the test problem in Chapter 5. This probably won't take a full session, but do try to get each journal entry right before going on to the next one. This kind of practice is absolutely vital to your understanding of accounting. If you find that you cannot make the entries, you may need to go back over some of the earlier material.

LESSON 8   Read Chapter 6 to the top of page 88. The working capital funds statement, which is the subject of this chapter, provides useful information for business managers in operating their businesses efficiently and effectively. It is worth your while to spend two study sessions on this chapter to gain an in-depth understanding of the nature of the funds statement, which is widely misunderstood.

LESSON 9 Finish Chapter 6 and work the test problem.

LESSON 10 Study Chapter 7. The accounting profession has promoted the cash flow funds statement to the same level of importance as the balance sheet and income statement. The accounting profession has specified the minimum requirements for the funds (cash flow) statement—particularly the requirement of adequate disclosure. The forms shown in this chapter comply with these requirements. Since this chapter is relatively short and builds on chapter 6, work the test problem in Chapter 7. Note how the statement varies when prepared on a cash flow versus a working capital basis.

LESSON 11 Study Chapter 8. The subject of inventories is always of enormous importance to companies that must carry stocks of merchandise or raw materials or work in process and finished goods. The methods of accounting for and finding the valuation of inventories have a dramatic effect upon reported earnings (as well as upon income taxes). We hope this chapter will be of value to you in pointing up (in accounting language) the critical aspects of the inventory control problem.

LESSON 12 Work the test problem in Chapter 8. This is a short assignment. After working it as prescribed (by using FIFO), you should rework it with average cost and then by using LIFO, and compare your resulting amounts of cost of raw materials used.

LESSON 13 Study Chapter 9. Depreciation probably heads the list of controversial subjects. There is a considerable variety of methods of computing depreciation, and they, like inventory valuation methods, may have enormous impact upon reported profit figures. Each method has its logic and its advocates. You owe it to yourself to understand the reasons for each method as well as to reach some conclusion as to your own preferences.

LESSON 14 Work the test problem in Chapter 9. It calls for two methods of recording depreciation. Because you'll have a lot of time left over, you should also work the problem a third way, by using the declining-balance method.

LESSON 15 Study Chapter 10. This chapter deals with the more frequently used types of capital stock and related transactions. Corporate executives, lawyers, bankers, accountants, regulators, and tax gatherers have created a bewildering maze of corporate investment securities. We can only scratch the surface here, but that should be enough to get you started in discussions with sundry members of the groups referred to above.

LESSON 16 Work the test problem in Chapter 10.

LESSON 17 Study Chapter 11 and work the test problem. This chapter is pretty straightforward. By now you should feel entirely at home with the debit-credit concept, and you should have no trouble with either the examples or the test problem. Please note, however, that the use of "reserves" has undergone decades of development, and only in the last decade have the abuses of the reserve category been fully recognized and publicly condemned. We're still having troubles with "deferred credits," an anomaly if there ever was one. Some day they will be outlawed, but the current tendency seems to be in the opposite direction.

LESSON 18 Read Chapter 12 to the bottom of page 175. This is a short reading assignment, but there's too much in the whole chapter for a single assignment. The subject of accounting for leases (under what circumstances should they be "capitalized") has evoked many years of argument and discussion. Here's hoping you can make up your own mind!

LESSON 19 Finish Chapter 12. Work the test problem.

LESSON 20 Read Chapter 13 to the bottom of page 190. This also is a short reading assignment, but the chapter needs to be split if only to have manufacturing overhead given extra attention.

LESSON 21 Finish Chapter 13 and work the test problem. In this section we accountants undertake the impossible, and don't ever forget it! The allocation of manufacturing (and administrative) overhead to departments, processes, cost centers, and, finally, units of product involves much that is arbitrary, pure estimate, and wishful thinking. Nevertheless, it appears that the allocations must be made if only to find the cost of goods sold and valuation of inventories. You should at least know what kinds of things the cost accountants are doing, and you should be aware of the weaknesses in their procedures.

LESSON 22 Study Chapter 14 to the top of page 206. This is a very short chapter, but it is a very important one regardless of your line of business. From it you should emerge with a familiarity with the notion of cost standards (as compared with the very misleading "actual" costs) and cost variances. The accounting involves enough complexities to justify your concentrating first on raw materials and direct labor and then on manufacturing overhead.

LESSON 23 Finish Chapter 14 and work the problem.

LESSON 24 Study Chapter 15 and work the test problem. This chapter skims over only a few of the special managerial decision aids that can be generated from a good accounting system. The six topics that are touched upon (responsibility accounting, standard costing, direct costing, differential costs, make-or-buy decisions, and capital budgeting) represent a set of fairly potent managerial activities in which the accountant should take a prominent part. We only mention operations research, which is simply the application of more or less rarefied mathematics to business problems. Any executive would be well-advised to become familiar with our six topics (as bread-and-butter items) and have at least a nodding acquaintance with the potentials of operations research.

LESSON 25 Read half of Chapter 16 on federal income tax concepts. This chapter deals entirely with the basic concepts. A familiarity with the concepts should be all that the typical businessperson needs, provided that good accountants, or tax practioners, are available for preparation of the tax returns and to help with tax planning.

LESSON 26 Read the rest of Chapter 16 and work out the short test problems. Read Chapter 17. This is a very short chapter designed to give you some helpful general information on useful software packages. No problems are assigned in Chapter 17.

LESSON 27 Study Chapter 18 to the middle of page 262. Consolidated financial statements constitute about the toughest part of accounting; but if you apply yourself thoughtfully to the material of this chapter, you should understand the fundamentals very well and should be able to comprehend the process used in the case of the company, or companies, that you are interested in by talking them over with the accountants in charge. It has been said that every company listed on the New York Stock Exchange presents consolidated statements.

LESSON 28 Finish Chapter 18 and work the test problem. This is a continuation of Lesson 27 with special attention to consolidated balance sheets *after* the date of acquisition and to consolidated income statements.

LESSON 29 Study Chapter 19. It's the rare company nowadays that does not practice income tax allocation in some form. You should spend two study sessions on this subject even though everything appears clear to you the first time over.

LESSON 30 Work the test problem in Chapter 19.

LESSON 31 Study Chapter 20. The 1970s and 1980s were notable for what might be termed "acquisition fever." One way to double your profits instantly is simply to combine with another company of approximately equal earnings potential and use the pooling-of-interests procedure to accomplish the combination. As in so many aspects of accounting, controversy over poolings versus acquisitions and the rules of the game has raged and apparently will continue forever.

LESSON 32 Work the test problem in Chapter 20.

LESSON 33 Study Chapter 21 to the middle of page 305. A modern term, "double-digit inflation," signals the necessity for accountants to adopt common-dollar (price-level adjusted) financial statements. The lack of adjustment for change in value of the monetary unit has undoubtedly been the most serious defect in accounting statements generally during the twentieth century. Finally, the need for accounting recognition of inflation (by methods other than LIFO) has become acknowledged by the majority of the leaders of the accounting profession. This subject is a must for you regardless of your involvement with accounting reports.

LESSON 34 Study the demonstration problem in Chapter 21.

LESSON 35 Read Chapter 22. So many of our larger corporations are involved in foreign operations that the average business executive is quite likely to have need for insight into some of the intricacies of such operations as well as the financial statements that are forthcoming. The translation of foreign currencies, when combined with adjustments for inflation, presents some especially fascinating accounting problems.

LESSON 36 Work supplementary problem 22-1.

LESSON 37 Take the final examination. You should allow up to two hours to do a thoughtful job. Send your solution in (see instructions on the first page of the examination) for grading.

THE McGRAW-HILL
36-HOUR
ACCOUNTING
COURSE

1
The Balance Sheet

What Is a Balance Sheet?

Imagine, first, that you have made a list of everything valuable that you own, and also the estimated dollar value of each thing, and have then added the dollar values to find their total. Second, you have made a list of the people, stores, etc., to whom you presently owe money, and also the amount owing to each party, and have determined the total of those amounts. Third, you have subtracted the smaller of the two totals from the larger to determine the *dollar difference* between the two lists. You now have all of the ingredients for a balance sheet.

Your first list can be labeled "assets"; your second list can be labeled "liabilities"; and the dollar difference can be termed your "net worth." If you arrange all that information in more or less orderly fashion, you will have a *balance sheet.* In the style customarily used by accountants, your balance sheet might appear as in Figure 1.1.

The Balance Sheet—What Good Is It?

A balance sheet is what accountants call a *financial statement.* Many accountants will assert that it is the most important of the various kinds of "statements" that they prepare. However, there's much uncertainty as to just how one arrives at the dollar figures that are assigned to the various assets. This could mean that not only are the individual asset valuations unacceptable to certain users of the statements but so also is the amount that we labeled "net worth" (since it was found by subtracting the liability total from the asset total as listed).

1

Figure 1.1 Balance sheet.

MY NAME Balance Sheet (date)			
Assets		Liabilities	
Cash	$ 10,000	Owed to stores	$ 1,200
Stocks and bonds	50,000	Owed to bank	60,000
Clothing	2,500	Total liabilities	$ 61,200
Furniture	28,000		
House	160,000	Net worth	244,300
Land	40,000		
Miscellaneous	15,000		
	$305,500		$305,500

In spite of disagreement on the matter of the dollar valuations (e.g., is our house worth $160,000 exactly or approximately?) the balance sheet is considered to be a statement of the "financial position" of the enterprise (or of the person or any other "entity" depicted) on the date noted in the heading of the statement. It goes without saying that the dollar measures that are assigned to the various assets must all be "as of" the same date; otherwise, we would have a mishmash and the total would have no meaning.

The balance sheet does not show how the subject—let's call it the "entity"—reached its displayed position. It also fails to show where the entity is heading (though a series of balance sheets on successive dates can be of help in that connection). Let's pursue this line of inquiry a bit more.

Does the Balance Sheet Really Show Financial Position?

Your own financial position is made up of the valuable possessions, or resources, owned by you, *offset by your debts.* As stated earlier, the *difference* between the dollar measure of your resources and the dollar measure of your debts is what is commonly called your *net worth.* If we apply the same formula to the company with which you are associated, we might, for example, find that the company's balance sheet shows assets totaling $1,000,000 and offsetting debts of $400,000, so that its net worth is $600,000. Accountants, particularly the teacher crowd, are so impressed by the algebra of this situation that they often refer to "the" accounting equation as: *Assets minus liabilities equals net worth,* or A − L = NW.

The balance sheet, basically, consists of a reporting of the dollar amount of assets *on the left-hand side* and all the existing debts *on the right-hand side;* the two sides *are then made equal* by filling in enough on the right-hand side to make them equal! The amount of the filler is the net worth. So if we want to flaunt our mathematical ability a bit, we may point out that, as mentioned above, A − L = NW. This can just as well be written as A = L + NW, which is a kind of arithmetic model of the standard balance sheet in which the assets, on the left, equal the sum of the liabilities and net worth, on the right.

So far it would appear that financial position means nothing more than a pair of totals (assets and liabilities) offset to show their difference (net worth). As a matter of fact, this arithmetic pattern constitutes only a minor aspect of any analysis of a company's financial position. The asset total has some meaning; the liability total has some meaning; and the net worth has some (very limited) meaning; but these are *gross* concepts, to say the least. Any analysis of a company's financial position will surely take into account, and with considerably greater interest, the relationships (ratios) that exist between some of the more detailed items within the asset, the liability, and the net worth categories. Financial position, in other words, is not to be construed as a mere difference between the asset and the liability totals. We'll look at that again later.

Does the Balance Sheet Actually Show What You Think It May?

We have just been commenting, with an apparent degree of confidence, on the service of the balance sheet in revealing a company's financial position. Before we become overly enthusiastic, let's slow down a bit and test our premises.

If the balance sheet does, in truth, show the *current value of all* the assets owned by a company and if it also shows all the company's debts, it would apparently qualify as an accurate statement of financial position—if the asset amount is correct and the liability amount is correct, then their difference, the net worth, must be correct. But now we come to the real hooker. The asset total (as well as many of the details which go to make it up) is *virtually never* equal to the current value of all the assets. If that isn't enough to discourage you, let us add that the *real worth* of a company depends on a great deal more than its list of assets and list of liabilities. You could probably imagine, in this age of leasing almost everything, a company which *owns* no assets at all, which has some real liabilities, and which, though its accounting net worth would then be a negative figure, might have a great deal of worth in the eyes of the expert investor. In other words, it takes more than tangible assets to make a company worth something—this essential ingredient is management. It would be perfectly ridiculous to expect, for example, that the stock of a company which has an accounting net worth of $100,000, with 10,000 shares outstanding, would have a market value *per share* that is exactly twice as much as that of another company with an accounting net worth also of $100,000 but with 20,000 shares of stock outstanding. The only time this relationship would be likely to hold true would be in case the $100,000 was in hard cash and the companies were about to be dissolved.

How Are Assets Valued?

Early in the preceding paragraph it was pointed out that the balance sheet fails to show true financial position, or true net worth, because the asset total is virtually never equal to the current value of all the assets owned. This admission might come as a surprise to almost everyone who has looked at a balance sheet but who has not had any experience or formal training in accounting.

The fact of the matter is that assets can be divided into two very general categories—the first being *cash and claims to cash* and the second being *assets that have been purchased* for use in the business (such as inventories, plant, and equipment). Roughly speaking, the first group is reported in the balance sheet *at the amount of cash funds they represent* (e.g., cash on hand, cash in bank, and amounts due from customers) and the second group is reported *at the amounts invested in them*—i.e., *at their cost.* Let's hasten to add that in making up the cost figures one must take into consideration (1) not only the amounts paid for the assets originally but also (2) the amounts (usually estimated) representing the using up of the assets. Thus, we buy a machine for $10,000, and that's its original cost. As the machine is used, it depreciates; on successive balance sheets we show the machine (probably combined with other related assets) at lower and lower amounts to reflect its inevitable depreciation or, as someone has phrased it, "its inevitable march to the junk heap."

It should be perfectly obvious that if some of the assets of the company are listed in the balance sheet as cash or near cash (such as accounts receivable) and the remainder are listed at what the company paid for them (in some cases years ago), the sum of the two groups simply won't equal the "present value" of the total assets. For purposes of discussion, let's refer to the two groups of assets as (1) the *monetary* assets and (2) the *nonmonetary* assets.

Why Are Nonmonetary Assets Reported at Cost?

Some accountants, particularly some of the folks in the ivory towers, sincerely believe that all nonmonetary assets should be reported in the balance sheet at their *current values.* It may be observed, however, that it is easier for the people in this group to tell *why* the assets should be so valued than it is for them to tell *how* current value, or current cost, is to be ascertained. They point out that the asset side of the orthodox balance sheet is a conglomerate mass of dollars representing not only the monetary but also the nonmonetary assets at costs that have been incurred sometimes over a span of 25 or more years, and they feel that these cost amounts may be far removed from current reality (the more modern expression is "irrelevant"). Certainly there's a good deal of truth to this accusation. But we must then examine the alternatives— that is, the utilization of current market value. (Some prefer to use the comparable term "current cost," or merely "current value.")

Surely no problem exists in listing cash at its current value because cash (and we're concerned here only with our domestic currency) is itself the ultimate measure of value. Similarly, marketable securities, such as the stocks and bonds that are listed on the organized stock exchanges or are traded in the over-the-counter market, can readily be listed at current values. Next, accounts and notes receivable can quite readily be listed at a close approximation of their current values—that is, at the amounts that will rather surely be collected from them within a reasonable period of time. However, when we move on to assets such as machinery and equipment—especially if those items were tailor-made for our firm—it becomes quite difficult to determine a reasonable market value. Particularly when the machinery is permanently affixed to the plant and would not conceivably be sold, the *relevance* of a current market value becomes pretty hard to recognize. Often the only market would be the secondhand, or junk, market. The land on which our buildings stand may have high potential value in the current real estate market. So what? Does the strength of our company lie in the fact that it could sell its site land for more than it cost, or does its strength lie in the day-to-day operations that it carries on? Needless to say, the market values of most buildings, so often designed for the special purposes for which they are being used, would be quite meaningless even if they were ascertainable. If the company is a going concern, it will not sell its building for the profit that is thus available, unless it is contemplating going out of business. Sometimes structures are appraised by a process of finding the present cost of the kinds of materials and labor that were originally expended in their construction, but such a procedure may result in a very poor representation of the current value of the structure.

Admittedly, this is only a sketchy, preliminary look at the subject of asset valuation, but it is intended to warn you, if not to soften the blow, that in most cases in dealing with accounting data we will be relying on *historical cost* where nonmonetary assets are concerned. The argument for cost can be expressed quite simply: First, there is no satisfactory means of determining current cost or current market value of most nonmonetary assets *economically on a continuous basis;* second, the essence, if not the quintessence, of profit determination lies in the matching of *cost* against *revenue.* Revenue is what we collect from the sale of something; cost is what we paid for something. "Buy low and sell high." In other words, a cardinal principle of accounting is that profit is not earned by mere *changes in the value* of things; it must be *realized by actual transactions* in which something is literally *sold* for an amount greater than its cost.

All this leads us to another conclusion. We had better stop using the term *net worth* in our balance sheets. Commonly in the balance sheets one now finds a term such as Stockholders' Equity or Capital Stock and Retained Earnings to represent the difference between the total assets and the total liabilities.

Balance Sheet Illustrations

Mainly for purposes of rounding out the present chapter, a few balance sheet illustrations will now be presented. Care is taken to exclude balance sheet items which might be unfamiliar or which might require special explanation at this point in our study. Here we are concerned mostly with the basic concept of the balance sheet, including content and structure.

Figure 1.2 is a balance sheet that is condensed beyond all reality but is intended to depict the skeleton structure of the orthodox balance sheet. As shown, the balance sheet in Figure 1.2 is in so-called *account* form. That is, the assets appear on the left-hand side and the liabilities and owners' equities are shown on the right. By the simple process of showing the liabilities and owners' equities below the assets, the form becomes known as the *report form,* as in Figure 1.3. Quite obviously, it makes little difference whether the balance sheet is presented in

Figure 1.2 Account form.

ORANGE PRODUCTS CO.
Balance Sheet as of December 31, 19XX

Assets		Liabilities and stock equity		
Current	$ 40,000	Liabilities:		
Noncurrent	60,000	Current	$20,000	
		Noncurrent	15,000	$ 35,000
		Stockholders' equity:		
		Capital stock	$50,000	
		Retained earnings	15,000	65,000
	$100,000			$100,000

Figure 1.3 Report form.

ORANGE PRODUCTS CO.
Balance Sheet as of December 31, 19XX

Assets	
Current	$ 40,000
Noncurrent	60,000
	$100,000

Liabilities and stock equity		
Liabilities:		
Current	$20,000	
Noncurrent	15,000	$ 35,000
Stockholders' equity:		
Capital stock	$50,000	
Retained earnings	15,000	65,000
		$100,000

account or in report form; the choice may depend solely on page size and convenience.

Figure 1.4 shows the same data, rearranged a bit more significantly, in "sequence" form. This form has a relatively small following, but it is used by some of the big companies. Some people feel that it is less clear than the others.

Figure 1.5 shows, in report form, a balance sheet with a few of the more common headings and explanatory notes included. This example might easily represent the balance sheet of a moderately large corporation as it would actually be presented in an annual report, or an interim report, to the company's stockholders.

Figure 1.4 Sequence form.

ORANGE PRODUCTS CO. **Balance Sheet as of December 31, 19XX**	
Current assets	$40,000
Less: Current liabilities	20,000
Working capital	$20,000
Noncurrent assets	60,000
	$80,000
Less: Noncurrent liabilities	15,000
Stockholders' equity (See Schedule A)	$65,000

Schedule A
Stockholders' equity

Capital stock	$50,000
Retained earnings	15,000
	$65,000

Balance Sheet Categories

Most people with a nodding acquaintance with accounting would define "current assets" as assets which "can be converted into cash within a year." Such a definition is both out of date and wrong. In the early days, the balance sheet was prepared mainly for use in dealing with creditors—in seeking bank loans or credit from suppliers—who were mainly interested in the "liquidity" of the borrower. Accordingly, current assets have traditionally been displayed ahead of the other assets in the balance sheet; from the creditor's standpoint, assets had to be liquid in order to be current. Now, however, we view the balance sheet as a conveyor of financial information to all parties with a legitimate interest in the company—not only the creditors but especially the owners and, at the same time, potential investors, the tax collectors, and the labor force. So, current assets now include the five classes of assets shown in Figure 1.5 on the assumption that the balance sheet should show the financial structure of the enterprise—that is, its circulating assets (current) and its relatively permanent plant assets. Thus, we toss out both the one-year rule as well as the "can-be-converted-into-cash" rule. In fact, the latter rule is nonsense from any point of view. Land, for example, is likely to be salable and in most cases *could* easily be "converted into cash within a year," but it is usually considered to be a leading example of the noncurrent group.

The noncurrent assets are more commonly called *fixed assets* and are placed under that heading.

Current liabilities can safely be defined as those which are to be paid

Figure 1.5 Annual or interim report.

ORANGE PRODUCTS CO.
Balance Sheet as of December 31, 19XX

Assets

Current:			
Cash		$ 5,000	
Marketable securities (at cost; market value is $12,500)		8,000	
Receivables (after subtracting $1,000 for estimated amount uncollectible)		10,000	
Inventories (at the lower of cost or market)		15,000	
Prepayments		2,000	$ 40,000
Plant:			
Land		$10,000	
Structures	$30,000		
Machinery and equipment	40,000		
	$70,000		
Less: Amount charged off as depreciation	25,000	45,000	55,000
Intangibles:			
Patents (at cost less $1,632 of amortization)		$ 4,999	
Goodwill (at nominal value)		1	5,000
			$100,000

Liabilities and stock equity

Current liabilities:		
Accounts payable	$12,000	
Taxes payable	4,000	
Dividends payable	2,500	
Miscellaneous	1,500	$ 20,000
Bonds payable, x%, due in 19XX		15,000
Total liabilities		$ 35,000
Stockholders' equity:		
Capital stock, par $10	$50,000	
Retained earnings	15,000	65,000
		$100,000

within a year from the date of the balance sheet, although some exceptions to this rule may occasionally arise.

Balance Sheet Relationships

Almost inevitably, routine note of certain fundamental relationships is made by a person who scans a balance sheet. First, a rough calculation of the *current ratio* is likely to be made. The current ratio is the arithmetic ratio of the total of current assets to the total current liabilities. (In our example the ratio stands at 40 to 20, or 2 to 1.) A rough determination of the amount of *working capital,* which is the difference between the total current assets and the total current liabilities, might also be made. (In our example the working capital is $40,000–$20,000.)

Another rather important relationship is that of owners' equity to total assets. (In the Orange Products Co. example this relationship, known as the *equity ratio,* is $65,000 to $100,000, or 65 percent.)

Financial analysts have invented dozens of "pet" ratios in addition to the three just described. Because this is a book on accounting and not a book on corporation finance or financial analysis, we won't worry about what the various ratios should be in any given case, but you should be warned *not* to settle for any predigested rules or standards. The analysis of any balance sheet rests first and most importantly on a knowledge of what underlies the reported figures, a knowledge of the industry that you are dealing with, a knowledge of what kind of *management* rules the firm (nothing is more important than that), and a lot of other things. At best, the ratios constitute supplementary or confirmatory data, and they should *never* be taken as complete answers in themselves.

Balance Sheet Terminology

In concluding this chapter, let's point out that different words are used by different accountants in referring to the same things. Incidentally, the very title, Balance Sheet, is often replaced by a title such as Statement of Financial Condition, Statement of Financial Position, or, simply, Position Statement. A satisfactory heading for the right-hand side of the position statement, to replace the clumsy Liabilities and Stock Equity, is the single word, Equities. In the examples in this chapter only the most common types of position statement items have been mentioned. This is lesson 1; we'll delve into matters such as reserves, LIFO, deferred federal income taxes, consolidated statements, and many other more complex and more exciting subjects as we pass on into our advanced lessons.

At this point it would be desirable for you to work the exercise that follows. It includes nothing new, and you won't know whether you're qualified for reading Chapter 2 until you have worked it. You'll find model answers in Appendix I, but, of course, you won't peek until you have finished working the problem.

TEST PROBLEM

Denton Bread Co. was organized early in 19XX, when 10,000 shares of $10 par common stock were issued for cash at par. During the remainder of the year, the company succeeded in earning $12,000, and it paid dividends of $8,000. Land was purchased for $5,000 cash; a building was erected for $50,000 cash; and machinery and equipment were purchased for $60,000 cash. To finance the fixed-asset purchases, a 20-year mortgage note for $30,000 was negotiated with the local bank. At the end of the year, assets other than those identified thus far consisted of cash $9,200, accounts receivable with a face value of $12,000, raw materials inventory which cost $5,000, miscellaneous supplies which cost $1,000, and prepayments of $500. Liabilities, in addition to the mortgage, consisted of wages payable $1,600, taxes payable $3,000, and mortgage interest payable $200. Depreciation of the fixed assets (other than land) was recognized in the amount of $3,400, and it was estimated that about $500 of the receivables might prove to be uncollectible.

Required

In the solution space provided, prepare a balance sheet, in excellent form, as of December 31, 19XX.

TEST PROBLEM Solution Space

DENTON BREAD CO.
Balance Sheet as of December 31, 19XX

Assets

Current:

Noncurrent:

Equities

Current liabilities:

Stockholders' equity:

2
The
Income
Statement

What Is the Income Statement's Purpose?

If you were to start a business concern by investing $100,000 in cash, it is conceivable, but unlikely, that you would be willing to operate it, or assign the job to a manager, and wait until the concern was finally dissolved before any computation of your earnings was made. Actually, such a delay in reckoning the earnings would have one virtue—the difference between the amounts of cash *invested* during the lifetime of the enterprise and the amount *finally realized* upon dissolution comes close to being the true profit (or loss) of the venture (assuming that you make proper allowance for any dividends or other withdrawals of funds during the lifetime of the venture). Rather than that, of course, owners and other interested parties demand *periodic* information on the progress of the enterprise; in short, they require a report of net income at least annually and in a great many cases quarterly or more often. The space of time covered by such a report is known as an *accounting period.*

It would be difficult to locate any truly authoritative statement of the purpose of the income statement, and it is best perhaps not to focus on any single purpose. If we want to be theoretical, we might state that the leading purpose is to show how much the *net assets of the enterprise have increased (or decreased)* during the accounting period—always with due allowance for any dividends paid or any additional investments or withdrawals by the stockholders.

Net assets and *net worth* are synonymous terms—each refers to the arithmetic difference between total assets and total liabilities. (Remember the equation, $A - L = NW$.) Possibly the term *net assets* is to be preferred because it avoids the word "worth," but it is less likely to be comprehended by nonaccountants.

Unfortunately, as we noted earlier, there is a wide range of opinions on the manner in which the A of the basic equation should be measured. Should the net assets reflect current *market* values, current *replacement* costs, historical costs, or historical costs translated into dollars of current purchasing power?

A more fruitful approach, it would seem, is to attribute more than a single purpose to the income statement and set out to prepare income statements that will, in fact, serve multiple purposes. This is achieved, basically, by avoiding overcondensation—*by disclosing the component elements* that go to make up the figure at the bottom of the statement rather than by limiting the report to a half-dozen or fewer figures.

The income statement is often referred to as the *operating statement,* and it should, indeed, portray the current operations of the enterprise to the degree that mere dollar figures can. The reader should be able to make some assessment of the size, growth, and perhaps the growth potential of the enterprise by analyzing the sales data. The relationship between the amount of a given expense, for example, and sales for the period may give some insight into the operating efficiency of the company. The relationship between net income and any "fixed charges" for bond interest or leasehold rents may be significant in evaluating the amount of risk inherent in making a stock investment, in lending funds to the enterprise, etc.

As in the case of the balance sheet, the financial analysts have developed a large number of "favorite" ratios relating particular income statement items to others and also relating certain income statement items with certain balance sheet items. For our purposes, then, let's not think of the income statement as a mere (and possibly frail) measure of financial growth through net income for the period.

What Is Net Income?

As you might guess, the term *net income* means different things to different accountants, so one can safely define it in a number of ways. One way relates to a possible purpose of the income statement—to show, at some point, *the earnings which management has produced* during the period *for all capital suppliers.* To illustrate, assume that, with assets of $100,000, management produces $10,000 of net income during a year; this is an important bit of financial information in itself. Then a separate question is, who is entitled to this $10,000 of net income? If some of the assets were acquired through the issuance of

$40,000 in bonds, then the interest on the bonds, assume $3,200 of the $10,000 net income, goes to the bondholders, which leaves a balance of $6,800 properly termed Earnings of Stockholders. This amount, in turn, might be subject to cumulative dividend claims of "preferred" stockholders (let's assume an amount of $2,500), leaving a balance to be labeled Earnings of Common Stockholders ($4,300).

Net income cannot really be described clearly without employing other accounting words that we are about to examine. Net income is made up of revenues, as the positive factor, from which are subtracted the negative factors, which are the expenses, most losses, and income taxes. Take particular note of the fact that the word "cash" has not been used at any time in this discussion; the reason is that cash has nothing, or at least very little, to do with the *determination* of net income.

A more popular definition, a variant of the one just presented, holds that net income consists of the earnings *after* interest on bonds, etc., has been subtracted. Thus, in the example the net income would be $6,800 rather than $10,000.

What Is Revenue?

First, let's shower you with words: sales revenue, interest revenue, rent revenue, dividend revenue, royalties revenue, and so on. The *total* revenues of a business are the sum of all the revenues from all sources during a given period. An enterprise can have billions of dollars of revenues in a given year and yet report a net loss for that year—because the dollars of expenses, losses, and income taxes must be deducted from the dollars of revenue before the amount of net income (or net loss) is determined. Thus, the sales revenue is the *total* amount collectible from customers for the delivery (sale) of goods and services during the period. This is *not* income in any proper sense of the word—it is revenue! For example, if we sell for $100 an object that cost us $70, our revenue from the sale is $100; whether or not we earn any *income* on the sale then depends on the total costs (including the $70) of the sale. Incidentally, many (perhaps most) accountants, in this simple example, would subtract the $70 from the $100 and call the remaining $30 "gross profit," which is a real corruption of the English language. There simply cannot be any profit until *all* related costs have been deducted from revenue, and the term "gross profit" should be jettisoned.

Revenue, then, is the total amount obtained by us from the sale of merchandise or other commodities or from the rendering of services to our customers. By itself, revenue gives no indication of the ultimate *net income*.

Just as revenue must be contrasted with net income, so must it be vigorously contrasted with the *inflow of cash.* Revenue for the period is the amount of revenue "earned" during that period, whether you get paid for it in cash during the same period, during the preceding period, or in the following period. True, if our apparent revenue amounts initially to $100,000 and it later becomes clear that one or more of our customers will fail to pay us a total of $1,000 owed us, our revenue can properly be described in two fashions: (1) Our *gross* revenue is $100,000 and (2) our *net* revenue is $99,000. In other words, gross sales revenue for a given period is a summation of all sales for the period, whether for cash or on charge account, and *net* sales revenue is the gross minus any portion deemed to be uncollectible. (Gross sales minus "bad debts" equals net sales.)

Our discussion of revenue leads conveniently to the noting of a word commonly applied to accounting. When a sale is made, cash need not be collected on the spot in order to recognize (record) the revenue. We *accrue* revenue *when the sale is made* or *when the service is rendered,* and this is the revenue that is recognized (reported) in the income statement. The time of collection of cash proceeds from the sale, while by no means unimportant, has no direct bearing on the amount or the timing of the revenue. This is one facet of the *accrual concept;* because the concept is widely applied in business accounting, it is not unusual to hear an accountant speak of *accrual accounting.*

The Accrual Concept

Accounting can be so performed that income is determined on either a *cash basis* or an *accrual basis.* Under the cash scheme, no income (revenue) is recognized in the accounts until it is received in the form of cash. (Note that a check is universally viewed as cash, unless doubt exists as to its worth.) And no expense is recognized in the accounts until cash payment has actually been made. The results of cash basis accounting range all the way from fairly logical to horrible.

Under accrual accounting, revenue is recognized in the period in which it is actually *earned,* i.e., when the services are performed, the goods are delivered, etc. Whether the corresponding cash is collected before, within, or after the earning period has no bearing on the timing of the revenue recognition.

The aim of accrual accounting is twofold: (1) to record and report in any given period the revenues (e.g., from sales, rentals, interest, and royalties) *earned* during the period and (2) to report the expenses (of whatever kind) that properly are *to be matched* against the reported revenues. Thus, the overall effort is to reflect the earnings performance of the entity for the period. The amount of earnings for a period may have little or no relationship to the amount of net inflow or outflow of cash for that period.

What Is an Expense?

First, consider some clear-cut examples of true expenses. Perhaps the most obvious example is the amount paid for goods that are sold at retail. The long title for this particular expense is "merchandise cost of sales." Thus, buy something for $12, sell it for $20, and you have two amounts to be accounted for: first, sales revenue of $20; second, an expense of $12, which will be designated as Merchandise Cost of Sales. (Note that the goods, as long as they remain unsold on your shelves, are assets except to the extent that they suffer deterioration or obsolescence.) Modify the example a bit by assuming that the sale was made as the result of placing an ad in the newspaper for $5. We now have, as before, Sales Revenue of $20, Merchandise Cost of Sales of $12, and Advertising Expense, a new expense, $5.

Note the distinguishing characteristics of the so-called expenses in our example. In both cases we made a sacrifice of some value ($12 and $5); also, the sacrifices were made to produce revenue ($20). Furthermore, the two expenses are recognized in the period in which the corresponding revenues were produced.

Reflect on this situation for a moment. Accountants are called upon to produce income statements which are intended to show the amount of income earned in the period covered by the particular income statement. In short, net income is the amount of gain produced by the revenues of the period minus the expenses of the period. Expenses of a given period are a kind of cost—amounts given up to produce the revenues (and resultant net income) of the period. Thus, the amount expended to buy, or construct, a manufacturing plant and manufacturing equipment is *not an expense*. But as time passes and these assets are used for the production of goods that are sold for revenues, the plant and equipment depreciate. To the extent that such depreciation is ascribable to the manufacture of goods that are sold, it is an expense.

Now let's take a quick test. If we construct a building for our own use in manufacturing, spending $1,000,000, is this an expense? Not immediately. The million dollars is properly referred to as the "cost" of construction, or cost of buying a fixed asset. If the building has an estimated useful life of, say, 50 years, it may be reasonable to transfer one-fiftieth of the $1,000,000 each year to an expense classification (as depreciation). If we have an inventory of goods that we have manufactured at total cost of $1,000,000 and the goods are destroyed by fire, with no insurance, does this represent expense? No. Although we have had a "cost" in the amount of $1,000,000, it is not a revenue-producing cost, so it is not an expense—it is a *loss.* Similarly, other cases of outlays, sacrifices, etc., can be expenses if they are incurred to produce the revenues of the period, or they can be losses, or manufacturing costs, purchasing costs, and payments of accounts payable—depending upon the circumstances in each case.

And so, given the amount of sales for a specific period, our task as accountants is to identify and report the kinds and amounts of expenses that were incurred to produce those revenues.

Expenses, then, in contrast with losses, are good things—they are beneficial in the sense that they create revenues. Needless to say, one does not incur expenses recklessly. They must be budgeted and carefully administered to the end that we maximize the difference between *total* revenues and *total* expenses—net income.

Some Other Offsets to Revenue

Revenues are good; losses are bad; expenses are in between. You always strive to reduce expenses, but you can't prosper unless you incur them, sometimes on a grandiose scale. Another kind of business negative is the *revenue contra,* by which we mean anything that happens which *cancels* out revenue that we have recorded earlier. For a simple example, let's sell merchandise for $100 and, at the time of sale, record it as sales revenue (even though the customer charged it). Within the next week, however, any of the following four events occurs:

1. The customer brings the goods back and we agree to cancel the charge against him. (This is a *sales return.*)

2. The customer skips the country and we know we'll never collect the $100, so we cancel the account from our records. (This is a *bad debt.*)

3. The customer pays his bill in cash within 10 days and we allow him a discount of $2, so our net revenue becomes $98 rather than $100. (The $2 is known as a *sales discount.*)

4. The customer finds the product isn't quite what he wanted and proposes to return it, but we say, "Keep it and we'll deduct $10 from your bill." (The $10 is known as a *sales allowance.*)

All four of these cases constitute revenue offsets (contras). They are not expenses or losses but revenue corrections—we had originally recorded $100 of revenue in each case but later events required corrective reductions. On an income statement they are properly shown as subtractions from gross sales in order to depict net sales. Contras of these kinds arise because, at the time of a given sale transaction, we can only assume that the customer will pay in due course (even though we know from experience that a certain percentage of our clientele will, for one of the four reasons, fail to pay the amount initially billed).

What Are Income Taxes?

If there's anything that everyone of us has experienced, it's income taxes, and we'll skim over the subject here as lightly as possible (with a full chapter on the subject to come later). The question here is, are income taxes an expense, a loss, or a revenue contra, or do they have their own unique status? Most accountants would probably classify income taxes as expenses. (But how, by any stretch of the imagination, do they produce revenues?) Some accountants would classify income taxes as pure loss—but that would deny that government makes any contribution whatsoever to our well-being. Other accountants assert that the government is a sort of partner in every profit-making enterprise and that the income tax claimed by government is, thus, merely its share or division of the earnings. In some cases income taxes take on the appearance of revenue contra, as when, for example, we make sales of war material to the government and then the government claims a refund in the form of income taxes on the profit from the sales. Given all those views, it becomes quite a problem to choose any single one, so we are going to propose simply that income taxes be shown as a separately reported subtraction from the total revenues of the period. You will note that treatment in the illustrative income statement soon to follow.

Interest and Dividends

Most accountants refer to interest as an expense, but interest is really a cost of borrowing money and surely in itself does not stimulate revenues as an expense should. In fact, the concept of interest cost is at least related to the concept of dividends. At one extreme, interest on first-mortgage bonds accrues as a contractual liability, with dire consequences in case of default; at the opposite extreme, cash dividends on common stock may be skipped year after year with virtually not a whisper from the stockholders. However, between those extremes is a whole range of securities, all more or less hybrid, which require interest or dividend payments more or less regularly and which constitute a virtual spectrum of financial investment instruments. No one can successfully establish a clear boundary between true debt instruments and true ownership instruments, although we tend to regard the two, respectively, as bonds and stocks. Our conclusion is that all interest and all dividends should be treated as *divisions of net income* of the company, that the net income is an amount determined by subtracting expenses, losses, and taxes from the net revenues, and that interest and dividends are then properly displayed as sharers in that net income in order of their contractual rights. It will be noted in the illustrative income statement to follow that both interest expense *and* dividends on preferred stock are subtracted from the revenue total before income is determined. Although, as argued above, income may be said to result before the subtraction of one or both of the above items, the statement as presented is designed to emphasize the earnings of the common stockholder and is in a form that nowadays has considerable authoritative support.

Income Statement Illustrated

There are very few rules to limit experimentation with income statement form, but only two basic forms are widely used for external reporting purposes. The first, and simplest, is usually called the *single-step form*. Highly condensed, the structure is more or less as shown in Figure 2.1. Alternatively, various subtotals may be shown with labels which are intended to identify them—a multiple-step statement.

Comments on Illustrative Income Statement

1. The statement as shown is in comparative form; that is, two years (or periods) are presented side by side for purposes of comparison and analysis of change. This is quite customary in present-day reporting.

2. Commonly the revenues are presented on two lines, viz., "net sales" and "other income."

3. The expenses are typically displayed on two or more lines, with "merchandise cost of goods sold" shown first and "selling and administrative expenses" next (subject to possible

Figure 2.1   Single-step form.

ALBANY COMPANY
Comparative Income Statements, Years Ended December 31

	19X4	19X5
Revenues (may list)	$xx	$xx
Revenue deductions:		
Expenses (may list)	$xx	$xx
Losses (may list)	xx	xx
Interest expense (may explain)	xx	xx
Income taxes	xx	xx
Preferred dividends	xx	xx
Income before extraordinary items	$xx	$xx
Extraordinary items (if any)	xx	xx
Net income	$xx	$xx
Retained earnings at beginning of period	xx	xx
	$xx	$xx
Common dividends	xx	xx
Retained earnings at end of period	$xx	$xx
Earnings per common share:		
Income before extraordinary items	$xx	$xx
Extraordinary items (gain or loss)	xx	xx
Net income	$xx	$xx

detailing either in the body of the statement or in a separate supporting schedule).

4. The expression "single-step form" refers to the fact that all the revenue deductions are added together and then deducted as a group from the revenues, so that an income balance is reached by a single subtraction. This is in contrast with "multiple-step" statements, in which the various expenses are subtracted successively from the revenues, with a resulting sequence of intervening subbalances that may or may not have any worthwhile significance.

5. "Extraordinary items" are gains or losses that occur within a given period which are so unusual, and so unrelated to the regular operations of the enterprise, that their inclusion with the revenues or revenue deductions might seriously becloud the analyst's interpretation of the degree of success with which the enterprise was administered during the period under review. Accordingly, extraordinary items are entered as a separate element in the statement. Examples of items that have been cited as extraordinary are the sale or aban-

donment of a significant segment of the business, a major devaluation of a foreign currency, and the lump-sum write-off of goodwill as a result of unusual developments within the period. It follows that the more commonplace losses and gains (such as inventory write-downs and fluctuations in foreign currencies) are listed in the upper portion of the income statement, so that they do affect the amount labeled "income before extraordinary items."

6. It is fairly common practice to terminate the income statement at the point labeled "net income" and then present, as a separate schedule, the remaining portion; so presented, the separated schedule is a Statement of Retained Earnings. Such a presentation has the virtue of emphasizing the net income figures for the year in contrast with the retained earnings, which consist of the accumulated earnings of past years.

7. It now is generally accepted procedure to calculate and report at the foot of the income statement the earnings per share of common stock for the period. Nowadays, with the invention of a number of hybrid types of stocks and bonds, as well as stock options and warrants, the determination of earnings per share can become a complex problem in itself. In the illustration it is merely assumed that no complexities exist.

8. Occasionally within a given year there becomes apparent a gain or loss that would have been "picked up" (accountants' slang for "recognized" or "reported") in a prior year had sufficient information to determine its nature and amount then been available. When such an item does turn up and its amount is clearly significant, it should be reported as an adjustment of retained earnings (the tail end of our illustrative statement) rather than as an element in the determination of net income for the current period. Such items are rare; and the result is that retained earnings is, for all practical purposes, kept "clean"—that is, rarely is its beginning-of-the-year balance modified to reflect currently discovered corrections of prior-year earnings determinations.

TEST PROBLEM

Revenue Data

During the year 19XX, Tarrant Co. sold its products for a total of $5,627,483. Of that amount, $525,480 had not been collected in cash by the end of the year and $24,000 was estimated to be uncollectible; during the year, the company collected $614,240 from sales made in earlier years. In addition to product sales, Tarrant earned $12,220 from dividends on stocks owned and $1,460 interest on bank deposits.

Expense Data

Assume that the company had no finished goods and no unfinished goods on hand at the beginning of the year. During the year, its manufacturing costs consisted of raw materials consumed, totaling $2,420,-000; factory labor, $1,115,000; and other factory costs (factory overhead) of $1,247,000. At the end of the year, unfinished goods on hand (i.e., the work in process inventory) were valued at $384,000 and finished goods on hand cost $418,000. Selling expenses totaled $592,-000, and general administrative expenses were $614,250 for the year. There were no interest expenses, and the company has no preferred stock outstanding. Income taxes were $154,000. During the year, the company suffered an uninsured flood loss of $125,000 and was required to pay $75,000 in damages resulting from litigation originating 2 years earlier. Retained earnings at the beginning of the year, according to the accounting records, stood at $1,500,000. Cash dividends paid were $1 per share on 100,000 shares. The common stock outstanding during the year, averaged to reflect fluctuations in number and time outstanding, was 102,000 shares.

Required

Prepare an income statement based on the data given above; assume that the company employs accrual accounting. Enter the data in the blank form provided on page 24.

TEST PROBLEM Solution Space

TARRANT CO.
Income Statement for the Year 19XX

Revenues:

$

$

Revenue deductions:
  Expenses:

$

_____ $

$

Income before extraordinary item $

Net income $

Retained earnings at beginning of year:
  As previously reported $

  Adjustment for
  As restated $

$

Cash dividends
Retained earnings at end of year $

Per share of common stock:
  Income before extraordinary item $
  Extraordinary item (flood loss)
  Net income $

3
The Accounting Structure

Management Decisions

As "boss," whether at the top, middle, or otherwise, you qualify for your title only because of the faith that one or more persons (including yourself) must have in your ability to make rational decisions. Bossing is essentially a combination of leadership and decision making or, if you prefer, leadership and the acceptance of responsibility. Some bosses are so ultracautious that they literally trust no one to make subdecisions or to assist them by supplying them with the right information for the exercise of their decision-making responsibilities. Those bosses finally get bogged down at their desks. Other bosses blithely delegate most of their decision making to their subordinates and concentrate on golf, racquetball, or martini formulas. The better bosses, and let's hope they constitute the majority, fit in between those two extremes.

All decisions, by definition, relate to the future—they invariably involve *judgments* as to the results of choice among alternative courses of action. When a decision situation arises, the good boss knows what kind of information is needed as a guide in applying *judgment* to the problem. Good bosses develop the supportive personnel necessary to be able to call for, and get, the relevant information in a hurry. They do not *develop* the information (with some exceptions); they *delegate* the job. But they should know what the information providers are doing with their time; they must understand what the information means *so that they can call for it as needed* rather than depend passively on their helpers to decide what they need. They will never allow their accountants to set up a private, impenetrable empire.

Accounting data are essential to a wide range of decisions, but the data that are stored by accountants are almost entirely the details of transactions, or events, that have occurred in the past. Well-trained accountants are capable of doing much more than perform the mere function of collecting and storing information for your use. They are also capable of "interpreting" the information for you, and, with the historical records plus current and probable future data, they should be of great help to you in your *planning* activities. Needless to say, planning covers a major portion of all executive activity, and we can merely mention it here.

However, the whole point of this section is to urge you, as an executive, to know what your accountants are doing so that you can call on them for information not only on a routine basis but, whenever necessary, on an emergency basis, and so that you can sensibly evaluate the information which they supply in response to your calls. To do so requires that you be able to talk the accountant's language. Perhaps that's the whole purpose of this book. Each chapter may involve getting you "over a hump," and we hope that you'll take the humps in stride. A major hump comes in the remainder of this chapter as we get down to the absolute elements of accounting, including the debit-and-credit lingo. We're going to review the elements of the typical accounting system—the forms, the journals, the ledgers, etc., and we probably will bore you.

Business Forms

Basic to all accounting is something we all view as unpalatable—the red tape. This is the deadly job of making notations on *business forms.* If you have good internal accounting help, they have designed the forms that are needed. Business forms are the seeds that produce the valuable crops—the decision-supporting reports. Probably it's a good thing for executives to keep the form producers in the company constantly on the defensive. You must respect the concept of business forms, but don't allow the forms to spring up and flourish like weeds around you. If, as an executive, you find that basic business documents are routinely flowing across your desk, the chances are you're being put upon by somebody. Business forms are designed for *routine processing.* This means they should flow automatically to bookkeepers, computer operators, or other individuals who may (1) merely file (store) them, (2) process them and prepare a report to you of any "exceptional" items that call for action on your part, (3) summarize them in the form of a routine report (headlines only) for you as an executive, or (4) make accounting entries from them.

Business forms, in the accounting sense, are "source" documents; they are the raw materials of the formal accounting records. All the documents that record transactions or events that will affect your financial statements and supporting schedules flow to the accounting department. (Carbon copies, of course, may go to other departments as needed.) And, most important, when computers are used for processing the accounting data, the forms must be designed to act as effective "input" media, or they may be omitted when the data are entered directly into the data processing equipment.

To record, in the formal accounting sense, means to *make an accounting entry* in a *journal* or in a *ledger.*

The Accounting Journal

Widespread computerization has, of course, greatly modified the physical trappings of accounting systems to the point where the traditional *journal,* as well as the various ledger forms, has virtually disappeared from the scene. However, the underlying need for some sort of journal-ledger structure has not been lessened, and the analysis of business transactions in the form of old-fashioned journal entries will be an important tool in the use of this book. In a later chapter we discuss computer software and how it can be used in businesses in a variety of ways.

When a transaction occurs, it must somehow be "recorded," usually as a whole, as an entry in some sort of business diary so that, at any future date, interested parties may refer back to the details of the transaction, in accounting form, when necessary. A given journal entry may be very simple, and the same entry, with varying dollar amounts, may be recorded many times daily; another journal entry may be very complex, as when a transaction involves changes in several financial aspects of the business. Actually, a complete journal entry always consists of two or more entries which are also to be recorded in the accounting ledger.

The Accounting Ledger

The journal, often referred to as a *book of original entry,* serves as a diary in which each transaction, or batch of similar transactions, is recorded intact. The next step is to take precisely the same transactions and record them over again in the ledgers, or *books of final entry.* The difference is that each piece of the entry recorded first in the journal is copied ("posted") in its own ledger account. So if a journal entry is composed of, say, five pieces, each of those five pieces will be posted to a separate ledger account. The journal is organized as a chronological record of transactions, as units, in the order of their occurrence; the ledger is organized into as many different pages (or "accounts") as are needed to accumulate the pieces posted (copied) from the journal but classified according to significant financial elements.

To illustrate. We borrow $1,000 from the bank. This is a transaction. It is recorded ("journalized") in the journal in technical form to show that two financial changes were caused by the bank loan: (1) The bank added $1,000 to our checking account, which is to say that our Cash in Bank increased by $1,000, and (2) counterbalancing the $1,000 addition to our bank account is an addition of $1,000 to our liabilities, under the technical heading of Bank Loans Payable. In the journal the two effects are recorded as a matched pair—a whole transaction—journalized as a unit. Next, the $1,000 increase of Cash in Bank is copied from the journal entry to a *ledger page* headed Cash in Bank and the $1,000 increase of Bank Loans Payable is copied (posted) to a ledger page (we set up a new sheet if we don't already have one) labeled Bank Loans Payable.

The *ledger*, then, consists of as many different sheets (accounts) as we feel we need to keep track of the many financial elements of the business. As a starter, let's assume that in our ledger we would, at least, have a separate account for each of the items to be listed in our balance sheet and our income statement. In fact, the ledger sheets (the ledger accounts) will be in loose-leaf form and will be filed in the same order as they appear in the financial statements. You see, the amounts shown in the financial statements are found by merely copying the balances of the ledger accounts into the arrangements chosen for the financial statements.

The Ledger Account

It is quite common for companies to have their ledger pages printed according to their own prescription, but the fundamental structure remains the same. The classical account has two sides—left and right —separated by a vertical line, and the account is topped by a horizontal line on which the account's name (and an assigned account number) is written. We cannot afford to be concerned about bookkeeping details, so we'll ignore the various forms in which the account may be designed and stick to the fundamental shape, which is that of a T. Just visualize a page divided down the middle, representing the stem of the T, with a horizontal line about an inch from the top of the page, representing the crossbar of the T, on which the title (e.g., Cash in

Bank) and the reference number (e.g., 101) are written. (See Figure 3.1.)

Now, how do we use this gadget? You will need to memorize the formula, and then we'll use it throughout the book; when you get through, it should have become second nature to you.

Here's the plan. One side of each account will be used to record *increases* in the content of that account and the opposite side will be used for *decreases*. The first thing to remember is that all asset and all expense accounts follow the same rule—to record an *increase in any asset or any expense* make an entry in the *left-hand* side of that asset's or that expense's account. To remember that shouldn't be too tough for you because, as you recall, in Chapter 1 (and throughout American practice) assets are displayed on the left-hand side of the balance sheet. Remember? Thus, assets may be thought of as "left-handed" items.

It's a bit harder to explain why expense accounts are operated the same as asset accounts, but think of expenses as "expired assets" and then show *increases in expenses by left-hand entries* (the same as assets).

Now, if increases in assets and increases in expenses are recorded by left-hand entries, their decreases will have to be recorded on the right-hand side of their Ts.

Asset and Expense Accounts

In Figure 3.1 you see a T account for Cash in Bank to which a number of postings have been made. (We could call it a "skeleton ledger account" because it's stripped down to bare bones.) You should be able to read this account as follows: The company had a bank balance of $1,242.50 at the beginning of the year, January 1. Its deposits, posted as summary totals for each month (asset additions are shown on the

Figure 3.1 Skeleton ledger account.

Cash in Bank			101
Jan. 1, Bal.		1,242.50	Jan. 31	7,214.20
Jan. 31		6,857.28	Feb. 28	4,114.18
Feb. 28		7,142.86	Mar. 31	7,212.15
Mar. 31		4,125.19	Apr. 30	3,756.92
Apr. 30		5,147.31		22,297.45
	2,217.69	24,515.14		

left-hand side of an asset account), were $6,857.28 for January, $7,142.86 for February, $4,125.19 for March, and $5,147.31 for April. The accountant has informally "footed" this column in small pencil figures showing a total of $24,515.14 on the left-hand side. The withdrawals from the bank account, also shown in the form of monthly totals, are recorded on the right-hand side of the account. Again informally totaled, the withdrawals footing is $22,297.45 for the period, leaving a left-hand balance of $24,515.14–$22,297.45, or $2,217.69. This should be the amount of cash in bank as of April 30, and it is the amount that would appear in the company's balance sheet dated April 30 were one to be prepared "as of" that date.

In Figure 3.2 you see a T account for Miscellaneous Office Expenses. Like asset accounts, the T accounts for all expenses are "left-handed." There's one big difference, however. At the end of an accounting period the closing balance then existing in each asset account (after any corrections, updatings, or adjustments that may be required) is "carried forward" as the beginning balance of the next period. Note again the January 1 balance shown in Figure 3.1. This is the "opening" balance for the current year, which, of course, began as the final stroke of midnight closed out the preceding year; thus, the closing balance of one year (or other accounting period) becomes the opening balance of the adjoining year *when the cumulative amounts are actually carried forward from one period to the next.* But the expenses of one period pertain to that period only (if we've done a good job of accounting for our expenses). Thus, we speak of the advertising expense, the depreciation expense, etc., of last year as compared with the advertising expense, etc., of this year. What this signifies is that each expense account *starts out each year with a zero balance.* The expense for one year is the expense for that year—it cannot at the same time be the expense for some other year. To repeat, all expense accounts have beginning-of-year (opening) balances of zero. During the year we make left-hand entries in them to keep track of each kind of expense as it builds up. Then at the end of the year we again empty the account (by simply making a right-hand entry in it sufficient to reduce its balance to zero) and we're ready to repeat the expense-recording process for the next period. These emptying-out entries are known as *closing entries.* Now note in Figure 3.2 that a number of entries have been made to record Miscellaneous Office Expenses as they were incurred throughout the year, but there was no opening balance. Note also that we've made a closing (right-hand) entry equal to the sum of the left-hand entries and thus ended up with a zero balance—the account is swept clean in readiness for next year's "charges." The number of left-hand entries in

Figure 3.2 in our case has no particular significance; only a few are needed to exemplify the accounting treatment of expenses.

To review, then, expenses (like assets) are recorded by entries on the left-hand side of each expense account involved; at the end of each accounting period (usually a year), a right-hand (closing) entry is made to reduce the account's balance to zero in readiness for the next period's entries to be made as a continuation of the same account. Note how the two sides of the expense account are footed and ruled to provide a clean start for the next year (Figure 3.2).

Figure 3.2 Expense account.

Miscellaneous Office Expenses			
Jan. 12, 19X1	175.20	Dec. 31 (to close)	720.63
Mar. 26	214.18		
Sept. 19	129.20		
Dec. 7	202.05		
	720.63		720.63

Equity and Revenue Accounts

In order to use the terms *debit* and *credit* as accountants do, we must apply the rules just illustrated for assets and expenses to the opposite side of the coin—that is, to the equity accounts and the revenue accounts, where they work exactly in reverse. To record asset increases, you make left-hand entries; but to record increases in liabilities, you make right-hand entries. We consider both the liabilities and the accounts showing the owner's equities to be forms of equities; the rule for increasing owners' equity accounts is the same as that for liabilities—increases are recorded by right-hand entries. In short, any equity account (liability or ownership) is increased by a right-hand entry. That is perfectly logical because on the balance sheet, as you have seen, all the equities are reported on the right-hand side. And, to wrap it all up, revenues are positive factors with respect to ownership accounts. That is, your sales revenue, your interest revenue, your dividend revenue, and your rent revenue all have the effect of increasing your ownership equity; so *revenue accounts* (the exact opposite of expense accounts in effect) also *are increased by right-hand entries.*

Figure 3.3 shows an important liability account, Accounts Payable, and an important revenue account, Sales Revenue, with illustrative entries which bear out what has just been said. Note that Accounts

Figure 3.3 Liability account and revenue account.

Accounts Payable

Jan. 31	27,380	Jan. 1, Bal.	20,267
Feb. 28	36,120	Jan. 31	35,200
Mar. 31	39,170	Feb. 28	29,600
Mar. 31, Bal.	24,537	Mar. 31	42,140
	127,207		127,207
		Apr. 1, Bal.	24,537

Sales Revenue

Mar. 31 (to close)	138,790	Jan. 31	43,010
		Feb. 28	39,640
		Mar. 31	56,140
	138,790		138,790

Payable, a balance sheet account, has an opening and a closing balance (just like Cash in Bank), whereas Sales Revenue starts each year at zero, builds up as sales are made, and is "closed out" at the end of the year just as expense accounts are closed out.

You should now have no trouble interpreting the entries in the accounts shown in Figure 3.3. Accounts Payable shows six amounts on the right-hand side. To keep the illustration short, it has been assumed that the accounting period is 3 months rather than a year, so the right-hand items consist of the opening balance of $20,267 carried forward from December 31, plus a lump-sum addition at the end of each month. The left-hand side shows three lump-sum entries representing amounts of accounts payable paid off (decreases) and a "plug" figure which is the *balance* at the end of our assumed 3-month accounting period. This plug figure makes the two sides equal; after footing and ruling both sides in fancy accounting style, the balancing figure is "brought down" on the right-hand side as the net amount owed at the start of the new period on April 1. Thus, the closing balance on March 31 becomes the opening balance on April 1.

The Sales Revenue account is easier to interpret. As in the case of expense accounts, there's never an opening balance in a revenue account at the start of a period; after entries are made on the right-hand side to record the revenue of each month, the whole amount is canceled out by a left-hand closing entry. To repeat, asset and equity accounts (balance sheet accounts) generally have opening and closing balances —amounts carried forward from one period to the next. Expense and revenue accounts have no opening or closing balances because they are swept clean at the end of each period by closing entries.

Figure 3.4 summarizes the rules that we have been examining.

Figure 3.4   Rules for accounts.

Any Asset Account		Any Equity (Liability or Ownership)	
Increases	Decreases	Decreases	Increases

Any Expense Account		Any Revenue Account	
Increases	Decreases	Decreases	Increases

The Process of Recording Complete Transactions

Now for a very basic rule: *At all times the sum of all amounts accumulated by left-hand entries must be kept equal to the sum of all amounts accumulated by right-hand entries.* This is the secret of the balance sheet—this is why the total of the asset side always equals the total of the equity side.

And now for a corollary rule: *Whenever any transaction is recorded, the accountant must make left-hand and right-hand entries that are equal in amount* (so that the basic rule is not violated).

Let's accustom ourselves to these rules by the process of making a few fundamental entries.

Assume (1) that a corporation is established by the issuance of common stock for cash in the amount of $100,000. To record this transaction (pretending that it is a single transaction), we must recognize the increase in the asset, Cash in Bank, by setting up a ledger account with that title and making a left-hand (increase) entry in the amount of $100,000. *And,* concurrently, we must record the creation of the owners' equity (they invested $100,000) by setting up a ledger account entitled Capital Stock and making a right-hand (increase) entry in it. Figure 3.5 shows the entire ledger of our new company after the first transaction has been recorded by equal left- and right-handed entries.

Could we prepare a balance sheet now by using the data in the ledger accounts? Certainly. The asset side would show a total of $100,-000, consisting entirely of cash in bank, and the equities side would show a total of $100,000, consisting entirely of the owner's equity, capital stock.

Figure 3.5 Ledger accounts.

Cash in Bank	Capital Stock
(1) 100,000	(1) 100,000

Let's try another. Assume (2) that the company spends $40,000 of cash to purchase a building worth $30,000 on land worth $10,000. Here our balanced transaction is made up of left-hand entries of $30,000 to Building and $10,000 to Land offset by a right-hand entry of $40,000 to Cash in Bank. The accounts now stand as in Figure 3.6.

Figure 3.6 Amended ledger accounts.

Cash in Bank		Capital Stock
(1) 100,000	(2) 40,000	(1) 100,000
Building		
(2) 30,000		
Land		
(2) 10,000		

Were we now to produce a balance sheet, it would show three assets totaling $100,000 and one equity with a balance of $100,000.

Now try some more basic entries. Assume that the following transactions occur—starting with (3) to carry on our illustration:

3. The company borrows $10,000 by giving the bank an x percent, 60-day, note payable. (See entry 3 in Figure 3.7.)

4. The company buys merchandise on account for $20,000. (See entry 4 in Figure 3.7).

5. The company sells merchandise on account for $30,000. (See entry 5 in Figure 3.7).

6. Cash is paid for miscellaneous operating expenses, $8,000. (See entry 6 in Figure 3.7).

Figure 3.7 Transactions added to ledger accounts.

Cash in Bank				Capital Stock		
(1)	100,000	(2)	40,000		(1)	100,000
(3)	10,000	(6)	8,000			
		✓ Bal.	62,000			
	110,000		110,000			
✓ Bal.	62,000					

Building		Retained Earnings			
(2)	30,000	(8a)	8,000	(8c)	30,000
		(8b)	15,000		
		✓ Bal.	7,000		
			30,000		30,000
				✓ Bal.	7,000

Land		Bank Loan Payable	
(2)	10,000	(3)	10,000

Merchandise				Accounts Payable	
(4)	20,000	(7)	15,000	(4)	20,000
		✓ Bal	5,000		
	20,000		20,000		
✓ Bal.	5,000				

Accounts Receivable		Sales Revenue			
(5)	30,000	(8c)	30,000	(5)	30,000

Miscellaneous Operating Expenses				Merchandise Cost of Sales			
(6)	8,000	(8a)	8,000	(7)	15,000	(8b)	15,000

7. A count (inventory) is made of the amount and cost of merchandise remaining on hand at the end of the period, which is found to be $5,000. This signifies that all the rest of the merchandise must have been transferred to customers in the sales transactions summarized in (5) above. In other words, the merchandise asset which cost $20,000 has been reduced

to $5,000; that is, of the $20,000 of merchandise asset, $15,-
000 has been given up and constitutes an *expense* known as
Merchandise Cost of Sales. (Many accountants call this Cost
of Goods Sold.) So entry (7) consists of a right-hand entry of
$15,000 in the Merchandise account and a left-hand entry to
Merchandise Cost of Sales.

8. Now we make closing entries. To do so, as you will recall,
we must reduce the balance of each expense account and
each revenue account to zero by making offsetting (closing)
entries on the "reducing" side of each account sufficient to
reduce the balance to zero. Query: When we make a right-
hand entry to Miscellaneous Operating Expense to close
that account, where do we make our required, equal left-
hand entry? Try Retained Earnings. Note that similar entries are made to close the other expense account, Merchandise Cost of Sales. And our only revenue account,
Sales, is closed by a left-hand entry which is accompanied
by a right-hand entry of the same amount to Retained
Earnings. So, essentially, expenses end up on the left-hand
(reducing) side of Retained Earnings and revenues end up
on the right-hand side; and the expense and revenue accounts are left in a zero (closed) condition in readiness for
the operations of the next accounting period.

The General Journal

It would appear that we're not getting first things first. Earlier it was
said that entries should be recorded first in the journal, from which the
items are posted to ledger accounts. That's true, but it's easier to depict
the left and right sides of a ledger account; so we just skipped the
journal for the time being. Now, in Figure 3.8 you'll find all the entries
as they would appear in formal, chronological order in a simple journal
form. Note that to symbolize left-hand entries, we merely write the
account title as far to the left as we can and put the corresponding dollar
amount in the left-hand money column on the same line. Right-hand
titles are simply indented a half-inch or so, and their corresponding
dollar amounts are entered in the right-hand money column. Dates (in
our case, transaction numbers) are inserted in a column on the left-hand
edge, and a brief explanation is written after each journal entry. The
complete journal appears in Figure 3.8.

Figure 3.8 Simple journal form.

The General Journal

Dates		LF	Left	Right
1	Cash in Bank	✓	100,000	
	Capital Stock	✓		100,-000
	To launch the corporation, $100,000 of capital stock is issued at par for cash.			
2	Building	✓	30,000	
	Land	✓	10,000	
	Cash in Bank	✓		40,000
	A building costing $30,000 on land, valued at $10,000, is purchased for cash.			
3	Cash in Bank	✓	10,000	
	Bank Loan Payable	✓		10,000
	Borrowed $10,000 from bank on x%, 60-day note.			
4	Merchandise	✓	20,000	
	Accounts Payable	✓		20,000
	Purchase of merchandise on account.			
5	Accounts Receivable	✓	30,000	
	Sales Revenue	✓		30,000
	Sales of merchandise on account.			
6	Miscellaneous Operating Expenses	✓	8,000	
	Cash in Bank	✓		8,000
7	Merchandise Cost of Sales	✓	15,000	
	Merchandise	✓		15,000
	Cost of merchandise asset given up in sales recorded in (5) above.			
8a	Retained Earnings	✓	8,000	
	Miscellaneous Operating Expenses	✓		8,000
	To close Miscellaneous Operating Expenses to Retained Earnings.			
8b	Retained Earnings	✓	15,000	
	Merchandise Cost of Sales	✓		15,000
	To close Merchandise Cost of Sales.			
8c	Sales Revenue	✓	30,000	
	Retained Earnings	✓		30,000
	To close Sales Revenue.			

Comments on Figures 3.7 and 3.8

From the illustration that you have just traced through, you should now recognize that in the journal (which we should have prepared first as the book of original entry) each transaction (or summary of a group of similar transactions such as sales) is recorded as a unit so that you can see all aspects of it in one place. Next, each left-hand entry and each right-hand entry is posted to a ledger account that carries *precisely the same title* as is used in the journal entry. At the end of the accounting period, journal entries are made to close the revenue and expense accounts, so that their net effect is reflected in Retained Earnings. The revenue and expense accounts now have zero balances and are ready for similar entries in the next period; the balance sheet accounts are left open, so that their balances will carry forward into the next period. Note that the balances to be carried forward are singled out by the formal ruling and balancing procedure.

Closing Entries Revisited

Instead of closing each expense account and each revenue account directly to Retained Earnings, it is customary to close them first to a temporary summary account called Income Summary, or Profit and Loss; then the net balance of that account is closed to Retained Earnings. This keeps Retained Earnings from becoming cluttered up with hundreds of entries. Closing entries performed this way are shown in Figure 3.9.

Use of Subsidiary Ledgers

So far we have examined transactions through the accounting procedures that lead to your periodic financial statements and we've made debits and credits to *general ledger* accounts only. However, business constantly needs detailed information for reasons other than preparing periodic financial statements, such as its dealings with individual customers and creditors. Consider charge (credit) customers for a moment. If a business has significant numbers of such customers, what would happen if we made debits for every one of them to the same general ledger account when they bought goods or services from us, and made credits for every one of them to that same general ledger account when they paid us? Wouldn't that account become a genuine mess? How could we hope to tell later from that account how much each customer

Figure 3.9 Closing entries.

8*a*	Income Summary (instead of Retained Earnings)	8,000	
	Miscellaneous Operating Expenses		8,000
	To close miscellaneous expenses to Income Summary.		
8*b*	Income Summary (instead of Retained Earnings)	15,000	
	Merchandise Cost of Sales		15,000
	To close cost of goods sold.		
8*c*	Sales Revenue	30,000	
	Income Summary (instead of Retained Earnings)		30,000
8*d*	Income Summary	7,000	
	Retained Earnings (finally, for net income only)		7,000
	To close Income Summary to Retained Earnings.		

owed us? Which ones were entitled to discounts for early payment? Clearly we must find some alternative, and that is to use *subsidiary ledger* accounts.

Here's how: As customers buy goods and services from us, all of them are debited in total to a single Accounts Receivable account in the general ledger—called a *Control* account (credits are made to Sales Revenue). We don't need to make an entry in the control accounts receivable account in the general ledger each time we make a sale. We can delay making the entry until the end of a month, for example, and then record it as a grand total, just so the account will be brought up to date for statement purposes. But let's systematically record *each* sale to a charge customer as a debit to that customer's *individual* subsidiary ledger account—we'll have one for each charge customer. And when the customer pays us, we'll credit that particular customer's subsidiary ledger account. These subsidiary ledger accounts look like, and are used like, the general ledger accounts we have been discussing.

Hence, at any time we should be able to go through each customer's subsidiary ledger account and find the complete story of each. However, if we're concerned only with our total (for financial statement purposes), we find it in our regular, general ledger control account for accounts receivable which is posted up to date through monthly journal entries that record debits for all sales on account and credits for all payments received from charge customers.

If you've followed this, you will recognize that at the end of the month we could take an adding machine tape of the balances of all the customers' subsidiary accounts, and its total should agree with the balance of the general ledger control account for accounts receivable. Notice two things: First, most of the accounts in our general ledger are control accounts, each receiving aggregate rather than detailed debits and credits and being "supported" by subsidiary ledgers on which we keep track of details needed to operate the business efficiently and effectively, just as is done with accounts receivable (such as for accounts payable, raw materials, and individual jobs performed in a manufacturing firm, among many others). Second, subsidiary ledgers can take many forms, the T form we have discussed, or cards, or sheets of paper, to name but a few. Control and subsidiary accounts are used very extensively in cost accounting, as we shall see in later chapters.

The Trial Balance

What should happen if we were now to make a list of all the ledger accounts and, opposite each account, show the net balance of each as it now stands? Answer: We would have prepared a *trial balance*, and the thing had better balance!

Fortunately, our illustration is a simple one and, because we made no mistakes, our trial balance does balance. See Figure 3.10.

Note that we have listed all accounts, though some have no balances.

Figure 3.10   Trial balance after closing.

	Balances	
Trial Balance after Closing	*Left*	*Right*
Cash in bank	$ 62,000	
Building	30,000	
Land	10,000	
Merchandise	5,000	
Accounts receivable	30,000	
Accounts payable		$ 20,000
Bank loan payable		10,000
Capital stock		100,000
Retained earnings		7,000
Sales revenue		—
Merchandise cost of sales	—	
Miscellaneous operating expenses	—	
	$137,000	$137,000

Customarily accounts with zero balances are not listed. However, a trial balance can be prepared any time that you want one; so let's see how ours would look had it been prepared *before* the closing entries (8a, b, c, and d) were made. See Figure 3.11.

Note that this trial balance shows no balance for Retained Earnings because (1) this is the first year of operation for our company and (2) the revenue and expense accounts have not yet been closed to Income Summary and to Retained Earnings.

It is customary to prepare a trial balance at the end of each month (1) to reveal the existence of bookkeeping errors which would "throw the trial balance out of balance" and (2) to aid in preparation of monthly financial statements.

The Financial Statements

Quite obviously, an income statement and a position statement can easily be prepared by copying the figures from Figure 3.11 (or from Figure 3.10) in the proper forms. Note, however, that we are for present purposes ignoring the fact that the building would have depreciated a bit during the year and we would owe some interest on the bank loan and some income taxes. The resulting income statement is shown as Figure 3.12 and the balance sheet as Figure 3.13.

Figure 3.11 Trial balance before closing.

Trial Balance before Closing

	Left	*Right*
Cash in bank	$ 62,000	
Accounts receivable	30,000	
Merchandise	5,000	
Land	10,000	
Building	30,000	
Accounts payable		$ 20,000
Bank loan		10,000
Capital stock		100,000
Retained earnings		—
Sales revenue		30,000
Merchandise cost of sales	15,000	
Miscellaneous operating expenses	8,000	
	$160,000	$160,000

Figure 3.12 An income statement prepared from trial balance.

OUR COMPANY
Income Statement for the Year Ended December 31, 19XX

Sales		$30,000
Expenses:		
Merchandise cost of sales	$15,000	
Miscellaneous operating expenses	8,000	
Depreciation (omitted)	—	
Interest on bank loan (omitted)	—	
Income taxes (omitted)	—	23,000
Net income (to retained earnings)		$ 7,000

Figure 3.13 A position statement prepared from trial balance.

OUR COMPANY
Balance Sheet, December 31, 19XX

Assets			Equities		
Current:			Current liabilities:		
Cash in bank	$62,000		Accounts		
Accounts			payable		$ 20,000
receivable	30,000		Bank loan		10,000
Merchandise	5,000	$ 97,000			$ 30,000
Noncurrent:			Stock equity:		
Land	$10,000		Capital stock	$100,000	
Building	30,000	40,000	Retained		
		$137,000	earnings	7,000	107,000
					$137,000

Conclusion

Now you have had a glimpse at the traditional accounting financial statements and at all the traditional accounting routines except one. We have mentioned the need for making *adjusting entries* at the end of each accounting period; but the entries deserve more than a passing glance, so we'll examine them in the next chapter. It should be noted, however, that entry 7, which recorded the cost of merchandise sold, is an adjusting entry; and adjusting entries would be needed to recognize depreciation of the building and the end-of-period liability for income taxes. Those financial developments, as was pointed out earlier in our book, occurred in a "flow" rather than "on-the-spot" form.

For your exercise, a set of data and forms appear below for you to use in performing the accounting tasks described in this chapter. Formal solutions, as usual, are presented in the appendix.

TEST PROBLEM

The problem that follows is designed to include only the barest essentials of the accounting cycle—a skeleton on which we can build, in logical sequence, to the end that we should be able to unravel the most perplexing of the problems of modern-day financial reporting and analysis. To solve this problem, you are asked merely to record a few basic transactions directly in the accompanying skeleton ledger accounts and to prepare a trial balance, statements, and closing entries in the forms provided. The assumed transaction data follow:

Transaction Data (Month of July)

(1) Empire Corp. is established and 10,000 shares of $10 par common stock are issued for cash which is deposited directly in the bank.

(2) A building is rented for $1,000 per month and July rent is paid. (Treat the rent as a miscellaneous expense.)

(3) Store equipment is purchased for cash, $30,000.

(4) Merchandise is purchased on account, $50,000.

(5) Sales, all on account, total $60,000.

(6) Miscellaneous expenses, all paid in cash, total $10,000.

(7) At the end of July, an inventory is taken and it is determined that, of the $50,000 of merchandise purchased, $15,000 remains on hand; that is, the merchandise inventory on July 31 is determined to be $15,000.

(8) The estimated useful life of the equipment is 20 years with no significant salvage value likely at the end of the life. Accordingly, the depreciation expense for July is determined to be one-twentieth of the cost divided by 12, or $1,500 ÷ 12, or $125. (Treat as a miscellaneous expense.)

(9) A trial balance is prepared.

(10) An income statement is prepared.

(11) A balance sheet is prepared.

(12) Closing entries are made.

TEST PROBLEM Solution Space

EMPIRE CORP.
Ledger

Cash in Bank	Capital Stock

Accounts Receivable	Retained Earnings

Merchandise	Sales

Store Equipment	Merchandise Cost of Sales

Accounts Payable	Miscellaneous Expenses

Income Summary

---

(9) EMPIRE CORP.
Trial Balance (before closing), July 31, 19XX

	Balances	
Account Title	*Left*	*Right*
	$	
		$
	$	$

(10) EMPIRE CORP.
Income Statement for July, 19XX

Sales		$
Expenses:		
Merchandise cost of sales	$	
Miscellaneous	_____	
Net income (and earnings retained)		$

(11) EMPIRE CORP.
Balance Sheet, July 31, 19XX

Assets		Equities	
Current:		Current liabilities:	
Cash in bank	$	Accounts	
Accounts		payable	$
receivable		Stock equity:	
Merchandise		Capital stock	$
inventory	$	Retained	
Store		earnings	_____
equipment			
	$		$

4
The Accounting Cycle

Elements of the Accounting Cycle

No matter what kind of accounting system the individual business enterprise maintains, the so-called *cycle* (or sequence) *of accounting activities* will be basically the same. The word "cycle" should not be defined too precisely, however.

Although a specific "bit" of accounting data will typically flow through the various stages of the cycle in consecutive order, such bits of data are being introduced into the accounting system at all times throughout the period, and thus, within the business as a whole, several parts of the cycle will be undergoing activity simultaneously.

In the order of their classical sequence, the stages of the accounting cycle are:

1. *Underlying documents.* Transaction data are recorded (stored) in underlying documents or in computer storage files.

2. *Journalizing.* The transaction data on the underlying documents are sorted and entered in the *journal*(s) either individually or in batches as summarized lists.

3. *Posting.* The transaction data are "posted" from the journal(s) to the ledgers. In some cases individual journal items may be posted; in other cases, the journals are so designed that much of the journal data can be summed and posted in total to the ledger. (Much posting time is thereby saved, and accuracy is improved.)

4. *Trial balance.* A trial balance is prepared to test bookkeeping accuracy and to aid in preparation of the work sheet and

statements. (Step 5 might well be labeled "Hunt for Errors," but we'll assume the trial balance did balance immediately.)

5. *Work sheet.* A work sheet may be prepared at the end of the period, before adjusting entries are made. The work sheet will be explained and illustrated later in this chapter.

6. *Adjusting entries.* The end-of-period adjusting entries are made. This means that they are *(a)* journalized and *(b)* posted to ledger accounts just as regular transaction entries are handled.

7. *Closing entries.* There's not much to be said about closing entries except that their purpose, at the end of an accounting period, is to sweep clean the income statement accounts (all revenue, expense, loss, tax, and interest accounts) to make them ready for the accumulation of similar information in the next period. The net result of the sweeping operation is entered in the Retained Earnings account as the net income for the year. (Here you can see why we must emphasize the need for care in the process of "matching" costs or expenses with revenues each period—to arrive at a sensible *net income* for the period.) The routine closing entry procedure was illustrated in Chapter 3.

8. *Financial statements.* After everything is shipshape, with all accounts adjusted up to date, with all liabilities determined, etc., financial statements are drafted. Fundamentally this operation involves no more than the copying of amounts, accumulated in the ledger accounts, into whatever forms the management elects to use in the structure of the income statement, the position statement, and the funds statement (see Chapter 6).

9. *Independent audit.* When all the above steps have been taken, it may be appropriate (or mandatory) to engage a firm of CPAs to perform an "independent" audit. What this means in essence is that outside, professional auditors examine your financial statements and, to the extent deemed necessary, your accounting records, the supporting documents, and whatever else is needed, and express their opinion (the so-called *accountants' certificate*) that your statements are prepared in accordance with generally accepted accounting principles. Over the years the CPA firms have expanded their activities to include tax-return preparation, accounting

systems design, budgeting, and a wide range of management consulting services.

What Is Meant by the Accounting Period?

We generally think of the accounting period as a year—a 12-month passage of time—whether the year be a regular calendar year ending on December 31 or a so-called *fiscal year* which closes at the end of whatever month suits the business. However, if 12 months is the formal accounting period, we must recognize that for the effective management of the business, as well as for effective disclosure of operations to absentee owners, financial reports are inevitably needed more frequently. Such reports are known as *interim statements;* and though the term is not too commonly used, we might refer to the time spanned by any report that covers less than a year as an *interim period.*

In the preceding section appears a list of the basic procedures that constitute a complete accounting cycle. From such a list it might be inferred that the only accounting activity within an accounting period is the accumulation of financial data on underlying documents followed by journalizing and posting of the data. However, depending upon the size and needs of the organization, the accounting staff may devote a substantial amount of time to what is known as *internal auditing* and to the preparation of routine as well as special-purpose reports for the various levels of management. Essentially, internal auditing consists of systematically checking the data that flow into the accounting records to assure their accuracy. In many situations, it involves the continuous testing of the organizational controls that have been set up to prevent the commission of recording errors or thefts of cash or other valuable resources. The nature of routine and special-purpose reports for internal management will be discussed in Chapter 15.

Again, referring to the list of activities that constitute the formal accounting cycle, let it be noted that some of the steps can be omitted or abridged when we are dealing with an interim period. For example, closing entries will *not* be made at the end of each month or each calendar quarter; and adjusting entries (which are necessary for any interim period no matter how short) may be made on a work sheet, which is then used directly for the preparation of the interim financial statements.

The balance of this chapter is devoted mainly to the nature of adjusting entries and the use of the work sheet.

What and Why Are Adjusting Entries?

If we do a good, thorough job of recording transactions as they occur, why should it ever be necessary to make adjusting entries at the end of the regular or interim period? The answer is that certain types of transactions (those that "flow" continuously) cannot be kept up to date; and for certain types of "spot" transactions, when they are repetitive and individually relatively insignificant, it is more efficient to allow the data to accumulate and record them in periodic batches (that is, by periodic adjusting entries which, in effect, treat the stream of spot transactions as if they constituted a continuous flow). A true flow-type transaction, of course, is something such as depreciation or interest expense or interest revenue, all of which "flow" continuously.

By merely scanning the list of accounts that make up a typical trial balance, you'll readily understand the inevitability of adjusting entries. Now let's look at a few as samples.

Start with cash in bank. If we have carefully recorded every collection or other receipt of cash, every deposit in the bank, and every check that we've written, should any end-of-period adjustment ever be called for? The answer is yes. Banks have the habit of making service charges (which may depend upon the number of checks, deposits, or other transactions handled in relation to the average balance maintained). Banks may make collections for you and report the collections via monthly statements. In short, any additions or reductions that the bank records with respect to your deposit account must be duplicated in your own accounting records, and the information for such "adjustments" may not be known to you until you receive the monthly bank statement.

Your company may hold, as temporary investments, marketable securities or other dividend- or interest-bearing investments as a means of obtaining some income on funds that are temporarily in excess of current operating needs. At the end of any accounting period, these investments must be reviewed to determine what interest and dividends may have been earned but have not yet been collected in the form of a spot-cash transaction. Adjusting entries are thus required to "accrue" interest and dividends receivable.

Accounts receivable are not always "good"—that is, almost every business is bound to have some deadbeats among its clientele. The recognition of so-called *bad debts* may be recorded on a spot basis (that is, whenever a specific account is determined to be uncollectible; it may be written off as a bad debt "expense"); or a periodic *blanket provision* may be made to reflect management's estimate of the portion of sales revenue that will never be collected. The latter procedure, which is the more common among larger companies, involves periodic adjustment to accrue the amount of bad debts estimated to have been accumulated within a given period. Typically this accrual adjustment is measured as a flat percentage (e.g., ½ percent) of the total credit sales for the period. Because this total is unknown until the end of the period, an end-of-period adjustment is required.

Next, consider merchandise. When an item of merchandise is sold, the event is, of course, a spot transaction. If you're a retailer of automobiles, it's likely that, when each sale is made, you'll not only record the revenue (remember, a left-hand entry to Cash or Accounts Receivable and a right-hand entry to Sales Revenue), but you'll also record the merchandise cost of the sale on the spot (by a left-hand entry to the expense account, Merchandise Cost of Sales and a right-hand entry to Merchandise or Car Inventory). But entries to record the individual costs of merchandise sold become highly impractical under many circumstances. Could an electric power company record the cost of each kilowatthour as the current flows through the customer's meter? Could the variety store record the cost of merchandise sold each time that it sells a ballpoint pen? Could a fabric shop make a cost of goods sold entry whenever it sells a yard of cloth? You can think of examples ad infinitum. The solution, of course, is to record only the revenue (and even that may be done in batches rather than individually) and *at the end of the period* make one big adjusting entry to record the cost of goods sold for the entire month (or longer period).

Almost every company pays in advance for various types of insurance. The moment the prepayment is made, the insurance begins to expire. We can't possibly record the expiration on a continuous basis—though we could make an accounting entry each day, or each week, or each month. Usually, we settle for the once-a-month solution. That, again, illustrates the fact that *the real purpose of adjusting entries is to update all accounts that have been allowed to lag as a practical necessity.*

The examples given so far should suffice as a demonstration of the *need* for periodic adjusting entries. Next, let's go through an illustrative problem dealing with adjusting entries. At the same time, we'll introduce the accountants' work sheet.

Problem Data

Tuesday Co. uses the calendar year as its formal accounting period, and management has asked the accounting staff to provide an interim income statement and a statement of financial position at the end of each month. Accordingly, at the end of January the accounting staff prepares a trial balance of the accounts as they stand before any adjusting entries have been made. The trial balance is as follows:

	Account Balances	
	Left	Right
Cash in bank	$ 5,000	
Marketable securities	20,000	
Accounts receivable	40,000	
Merchandise	60,000	
Prepaid insurance	3,000	
Land	8,000	
Equipment	60,000	
Buildings	80,000	
Allowance for depreciation		$ 30,000
Accounts payable		35,000
Notes payable		25,000
Capital stock		100,000
Retained earnings		21,000
Sales		85,000
Selling expenses	10,000	
Administrative expenses	10,000	
	$296,000	$296,000

It is determined that adjusting entries must be made as follows for the reasons listed:

1. Bank service charges, in the amount of $72 for the month of January, are shown on the monthly bank statement which has just been received. The required adjusting entry must record a $72 reduction of Cash in Bank (this calls for a right-hand entry) and a recognition of $72 of expense which, for our purposes, we'll classify as administrative expense (a left-hand entry). The entry, in skeleton journal form, is:

Administrative Expenses   72
    Cash in Bank   72

2. The marketable securities consist entirely of government, industrial, and public utility bonds. The interest earned in January (on an accrual basis) is determined to total $130. The required adjusting entry, to show the receivable of $130 and the corresponding interest revenue, is:

Interest Accrued Receivable	130	
Interest Revenue		130

Note that this entry depicts an increase in the asset Interest Accrued Receivable by a left-hand entry and an increase in the revenue account, Interest Revenue, by a right-hand entry.

3. This company's experience has shown that the bad debt rate has tended to be about 1 percent of total sales. Since any uncollectible receivables that came into being during January would still be "on the books," an adjusting entry must be made to show that receivables totaling approximately 1 percent of sales for the month of January are *probably* uncollectibles. The entry to record this adjustment is made as follows:

Bad Debts	850	
Allowance for Bad Debts		850

The left-hand entry, the charge to Bad Debts, represents not really an expense but a cancellation (offset or reduction) of the month's recorded sales revenue of $85,000. The accounts receivable must also be reduced by $850, but this is just an estimate; we don't yet know which specific accounts are uncollectible. We perform an accounting trick: we make the right-hand entry not to Accounts Receivable but to an offsetting account, which is named Allowance for Bad Debts. You should note that this is the practical equivalent of making a direct reduction of the accounts receivable balance; but since the accounts receivable are made up of accounts with, perhaps, hundreds of customers, we *achieve the effect* of a reduction by using what all accountants call a *contra* account —Allowance for Bad Debts. On the balance sheet this account shows up as follows:

Current assets:		
Cash in bank		$ 4,928
Accounts receivable	$40,000	
Less: Allowance for bad debts	850	39,150

By the procedure just demonstrated, we are able to keep the (so far unidentified) uncollectible accounts receivable on the books and, at the same time, achieve the financial effects of recognizing their worthlessness. (We'll soon see other uses for contra accounts.)

4. The $60,000 balance in the merchandise account consists of $20,000 carried over from last year plus $40,000 purchased in January. We have not attempted to record the merchandise cost of sales accompanying each recorded sale. We now determine, either by physical count or by estimate, that the cost of merchandise remaining on hand on January 31 is $10,000. This means that $50,000 has disappeared, we hope as the result of sale. Needless to say, the $50,000 may also include disappearance by theft, spoilage, and other forms of shrinkage. For the present we'll be charitable and pretend the whole $50,000 represents cost of goods sold. Then our required adjusting entry is to reduce the merchandise (asset) account to $10,000 by a right-hand entry and increase Cost of Goods Sold, an expense account, by a left-hand entry, as follows:

Cost of Goods Sold	50,000	
Merchandise		50,000

5. It is determined that the balance of Prepaid Insurance (often termed Unexpired Insurance) should be reduced by $100 to represent the amount that expired during January. A right-hand entry is made to reduce the asset, Prepaid Insurance, and a left-hand entry is made to increase our administrative expense, thus:

Administrative Expenses	100	
Prepaid Insurance		100

6. Equipment and buildings depreciate through use and with the passage of time. We'll look into this phenomenon later, but for the present let's assume that the depreciation for January totals $800. Now, rather than subtract the $800 directly from the numerous accounts that our company keeps for the various categories of equipment plus an account for the building, we again use the offset technique—the contra account—and make our right-hand entry to Allowance for Depreciation, and we split the left-hand entry (we'll assume it's a reasonable split) 80 percent to Selling Expenses and 20

percent to Administrative Expenses. Here's the entry in journal form:

```
Selling Expenses                    640
Administrative Expenses             160
    Allowance for Depreciation              800
```
To record equipment and building depreciation of $800, charging 80% to selling and 20% to administrative expenses.

7. Our salesclerks are paid weekly; and because January ended in the middle of a week, we must recognize "accrued wages payable" of $1,000, as follows:

```
Selling Expenses                  1,000
    Wages Accrued Payable                 1,000
```

You'll recognize the effects of this event—to increase Selling Expense by $1,000 and to increase a liability, Wages Accrued Payable, by $1,000. Note again that the word "accrued" is used to indicate an interim recognition of a liability that is growing through time and is to be paid later.

8. Interest on our notes payable was paid on last December 31, but by the end of January we must recognize the accrual of (assume) $200 of fresh interest expense. The entry is:

```
Interest Expense                    200
    Interest Accrued Payable                200
```

9. To round out our adjusting entries, we must recognize that we'll probably owe some income taxes. It's not easy to make a reliable estimate of the amount attributable to the first month of the year, but let's accept $2,500 as a reasonable guess. Our adjusting entry then is:

```
Income Tax Expense                2,500
    Income Tax Accrued Payable            2,500
```

Now if we can safely assume that there are no more adjusting entries to be made, we are ready to post entries 1 through 9 in our ledger accounts and prepare our monthly statements. But purely for educational purposes, let's now demonstrate the use of a work sheet as an instrument for the preparation of interim statements.

The Work Sheet

The accountant's work sheet is a most useful gadget, and it's something you are now well-equipped to handle. Here's the concept. We start with a sheet of columnar paper—one with a wide column at the left for the listing of our account titles followed by from a half-dozen to a dozen narrower money columns to the right. In the first pair of money columns, we list the amounts which make up our unadjusted trial balance as of any given date. In the next pair of columns we make left- and right-hand entries (adjusting entries) to adjust the raw trial balance figures; then, we copy the trial balance figures, *as modified by the adjusting entries,* into the third pair of columns (which are headed Income Statement) and into the final pair (which are headed Balance Sheet). Whether a given item is copied in an income statement column or a balance sheet column depends simply on whether the item is to appear in the income statement or in the balance sheet. Thus, the adjusted amount for Cash in Bank would be carried to the left-hand (asset) column under the heading Balance Sheet, and the amount for Sales and for each class of expenses would be entered in the Income Statement columns. Then all that remains to be done is to copy the sorted amounts into your regular income statement and balance sheet formats, and there you have your financial statements all done.

Let's illustrate this procedure with the example in the preceding section on adjusting entries. Figure 4.1 is an eight-column work sheet in finished form. Note the trial balance in the first pair of columns, the adjusting entries in the second pair, the income statement amounts (as adjusted) in the third pair, and the balance sheet amounts (as adjusted) in the fourth pair.

The Work Sheet—Comments

In order to be thoroughly familiar with work sheet procedure, you ought to follow through the details in Figure 4.1. For example, note that Cash in Bank, on the first line, had a balance of $5,000 but that, in adjusting entry (1), we made a right-hand entry of $72 to record the reduction caused by the bank's service charges. This same adjusting entry is shown in the right-hand adjusting entry column. Then, after all other adjusting entries have been entered in the work sheet, Cash in

Figure 4.1 Eight-column work sheet.

TUESDAY CO.
Eight-Column Work Sheet, as of January 31

	Trial balance		Adjusting entries		Income statement		Balance sheet	
	Debit	Credit	Debit	Credit	Debit	Credit	Debit	Credit
Cash in bank	5,000			(1) 72			4,928	
Marketable securities	20,000						20,000	
Interest accrued receivable			(2) 130				130	
Accounts receivable	40,000						40,000	
Allowance for bad debts				(3) 850				850
Merchandise	60,000			(4) 50,000			10,000	
Prepaid insurance	3,000			(5) 100			2,900	
Land	8,000						8,000	
Equipment	60,000						60,000	
Building	80,000						80,000	
Allowance for depreciation		30,000		(6) 800				30,800
Accounts payable		35,000						35,000
Notes payable		25,000						25,000
Interest accrued payable				(8) 200				200
Wages accrued payable				(7) 1,000				1,000
Income tax accrued payable				(9) 2,500				2,500
Capital stock		100,000						100,000
Retained earnings		21,000						21,000
Sales		85,000				85,000		
Interest revenue				(2) 130		130		
Bad debts			(3) 850		850			
Cost of goods sold			(4) 50,000		50,000			
Selling expenses	10,000		(6) 640 (7) 1,000		11,640			
Administrative expenses	10,000		(1) 72 (5) 100 (6) 160		10,332			
Interest expense			(8) 200		200			
Income taxes			(9) 2,500		2,500			
Net income					9,608			9,608
	296,000	296,000	55,652	55,652	85,130	85,130	225,958	225,958

Bank, as adjusted by $72, is carried way over to the left-hand balance sheet column (because Cash in Bank is an asset). Exactly the same procedure was followed through the whole illustration.

But note two technical matters. First, each left-hand column is headed "Debit," and each right-hand column is headed "Credit." It's as simple as that—these two words mean nothing more than "left" and "right," and don't let anybody try to convince you otherwise. So, from now on instead of saying that we're going to make a left-hand entry in a journal entry or in an account, we're going to say that *we're making a debit entry*. Instead of right-hand, we'll say *credit*.

Second, please note how the last two pairs of columns are "balanced." Obviously, if you carry the adjusted revenue balances to the credit (right) side of the income statement and carry the expenses to the debit side, the two sides won't be equal—you have to *plug* them to make them equal, and the amount of that plug is your net income (or loss). Also, if you carry the assets, the liabilities, the capital stock, and the retained earnings to the balance sheet columns, they won't have equal totals until you plug them for the net income (addition to retained earnings) for the period. You see, the retained earnings balance in the raw trial balance is the amount carried forward from December, and it is brought up to date as of the end of January only when you add January's net income to it.

Financial Statements

The financial statements for Tuesday Co. are prepared by copying the data in the last four columns of the work sheet into blank income statement and balance sheet forms. They appear as Figures 4.2 and 4.3.

Figure 4.2 Income statement prepared from the work sheet.

TUESDAY CO.
Income Statement, January, 19XX

Sales (less bad debts of $850)		$84,150	
Interest revenue		130	$84,280
Expenses:			
Cost of goods sold	$50,000		
Selling	11,640		
Administrative	10,332	$71,972	
Interest		200	
Income taxes		2,500	74,672
Net income			$ 9,608

Figure 4.3   Balance sheet prepared from the work sheet.

TUESDAY CO.
Balance Sheet, January 31, 19XX

Assets

Current:			
Cash in bank		$ 4,928	
Marketable securities		20,000	
Interest accrued receivable		130	
Accounts receivable	$ 40,000		
Less: Allowance for bad debts	850	39,150	
Merchandise		10,000	
Prepaid insurance		2,900	$ 77,108
Noncurrent:			
Land		$ 8,000	
Equipment	$ 60,000		
Building	80,000		
	$140,000		
Less: Allowance for depreciation	30,800	109,200	117,200
			$194,308

Equities

Current liabilities:			
Accounts payable		$ 35,000	
Notes payable		25,000	
Interest accrued payable		200	
Wages accrued payable		1,000	
Income taxes accrued payable		2,500	$ 63,700
Stockholders' equity:			
Capital stock		$100,000	
Retained earnings, January 1	$21,000		
Earnings retained, January	9,608	30,608	130,608
			$194,308

Are Interim Statements Dependable?

The extent to which interim balance sheets and income statements are dependable is arguable. One thing is certain: They do have their weaknesses. Business executives, who should be making use of them, should certainly know enough about them to be aware of their weaknesses—in other words, not to make decisions on the basis of unreliable data, at least without knowing that minor, or even major, weaknesses exist.

It's too early in the game for us to explore the weaknesses of interim statements in detail, but if you're willing temporarily to take an opinion on faith, a couple of observations will be presented now and we'll examine the question of reliability more thoroughly later.

First, if we are going to divide the total lifetime of the enterprise into segments for financial reporting purposes, the most natural segment length would appear to be the year—whether or not December 31 is chosen as the annual cutoff date. However, statements prepared to report the results of operations even for a whole year (as well as balance sheets at year-ends) inevitably involve the exercise of judgment, the making of estimates, and some arbitrary decisions. To cut the year, in turn, into two, four, or even twelve segments for reporting purposes amplifies the level of uncertainty for a number of reasons, and it may well be contended that reports for periods shorter than a year should be prepared on a special-purpose basis only—that is, they should contain only data that pass the test of reliability. Data that do not pass the test should be clearly labeled as conjectural or speculative.

Internal Control Structure

We have spent a significant amount of the preceding chapters discussing major aspects of the accounting system and the accounting cycle. We would be remiss if we didn't briefly discuss the *internal control structure*, which, briefly defined, is a combination of the attitudes, environmental factors, and accounting procedures and techniques utilized to ensure that the business objectives are attained in the most efficient and effective manner. The structure developed must depend on many things: use of computers versus manual processing of transactions; number of employees available to perform various functions; size of the business; nature of the business and its objectives; management's philosophy and operating style; and many others. Here we can only briefly present a few of the major factors involved.

There are two broad elements in the internal control structure: the control environment and control procedures. The control environment is extremely important, encompassing such things as developing an organizational structure which best leads to fulfilling the business objectives; assigning authority and responsibility for performing certain functions; having an adequate internal audit function; having a good system for hiring, training, and promoting employees; and providing proper monitoring and compliance with requirements imposed by external authorities, such as legislative and regulatory bodies. After this brief listing, however, we'll spend the balance of our time on *control procedures*, since these tie more directly into the accounting system.

Control procedures are utilized, first, to reduce the number of errors that are made in the accounting process and to find and correct those that are made and, second, to discourage those who might be inclined to defraud the business in some manner and to uncover fraud and embezzlement and those responsible when they do occur.

There are five major categories of control procedures: (1) *Proper authorization of transactions and activities*—only certain individuals should have the authority to initiate certain transactions. These transactions should be well-documented so that such individuals can be held accountable for their actions. (2) *Segregation of duties*—*different* individuals should be assigned to the responsibilities of authorizing transactions, recording transactions, and maintaining custody of the related assets. For example, subsidiary ledgers make it possible for one individual to post to the general ledger and a different employee(s) to post to the subsidiary ledger, each acting as a check on the other. Or, the individual who deposits cash receipts in the bank *should not* make entries to the Cash in Bank account or reconcile the bank balance. (3) *Adequate documents and records*—proper documentation allows the business reasonable assurance that all transactions have been recorded. (4) *Safeguards over assets*—for example, allowing only certain individuals to make cash disbursements, using a mechanical check protector, and appropriate physical segregation of assets. (5) *Independent checks on performance*—these include making timely periodic comparisons of book records with the physical assets represented by those records, such as inventories, securities, cash, and plant and equipment.

Conclusion

If you're still with us, you have now suffered through just about all of the mechanical details (call it bookkeeping if you wish) that we're going to deal with. No apologies are offered for the amount of bookkeeping that we have analyzed, because it will help us immeasurably in the discussion of the sequence of topics that follow. If you will apply your pencil to the summary test problem on the following pages and if you find that it presents no major difficulties, you should be all set to explore some of the more interesting aspects of accounting—particularly the ways in which accounting should be useful to you in your work.

TEST PROBLEM

The trial balance of Blitz Co. on December 31, before adjustments, is shown in the first two columns of the work sheet on page 60. Data on which end-of-year adjusting entries are to be based are as follows. (Assume that the company did not make interim adjusting entries in its formal records.)

(1) Unrecorded bank service charges amount to $25.
(2) The $100 balance in Allowance for Bad Debts is the amount remaining from last year's provision. The proper increment for this year is estimated to be 1 percent of total sales for the year.
(3) The inventory of merchandise at year-end is determined to be $10,000.
(4) Depreciation for the year is determined to total $4,000, of which 90 percent is selling expense and 10 percent is administrative.
(5) Interest accrued payable on the bonds at the end of the year is $1,000.
(6) Income taxes are to be accrued in the amount of $650.

Required

In the spaces provided, prepare a complete work sheet, an income statement, and a balance sheet.

TEST PROBLEM Solution Space

BLITZ CO.

Work Sheet for the Year Ended December 31, 19XX

	Trial balance		Adjusting entries		Income statement		Balance sheet	
	Debit	Credit	Debit	Credit	Debit	Credit	Debit	Credit
Cash in bank	2,500							
Accounts receivable	40,000							
Allowance for bad debts		100						
Merchandise	40,000							
Plant	100,000							
Allowance for depreciation		35,000						
Accounts payable		20,000						
Interest accrued payable								
Income tax accrued payable								
Bonds payable		25,000						
Capital stock		50,000						
Retained earnings		13,400						
Sales		60,000						
Bad debts								
Cost of goods sold	10,000							
Selling expenses	11,000							
Administrative expenses								
Interest expense								
Income taxes								
Net income for year								
Totals	203,500	203,500						

BLITZ CO.
Income Statement, Year Ended December 31, 19XX

Sales		$
Less: Bad debts		
Net sales		$
Expenses:		
Cost of goods sold	$	
Selling		
Administrative		
	$	
Interest expense		
Income taxes		
Net income (and earnings retained)		$

BLITZ CO.
Balance Sheet, December 31, 19XX

Assets

Current:			
Cash in bank		$	
Accounts receivable	$		
Less: Allowance for bad debts			
Merchandise			$
Plant (cost)		$	
Less: Allowance for depreciation			
			$

Equities

Current liabilities:			
Accounts payable		$	
Interest accrued payable			
Income tax accrued payable			$
Bonds payable			
Total liabilities			$
Stockholders' equity:			
Capital stock		$	
Retained earnings, January 1	$		
Earnings retained, 19XX			
			$

5
Working Capital

What Is Working Capital?

When accountants speak of working capital (or net working capital), they mean *the algebraic difference between the total of the current assets and the total of the current liabilities.* The term is used a great deal and, as a business executive, you should be quite familiar with it. However, it is a poor one because it simply doesn't convey its real meaning. "Capital" has several different meanings (e.g., the invested capital of the company and capital assets—the noncurrent assets), and to put the word "working" in front of "capital" doesn't seem to add much. But as the saying goes, we must see it "like it is," and that means "current assets minus current liabilities equals working capital."

To add to our difficulties, it is not unheard of for the banker, or other lender, to insist that you maintain a certain specified amount of working capital at all times. That not only leads to occasional arguments over what should be included in working capital but may also require you to be stingy with dividend payments to your stockholders and perhaps to accumulate more working capital than you can use economically.

Let's spend the next several paragraphs on simple illustrations of the more common transactions that affect our working capital. Just for practice in the use of accounting language and form, for each common working capital element we'll run through a few typical transactions. Part of the reason for this exercise will be to build up your familiarity with "debit" and "credit." Our aim in each case will be to list the more common transactions and show how they would be recorded in simple journal form.

Cash Receipts Transactions

Cash, a current asset, comes from many sources. The more common sources are depicted in the journal entries (with their explanations) that follow. Because the dollar amounts involved are of no importance to us at this point, in most cases, we'll just use x's in place of assumed figures.

(1)

Cash on Hand	xxx	
Capital Stock		xxx

To record the issue of capital stock when a corporation is formed. A debit (left-hand) entry is made in the Cash account as an asset increase, and a credit (right-hand) entry is made in the Capital Stock account as an equity increase.

(2)

Cash on Hand	xxx	
Bonds Payable		xxx

We borrow money by issuing bonds. Bonds Payable is a liability, and we must make a credit to record the increase. The debit to cash is obvious.

(3)

Cash in Bank	xxx	
Bank Loan (Notes Payable)		xxx

We borrow money from a bank. Our bank account (an asset) is increased (debit) and a current liability (Bank Loan Payable) is increased (by a credit).

(4)

Cash on Hand	xxx	
Sales Revenue		xxx

When we sell merchandise for cash, in addition to debiting cash we must record the *increase in revenue* by a credit.

(5)

Cash on Hand	xxx	
Accounts Receivable		xxx

This entry records the collection of cash from a customer who at an earlier time purchased merchandise from us "on account."

(6)

Cash on Hand	1,200	
Marketable Securities		1,000
Gain on Sale of Marketable Securities		200

We sell for $1,200 securities that cost us $1,000, and
we realize a gain of $200 (which is shown as a credit
because the gain constitutes an *increase* in the
owner's equity).

(7)

Cash on Hand	800	
Loss on Sale of Marketable Securities	200	
Marketable Securities		1,000

We sell for $800 some securities that cost us $1,000,
and we incur a loss of $200 (which is shown as a
debit because the loss constitutes a *decrease* in the
owner's equity).

(8)

Cash on Hand	3,000	
Allowance for Depreciation	6,000	
Retirement Loss	1,000	
Machinery		10,000

We sell for $3,000 machinery which some time ago
cost us $10,000 but which has been depreciated
down to $4,000, and our apparent loss is the
$1,000. Note that the accumulated depreciation
over the years had been recorded in a contra account (as an offset to the machinery account); and
when we dispose of the machinery, our contra account must be reduced along with the reduction of
the machinery account. (We'll spend more time on
this later.)

(9)

Cash in Bank	xxx	
Cash on Hand		xxx

To record a bank deposit.

Cash Disbursement Transactions

Although statistical evidence of cash disbursement transactions is hard
to find, it is likely that the bulk of all purchases of merchandise, raw
materials, supplies, and services made by business firms are made on
credit—that is, on account. As a matter of fact, when the company
employs the so-called *voucher system* in formal fashion, even its cash

purchases are recorded initially as if they were on account; this means that, at least theoretically, every cash disbursement is a payoff of an account payable. To illustrate, assume that our company buys $100 of merchandise for cash. The entry in journal form would be:

Merchandise	100	
Cash in Bank		100

But if the voucher system is in operation, this entry would be recorded in two steps. First, as the assumed incurrence of an account payable when title to merchandise is received:

(1)

Merchandise	100	
Vouchers Payable		100

Second, the follow-up entry eliminates the account payable (voucher payable) by a debit, with a corresponding credit to Cash in Bank.

(2)

Vouchers Payable	100	
Cash in Bank		100

Two observations are pertinent at this point. First, good business practice dictates that *every* disbursement be made by check. This assures us of a formal record of the payment. Second, a voucher is *any document* that serves as evidence of a given transaction. Thus, if every check we issue is documented by an invoice (bill) or other piece of documentary evidence, we are likely to be in pretty good shape when the auditors come around to check up on our records. As documentary support of a cash disbursement, a voucher consists of one or more business forms detailing the transaction, and at some point, as a rule, some or all of the forms may bear signatures of vendors, officers of our company, or other parties. Such signatures constitute authorization for the issuance of a check. The use of the voucher system (with disbursements by check only) constitutes part of what is known as a system of *internal check and control.* We'll further develop this later.

To repeat. Under a strict voucher system, *since every payment is preceded by the setting up of a liability* (which may be a very temporary one) called *vouchers payable,* the only account that can be debited when we make a credit to Cash in Bank is Vouchers Payable.

In the absence of a voucher system, we will, of course, have credits to Cash in Bank accompanied by debits to whatever thing or service was acquired for cash. Thus, in addition to debits to Merchandise, we might make cash purchases of materials (debit Raw Materials), public utility services (debit Heat, Light, and Power), labor services (debit Labor Services), and so on. Also, we might have cash payments for dividends, interest, income taxes, or the payment of long-term debt. In each case Cash in Bank would be credited and the appropriate account (Dividends, Interest, Income Taxes, Bonds Payable) debited.

Marketable Securities

Only four transactions with respect to marketable securities are common. They are (1) purchase, (2) collection of interest and dividends, (3) resale at a gain or loss, and (4) end-of-period markdown to reflect loss of value. These may be illustrated in simple journal entries as follows (with assumed amounts):

(1)

Marketable Securities—Cost	12,000	
Vouchers Payable		12,000

We purchase nonspeculative, marketable securities to be paid for out of excess of cash currently on hand during a lull in business activity and to build up a fund for payment of income taxes at a later date.

(2)

Cash	600	
Interest Revenue		400
Dividends Revenue		200

To record receipt of interest and dividends earned on marketable securities.

(3)

Cash	9,300	
Marketable Securities—Cost		8,750
Gain on Sale of Marketable Securities		550

To record sale, for $9,300, of securities that cost $8,750.

(4)

Loss from Decline in Value of Marketable Securities	400	
Marketable Securities—Cost		400

Entry made at end of accounting period so balance

sheet will show marketable securities at *the lower* of
their cost or their current market value, per accounting convention of conservatism.

Accounts Receivable

Only three transactions commonly involve accounts receivable: (1)
their origination at time of sale, (2) collection, and (3) charge-offs when
found uncollectible. To illustrate each of these, observe the following:

(1)

Accounts Receivable	10,000	
Sales Revenue		10,000

To record our sales of merchandise for given dates, all
subject to terms 2/10, *n*/30.

In the explanation to entry (1), note the terms, 2/10, *n*/30. This simply
means that a 2 percent discount will be allowed if the bill is paid within
10 days and that in any case the whole bill is due within 30 days. Such
terms vary. Thus, we could have 3/10, 2/30, *n*/60, which means the
face of the bill is "net" if the customer waits more than 30 days but the
net amount is 3 percent smaller if the bill is paid within 10 days and is
2 percent smaller if paid between 10 and 30 days from the date of the
invoice (bill).

(2)

Cash	89,000	
Sale Discounts	1,000	
Accounts Receivable		90,000

To record collections from customers of invoices totaling $90,000 face, less discounts totaling $1,000.

With respect to the elements of entry (2), note that we have collected
$1,000 *less* than the amount originally charged to the customers. Since
the original charge was recorded by a debit to Accounts Receivable and
a credit to Sales Revenue of $90,000, we must now reduce the recorded
revenue by $1,000 because we are permitting the customers to pay off
this debt *in full* by remitting only $89,000. In other words, when we
sell goods or services with the understanding that the customer can take
a cash discount if he pays, say, within 10 days, our initial recording of
sales revenue (at gross) must be revised if we collect a smaller amount.
We could simply debit Sales Revenue for the $1,000; but for purposes

of keeping management informed on the amount of discounts the customers are actually taking, it may be better to make the debit to a contra account, Sales Discounts, which is treated as a subtraction from Sales in our income statement.

In Chapter 4 one of the end-of-period adjusting entries that was used for illustration showed how we recognize the probability that some accounts receivable will turn out to be uncollectible. To refresh your memory, the adjusting entry shown there was:

Bad Debts	850	
Allowance for Bad Debts		850

As was explained, the "allowance" constitutes an estimated blanket *offset* to Accounts Receivable—a substitute for making a credit directly to Accounts Receivable—at a time when you are sure some of the receivables will not pay off but you don't yet know which ones. You can't make a direct credit to the receivables; therefore, you employ the bookkeeping trick of using a contra account.

Now let's assume that, after the lapse of a few weeks, we become certain that John Doe, who owes us $150, will never pay his bill. This means that $150 of the $850 is now identifiable with a specific account receivable, so we can transfer $150 from the blanket contra account to the credit side of Accounts Receivable. Our entry is:

Allowance for Bad Debts	150	
Accounts Receivable		150

The balance of the allowance account now stands at $700, which means that we expect to have additional write-offs of approximately $700 from sales made in the past period.

Inventories

The routine transactions involving inventory items (such as merchandise, raw materials, work in process, and finished goods) consist of their acquisition (by purchase or by manufacture) and their consumption (by sale or by internal usage). Following are illustrative entries:

(1)

Merchandise	xxx	
Accounts Payable		xxx
To record purchase of merchandise.		

(2)

Raw Materials	xxx	
Accounts Payable		xxx

To record purchase of raw materials.

(3)

Supplies	xxx	
Accounts Payable		xxx

To record purchases of supplies.

(4)

Cost of Goods Sold	xxx	
Merchandise		xxx

A physical inventory of goods remaining on hand is taken in order to determine the cost of goods that have been sold.

(5)

Work in Process	xxx	
Raw materials		xxx

To record cost of raw materials requisitioned for processing into finished goods.

(6)

Work in Process	xxx	
Factory Labor		xxx

To transfer cost of factory labor into the account representing the cost of making finished goods.

(7)

Work in Process	xxx	
Manufacturing Overhead		xxx

To transfer miscellaneous manufacturing costs into the account representing the cost of making finished goods.

(8)

Finished Goods	xxx	
Work in Process		xxx

To transfer from the work in process account to the finished goods account the cost of goods actually finished this period.

(9)

Cost of Goods Sold	xxx	
Finished Goods		xxx

To recognize the cost of finished goods that have been
sold during the period.

Prepayments

To round out the accounts that make up the current asset sector of
working capital, we must mention various kinds of prepayments.

In general, prepayments (commonly called *prepaid expenses*) consist
of amounts that have been paid in advance to suppliers of services. The
most common examples are prepaid insurance, prepaid rent, and prepaid property taxes. Under normal circumstances only two common
transactions affect the prepayment accounts: (1) the payment made in
advance and (2) the amortization of the prepayment as it expires. To
save space and your time, the first of these will be illustrated in a single
bundle.

(1)

Prepaid Insurance	xxx	
Prepaid Rent	xxx	
Prepaid Property Taxes	xxx	
Cash in Bank		xxx

To record payments in advance for services to be received over various periods of time in the future. Entries made later to record the expiration of each of
these follow.

(2)

Insurance Expense	xxx	
Prepaid Insurance		xxx

To record expiration of the portion of prepaid insurance
allocable to past period.

(3)

Rent Expense	xxx	
Prepaid Rent		xxx

To record expiration of prepaid rent.

(4)

Property Tax Expense	xxx	
Prepaid Property Tax		xxx

To record expiration of prepaid property tax.

Current Liabilities

The negative element in working capital is made up of all the current liabilities. Although the cash needed to pay the liabilities may not always be easy to find, the accounting entries for current liabilities present no significant difficulties. Examples are:

(1)

Merchandise	xxx	
Raw Materials	xxx	
Telephone Expenses	xxx	
Accounts Payable		xxx

To record amounts owed for purchases of merchandise, materials, and telephone services.

(2)

Accounts Payable	xxx	
Cash in Bank		xxx

To record payment of accounts payable.

(3)

Interest Expense	xxx	
Interest Payable		xxx

To record amount of interest payable as of end of period.

(4)

Labor Services	xxx	
Wages (Payroll) Payable		xxx

To record liability for unpaid wages as of end of accounting period.

(5)

Dividends Charge	xxx	
Dividends Payable		xxx

To record the declaration of a dividend to be paid on (date).

Entries to record payment of each of the illustrated current liabilities are the same—simply debit the liability account (to show that you are reducing it) and credit Cash in Bank.

These examples do not by any means exhaust the possible kinds of current liabilities; however, you should have no trouble in applying the same pattern of entries to any other current liabilities that come to your attention.

What Can Your Accountants Do for You?

So far in this chapter we have really been doing nothing more than drill on the technique of depicting a transaction in journal entry form. By now you should begin to feel more or less at home with the notion of debit and credit.

Essentially, what we have done so far is study the procedure followed in recording *historical events*. This is the accountant's data-storage function, and by no means should it be sneered at. In order to know how much cash you have in the bank, you must keep some kind of record; in order to be able to send bills, you must keep accounting records of your customer's purchases and payments; in order to keep track of merchandise, raw materials, and other inventories, you need a record of your purchases; and you must either keep perpetual inventory records or take periodic physical inventories. All of this the accountant takes for granted, and it's done in the regular course of business.

On the other hand, your accounting staff should stand ready to supply you with special-purpose studies and reports whenever you need them, as well as with other reports of a more or less routine nature. We'll hope to tick off quite a number of such reports as we progress from chapter to chapter. They should give you a fairly good acquaintance with the things your accounting staff is capable of doing to assist you in the performance of your managerial functions; on the other hand, *you should never make the mistake of relying solely on accounting information when making a decision which should actually rest on information from additional sources as well.* Such a mistake is altogether too common in business practice.

Two examples of routine accounting schedules that commonly prove useful to management are the cash budget and the accounts receivable aging schedule. A brief section will now be devoted to each.

The Budget

While this is by no means intended to be a book on corporation finance, it is inevitable that certain aspects of financial management will crop up as we progress from one aspect of accounting to another.

A budget stands midway between the accounting function and the financial management function in an enterprise. Usually you would expect the accountants to perform the actual task of *compiling* the budget. If, however, your company is large enough to have any job specialization whatsoever, the raw data that are to be fed into the budget must come from a variety of sources (including, for example, the treasurer, the sales manager, the production manager, and all others who are in a position to have a significant influence on financial affairs). Often the budgeting process is performed by a budget committee, which may begin its work 3 months or more before the start of the year for which the budget is being prepared.

Let there be no misunderstanding—*budgeting is absolutely essential to the welfare of the enterprise.* In case you don't share that enthusiasm for budgets, contemplate the following quotation from someone unknown: "Not to budget is not to plan." Do you believe in planning?

Budgets take various forms and are often prepared in segments prior to being brought together to form a "comprehensive" budget. One very important segment is the *cash budget,* which we'll now explain.

The Cash Budget

The portion of the comprehensive budget which "plans" the *outflows, inflows,* and *balances* of cash as it stands at various points throughout the period is covered by the cash budget. Opinions vary as to the most satisfactory budget period, but in one scheme, which perhaps is the most popular, fairly detailed plans for a full year are developed in advance and the budget schedule shows the flows and balances for each month. Visualize a 13-column schedule with a column for each of the 12 months and a thirteenth column for aggregates and planned end-of-year balance.

The generalized form of the budget schedule is the essence of simplicity. If we assume a year starting on January 1, the first figure in the first column should be the amount of cash held at the beginning of the year; this is the opening balance. For budgeting purposes the opening balance includes both cash on hand and cash in bank.

Following the opening balance, we list the various sources from which we plan to receive cash during the month of January and also list the anticipated amount from each source. Naturally, we next list the planned amounts to be disbursed during January. Needless to say, the formula Opening Balance + Receipts − Disbursements gives us a resulting end-of-month balance. This balance is, of course, automatically the start-of-month balance for February, and the adding and subtracting process is repeated. So it goes throughout the 12-month period. The form of the cash budget is illustrated in Figure 5.1 for the first quarter of a year, with a total column appended.

Certainly a most important reason for the *forward-looking* cash budget is to detect possible future cash stringencies and to make arrangements well ahead of time for coping with such shortcomings. Bankers

Figure 5.1 Cash budget form.

PSEUDO CO.
Cash Budget, First Quarter, 19X1

	January	*February*	*March*	*Summary*
Cash balance, first of month	$ 5,000	$ 5,400	$10,165	$ 5,000
Cash receipts, routine:				
Collections on account	$28,000	$30,000	$27,000	$ 85,000
Cash sales	8,000	9,000	7,500	24,500
Miscellaneous	1,400	1,800	1,500	4,700
Total receipts	$37,400	$40,800	$36,000	$114,200
Total available (before financing)	$42,400	$46,200	$46,165	$119,200
Cash disbursements, routine:				
Payments for:				
Merchandise, materials, and				
supplies	$30,000	$20,000	$23,000	$ 73,000
Advertising	1,500	1,000	1,000	3,500
Utilities	300	350	350	1,000
Other outside services	1,200	1,200	1,200	3,600
Wages and salaries	6,000	6,000	6,000	18,000
Property taxes	—	—	2,000	2,000
Rent	500	500	500	1,500
Income taxes	—	—	3,500	3,500
Land purchase contract	1,000	1,000	1,000	3,000
Miscellaneous	1,500	950	550	3,000
Total disbursements	$42,000	$31,000	$39,100	$112,100
Minimum operating cash balance	5,000	5,000	5,000	—
Total cash requirement	$47,000	$36,000	$44,100	$ —
Anticipated cash excess or				
(deficiency)	$ (4,600)	$10,200	$ 2,065	$ —
Financing:				
Short-term bank loans	$ 5,000			$ 5,000
Loan repayments		$ (5,000)		(5,000)
Interest payments		(35)		(35)
Total financing	$ 5,000	$ (5,035)	$ —	$ (35)
Cash balance, end of month	$ 5,400	$10,165	$ 7,065	$ 7,065

insist upon copies of up-to-date financial statements which they will want to analyze carefully before agreeing to make a loan, but nothing is more useful than a detailed cash budget which shows the proposed loan, as a cash receipt within a given month, and then proceeds to show the repayment of the loan with interest, on schedule, among the disbursements of one or more later months. You will note that both a borrowing and a repaying transaction are illustrated in Figure 5.1, along with the routine cash flows, in and out, from collections as well as various types of payments. Note also that the schedule has a line for minimum operating cash balance. Such a balance may be formally decided upon by your company, and its introduction in the budget schedule works out well mechanically if it is added to the disbursements. (Money set aside or held as reserve is, in a rather farfetched sense, a sort of internal disbursement.) This treatment complicates the schedule a bit, but it soon becomes routine.

Comments on Cash Budget Illustration

Note first that the amounts used in our budget illustration are purely hypothetical. In your own situation you must be supplied with acceptable predictions (plans) of sales for each month and a calculation of probable cash flow resulting from cash sales and collections from sales that are made on account. Past experience, the market outlook, and *plans for improvement* go into the preparation of the budgeted figures. Similar considerations govern the various classes of disbursements. Isn't it amazing, the number of newly formed businesses that fail before they ever get off the ground? If everyone who contemplates setting up in business could somehow be required to prepare in detail a comprehensive budget for the first year or two, and in rough form for the first five years, what a lot of business failures would be avoided simply because they would not be started in the first place! Wouldn't you agree that, in general, a profitable business is an asset to society because it puts together raw materials and labor and management and converts them into something of *greater value* to society? An unprofitable (loss) enterprise is a detriment to society because it consumes materials and labor but its output is worth *less* than the materials and labor consumed! The loss enterprise, in effect, wastes valuable resources. All hail the budget as a means of avoiding losses by planning in advance.

One more word about cash. It's very poor business practice to have too much of it around for too long. Unused cash is nonproductive and, worst of all, it actually shrinks in value as that old bugaboo *inflation* eats its way into our economy. If the general price level goes up 9 percent in a year, it means that any cash that we've held throughout that year has lost approximately 9 percent of its power to buy goods and services. Also, claims to cash (accounts receivable) suffer the same shrinkage as does cash itself. So it's of real importance that we plan our cash flows in such a way as to minimize any cash balances in excess of current working-capital needs. Obviously, the cash budget is a prime tool in accomplishing this aim.

Control of Receivables

As we progress in this book, we should be able to present new topics with lesser amounts of introductory explanation because you are accumulating a fundamental understanding of the rituals and concepts of accounting. You should soon need only to see a journal entry or an accounting report in order to understand it with minimal explanation.

Let's try this approach with another valuable accounting schedule, the widely used accounts receivable aging schedule. As in all cases, the scope, detail, etc., must be adapted to the size and complexity of your company, but whether your accounting system is operated strictly by pen and ink or is thoroughly computerized, an aging schedule is a great device for control of receivables.

The accounts receivable aging schedule lists the name of each customer and, in a series of columns after the name, shows (1) the total amount owed you and (2) a breakdown of that amount in terms of the length of time it has been owing. Space at the right-hand end of the schedule may be provided for comments, which may include references to communications with the customer, recommendations for actions to be taken, etc. In very abbreviated form such a schedule is shown in Figure 5.2.

Comments on Aging Schedule

If the company is small enough for such attention, the aging schedule may be useful in providing management with details that lead to managerial (or legal) action with respect to individual customers. In all situations the column totals should prove useful in determining the quality of the accounts receivable total. What portion is in the older categories and in risk of becoming uncollectible? Are the proportions in the older, or more recent, categories changing for the better or for the worse? Should credit terms and credit pressure be modified? Is our present allowance for bad debts adequate? The schedule is commonly used to check out those questions by making estimates of the portion of each column total that is likely to be uncollectible. For example, we might derive the schedule shown in Figure 5.3 from the details shown in the aging schedule.

The aging schedule can be prepared as often as necessary to assist the credit or other manager to "keep on top" of the accounts receivable situation.

Figure 5.2 Accounts receivable aging schedule.

PSEUDO CO. CUSTOMER ACCOUNTS
Aging Schedule, March 31, 19XX

Customer (or number)	Present balance	Under 31	31–60	61–90	91–180	181–360	Comment
A. A. Adams	$ 100	$ 100					
B. B. Black	50			$ 50			Paid in full on April 10
C. A. Cream	70	30	$ 20	20			
D. C. Duke	150					$ 150	Can't locate customer
Z. A. Zohn	220	220					
Totals	$58,120	$27,170	$16,420	$7,160	$5,400	$1,970	
Percentage of total	100%	47%	28%	12%	9%	4%	

Age of balances, days

Figure 5.3 Bad debt allowance prepared from aging schedule.

Test of Adequacy of Bad Debt Allowance
March 31, 19XX

Age group, days	Total	Estimated uncollectible, %	Estimates
1–30	$27,170	1	$ 270
31–60	16,420	3	500
61–90	7,160	5	350
91–180	5,400	10	540
180–1 year	1,970	50	1,000
Total	$58,120		$2,660
Present allowance			1,600
Addition needed			$1,060

TEST PROBLEM

In the space provided for your solution, make simple journal entries to record the following transactions, all of which involve working capital items:

(1) Sales of merchandise for $500 cash
(2) Sales of merchandise for $600 on account
(3) Collection of $196 from customers after allowing $4 of sales discount
(4) Borrowing $5,000 from the bank by giving a 90-day, 8 percent note payable
(5) Payment of the note in (4) at maturity
(6) Sale, for $800 cash, of a machine which originally cost $2,000 and on which we have so far recorded (accrued) depreciation of $1,100
(7) Provision for $500 of estimated bad debts
(8) Write-off of an account receivable, $120
(9) Recognition of end-of-year merchandise cost of goods sold based on opening inventory of $1,000, purchases of $10,000, and final inventory of $2,000
(10) Recognition of insurance expiration of $300

TEST PROBLEM Solution Space

Entry Number	Debits	Credits
(1)		
(2)		
(3)		
(4)		
(5)		
(6)		
(7)		
(8)		
(9)		
(10)		

6
The Funds Statement— Working Capital Flows

What Are Exhibits and Such Things?

An *exhibit*, or *statement*, is usually a financial report of major rank. Thus, in the annual report to stockholders, your company will invariably present a balance sheet (statement of financial condition) and an income statement. These are the omnipresent major exhibits, or statements.

Your report to stockholders may or may not also include one or more *supporting schedules*. All this means is that typically your major exhibits show very little detail; most of the titles or captions cover broad classes of data such as "plant," "equipment," and "investments." If you wish to disclose the component *elements* of a given class, you may present such elements in a supporting schedule. Thus, the major statements tend to report the headlines; for the inside details of the story, you must look to supporting schedules (if you feel the need).

Undoubtedly, you already realize that the amount of detail, whether in supporting schedules or otherwise, depends a great deal upon the person to whom the report is directed. If the statements are for internal use by management, supporting schedules should be made available in whatever form and degree of detail are called for by the positions and responsibilities of the individual recipients; on the other hand, the general stockholder of a large corporation is usually content to receive highly condensed data with little by way of supporting schedules. It's sad, but true, that most stockholders know very little about financial statements and may look at nothing more than the *footings* (totals) of the balance sheet and the final net income figure of the income sheet plus possibly the reported earnings per share.

So we have exhibits, or statements, supplemented by schedules. For internal purposes, a supporting schedule is often called a *proof.* Thus, if your balance sheet shows accounts receivable of $25,620 and you have something to do with customer credit problems, you may ask your accountant for a proof of the customer total. Don't be surprised if what you get is a simple list of all the customers who now owe money to your firm and, for each customer, the amount owing as of the date specified in the heading of the proof list. Thus, a proof (which "proves" the accuracy of the total shown in the balance sheet) is just another supporting schedule. Proofs are also prepared in considerable quantities by auditors for verification purposes.

All this chitchat is designed to lead us to a discussion of cash and working capital flows. A funds statement on a cash basis (a *cash flow statement*) is now required to be presented in the annual report to stockholders. We discuss this fully in Chapter 7. Here we discuss a funds statement on a working capital basis (a *working capital flow statement*) because it is useful (as we will see in the following pages) to management for internal use. In any case, let's work our way into the subject systematically by starting with something you've handled earlier in this text.

Working Capital Changes

In Chapter 1 we had a brief introduction to the balance sheet terms, current assets and current liabilities, and in Chapter 5 we examined the arithmetic difference between the sums of the current assets and current liabilities, commonly known as *working capital.*. One might well believe that the current assets should be known as the working capital of the firm and that if from the current assets we subtracted the current liabilities, the difference would be termed *net* working capital. Sure it's logical, but that's not the way it's done. Working capital and net working capital refer to the same quantity—the difference between current assets and current liabilities.

Now for a bit of exercise. What events, or transactions, cause (net) working capital to change? Obviously, any transaction that changes the total current assets (without a simultaneously offsetting change in current liabilities) changes the working capital. Obviously, any transaction that changes the total current liabilities (without a simultaneously offsetting change in current assets) changes the working capital. Thus, viewed alone, current assets+ and current assets— transactions respectively increase and decrease working capital. Current liabilities+ and current liabilities— transactions, happening alone, respectively decrease and increase working capital. Samples follow.

Current asset increases (that are not offset by current liability increases) occur when a company issues capital stock or long-term (not a current liability) bonds for cash or short-term receivables and also when land, buildings, equipment, or other noncurrent assets are disposed of for cash. Most important, current assets flow in when the company sells its goods and services for cash. All the transactions listed so far would also cause increases in working capital if they were performed on a credit basis instead of for cash, because accounts receivables, like cash, are current assets. Therefore, most sales and other revenue transactions increase current assets and increase our working capital, as do most sales of noncurrent assets and issues of capital stock and bonds.

Net decreases in current assets (which means decreases in working capital) occur when we buy noncurrent assets for cash, when we incur expenses for cash, and when we retire bonds or capital stock for cash.

An increase in current liabilities (without compensating increases in current assets) *reduces* working capital in such transactions as when we incur expenses (advertising, wages, etc.) on account, when we declare dividends payable, and when we recognize "accrued" income taxes payable.

A decrease in current liabilities (without offsetting decreases in current assets) occurs only in rare instances, because almost always current liabilities are paid off in cash. Let's skip this one.

Finally, there is *no change* in *net* working capital when we (1) borrow money on a short-term bank loan or (2) buy materials or merchandise on account. Either transaction involves current liability and current asset increases of equal amount. Similarly, when we pay off a current bank loan or any other current liability in cash, the working capital remains unchanged in amount because we have merely subtracted the same amount from each element in the formula, $CA - CL = WC$.

Again, then, "funds" can be a synonym for working capital; it follows that a working capital funds flow statement is a statement which portrays the opening balance, the inflows, the outflows, the net change, and the closing balance of working capital or funds.

One final word: As a synonym for "working capital," accountants very often use the expression "net current assets."

The Working Capital Funds Statement—Purpose

Does the funds statement serve any particular function other than to show the flow of working capital for the period? Yes. It serves a most important additional function. What it does is fill in a tremendous gap not provided for by the income statement cum balance sheet. Typically, the annual report shows not only the current balance sheet but, in a parallel column, the balance sheet of a year ago—so we have "comparative" balance sheets at the beginning and end of the year. The income statement, with its listing of revenues, expenses, losses, taxes, interest, and dividends, serves to link the retained earnings balance at the start of the year with the balance at year-end. In other words, the income statement more or less explains what brought about the transformation of the retained earnings balance on January 1 into the retained earnings balance one year later, on December 31. But where, then, do we find any information to account for the changes in the other portions of the comparative balance sheets? The answer is, in the funds statement. The funds statement details the changes in working capital (which covers all the current assets and current liabilities), and in so doing it tends to reveal the events that account for the changes in all other categories.

Because you are unlikely to become a professional accountant, and therefore may never again read an essay on the funds statement, we're going to take a fairly complete tour here. We hope you'll stick with it on the assumption that whatever insight you may gain will remain with you and will be useful to you in the future. Later on, we'll take a general view of the whole subject of funds flow and try to determine the uses and limitations.

The Funds Statement—Horseback Version

A quick estimate of the "working capital flow" of a company for a given period can be made by little more than a glance at the company's income statement. Let's take a look at this horseback procedure and then appraise its usefulness.

Assume that you are interested in the financial soundness of a company and your financial advisers have told you that you should be sure to check on the company's working capital flow. The quick-and-easy method is simply to take the reported net income of the company and to that figure add the amount of depreciation for the period of the income statement. To do that is easy; to understand what you're doing is less easy. (A great many people do it, and their lack of understanding is evidenced by the misleading inferences that they derive and proclaim from their quickie analysis.)

Here's an example. Camel Products Co. presents the following condensed income statement for the year:

CAMEL PRODUCTS CO.
Income Statement, Year Ended December 31, 19X1

Sales and other revenues		$256,000
Cost of goods sold*	$120,000	
Selling and administrative expense*	85,000	
Interest expense	7,000	
Taxes	15,000	227,000
Net income		$ 29,000

*Depreciation included in these accounts totals $14,000.

By quick arithmetic, one determines the flow of funds to have been $43,000 for the year. Let's examine the mechanics of this determination. First, the gross inflows of working capital funds are probably quite well measured by the $256,000 figure labeled "sales and other revenues." You, of course, know as well as I do that *revenues are not synonymous with cash,* so immediately you can assume, with no fear of contradiction, that it could be seriously misleading to say the company had gross *cash* inflow of $256,000. Accordingly, unless we modify this amount to exclude sales on a credit basis (and to include collections from the credit sales of the year before), we cannot properly label our quickie calculation a determination of cash flow. Second, the cost of sales (or manufacturing cost of goods sold) should include all outlays, or outflows, of funds incurred in the manufacture of the goods actually sold. Note again that if we stick to the phrase "working capital funds," we're on fairly safe ground, since a reduction of working capital occurs when we pay out either cash or other current assets or when we increase our current liabilities. Third, the other expenses (selling and administrative, interest, and taxes) as listed should include all funds outflows traceable to these categories of expense. But, fourth, as the footnote indicates, some $14,000 of depreciation is buried in the expense accounts. Let's pay special attention to this depreciation.

Does depreciation expense involve an outflow of funds? Yes, it certainly does—but the outflow occurs *when the depreciable assets are paid for,* rather than when they are used. In other words, the *purchase* of depreciable assets requires an outflow of funds sooner or later, but the subsequent accounting recognition of the *depreciation* of those assets does not. Depreciation is the "write-off" of the cost of assets, systematically, over the lives of the assets; the amounts and timing of the depreciation charges would almost never be related in any way to the timing of the amounts paid for the assets. In other words, the *purchase* of an asset normally involves an outflow of funds and the depreciation of the same asset does not. *Depreciation is a "nonfund" charge.*

What has just been said is intended to convince you that, from the expenses for the year, $227,000, we must deduct the $14,000 of depreciation because it is a "nonfund" expense. If you accept this as valid, you can then go directly to the conclusion that a quick way to estimate the net working capital funds inflow (or outflow) of a company for any reported period is simply to remove (subtract) the amount of depreciation from the reported expenses (or just add their amount to the reported net income). The flow of funds of Camel Products Co. for the year was accordingly $43,000. In certain situations there may also be other types of nonfund charges that must be added back.

How to Milk a Company

It would be within the realm of reason to say that those in control of Camel Products Co. have roughly $43,000 of cash at their discretionary disposal ("roughly" because working capital funds and cash are not synonymous). This sum could be used (1) to make payments on any long-term debt that is outstanding and subject to redemption, (2) to purchase items of plant and equipment, or (3) to pay cash dividends, within legal limitations. (We must have at least the same amount of retained earnings.) Let's repeat—the $43,000 does provide a measure of the funds available for discretionary disposition as the result of the operations for the year. *But it does not represent the earnings of the year!*

The science of milking a company consists simply of using funds flow (rather than net income) as the standard for dividend payment—it consists, in effect, of saying that you can ignore depreciation and can budget your dividend payments without providing for the replacement (and, of course, without providing for any expansion) of the plant assets. An expert milker goes a step farther: he "reduces" his expenses by neglecting the normal maintenance and upkeep of the plant assets. So the combination of failure to replace and failure to maintain hastens the demise of the corporate victim.

To summarize, then, working capital funds flow has meaning in the minds of those who take the pains to understand it; at the same time, funds flow when misunderstood is susceptible to wicked abuse. Some analysts even go so far as to report the "funds flow per share" of common stock outstanding. That is utter nonsense. As you must surely realize, a company which is declining, in fact a company which is regularly suffering operating net losses, may show a "beautiful" record of funds flow per share!

The Working Capital Funds Statement—Balance Sheet Version

In our example of funds flow by the horseback, or quickie, method did we leave out something? Yes! Such a determination completely overlooks some very important sources of funds. Three such sources (none of which would normally be revealed in the income statement) are (1) issues of capital stock for cash, (2) issues of bonds, or other long-term borrowing, and (3) sale of corporate property (e.g., land, buildings, and equipment), for cash or on account. Similarly, certain very important outflows of funds are excluded from our income statement version of working capital flow. They are (1) retirements of capital stock for cash, (2) payment of long-term debt (e.g., retirement of bonds), and (3) purchases of noncurrent assets such as land, buildings, and equipment.

It is evident that, with its omissions, the income statement, or horseback version, is of limited usefulness. It does serve to show the amount of funds "generated" by routine current operating activities, but it fails to show several important classes of inflows and outflows. On the other hand, the limited analysis may provide information of importance to the sophisticated analyst, since it emphasizes the magnitude of the funds flow from the regular, recurring operation of the company exclusive of sporadic purchases and disposals of long-term assets, capital stock transactions, and the like.

For a more nearly complete portrayal of the company's funds flow, let's see if we can prepare something of a formal funds statement directly from a pair of comparative balance sheets. Again we'll use the amounts of Camel Products Co. Assume now that our only available information is the following pair of balance sheets prepared at the end of the year corresponding to the income statement we have been discussing and also at the end of the preceding year.

To solve this problem, let's abide by the following rules:

1. Use a formal, two-section form showing *(a)* increases (sources) of working capital funds and *(b)* decreases (disposi-

CAMEL PRODUCTS CO.
Comparative Balance Sheets, December 31

	19X1	19X2	Increase (Decrease)
Current assets	$ 80,000	$ 75,000	$(5,000)
Buildings (after depreciation)	50,000	63,000	13,000
Equipment (after depreciation)	110,000	120,000	10,000
Land	10,000	12,000	2,000
	$250,000	$270,000	$ 20,000
Current liabilities	$ 40,000	$ 31,000	$(9,000)
Bonds payable	50,000	40,000	(10,000)
Capital stock	100,000	120,000	20,000
Retained earnings	60,000	79,000	19,000
	$250,000	$270,000	$ 20,000

tions) of working capital funds and define the net funds flow as the net change in working capital.

2. To account for any change that is not explained by the available data, make an "educated" guess as to the cause of the change.

So we proceed. Our first step might be to prepare a very elementary "schedule of change in working capital," since the amount of working-capital change is the target figure of our derived funds statement. The necessary schedule is prepared automatically, and with no difficulty, as follows:

CAMEL PRODUCTS CO.
Schedule of Change in Working Capital, 19X2

	19X1	19X2	Increase (Decrease)
Current assets	$80,000	$75,000	$(5,000)
Current liabilities	40,000	31,000	9,000
Working capital	$40,000	$44,000	$ 4,000

Only one point of explanation may be called for. In the comparative balance sheets the decline in current liabilities is shown in parentheses as a *decrease*, but in the working-capital schedule the current liability decline is shown as a $9,000 *increase*. That is so because, as you may remember, the smaller the amount of your current liabilities the larger the amount of your working capital, and thus the liability decline, viewed alone, constitutes an *increase* in working capital. In any case, the target figure for our funds statement is the $4,000 change in working capital, since that figure represents the net result of all funds inflows and funds outflows for the year 19X2.

Our next step is to observe the amounts of the changes of *all other items*, one at a time, and with our "educated" guesses list those changes as being the contributory factors (the sources and dispositions) that change the net amount of funds. So let's examine the balance sheet items (excluding the working capital items), in order.

Buildings increased $13,000. We know from our examination of the income statement that the company recorded $14,000 of depreciation. That could affect both the buildings and the equipment; but we've agreed to prepare our statement from the balance sheets alone, and so we either make an arbitrary guess as to the depreciation or ignore it. Let's ignore it. Then, if buildings increased by $13,-000, we simply *assume* the company spent $13,000 for new buildings. Thus, we have our first disposition of funds—Purchase of Buildings, $13,000.

Equipment increased $10,000. If we reason as we did with buildings, we will conclude that the company spent $10,000 for equipment. Thus, we have our second disposition of funds—Purchase of Equipment, $10,-000.

Land increased $2,000, and our educated guess is another purchase, or disposition of funds—Purchase of Land, $2,000.

That completes the scrutiny of the assets; we proceed to the equity portion of the balance sheets and, after skipping current liabilities, find that bonds payable decreased by $10,000. The decrease in bonds could easily be "guessed" as a payoff of part of the company's debt for cash, which amounts to another disposition of funds—Redemption of Bonds, $10,000.

The capital stock increased $20,000. Our guess should probably be that cash of $20,000 was collected through the issuance of capital stock. This is the first "source" item we've encountered—Issue of Capital Stock, $20,000.

The final balance sheet item, Retained Earnings, increased by $19,000. Under our current artificial restriction against referring to the details of the income statement, we cannot modify that figure for depreciation, as we did when dealing with only the income statement. So let's just list, as our final item, Net Income (source funds), $19,000.

CAMEL PRODUCTS CO.
Funds Statement, Year Ended
December 31, 19XX

Source of funds:	
Issue of capital stock	$20,000
Net income	19,000
	$39,000
Disposition of funds:	
Purchase of buildings	$13,000
Purchase of equipment	10,000
Purchase of land	2,000
Redemption of bonds	10,000
Added to working capital	4,000
	$39,000

All that now remains to be done is to organize the data in formal style, as follows:

Comments on Balance Sheet Version

The income statement version merely computed a final total of working capital flow from operations for the year, $43,000. Obviously, this is a far cry from the balance sheet version, which attempts to reveal not only the flow from operations (net income) plus all other sources but also the dispositions that were made of the funds collected. This form, though loaded with inaccuracies resulting from educated guesses based on very sketchy information, comes much closer to the aim of the funds statement set forth earlier in this chapter—including, broadly, an analysis of the changes in major balance sheet items for the period under review.

The Funds Statement—Complete Version

Now forget what has gone before. Let's remove the blinders and prepare a funds statement on the basis of the complete internal records of our company. In other words, assume that we have not only the income statement and comparative balance sheets but also all the ledger information needed to account for the changes in the major balance sheet items.

To keep our illustration within bounds, assume that the "additional information" consists of the following:

1. No equipment or buildings were disposed of. Of the $14,000 of depreciation, $2,000 was deducted from buildings and $12,000 from equipment. A building was purchased for $15,-000, and equipment was purchased for $22,000.

2. Land was purchased for $2,000.

3. Bonds were retired at par, $10,000.

4. Capital stock was issued for $20,000.

5. Dividends of $10,000 were paid.

With that much information to keep track of, the best procedure in developing a solution consists of setting up a skeleton form with plenty of space in which to record the various sources and the dispositions. Then, directly in the skeleton form, start making the entries that you can discern, first, from the "additional" information, second, from the income statement, and, finally, from the balance sheet. The combined form is shown as Figure 6.1.

Figure 6.1 Camel Products Company funds statement.

CAMEL PRODUCTS CO. Funds Statement, Year Ended December 31, 19XX		
Sources of funds:		
Net income (per income statement)	$29,000	
Add back all nonfund charges: Depreciation	14,000	
"Cash flow" from operations		$43,000
Capital stock issued (details)		20,000
Total funds acquired		$63,000
Disposition of funds:		
Purchase of building		$15,000
Purchase of equipment		22,000
Purchase of land		2,000
Retirement of bonds (details)		10,000
Cash dividends paid		10,000
Net addition to working capital (see schedule)		4,000
		$63,000

Comments on Complete Version

The version of the working capital funds statement that is based on free access to all accounting information is, of course, superior to all others.

What it does is to incorporate the horseback version as the lead-off entry in the source section and so provide, for whatever it may be worth, the financial analyst's desired computation of working capital flow for the year. However, the form, by also detailing the balance sheet changes for the year, makes the statement a complete report of the financial activities of the year insofar as these activities went through the working capital funnel.

TEST PROBLEM

The following data are from the accounting records of Decatur Co. covering the calendar year 19X2.

Income Statement, 19X2

Sales		$300,000
Expenses:		
Cost of goods sold	$170,000	
Selling and administrative	75,000	
Interest	4,000	
Taxes	21,000	270,000
Net income		$ 30,000

NOTE: Depreciation of $10,000 was accrued in 19X2.

Comparative Position Statements

	19X1	*19X2*
Current assets	$ 80,000	$100,000
Plant (after depreciation)	300,000	340,000
Land	20,000	10,000
	$400,000	$450,000
Current liabilities	$ 40,000	$ 40,000
Mortgage payable	60,000	50,000
Capital stock	200,000	250,000
Retained earnings	100,000	110,000
	$400,000	$450,000

Additional Data

Cash dividends of $25,000 were paid in 19X2.
Plant was purchased in the amount of $50,000.
Land which cost $10,000 was sold for $15,000 cash.
Mortgage principal payments of $10,000 were made.
The increase in capital stock resulted from the issue of new shares for cash.

Required

Prepare a funds statement in the following blank form.

TEST PROBLEM Solution Space

DECATUR CO.
Funds Statement, Year Ended December 31, 19X2

Sources of funds:

$

$

$

Applications of funds:

$

$

Schedule of Working-Capital Changes

	19X1	*19X2*	*Increase (Decrease)*
	$	$	$
Current assets			
Current liabilities			
Working capital	$	$	$

7
The Funds Statement— Cash Flows

The Cash Receipts and Disbursements Statement

We might call the cash receipts and disbursements statement "the club person's delight." Every club, society, and fraternity has a treasurer of sorts, and the financial report, be it presented monthly, quarterly, semi-annually, or annually, consists of nothing more than a statement of cash receipts and disbursements. In this chapter we hope to start with a quick look at such a statement and then work upstairs to the technical details of such a statement.

Essentially, a cash receipts and disbursements statement, not too surprisingly, consists of two offsetting lists: (1) the amounts of cash received (receipts), showing the sources in as much detail as is desired, and (2) the amounts disbursed, again in whatever detail is called for. The difference between list 1 and list 2 equals the net increase or decrease in cash during the period covered by the statement. Mechanically, if we show the opening (beginning-of-period) balance of cash at the top of the page and then enter the two lists, one below the other, so that their difference can be computed, the difference is shown as an addition to, or subtraction from, the opening balance to give us the final balance (as of the close of the period covered by the report). In the truest sense of the term, this describes a *cash flow statement.* By major types of events and transactions, it is designed to show what brought about the change in the cash balance during the period.

Without concerning ourselves with the amounts or the captions, we see the basic structure of a true cash flow statement in Figure 7.1.

Let's make a few observations by reference to the cash flow statement:

Figure 7.1   Basic Structure of a Cash Flow Statement

JONES BIKE AND HIKE CLUB
Cash Flow Statement for the Summer of 19XX

Cash balance at beginning of season		$ 25.17
Cash receipts:		
Dues (see schedule 1* for details)	$175.50	
Picnic lunches sold	87.28	$262.78
Cash disbursements:		
Food (see schedule 2* for details)	$ 75.45	
Park rentals (see schedule 3* for details)	60.00	
Band-aid adhesive bandages	2.00	137.45
Net increase in cash		125.33
Cash balance at end of season (before banquet)†		$150.50

*These schedules are on file at your treasurer's house.

†The amount of $150.50 is now on deposit in the County Savings Bank.

1. As far as the Jones Bike and Hike Club is concerned, the statement really serves two purposes: It gives a complete summary of the cash activities of the club for the season (prior to the banquet!). Anyone who really wants the complete details can visit the treasurer's house and examine the supporting schedules (or proofs); also, because of the simplicity of the operations, the statement probably serves as an income statement (unless some dues are yet to be collected).

2. The form, or formula, of the funds flow statement could be used to depict the "flow" of any other balance sheet item. Thus, one might prepare an inventory flow schedule or a marketable securities flow schedule or an accounts receivable flow schedule; the possibilities are virtually limitless.

   Now, let's take leave of the Bike and Hike Club and think again in terms of a modern business enterprise. Should the report to stockholders include a cash flow statement which shows every penny collected from every source and every penny spent for whatever purpose? Should the report also include flow statements for receivables, inventories, and all the other assets? In general, the answer is no. Such reports may, in truth, be of service to various levels of management, but to the inactive stockholder (and the general public) this kind of information could be overwhelming and of very limited use.

   However, the accounting profession has concluded that cash flow information, by broad categories of inflows and outflows, is important to stockholders and creditors in making investing and lending decisions; therefore, now a *cash flow statement* must be presented in the annual report as a major third statement, along with the balance sheet and income statement.

Let's Review

Understanding the material here depends on understanding the material we have just covered in Chapter 6. So let's review briefly in order to see the differences and similarities between the funds statement prepared on a working capital basis and one prepared on a cash flow basis.

When a funds statement is prepared on a working capital basis, the primary purpose is to reflect the events and transactions which caused working capital (i.e., current assets minus current liabilities) to increase or decrease during the year. When prepared on a cash flow basis, the purpose is to reflect what brought about changes in *only one* working capital item, namely, *cash.*

Let's think about this a little more. If a company, say, pays cash of $10,000 for a piece of land, *cash decreases by $10,000,* but, and here is a critical point for things to follow, *working capital also decreases by $10,000.* Why? Because cash is one of the working capital items (a current asset), and since cash decreased $10,000 without a corresponding decrease in another current asset or increase in a current liability (land is a noncurrent asset which increased), then working capital also decreases by $10,000.

Or, think of this situation. If 10-year bonds are issued for $100,000 cash, it is obvious that *cash increases $100,000.* But since bonds payable are long-term liabilities, *working capital also increases $100,000.*

Note, therefore, that whether you are preparing a funds statement on a cash flow *or* a working capital basis, the acquisition of the land, and the issuance of the bonds, would be reflected in exactly the same manner.

Major Sources and Uses of Cash and Working Capital

What are the major sources and uses of cash and working capital? The answer is the same in both cases. Cash and working capital flows in and out of the entity are due to three major activities—investing, financing, and operating activities.

Investing activities normally are those concerned with changes in non-current assets. When you acquire land, buildings, machinery, or any other non-current asset, these are investing activities. As you learned in Chapter 6, such assets are normally acquired by the use of cash (cash flows out) which has been borrowed on a long-term basis, generated by operations, or obtained through the issuance of common or preferred stock. If you dispose of such assets, cash often flows in. Such dispositions are part of investing activities, in a broad sense, but might better be called dis-investment activities. In any case, notice once again that working capital and cash are both impacted, in the same direction and in the same amount, and therefore would be shown in the "funds" statement in the same way whether prepared on a cash *or* a working capital basis.

Financing activities usually are those concerned with changes in long-term liabilities, preferred stock and common stock. When these securities are issued, normally cash flows in (cash is increased), but so is working capital increased. On the other hand cash is frequently used (cash is decreased) by a business when it buys back some of its bonds for example, or preferred or common stock. Therefore, once again, cash and working capital both change in the same direction in the same amount, and such changes would be reflected in both types of "funds" statements in the exact same way.

What all of this builds up to is this: with a few minor exceptions we will not discuss, *the results of investing and financing activities do not change* depending on whether you are preparing a cash flow funds statement or a working capital funds statement. *They remain the same.*

The obvious corollary is: *Cash flow from operations is likely to be different, often significantly different, than working capital provided by operations.* So let's concentrate mainly on that difference for a while.

"Funds" Provided by Operations

Operating activities include all earnings-related activities of producing and selling goods and services to customers. For income statement proposes, all such activities are reflected on an accrual basis of accounting, as you learned in earlier chapters. Thus, net income is measured on an accrual basis of accounting.

In this chapter, we want to convert net income from an accrual to a cash basis in order to obtain *cash flow from operations.* In other words, we want to include all the cash inflows and outflows entering into the determination of net income, while excluding all those things affecting the determination of net income which do not affect cash.

Let's start by considering an easy illustration: Simple Company began operations on 1/1/1. Simple Company was indeed simple. All sales were for cash, and all expenses were immediately paid in cash. Simple Company operates in a no-tax economy and rents the building and equipment it needs on an operating lease basis. It sells all the inventory it buys. It obtained the cash for operations by issuing no-par common stock on 1/2/1 for $300,000. The company had no other transactions during year 1 other than operating transactions. Comparative balance sheets and the income statement for year 1 are shown in Figures 7.2 and 7.3.

Obviously, cash increased by $500,000 during the year, and so did working capital. What caused these increases? First, common stock was issued for $300,000 cash—a financing activity. Working capital also increased $300,000. Second, operations provided a net cash inflow of $200,000 since *all* sales of $1,000,000 were for cash, and *all* expenses of $800,000 were paid in cash. Note that net working capital also increased $200,000. If we prepare both types of "funds" statements, they would be identical except for a few differences in terminology as shown in Figure 7.4.

Figure 7.2   Year 1 comparative balance sheets.

SIMPLE COMPANY
Comparative Balance Sheets

	At *12/31/1*	*At* *12/31/0*
Current assets:		
Cash	$ 500,000	-0-
Noncurrent assets:	-0-	-0-
	$ 500,000	-0-
Current liabilities:	-0-	-0-
Noncurrent liabilities:	-0-	-0-
Stockholders' equity:		
Balance, January 1	-0-	-0-
Stock issued 1/2/1	$ 300,000	-0-
Retained Earnings	200,000	-0-
	$ 500,000	-0-

Figure 7.3

SIMPLE COMPANY
Income Statement for the Year Ended 12/31/1

Sales revenue	$ 1,000,000
Operating expenses	800,000
Net income	$ 200,000

Figure 7.4 Comparative "funds" flow statements.

Simple Company cash flow statement for 19×1		Simple Company working capital flow statement for 19×1	
Sources of cash:		Sources of working capital:	
Operations	$ 200,000	Operations	$ 200,000
Issuance of common		Issuance of common	
stock	300,000	stock	300,000
Total sources of cash	$ 500,000	Total sources of working capital	$ 500,000
Uses of cash:		Uses of working capital:	
To increase cash		To increase working	
balance	$ 500,000	capital	$ 500,000

Now, let's make a slight, but important, change in the preceding illustration. Assume everything remains the same *except* that $75,000 of the sales were made on credit rather than for cash, and that the resulting accounts receivable had not been collected by 12/31/1. Comparative balance sheets and the income statement for year 1 would then be as shown in Figures 7.5 and 7.6.

Figure 7.5 Amended comparative balance sheets.

SIMPLE COMPANY
Comparative Balance Sheets

	At 12/31/1	At 12/31/0
Current assets:		
Cash	$ 425,000	-0-
Accounts receivable	75,000	-0-
Total current assets	$ 500,000	-0-
Noncurrent assets:	-0-	-0-
	$ 500,000	-0-
Current liabilities:	-0-	-0-
Noncurrent liabilities:	-0-	-0-
Stockholders' equity:		
Balance, January 1	-0-	-0-
Stock issued 1/2/1	$ 300,000	-0-
Retained earnings	200,000	-0-
	$ 500,000	-0-

Figure 7.6 Amended income statement.

SIMPLE COMPANY
Income Statement for the Year Ended 12/31/1

Sales revenue	$ 1,000,000
Operating expenses	800,000
Net income	$ 200,000

Let's analyze the situation: During the year, the business had $1 million of sales on an *accrual basis,* but $925,000 ($1 million − $75,000) on a *cash basis.* During the year, cash increased $425,000: ($300,000 from the issuance of stock) and $125,000 (net income of $200,000 − $75,000 ending accounts receivable balance). Notice, however, that working capital still increased $500,000 ($300,000 from the issuance of stock, and $200,000 from operations) during the year. In a word, you must convert net income from and accrual to a cash basis to obtain *cash flow from operations.* The "funds" statements would now look as shown in Figure 7.7.

Figure 7.7 Amended comparative "funds" flow statements.

Simple Company *cash flow statement* *For 19×1*		*Simple Company* *working capital flow statement* *For 19×1*	
Sources of Cash:		Sources of Working Capital:	
Net Income $ 200,000		Net Income $ 200,000	
Deduct:		Deduct: $0	
Ending			
Accounts			
Receivable		Add: 0	0
balance	75,000		
Cash flow		Working	
from		Capital from	
operations	$ 125,000	Operations	$ 200,000
Issuance of		Issuance of	
Common		Common	
Stock	300,000	Stock	300,000
Total		Total	
Sources of		Sources of	
Cash	$ 425,000	Working	$ 500,000
		Capital	
Uses of Cash:		Uses of Working Capital:	
To Increase		To Increase	
Cash Balance	$ 425,000	Working	
		Capital	$ 500,000

Let's expand the illustration a bit more, by assuming the following:

Net income for 19×2:		
Sales revenue	$ 1,500,000	
Operating expenses	900,000	(includes depreciation expense of $100,000)
Net income	$ 600,000	

All other operating expenses were paid in cash.

Accounts receivable:	
12/31/1	$ 75,000
12/31/2	$ 125,000

What would cash provided by operations be for the year 19x2? The $75,000 resulted from sales on account during 19x1, but which was collected in cash during 19x2. Therefore, net income on a cash basis for 19x2 is $75,000 higher than on an accrual basis, so the $75,000 must be added to the net income of $600,000. The $125,000 resulted from sales made on a credit basis during 19x2, but the cash will not be collected until 19x3. Consequently, net income on an accrual basis is $125,000 higher than on a cash basis, and therefore the $125,000 must be deducted from net income of $600,000 to arrive at cash flow from operations for 19x2. Again, since accounts receivable is a working capital item, nothing must be added to or subtracted from net income to determine working capital provided by operations during 19x2. Since neither cash nor working capital is impacted by depreciation, $100,000 must be added to net income to determine both cash and working capital provided by operations for 19x2. Compare the following partial "funds" statements:

"Funds" Provided by Operations for 19×2				
Cash flow			*Working capital flow*	
Net income		$ 600,000	Net income	$ 600,000
Add: depreciation	$ 100,000		Add: depreciation	100,000
Beginning accounts receivable	75,000	175,000		
Deduct: Ending accounts receivable		(125,000)		
Cash flow from operations		650,000	Working capital from operations	$ 700,000

Of course, when expenses are converted from an accrual to a cash basis, the impact goes the opposite direction in terms of converting net income to cash flow from operations.

Assume the same facts as in the preceding illustration, but add the following balance sheet accounts:

Wages payable 12/31/1	$ 65,000
Wages payable 12/31/2	$ 85,000

When must the wages payable amount of $65,000 have come into existence? The answer is sometime during 19x1 when wages expense was increased (debited). When would the $65,000 have been paid? Answer: In early 19x2. Consequently, cash outflow for wages was $65,000 higher in 19x2 than wages expense on an accrual basis. Keeping this in mind, it is easy to see that the $65,000 would have to be *deducted* from net income to convert to cash flow from operations.

The opposite is true, of course, for the ending of the year balance in wages payable of $85,000. The $85,000 was debited to wages expense and credited to wages payable sometime in 19x2, probably late in the year, and therefore impacted net income on an accrual basis in 19x2. However, the $85,000 will not be paid (no cash outflow) until 19x3, that is, will not reduce *net* cash inflow from operations until 19x3. Therefore, wages expense is higher on an accrual basis than on a cash basis and would have to therefore be *added* to net income to convert to cash flow from operations.

Note, finally, that wages payable is a working capital item, so no additions or deductions to net income would be necessary to derive working capital provided by operations. The "funds" provided by operations section would now appear as shown in Figure 7.8.

The question remains: Which balance sheet account balances must be used to convert net income to cash flow from operations? Although there are some exceptions, the answer is current assets [accounts receivable (net), inventories, and prepayments] and current liabilities (accounts payable, wages payable, interest payable, taxes payable, etc.).

You have probably noted a pattern in converting net income to cash flow from operations. You *add* the beginning balances in current asset accounts and *deduct* the ending balances (or, if you prefer, *add* the *decrease* in current asset account balances, and *deduct* the *increase*). For current liabilities, the opposite is true—*deduct* the beginning balances and *add* the ending balances (or, again, if you prefer, *deduct* the *decrease* in current liability account balances, and *add* the *increase*).

Figure 7.8 "Funds" provided by operations for 19×2.

Cash flow			Working capital flow	
Net income		$ 600,000	Net income	$ 600,000
Add: depreciation	$ 100,000		Add: depreciation	100,000
Beginning accounts receivable	75,000			
Ending wages payable	85,000	260,000		
Deduct: ending accounts receivable	125,000			
Beginning wages payable	65,000	(190,000)		
Cash flow from operations		$ 670,000	Working capital from operations	$ 700,000

EXTENDED EXAMPLE

You are now ready for a somewhat more complex example: Assume Complex Corporation, during 19x3, used some of the cash it had generated in past years, borrowed $620,000 on long-term bonds issued at par, issued additional no-par common stock for $800,000, and used most of the money to acquire buildings and machinery. Complex Corporation determined it was less expensive to do this than to continue to lease assets. All of these events took place on 1/1/3. Figures 7.9 and 7.10 are comparative balance sheets and an income statement for year 3.

Based on these data, the statement of cash flows would be as shown in Figure 7.11.

Certain Noncash Items

One final note. The accounting profession feels there are certain events and transactions which could have such a material impact on the investing and lending activities of owners and creditors that their impacts should be reflected in the cash flow statement *even though cash is not affected.* These events and transactions encompass such things as exchanges of long-term assets, conversion of bonds payable to common stock, and the acquisition of noncurrent assets in direct exchange for bonds, preferred stock, or common stock issued. Obviously, these cannot be placed in the *body* of the cash flow statement, since cash is not impacted by them. Rather, they are reflected in footnote disclosure in the statement such as follows:

"Conversion of bonds into common stock—$1,000,000"

"Exchange of buildings for land—$500,000"

"Acquisition of land in exchange for common stock—$750,000"

Figure 7.9 Year 3 Comparative balance sheets.

COMPLEX CORPORATION
Comparative Balance Sheets

	At 12/31/3	At 12/31/2
Current assets		
Cash	$ 255,000	$ 765,000
Accounts receivable (net)	95,000	75,000
Merchandise inventory	96,000	150,000
Total current assets	$ 446,000	$ 990,000
Noncurrent assets		
Buildings (net of accumulated depreciation of $40,000)	$ 1,870,000	$ -0-
Machinery (net of accumulated depreciation of $50,000)	450,000	-0-
Total noncurrent assets	$ 2,320,000	$ -0-
	$ 2,766,000	$ 990,000
Current liabilities		
Accounts payable	$ 35,000	$ 50,000
Wages payable	45,000	40,000
Income taxes payable	50,000	-0-
Total current liabilities	$ 130,000	$ 90,000
Noncurrent liabilities		
Bonds payable	$ 620,000	-0-
Total noncurrent liabilities		
Total liabilities	$ 750,000	$ 90,000
Stockholders' equity		
Common stock—no par	$ 1,100,000	$ 300,000
Retained earnings	916,000	600,000
Total stockholders' equity	$ 2,016,000	$ 900,000
	$ 2,766,000	$ 990,000

Figure 7.10   Year 3 Income statement.

COMPLEX CORPORATION
Income Statement for the Year Ended 12/31/3

Sales Revenue		$ 1,700,000
Operating expenses:		
Cost of goods sold expense	$ 900,000	
Wages expense	250,000	
Insurance expense	20,000	
Depreciation expense	90,000	1,260,000
Operating Income		$ 440,000
Non-Operating Expense—Interest		24,000
Income before taxes		$ 416,000
Tax expense		100,000
Net Income		$ 316,000

Figure 7.11   Year 3 cash flow statement.

COMPLEX CORPORATION
Cash Flow Statement For 19x3

Sources of cash:		
Net income		$ 316,000
Add: *depreciation expense ($40,000+$50,000)	$ 90,000	
Increase in wages payable	5,000	
Increase in income taxes payable	50,000	
Decrease in merchandise inventory	54,000	199,000
Deduct: increase in accounts receivable (net)	$ 20,000	
Decrease in accounts payable	15,000	(35,000)
Cash provided by operations		$ 480,000
Issuance of bonds		620,000
Issuance of common stock		800,000
Reduction in cash balance during 19x3		510,000
Total sources of cash		$ 2,410,000
Uses of Cash:		
*Acquisition of buildings ($40,000 + $1,870,000)		$ 1,910,000
*Acquisition of machinery ($50,000 + $450,000)		500,000
Total uses of cash		$ 2,410,000

TEST PROBLEM

The data in Figures 7.12 and 7.13 are from the accounting records of the Tipton Company, covering the calendar year 19x2.

Figure 7.12 Year 2 income statement.

Sales		$ 400,000
Expenses		
Cost of goods sold	$ 220,000	
Selling and administrative	90,000	
Interest	4,000	
Taxes	23,000	337,000
Net income		$ 63,000

Figure 7.13 Year 2 comparative balance sheets.

	19x1	*19x2*
Cash	$ 20,000	$ 35,000
Accounts receivable (net)	25,000	20,000
Inventories	35,000	83,000
Total current assets	$ 80,000	$ 138,000
Plant (after depreciation)	300,000	340,000
Land	20,000	10,000
	$ 400,000	$ 488,000
Accounts payable	$ 25,000	$ 35,000
Wages payable	15,000	10,000
Total current liabilities	$ 40,000	$ 45,000
Mortgage payable	60,000	50,000
Capital stock	200,000	250,000
Retained earnings	100,000	143,000
	$ 400,000	$ 488,000

Some additional data about the Tipton Company include the following:

Cash dividends of $25,000 were paid in 19x2.

Plant was purchased in the amount of $50,000.

Land which cost $10,000 was sold for $15,000 cash

Mortgage principal payments of $10,000 were made.

The increase in capital stock resulted from the issue of new shares for cash.

Required

Prepare a cash flow funds statement in the following blank form.

TEST PROBLEM Solution Space

TIPTON COMPANY
Cash Flow Funds Statement, Year Ended December 31, 19x2

Sources of cash: $

$

$

Applications of cash: $

$

8
Inventories

What Are Inventories?

The term *inventories*, like so many terms that we find in accounting, is widely used in ordinary conversation. It tends to refer to our "supply" of almost anything; thus, we might refer to our inventory of battleships or houses. Let's be more precise for accounting purposes; the best example of inventories is our stock of merchandise held for sale to customers, i.e., our merchandise inventory (often referred to as our *stock in trade*). And if we're connected with a manufacturing company, the term embraces our raw materials, our semifinished goods (work in process, or "in progress"), and our finished goods. A dealer in marketable securities, such as stocks and bonds, would have a marketable securities inventory. Added to that, we generally allow the inclusion of various kinds of consumable supplies under the inventory heading. Supplies (not to be confused with *equipment,* which means more or less permanent assets) include auxiliary goods such as stationery, fuel, lumber, and repair parts. Technically, we should not include as inventories stores of lumber and building supplies that we may have purchased for use in the construction of our own buildings or manufacturing plant, because inventories are limited to the stocks of goods which qualify as current assets and which are part of working capital. Public utility companies regularly err in their balance sheet presentation of construction materials and supplies by showing them as a current asset.

Typical Inventory Transactions

Without paying much attention to reasons or theory, let's now skim through a series of unrelated transactions represented in the form of

110

simple journal entries. As in the series of journal entries presented in Chapter 5, no dollar amounts will be assumed in most cases because they would not be of significance to the illustrations.

(1)

Merchandise	1,000	
Accounts Payable		1,000
Purchase of merchandise at invoice price of $ 1,000,		
terms 2/10 eom.		

The notation 2/10 eom means that if the account payable ($1,000) is paid within 10 days after the end of the month (eom), the buyer is granted a cash discount of 2 percent. Often you'll see terms such as 2/10, *n*/30 or 3/20, *n*/60. The first means that the bill is due in 30 days but the buyer can deduct 2 percent if he pays within 10 days from the date appearing on the invoice. The second is similar: 3 percent off if paid within 20 days; but if payment is delayed beyond 20 days, the face of the invoice becomes the net price. Thus, in the case of our $1,000 account payable, the net price is $980 until the tenth of the next month; after that, the net price becomes $1,000. When no discount is offered, the bill may merely bear the notation "terms net."

(2)

Accounts Payable	1,000	
Cash in Bank		980
Merchandise Discount		20
To record payment of account within 10 days after end		
of month to take advantage of cash discount.		

How would you classify the account Merchandise Discount? Your logical conclusion should be that the credit constitutes a *correction* of the overstated $1,000 original debit to Merchandise. We recorded the purchase of merchandise at "gross," or $1,000. As things turned out, however, our cost of merchandise was only $980, so we could make a $20 credit directly to the merchandise account or (you guessed it) use a contra account to reflect the reduction in recorded cost. In the old days most accounting texts said, incorrectly, that a cash discount is a form of gain or revenue.

A better way to record the two transactions is to debit merchandise for the *net amount* initially and show accounts payable also at net. Surely under the terms of the purchase *we owe only $980* until the tenth of next month has passed. If you want to debate this point with your accountant, the proper "buzz words" are gross versus net. Barring some peculiar set of circumstances which make recording at net impractical, the net method is far superior, as the following entries show.

(1a)

Merchandise	980	
Accounts Payable		980

Purchase of merchandise at invoice price of $1,000
less 2% if paid by 10 eom.

(2a)

Accounts Payable	980	
Cash in Bank		980

Payment of invoice within discount period.

To add to your side of the argument, let's assume that payment of the bill is delayed until the discount period has expired. Then we must pay the entire $1,000, of which $20 is a *penalty* for waiting until the last minute. Under the net method, as the accounts will show, we now will pay off a debt that we recorded at $980 by giving up $1,000 for a *loss* of $20; let's label that loss Loss from Lapsed Discounts. The entry is:

(2b)

Accounts Payable	980	
Loss from Lapsed Discounts	20	
Cash in Bank		1,000

Wouldn't you argue that the accounts should show discounts that have been lost through neglect rather than to emphasize, as the gross method does, the routine "taking" of cash discounts? Do you realize that with terms 2/10, n/30 the 2 percent amounts to an annual rate of 36 percent? (Payment 20 days earlier than necessary saves you 2 percent of the face of the bill. A 360-day year contains eighteen 20-day periods, and 18 times 2 percent is 36 percent.)

(3)

Accounts Payable	xxx	
Merchandise Returns and Allowances		xxx

To record returns of merchandise for credit and to record reductions in price (allowances) granted by the suppliers on goods found to be defective or not in accord with specifications.

(4)

Merchandise	xxx	
Accounts Payable		xxx

To record freight and transportation charges as an
added cost of merchandise purchased.

(5)

Merchandise Inventory	27,000	
Cost of Goods Sold	116,000	
Merchandise		143,000

To allocate cost of merchandise pool between goods
left over (inventory) at the end of the period and the
goods sold.

The amounts in (5) are determined by taking a physical inventory at the
end of the period, finding its cost, and assigning the remainder of the
total cost pool (opening inventory plus purchases) to Cost of Goods Sold.
This is known as the physical, or periodic, inventory method. When we
are dealing with items that are individually significant, we may use the
continuous (or perpetual) inventory procedure. Then, each time that a
sale is recorded, the corresponding cost of goods sold is recorded simultaneously.

(6)

Supplies	xxx	
Accounts Payable		xxx

To record purchases of various kinds of supplies.

(7)

Selling Expenses	xxx	
Administrative Expenses	xxx	
Supplies		xxx

To record consumption of various kinds of supplies for
various purposes as measured by amounts recorded
on requisitions (underlying documents).

(8)

Manufacturing Overhead	xxx	
Supplies		xxx

To record consumption of supplies by various factory
departments, with the cost charged to Factory Overhead because it cannot be traced directly to units of
product manufactured.

(9)

Raw Materials	xxx	
Accounts Payable		xxx

Purchase of various kinds of raw materials for use in
production in our factory.

(10)

| Work in Process | xxx | |
| Raw Materials | | xxx |

To record cost of raw materials used in production, as measured by amounts shown on requisitions issued and traceable directly to specific jobs in process.

(11)

Work in Process	xxx	
Payroll Payable		xxx
Manufacturing Overhead		xxx

To recognize direct labor and factory overhead costs chargeable to work in process.

(12)

| Finished Goods | xxx | |
| Work in Process | | xxx |

To recognize cost of goods finished during the accounting period.

(13)

| Cost of Goods Sold | xxx | |
| Finished Goods | | xxx |

To record the factory cost of goods sold during the period.

Inventory Valuation

The values at which the inventories of merchandise, materials, work in process, finished goods, etc., are recorded have a dual significance in financial reporting. First, the amount shown in the balance sheet as a current asset is likely to be a significant working-capital component. Statement analysts may be expected to pay considerable attention to your working-capital position and special attention to the proportion of your current assets that consists of inventories. Thus, to the degree of choice that you have in reporting a valuation figure for your inventories, you will be in a position to influence the decisions of creditors and investors who look to your financial statements as a prime source of financial information. Second, and perhaps even more important, the accounting valuation which you place on your inventories directly affects the amount of net income for the period. Recall the following formula:

Inventory at start of period	xxx
Add: Cost of goods purchased (or manufactured)	xxx
Total goods to be accounted for	xxx
Less: Inventory at end of period	xxx
Cost of goods sold	xxx

Quite obviously, the amount shown as inventory at end of period directly affects the final amount, cost of goods sold. The greater the cost of goods sold the lesser the net income. Or, to get right to the point, the greater the amount shown as ending inventory the greater the net income, the lower the ending inventory the lower the net income.

The fact is that you do have substantial leeway in the valuation of your ending inventory, and the leeway is derived from the variety of choices available to you in your expressed assumption as to the manner in which the goods flow through your establishment. Let's examine the flow assumptions one by one, but first let's acknowledge one cardinal rule: Basic to all good accounting is *the rule of consistency;* we cannot shift back and forth from one flow assumption to another as suits our wishes or whims each year. This is a real handicap for anyone who wants to manipulate the reported net income figures of his company.

Identified Cost

It is almost universally acknowledged that inventories should be reported at their cost (with due allowance for physical shrinkage, wear and tear, and shrinkage in value). If we acknowledge that cost is the appropriate target for inventory valuation, we may next ask, cost of what? The amount would seem to be *the cost of the goods on hand.* This is our inventory at any point in time. Many people overlook the fact that, carried to its logical conclusion, the expression "cost of the goods on hand" must mean *the amount that we paid for the specific goods* that remain unsold at the end of the period. Now, we may have bought several batches of certain items, and the prices that we paid per unit may have been different for each batch. Suppose at the end of the year we have on hand a few units from each batch. Because the units (though otherwise identical) cost different amounts, the identified cost concept requires that we inventory them at their respective costs. Thus, if we have on hand five units of material X and know that we paid $2 each for two of them, $3 each for two of them, and $4 for the fifth, our identified cost inventory of material X is $14. Some people like to argue that it is perfectly ridiculous to list a series of identical items at different values. Yes, it would be ridiculous if our balance sheet were intended to show the *current values* of all our assets, but the balance sheet makes no such pretense. The general rule for nonmonetary assets is to record the assets *at their cost.* Under that view, the identified cost method is absolutely great except for one thing, *it's usually not practical!* Surely if you're a speculator in real estate, you can easily keep track of the cost of each lot, each house, or each farm that you buy, but it's just not feasible to identify the specific costs that attach to such things as specific gallons of gasoline, cubic feet of gas, pounds of flour, barrels of cement, or yards of cloth.

What do we do, then, when we want to apply the identified cost concept but find it totally impractical? Answer: We make a whopping big assumption as to *the order in which the goods flow* through our business and we "price" our inventory on the basis of our chosen flow assumption. Let's examine the popular assumptions.

First-in, First-out

As a matter of physical fact, all goods, unless they are allowed to rot or rust in the storage bins, flow through the business in a first-in, first-out (FIFO) procession. Of course, the flow is not perfect—some goods never become used or sold and are finally discarded or sold as scrap; some goods are slower moving than others. But the realistic assumption is that your raw materials, your supplies, your work in process, and your finished goods pass through your hands in an orderly first-in, first-out parade. The oldest goods of a given category are constantly cleared from the shelves, and the inventory at any date may reliably *be assumed* to consist of *the most recent purchases.*

The first-in, first-out assumption has no magic significance in itself; it is an assumption for the sake of convenience. It is a convenient way to *simulate* identified cost. Let's demonstrate the method by a simple example.

At the end of the year our company has 1,000 units of a particular item left over after starting with a beginning-of-year inventory of 800 and adding 9,000 that were purchased during the year. Clearly, a total of 8,800 have disappeared if we can now find only 1,000 of the 800 plus 9,000. If the 800 units on hand at the beginning of the year cost $1 each and we bought the 9,000 units in three batches of 3,000 each, costing $1.10, $1.20, and $1.40 per unit, what is the FIFO (first-in, first-out) cost of the 1,000 in the final inventory? The answer is, 1,000 at $1.40, the invoice price of the most recent purchase. The cost of goods sold is then assumed to be the difference between $1,400 (1,000 at $1.40) and the grand total cost ($11,900) of all units to be accounted for, or $10,500. The details may be displayed in schedule form as follows:

	Units	Per Unit	Total
Initial inventory	800	$1.00	$ 800
Purchase 1	3,000	1.10	3,300
Purchase 2	3,000	1.20	3,600
Purchase 3	3,000	1.40	4,200
Total to be accounted for			$11,900
Final inventory at FIFO	1,000	1.40	1,400
Cost of goods sold (or used)			$10,500

If it had been feasible to mark the cost on each unit as we purchased it, we could have totaled up the costs of the 1,000 left over at the end by examining each one and running an adding machine tape to get the total. But if we followed good housekeeping practice during the year, the likelihood is strong that almost all of the 1,000 remaining on hand at year-end came from purchase 3. And note this: If our assumption creates no significant error, we should employ it rather than go through the clerical process of marking and identifying each item as if it were an important individual.

What Are Inventory Profits and Holding Gains?

In a great many articles that have been written the authors point out that net income is often affected significantly by the fact that the replacement costs and the selling prices of goods may rise (or fall) while the goods are being held in stock by the company. Such a development, so it is argued, creates *holding gains* or, as they are more commonly termed, *inventory profits.* The concept is more elusive than you might think. Let's dive into it with a mini-example.

Our company buys one unit of an item for $100, wholesale, when the retail price is $130. This specific item is not sold until later when the wholesale price has risen to $120 and, obediently, the retail price has gone to $156 (30 percent over cost). By traditional accounting, on a strict cost basis, our company would show a gross margin of $56 on the sale ($156 —100) which, of course, would be offset in the determination of net income by various operating expenses and taxes. The point is that $20 of the gross margin (and a corresponding portion of the net income) could be attributed solely to the wholesale and retail *price rises* that occurred while we were "holding" the item. Out of this phenomenon have evolved three distinct schools of accounting thought. Let's take a look.

THE HOLDING GAIN SCHOOL: One crowd says that holding gains are quite different from "trading" gains, which are the result of normal buy-and-sell transactions. (Trading gains are deemed to represent the fruits of managerial effectiveness—they are the real "operating" gains.) Our income statements should divide the gross margin into two parts: (1) holding gain and (2) trading gain. In our example, this school would report the gross margin as follows:

Sales	$156
Cost of goods sold, on replacement-cost basis	120
Gross trading margin	$ 36
Add: Given holding gain ($120 − 100)	20
Gross margin	$ 56

THE INVENTORY PROFITS SCHOOL: Another crowd says that inventory profits are illusory. To them the *real* cost of goods sold is not the identified (or FIFO) historical cost of the goods sold but, rather, the current, *or near-current,* replacement cost as *measured by the amounts we have actually paid most recently for identical goods.* To illustrate this notion, we must make an added assumption: that our company did buy a second item for $118 not long *before* it sold the first one. This group does not want to abandon the hallowed historical cost principle; so as a substitute for the current $120 replacement cost employed by the holding gain school, cost of goods sold is calculated as being made up of the actual cost(s) of the goods *most recently purchased.* In other words, these folks would avoid the need for showing holding gain (which they consider to be a mirage) by making the highly artificial assumption that we didn't really sell the old $100 item—what we actually sold was the latest one we bought, the $118 item. This assumption is the reverse of FIFO and is known as LIFO (last-in, first-out). It really should be known as *artificial* LIFO because, actually, goods don't flow through a company in that cockeyed order. In our example, the anti-inventory profits (LIFO) school would report their gross margin as follows:

Sales	$156
Cost of goods sold, on LIFO basis	118
Gross margin	$ 38

THE IDENTIFIED COST SCHOOL: Now let's get back to basics. Most businesses are constantly buying, fabricating, and selling goods. Under the most common circumstances the stock of goods is maintained at minimum levels (to minimize costs of storage, protection, interest on investment, deterioration, and obsolescence); in other words, most enterprises are in business to trade, in the normal sense of the word, rather than to speculate on price increases. Fluctuations, up and down, in wholesale and retail prices are part of the economic environment, and there seems to be little reason for undertaking the complicated bookkeeping procedures that would be required to determine with any precision the amount of gross margin that is caused by holding gains. Nor would the reporting of such information often be of any real service to the statement analyst; on the other hand, it is totally wrong to deny that such gains have occurred and to repress their recognition (by use of LIFO). The identified cost group, then, would report as follows:

Sales	$156
Cost of goods sold, on FIFO basis	100
Gross margin	$ 56

COMMENTARY: Now that you've had a glimpse at three interesting schools, perhaps you could be convinced that the third would be best *if those who use it would only adjust their historical dollar costs to reflect changes in the value of our measuring unit—the dollar.* Unfortunately, we must delay full explanation of the problem of our shaky dollar until Chapter 21. Please, therefore, keep in mind the italicized words in the preceding sentence.

Last-in, First-out

Although LIFO was touched upon in the preceding section, it's much too prominent in current usage to be dropped so quickly. The LIFO inventory valuation procedure is acceptable for income tax purposes and has widespread endorsement. We must at least scan the highlights of LIFO.

During periods of persistent inflation (which seems to be almost constant), our costs and selling prices tend to rise in parallel fashion. As was demonstrated in the preceding section in simplified form, use of the FIFO flow assumption, realistic as it may be, matches costs that may have been incurred days, weeks, or months ago against revenues from current sales—simply because, for each sale that is made, the accountant checks off against that sale the cost of the unit of inventory that has been on the shelves for the longest time. The result is a gross margin determination that includes the full amount of holding gain (or, as we'll see later, the *illusory* gain from deterioration of the purchasing power of our currency).

LIFO, on the other hand, artificially assumes that the oldest goods remain on the shelves (forever?). In fact, some refer to LIFO as FINO —first-in, never-out! If, for example, our company begins to use LIFO at a time when it has on hand 100 tons of steel that cost $500 per ton and if its ending inventory of steel for the next 20 or more years never goes below 100 tons, on its balance sheet for every one of those years the same 100 tons at $500 will be included in the inventory.

In its favor, it may be admitted that LIFO tends to suppress recognition of illusory gains from inflation. At best, however, it does so in a makeshift fashion, since prices of steel and other specific commodities do not move in concert with changes in the purchasing power of the dollar. Strongly in favor of LIFO is the possibility of stalling off payment of income tax on illusory gains, since LIFO is an allowable procedure for income tax purpose.

In very strong opposition to LIFO is the fact that the FINO inventory figures, which appear as current assets in the balance sheet, are farcical.

Let's look at one more example. Assume that a newly formed company makes the following purchases of a given item during its first year of existence:

Date	Quantity	Price per Unit	Amount
Jan. 1	1,000	$2.00	$ 2,000
Feb. 10	3,000	2.40	7,200
June 15	4,000	3.00	12,000
Nov. 5	3,500	3.50	12,250
Totals	11,500		$33,450

Assume also that sales of this item during the period, when price varied from $3.00 to $4.50 per unit, amounted to $40,000 and that on hand on December 31 there remain 1,500 unsold units. First, let's see what our gross margin would be if we used FIFO. Following is the FIFO schedule.

Sales		$40,000
Cost of goods sold:		
Purchases	$33,450	
Inventory, December 31 (1,500 @ $3.50)	5,250	28,200
Gross margin		$11,800

Next, the same schedule shows the gross margin if LIFO is employed.

Sales		$40,000
Cost of goods sold:		
Purchases	$33,450	
Inventory, December 31		
(1,000 @ $2 + 500 @ $2.40)	3,200	30,250
Gross margin		$ 9,750

As you should recognize, the LIFO procedure shows $2,050 less gross margin. The difference is equal to the difference in the amount assigned to the 1,500 units of closing inventory. Under LIFO procedure the 1,500 units will constitute the beginning inventory for the following year at the same $3,200 valuation, and the same units and same value could, theoretically, remain in the financial statements for all time. FIFO procedure, on the other hand, tends to provide inventory costs that are continuously up to date.

Dollar Value LIFO

It does not seem appropriate here to explore the intricacies of so-called *dollar value LIFO*, but the rationale should be noted. For companies that handle standard materials or standard merchandise year after year, the LIFO procedure that we have just scanned is entirely feasible. However, many companies, especially retail stores, have more or less constant changes in the *variety* of goods handled. LIFO would be of little use to them, since they are persistently "selling out" their complete stock of items that are dropped from their line. In short, as originally conceived, a somewhat limited number of taxpayers could employ LIFO and all others were in a true sense being discriminated against. To remedy the discrimination, dollar value LIFO was invented. Essentially, dollar value LIFO treats a complex variety of materials or merchandise as a pool of dollars rather than as a quantity of physical units. By use of a series of price index numbers, goods on hand at the end of each year are valued at costs which are translated into earlier years, with an end result which simulates LIFO on a physical unit basis.

Average Cost

To round out the discussion of inventory valuation procedures, it must be noted that some companies value their ending inventories on a moving average cost basis. This may mean that, for each class of materials or merchandise, the cost of the purchases for the year is added to the cost of the opening inventory and the sum is divided by the corresponding total number of units to obtain an average unit cost. This average unit cost is then applied to the number of units remaining on hand at year-end to determine the dollar valuation of the ending inventory. Where continuous (perpetual) inventory procedure is used, the average cost per unit may be changed whenever a new batch of a given item is purchased, and then the final inventory is priced at the average cost in effect at the year's end. Needless to say, the use of an average cost procedure is bound to result in a cost of goods sold figure (and a gross margin) that lies somewhere in between the corresponding amounts resulting from FIFO and LIFO.

Cost or Market, the Lower

Let's face it. Businessmen in general, and almost all accountants, are conservative in their financial affairs. An old-time guiding principle of accounting goes somewhat as follows: Recognize all losses, anticipate no gains. As translated, this means, "Write assets down and liabilities up, whenever any glimmer of doubt appears, but don't ever acknowledge any gain until it has been unquestionably realized in the form of cash (or claim-to-cash) proceeds." We could debate the doctrine of conservatism for hours, but that would be inappropriate here. Rather, as we pass from one area to another, we'll simply take note of the implications of conservatism as they are reflected in the current "generally accepted" practice.

As a prime example of accounting (and business) conservatism, it is generally assumed that inventories, unless valued at LIFO, must be valued at *the lower of cost or market.* The bulletin which prescribes the rules for determining the valuation is too technically complex for our detailed consideration. In simplified terms, however, the rule boils down to a requirement that if the goods on hand at the end of the period could be replaced (in customary quantities and through customary channels) at prices that are lower than those that were actually paid, the recorded costs of the goods on hand should be written down to their replacement costs (and a corresponding loss shown). The theory is that if your buying price for goods has dropped, it is likely that your resale price for the goods will drop also. Many comments (not all flattering) could be made about this rule, but one point stands out. If the replacement cost (market price) of goods has *fallen,* we must accrue a corresponding assumed loss; should the reverse occur—forget it! It should be added that income tax rules do not permit the use of cost or market if the taxpayer is "on LIFO."

Inventory Turnover

One of the relationships which financial analysts frequently use in appraising the financial quality of a firm is the ratio of the cost of goods on hand (inventory) to the cost of goods sold for an entire year. If, for example, the company now has on hand goods inventoried at $20,000 and the cost of all goods sold during the past year was $240,000, the ratio of 20 to 240 (1 to 12) indicates that the company's inventory approximates the needs for a month's sales. The relationship may be reported as a "30-day supply" (since accountants usually assume a 360-day year for ease in quoting such approximate relationships), or the term *turnover* may be used. In our example the evidence indicates an inventory turnover rate of 12 times per year. Turnover is computed by dividing cost of goods sold for the year by the amount of inventory at year-end or, better, by the average of the initial and ending inventories (or even by the average of the inventory quantities at the ends of all 12 months). In general, of course, the higher the turnover rate the better. If a company can operate successfully with a 10- or 20-day inventory, this means less funds tied up in merchandise and materials and, accordingly, lower costs. Needless to say, one important function of management is to seek and maintain *optimum* inventory levels. Overstocking means excessive interest costs, obsolescence, and high storage costs; understocking leads to loss of customers and loss of sales. The buzz word for understocking is "outages," and our current crop of management scientists delight in seeking to measure the cost of outages.

Inventory Reports for Management

If perpetual inventory records are kept or if inventory records are computerized, accountants should be able to keep management currently apprised of the firm's inventory position not only in terms of inventory totals but also in reports of significant over- or understock of specific items that are important to the welfare of the company. Quite a bit of research has been done by the operations research (OR) folks with respect to inventory management, including, for example, the development of formulas for determining the optimum quantity of goods to be purchased at a time.

TEST PROBLEM

On January 1 the raw materials inventory of a company, valued at FIFO cost, is $12,000; it consists of 20,000 pounds of material. The company buys 25,000 pounds at 80 cents per pound on January 10 (terms 2/10, n/30) and pays for them on January 19; the company buys 20,000 pounds at 90 cents per pound on January 20, under the same terms, and pays for them on January 31. All raw material purchases are *recorded at net* prices. Perpetual inventory records show a balance of 22,000 pounds of the material on hand on January 31.

Required

In simple journal form, record the purchases, the payments, and the usage during January with respect to the raw materials.

TEST PROBLEM Solution Space

	Debit	Credit
January 10		
January 19		
January 20		
January 31		

9
Fixed Assets and Depreciation

Classes of Fixed Assets

In a very broad sense accountants divide assets into two major groups: current and noncurrent. By tradition the noncurrent assets have come to be termed *fixed assets,* a term which is not particularly apt since, with the possible exception of land, no asset is permanently fixed or permanently attached to a particular owner. There is no established rule as to terminology; you may take your choice.

In the noncurrent category five principal subdivisions stand out. A corporation, a partnership, or a person, for that matter, may acquire the capital stock, bonds, notes receivable, or mortgages issued by other companies or persons, and the intent may be to hold the "securities" for a considerable period of time for their investment value—that is, for the interest and dividends or possible value growth that will be obtained. In contrast with purchases of marketable securities for the short-term employment of temporarily excessive cash funds, these securities are *long-term investments,* and they are properly classified as fixed assets in the balance sheet. Because we will be looking at these same securities from the standpoint of their issuers later, we will give them no special consideration in this chapter.

A second major category of fixed assets consists of all types of *natural resources.* Most commonly in this category we think of the land on which our buildings rest—site land—but this group also includes agricultural land, mining land, rights-of-way, etc. For most companies these assets present no major accounting problems, and we'll touch on them only lightly in this chapter.

The third category includes all types of *depreciable structures,* of which buildings constitute the principal subgroup. We'll concern ourselves with the questions of the valuation of structures when they're first acquired and as they age.

The fourth category consists of *machinery and equipment* of all types. As with structures, we'll be concerned with both the initial and the subsequent valuation of items in this group.

The fifth category is made up of all kinds of so-called *intangible assets*. It is very difficult to concoct a satisfactory accounting definition of intangibles because, for example, both accounts receivable and cash in bank are intangible but neither is included within the technical accounting category of intangibles. The best way out seems to be just to list the things that accountants usually classify as intangibles. They are goodwill, patents, trademarks, trade names, franchises, secret processes, and, possibly, leaseholds and long-term prepayments. You may think of others. In any case, we'll devote no more time to this category here but will take a closer look at goodwill at a later point in the book. Essentially, then, this chapter will be concerned with the initial and subsequent valuations of structures, machinery, and equipment.

Initial Valuation of Fixed Assets

There tends to be very little disagreement as to the proper initial accounting for depreciable and nondepreciable fixed assets of all types. "Cost" has almost universal acceptance. (A few accountants believe that there may be numerous instances in which the buyer either clearly outwits the seller or is obviously outwitted and that accounting recognition should immediately be made of the implied gain or loss in the act of making the purchase. The vast majority of accountants rebel at that idea and prefer to let any "purchase gain" or "purchase loss" show up in the subsequent accounting for the asset.)

The determination of acquisition cost can be tricky sometimes. The easiest case, of course, is when we buy land, buildings, or equipment for cash (or by a down payment plus a mortgage or installment purchase contract). Be sure to include ("capitalize") *all* costs of acquisition up to the point at which the asset is *in place and ready for use*. Costs that should be capitalized include transportation, installation, and break-in, as well as basic construction costs when the company builds its own structures or equipment.

A more difficult determination of acquisition cost arises in the less common situation in which we issue capital stock to someone in exchange for an asset or a "basket of assets." In these days of intensive merger activity, it is not at all unusual for one company to acquire the "net assets" of another company by giving the other company an agreed-upon number of shares of capital stock. Two questions present themselves: (1) What actually is the *cost* to us of the assets that we acquire in this fashion (whether we get a basketful or a single asset)? (2) How do we allocate the total cost of the entire group of assets to the individual assets that make up the group? The usual (and apparently sound) accounting answers to these questions may be stated quite briefly. First, when capital stock is issued in the acquisition of assets, the assets should be recorded at their estimated *current market values* (with due allowance, of course, for their physical condition). If current market value is not ascertainable, an acceptable alternative is to determine the current market value of the capital stock that is being given and assign the same value to the assets that are acquired. The answer to the second question is that once the aggregate cost of a group (basket) of assets is known, the cost should be allocated to the component elements of the group in proportion to their respective market, or appraised, values.

The final acquisition deal for us to consider is the one in which we trade in an old asset on a new one—that is, a barter transaction in which, usually, we must give cash to boot. Here it is a great temptation to argue that the cost of the new asset is equal to the amount of cash (or future cash) we give plus the book value of the old asset traded in. Thus, if we trade an automobile that originally cost us $12,000, which we have depreciated down to a book value of $4,000, and if we give cash or notes payable to boot of $18,000, the cost of the new asset would be recorded at $22,000. That may be appropriate for income tax purposes, but it's poor accounting theory. Our real cost is the amount of cash paid ($18,-000) plus the *current market value* (rather than our book value) of the asset traded in. If we assume the asset traded in had a current market value of $2,500, the correct cost of the new asset is $20,500. Many folks go astray in this same situation by being overly impressed by the list price of the new automobile. We all know that list prices are not to be taken very seriously. Thus, if the new car had a list price of $20,000, another wrong recording of the trade-in would be the following:

Loss on trade-in	2,000	
Automobile (new—at list price)	20,000	
Allowance for Depreciation (old)	8,000	
Cash in Bank		18,000
Automobile (old)		12,000

This concludes our discussion of the initial valuation of fixed assets. In every transaction, you are bound to encounter special circumstances that present difficulties. We have touched upon the major high points, and we hope that you'll be able to resolve the unique problems of each situation as they arise. Next we take a look at some of the alternatives with respect to asset valuation subsequent to acquisition.

Historical Cost Less Depreciation

Accountants have strongly favored carrying fixed assets on the books and on the financial statements at their historical dollar cost as adjusted for the amount of depreciation that has been recognized. In favor of this position is the ever-present affection that accountants have for "objectivity." They like to present figures that can be audited and confirmed. They also like to avoid estimates and appraisals as much as they can, because these tend to be "subjective" valuations subject to bias and manipulation which may be detrimental to the interests of investors and creditors. Further, they favor historical cost because, they say, profit is earned only as we make use of our assets and write off (depreciate) their cost against the amounts (revenues) that we receive for their use. In other words, business profits are made through the current operations of the business, and not by the purchase of assets at a bargain or by the subsequent (assumed) increases in the values of the assets (most of which are no more than reflections of inflation). Many accountants who favor historical cost believe that cost should be restated in terms of the current value of the measuring unit—the dollar. We'll spend a whole chapter on this interesting subject later. Nothing has been so thoroughly neglected by accountants as the undeniable fact that our measuring unit has been changing in size by anywhere from 1 to over 20 percent each year (always shrinking) and that it is simply ridiculous to add together dollars of different vintages and treat them as if all of them had the same meaning.

Replacement Cost

Practicing accountants have traditionally shown little enthusiasm for making formal recognition of appraised values for fixed assets in the accounts and financial statements. Admittedly, some knowledge of current values of the fixed assets of a business is important internally for purposes of getting adequate insurance coverage, and such information may be of considerable interest if property is the basis for rate regulation or is to be mortgaged in connection with a loan or bond issue. There are those (for example, the theoretical economists) who argue that the true income for any period is best defined as the difference between the amount of the net assets at the beginning and end of the period. (Net assets, to repeat, is the expression for the amount found by subtracting total liabilities from total assets—a difference frequently termed *net worth.*) The economists would, of course, require that the assets be recognized at their current values for their purposes in determining the net assets. Again we are faced with the question of recognizing holding gains as the fixed assets (which we intend never to sell) fluctuate in value. Many accountants have strongly resisted the notion that appraisal (versus historical cost) valuations be displayed even in the form of footnotes to the formal statements. Let's note some of their arguments against deviation from historical cost.

First, it would be quite costly to employ appraisers as often as once a year to supply us with their "educated" estimates of the current replacement costs of our properties.

Second, the basic definition of current value is most elusive: Does it mean replacement cost? Do we mean the *literal reproduction* of our existing buildings and machinery by using the same building materials, the same hand labor, the same building methods, etc? Or do we mean the cost of buying, in the present market, closely similar assets that will provide the same amount of service as the assets we are now using and with due allowance for the amount of depreciation that our assets have sustained to date? Or do we mean the amount for which we could sell the asset now? Needless to say, this question presents very major complexities.

Third, if we were to report the fixed assets in our balance sheet at their replacement values, would our investors have a significantly better basis for estimating *the value of their company?* Or does the value of the company depend more heavily upon the effectiveness and excellence of the management?

Fourth, if we were to make the necessary adjustments for recognition of the change in the value of our monetary unit (which we'll explore in Chapter 21), wouldn't that pretty well solve the problem? It can be argued quite successfully that reproducible fixed assets never, or at least rarely, increase in true value, though their cost, restated in dollars of current purchasing power, is very much subject to change. In other words, true holding gains, even if we wanted to recognize them, are likely to be quite immaterial when allowance is first made for deterioration of the monetary unit.

Possibly a good compromise between historical and current costs would be to agree to recognize changed fixed asset values when and if it becomes perfectly obvious that some very substantial value changes have occurred—to the point at which the company should be asking itself if it might be better to dispose of certain assets in order to realize the big gains rather than continue to employ the assets in the business. It is quite probable that such value changes would almost never be called for except in rare cases when the company's land had undergone dramatic value increase.

DEPRECIATION OF FIXED ASSETS

Any formula for the computation of depreciation must make use of at least four factors: asset cost (or alternative valuation basis), useful life, probable terminal salvage, and timing of service extraction. It's sad, but true, that every one of those factors presents difficulties (in many cases absolute impossibility) of accurate measurement. Nevertheless, we must recognize depreciation. Because of the vast amount of uncertainty, a lot of different methods of measuring depreciation have been proposed, and it would seem quite important for any executive to have a nodding acquaintance with the more common procedures and to be on guard against being misled by the numerous false impressions that so many people have with respect to the accounting for depreciation.

What Is Depreciation?

Depreciation is the exhaustion of the useful service potential of an asset through the combined effects of utilization, wear and tear, aging, and obsolescence. The first three of those factors tend to cause the asset to deteriorate physically, and obsolescence means the loss of usefulness from all other causes. For example, the asset becomes obsolete because it is no longer large enough for our needs (our first computer), our competitors have acquired a more efficient machine and we must replace ours in order to match their reduced costs of production, or the output of our equipment has gone out of style. Depreciation does not include breakage or other casualty loss; these are losses rather than depreciation.

Accounting for depreciation consists in making accounting entries to recognize, with reasonable accuracy and in dollar amounts, the depreciation cost that should be assigned in each accounting period. Every depreciable asset has its *depreciable cost,* which means original cost minus the amount we expect to get for the asset when we retire it—the so-called salvage. If an asset costs $100 and we predict that we will use it for 4 years and then sell it secondhand for $20, the depreciable cost is $80 so far as we are concerned. So accounting depreciation boils down to this. Assuming use of historical cost of a given asset (or collection of assets), we must have a record of the cost, we must make an estimate (or assumption) as to the prospective terminal salvage (which, subtracted from the cost gives us the *depreciable cost*), we must make an estimate (or assumption) as to the useful life (that is, how long the asset will be useful *to us*), and we must then determine the most *appropriate pattern* to be followed in the allocation of the depreciable cost to the individual accounting periods making up the useful life of the asset or collection of assets.

Depreciation Patterns

Four general patterns are possible in the allocation of depreciable cost to the periods of useful life. One pattern assumes that each period realizes the same benefit from the asset and, accordingly, should bear the same depreciation charge. This pattern, logically enough, is termed *straight-line* depreciation. At the opposite extreme, one may predict that the utilization of the asset will vary in uneven fashion from year to year and that, instead of a straight line, we should contemplate use of a pattern of charges best depicted by a *wavy line*. This leaves only two other realistic choices. One is based on the assumption that most assets perform most effectively when new and that their effectiveness declines more or less continuously as they age, so that a *decreasing line* (to represent decreasing charges per period) may be appropriate. Lastly, in certain rare cases an *increasing line* may be chosen. From here on this chapter will be devoted to the respective merits and shortcomings of the various depreciation line assumptions.

Straight-Line Depreciation

The periodic straight-line depreciation accrual is determined by dividing the depreciable cost of the asset by the number of accounting periods contained in the estimated useful life of the asset. Depreciable cost, as defined earlier, is the total cost of the asset minus the expected *net* salvage. Gross salvage is the total amount that we hope to recover from the asset at the time of its final retirement and disposition; net salvage is gross salvage less any costs that are incurred in the process of obtaining the gross salvage. For example, in the razing of a structure we might plan to recover used bricks worth a total of $500 (gross salvage); but if the probable labor cost of razing the structure is $400, then the net salvage, to be used in the straight-line depreciation calculation, is only $100.

Straight-line is by far the most popular depreciation method used by American industry; oddly enough, such popularity is not really warranted. It has only two arguments going for it, and neither is laudable. First, it's the simplest method, and this may be true. To work a problem in straight-line depreciation would perhaps require education in arithmetic through the second grade in school, whereas the other popular methods might demand the higher mathematics covered in the third or fourth grade. Second, straight-line depreciation constitutes a compromise in a sea of uncertainty. We don't really know the useful life of an asset at time of acquisition and we don't know the pattern in which the asset's services will be extracted, so we make the unwarranted assumption that over the uncertain life the same amount of service will be extracted in each period.

On the other side, there are some fairly potent arguments against straight-line depreciation. First, assets typically perform most efficiently and productively when they are new; and if a given period receives the benefit of superior service, it should bear a correspondingly high depreciation charge. As the asset ages and performs less effectively, each period should receive a smaller depreciation charge. Certainly the straight-line pattern fails to match this performance picture. Compounding the inequity of straight-line depreciation charges is the typical pattern of repair and maintenance charges, which tend to increase perceptibly as the asset ages. So with straight-line depreciation we end up with *increasing charges for decreasing services* as time passes! A final argument against straight-line depreciation is a relative one. It is a less conservative method than certain others. It delays the write-off of the asset, and, if used for tax purposes, fails to capitalize on tax benefits that may possibly be derived from use of the accelerated depreciation methods allowed (we'll discuss these allowable accelerated depreciation methods in Chapter 16).

Wavy-Line Depreciation

A method of depreciation that results in a wavy line is commonly referred to as the *production units method*. The formula is similar to straight-line except that the depreciable cost is divided not by the expected number of accounting periods in the asset's life, but by the total number of *units of output* that the asset is expected to render. Thus, in the case of a taxicab the depreciable cost might be divided by, say, 200,000 miles to obtain the estimated depreciation cost per mile. Then the total depreciation charge for a given accounting period would be found by multiplying the miles driven by the depreciation cost per mile. The production units method has considerable theoretical appeal. It is based on the sound premise that when you buy a depreciable fixed asset, you are acquiring a "bundle of services"; and it follows logically that, if the services are identical, one unit of depreciation occurs as each unit of service is detached from the bundle. For a useful analogy, think of the purchase for $100,000 of a mine that contains 100,000 tons of coal. As each ton of coal is extracted, the cost of the mine content remaining would naturally be written down by $1. (The exhaustion of mines, oil and gas wells, etc., is called *depletion* rather than depreciation.) And so we find strong support for the units-of-production, wavy-line, method of booking depreciation *when the units of service output are identical and the total, original service-unit content can be ascertained within reasonable limits of accuracy.* The unfortunate fact is that industry has found relatively few situations in which those requirements can be met. It's virtually impossible to find a satisfactory definition of a service unit in the case of almost any structure, and it's even more difficult to make anything like a reliable estimate of the total number of service units that will be extracted from any piece of machinery. In short, the production units method has failed to gain widespread acceptance because of its apparent impracticability. In that respect it is similar to the identified cost method of valuing inventories, in which, as you will recall, accountants are prone to adopt flow assumptions which they believe satisfactorily *approximate* the realistic movement of goods. Something of the same thing is done in the realm of depreciation when accountants adopt either a straight-line assumption or the decreasing-line assumption, which we are to examine next.

Decreasing-Line Depreciation

As we've noted repeatedly, most depreciable assets tend to turn out less and less service as they grow older. Such service deterioration may manifest itself in several ways. Some machines simply run slower and slower; some have more breakdowns and more downtime; most require more attention as they age—more maintenance and repair; and some get out of adjustment and cause more defective products as time passes. Few depreciable assets escape what we might term *service deterioration* as they age, and such deterioration shows up in different ways for different assets. Buildings used for offices, apartments, and other purposes lose their attractiveness as they cease to be "modern." In many ways, assets perform less satisfactorily as they get older; they may produce a reduced flow of services, or they may render an undiminished amount of service but at a higher operating cost, or the same physical service may have lower and lower market value. The old apartment house or the old motel, for example, provides just as much space for occupancy as when new, but the revenue (and net income) to the owner suffers because customers can be attracted only in fewer numbers and at reduced rents. This tendency, then, for a depreciable asset to render considerably more than half of its total service during the first half of its life strongly encourages the conclusion that the depreciation line, or curve, should have a downward slant. The plans are variously known as *accelerated depreciation, liberalized depreciation,* and *decreasing charges depreciation.*

There are two common plans for calculating the periodic depreciation charges under the liberalized concept. First is one which appears to be (and perhaps is) almost idiotic. It's called the *sum-of-years'-digits* method. If an asset has a 4-year life, you add the digits 1 through 4 (which equals 10) and your depreciation each year is found by applying a fraction, which consists of the numbers of years taken in reverse order over 10, to the depreciable cost of the asset. Assume that an asset costs $100 with an estimated life of 4 years and probable salvage of $10. Then the depreciation series for the 4 years would be: year 1, $4/10$ of $90, or $36; year 2, $3/10$ of $90, or $27; year 3, $2/10$ of $90, or $18; year 4, $1/10$ of $90, or $9, for a total of $90.

If you're unhappy with sum-of-years' digits, use the *declining-balance* method. In many cases, it allows you more depreciation earlier than is allowed under sum-of-years' digits. Again the calculation is easy: If an asset has a 5-year life, the straight-line depreciation rate would be 20 percent each year applied to the initial cost of the asset minus its salvage. The (double) declining-balance method permits you to use *double the straight-line rate,* but the double rate is applied each year to the amount remaining in the asset account, and no salvage value is fed into the calculation. If we apply the declining-balance method to the $100 asset used in the preceding paragraph, the succession of depreciation charges will be: year 1, 40 percent of $100, or $40; year 2, 40 percent of ($100 − $40), or $24; year 3, 40 percent of ($60 − $24), or $14.40; year 4, 40 percent of ($36 − $14.40), or $8.64, for a total of $87.04. Note that in this example there is a built-in salvage residual of $12.96 as compared with the $10 that was preselected in the sum-of-years' digits plan. The relative amounts recorded under the two plans are as follows. (SYD = sum-of-years' digits plan; DB = declining-balance plan.)

Year	SYD	DB
1	$36	$40.00
2	27	24.00
3	18	14.40
4	9	8.64
	$90	$87.04

Composite and Group Depreciation

In spite of the availability of computerized depreciation accounting, common practice is to apply a single straight-line depreciation rate to all of a firm's assets or to subdivide the assets into related collections and apply an appropriate rate to each collection. Such procedure is known as *composite depreciation,* and the rates are supposed to be determined for each collection of assets by an averaging process.

Group depreciation is similar to composite depreciation except that, under group depreciation, the assets are classified into closely related groups in which, for example, each asset in a group has the same approximate useful life. The selected depreciation rate for the group then depends upon the probable mortality of the component units within the group. Thus, one might apply group depreciation to all of the utility poles owned by a public utility company and, though the useful lives might range from 8 to 20 years, the average life used to determine the group rate would depend upon the shape of the expected retirement curve for the poles.

One important characteristic of composite and group depreciation plans is that *no loss or gain is recognized* when a given member of the collection is retired. The reason is that the depreciation rate employed rests on the assumption that some of the assets will be retired sooner than average and some later than average—all to come out even in the long run.

Typical Depreciation Entries

Some of the most common entries involving depreciation accounts are shown in the following illustrations:

(1)

```
Depreciation                                        xxx
    Allowance for Depreciation                              xxx
To record periodic depreciation by any method.
```

(2)

Allowance for Depreciation	900	
Cash	200	
Retirement Loss	400	
Machinery		1,500

To record sale of machinery in secondhand market for
$200 when book value is $1,500 — $900, or $600,
for a loss of $400.

(3)

Allowance for Depreciation	900	
Cash	800	
Machinery		1,500
Retirement Gain		200

To record sale of machinery in secondhand market for
$800 when book value is $600, for a gain of $200.

(4)

Allowance for Depreciation	1,300	
Cash	200	
Machinery		1,500

To record sale of machinery in secondhand market for
$200 with no gain or loss recognized, since the ma-
chinery is being depreciated by composite plan.

(5)

Allowance for Depreciation	700	
Cash	800	
Machinery		1,500

To record sale of machinery in secondhand market for
$800 with no gain or loss recognized, since the ma-
chinery is being depreciated by composite plan.

A Caveat

In spite of the arguments, pro and con, for using one method of depreciation for book purposes rather than another, many businesses
generally, and most small business in particular, elect to use the same
method for book purposes that they use on their tax return. This approach not only is simpler and less costly, eliminating the need to
keep two sets of records for depreciation, it also avoids the major differences giving rise to an income tax allocation problem, as we discuss
in Chapter 19.

Depreciation Fallacies

Some companies persist in using the term *reserve for depreciation* in their financial statements; many are now using *accumulated depreciation*. The former title is fast disappearing because of its misleading nature. When it is used, it leads many people to assume that the company always has reserved an amount of cash equal to the amount shown as the reserve for depreciation. That is totally foolish, but it is too common to be ignored. Should there be any misgivings in your own mind, just assume that in your balance sheet you show an allowance, or reserve, for depreciation in the amount of $100,000 and that you actually do have exactly $100,000 in the cash accounts—so they do match. What, now, is the entry to record the purchase of $100,000 worth of merchandise for cash? Obviously, it's a debit to Merchandise and a credit to Cash in Bank—with the allowance for depreciation completely undisturbed even though your cash has gone down to zero.

One of the more hideous fallacies related to depreciation is that depreciation in some way is capable of generating cash, or funds. Probably most nonaccountants (who give the matter any thought) have this misunderstanding. Cash flows in from the sale of merchandise and the collections from customers, whether you show $1 of depreciation or $100,000. The amount of depreciation recorded has absolutely no effect on the amount of cash inflow. True, depreciation is deductible for tax purposes with the result that fewer tax dollars are paid out as more depreciation is deducted, but this is not what the mistaken people have in mind. If depreciation produces funds, one should find at least a few dimes lying under his car at the end of each day at the office! Certainly, if a firm has an oversupply of cash, and poor management, it may hoard an amount of cash each year equal to the recorded depreciation, but the depreciation does not create the cash in any way.

A third fallacy, which actually stems from the one just mentioned, is that depreciation does, or must, provide for the *replacement of an asset*. That is simply impossible. Depreciation is nothing more or less than the spreading, or allocation, of the *cost* of an asset over the asset's useful life. If you want to "provide" for the replacement of an asset, you must set aside in a sinking fund, or in a portfolio of investments, cash that you collect from your customers. But that has nothing to do with depreciation. To illustrate the point, if you record depreciation of a given asset as $10,000 per year and at the same time want to dedicate some cash to the future replacement of that asset, you must make two separate and unrelated entries each year as follows:

(1)

Depreciation	10,000	
Allowance for Depreciation		10,000
To record depreciation.		

(2)

Asset Replacement Fund (bank account)	10,000	
Cash in Bank		10,000

TEST PROBLEM

At the beginning of a year Our Company buys a machine for $10,000 cash. The estimated useful life is 5 years, and probable salvage is $1,500. At the beginning of the fourth year, the machine is sold for $3,000.

Required

In simple journal form record the depreciation for each of the 3 years and record the sale. Use the straight-line procedure. Repeat, but use the sum-of-years' digits method.

TEST PROBLEM Solution Space

	Debit	*Credit*

Straight-line procedure:

Year 1

Year 2

Year 3

Year 4

Sum-of-years' digits procedure:

Year 1

Year 2

Year 3

Year 4

10
Corporation Accounts

What Is Unique about Corporation Accounting?

The unique aspects of corporation accounting rest entirely upon one characteristic—the manner in which the enterprise raises its capital. Neither the sole proprietorship nor the partnership issues capital stock, but the corporation does. Neither the sole proprietorship nor the partnership employs a surplus (retained earnings) account, but the corporation does. The unincorporated enterprises do not issue bonds, as the corporation does if necessary. The financial statements of a partnership or proprietorship are usually not made available to the general public, whereas a corporation which is listed on one of the stock exchanges, or which otherwise has the requisite characteristics, must publish its financial statements regularly and may be required to submit to annual audit by independent public accountants.

In spite of the fact that the corporate form of organization has certain drawbacks, such as being subject to income taxation, lawsuits, etc., it dominates the American financial scene, which includes several million corporations ranging from corner grocery stores to large farms, to giant conglomerates, to even larger nonconglomerates such as General Motors, Standard Oil, and American Telephone and Telegraph. The principal reasons for popularity of the corporate form include the facts that the owner's liability is limited to the amount of the individual's investment, ownership interests are readily transferable, and the value of one's investment (in the case of "listed" securities) is readily determinable on a day-by-day basis.

In recent years the managers of corporations have surely taken full advantage of the powers to issue securities of all shapes and sizes. Indeed, the tendency to invent special classes of securities has created some tough problems for the accountants and the financial analysts. In this chapter we'll look at the major types, but by no means can we exhaust the arsenal.

The Issue of Capital Stock with Par Value

Much of the power of the corporation rests on the provisions of the charter and bylaws. The charter may provide for the issuance of shares of stock that do, or do not, have a par value. As a matter of fact, par value means very little aside from the fact that it sets a minimum issuing price for the shares. State corporation laws, almost without exception, stipulate that shares with a par value may not be issued at a discount; that is, they may not be issued for consideration that has a value less than the par value of the stock. Many companies establish what amounts to a nominal par value for their stock, which may be issued for many times the par value. In other cases the par value of the capital stock may start out at, say, $10 or $100 and then, as the result of several stock "splits," be repeatedly reduced. It may even become an almost inconsequential part of the overall stockholders' equity of the company.

When capital stock is issued at a price higher than its par value, the excess over par is typically recorded and reported as Capital Stock—Premium, or as Capital Paid In in Excess of Par, or simply as Capital Surplus. Use of the last title, because it contains the word "surplus," has been strongly discouraged. For example, the Committee on Terminology of the American Institute of Certified Public Accountants, in its discussion of the undesirability of "surplus" as an accounting term, simply said, "The use of the term *capital surplus* (or, as it is sometimes called, *paid-in surplus*) gives rise to confusion." The committee went on to point out the obvious fact that the word "surplus" (like surplus fat) implies too much of something—something that the corporation plans, or should plan, to eliminate as soon as possible.

For an example of low-par stock as well as use of the term "capital surplus," a well-known company in its consolidated balance sheet showed common stock with par value of $.50, totaling $1,212,000, and on the next line showed capital surplus of $234,150,000—more than 200 times the amount of the capital stock par. In these days when so much emphasis is being placed on the market value and trading volume, it is doubtful that many new corporate stock issues will carry the once-familiar $100 par value designation.

Common stock is known as the *residual equity* of the corporation.

This means that in the event that the corporation is dissolved, either voluntarily or involuntarily, the common stockholders get "what's left" (if anything) after the claims of all creditors and preferred stockholders (in that order) have been met as fully as possible. Preferred stock ranks senior to common stock with respect to dividend payments as well as in dissolution, and the dividends on certain forms of preferred stock may "accumulate" from year to year if they remain unpaid.

Entries to record the issue of common and preferred stock are the same. Assume, for example, that 100 shares of $10 par common stock are issued for $12 each, in cash. The entries are:

Cash in Bank	12,000	
Capital Stock—Par		10,000
Capital Paid In in Excess of Par		2,000

The Issue of Capital Stock with No Par Value

No-par stock was invented in the hope of eliminating the confusion and opportunities for fraud that par-value stock appeared to create. It was thought that avoiding the expression "par value" would cause shareholders to view their shares as nothing more than evidence of fractional interests in the total common stock ownership of the corporation. Soon, however, it became common practice to establish a "stated value per share" for no-par shares and, as in the case of par-value stocks, amounts received in excess of the stated value were credited to Capital Surplus or to Paid-In Surplus. The practice is commonplace today, although the word "surplus" has nearly disappeared.

When no-par stock is issued for cash, the most logical entry is to debit Cash for the amount received and to credit Capital Stock—No Par *for the same amount.* If, however, there is an established stated value per share, it is almost unavoidable that only the stated-value portion of the proceeds of issue will be credited to the Capital Stock account and the excess will be credited to Capital Paid In in Excess of Stated Value or a similar account.

The Issue of Capital Stock for Property

When capital stock is issued for cash, there is no question as to the dollar amounts involved, even though there may be some choice as to the accounts to be credited. However, when stock is issued in exchange for land, buildings, machinery, securities, or other forms of property, uncertainties can arise. One thing ought to be certain: When we issue stock for cash, we record the transaction for the amount of dollars that actually change hands, and few people would have the courage to argue that any different figure should be used. When, therefore, we issue stock for something other than cash, we should surely record the transaction, as accurately as we can, *at the cash value* of the thing received. Unfortunately, there is a school of thought that believes the absence of cash in the case of a stock issue gives license to pick a valuation of the thing received that may not bear even a remote relationship to its current value. We'll take a closer look at this phenomenon in Chapter 18 when we deal with mergers and acquisitions.

For the time being, let's be purists and at least attempt to record the noncash assets received in exchange for stock at their current cash values. If, for example, we issue 10,000 shares of common stock with a par value of $.50 per share for a tract of land worth $25,000, our entry should be:

Land	25,000	
Capital Stock Common—Par		5,000
Capital Paid In in Excess of Par		20,000

Or if we issue 100,000 shares of no-par stock to the stockholders of another corporation in exchange for all the stock of that corporation that they hold, and if their stock has as aggregate market value of $2,500,000, our entry should be (ignoring pooling-of-interests rules):

Investment in Common Stock of X Co	2,500,000	
Capital Stock—No Par (and no stated value)		2,500,000

Sometimes the current market value of the property received may not be readily ascertainable, whereas the current market value of the stock that we issue in exchange is known. Then there should be no objection to using the latter value in recording the acquisition of property.

Treasury Stock—What, Why, and How?

Sometime ago the *Wall Street Journal* devoted one of its splendid feature articles to the subject of "buying yourself," with the headline, "More Companies Find Their Shares Are Rewarding Investment." The first sentence of the article reads: "Keebler Co., a Chicago-based cookie and cracker maker, has found what it considers a hot invest-ment for some extra cash it has on hand. The investment is called Keebler Co."

To "buy itself," a corporation merely places an order for some of its own outstanding shares in the stock market, much as any of us might purchase shares through our broker. When the corporation does ac-quire its own shares, they may be canceled and retired or they may be held in an inactive state in the corporate treasury (wherever that may be). Shares held in the treasury are aptly termed *treasury shares* or *treasury stock.*

Treasury shares have no voting rights and dividends cannot be paid on them, since such an act would constitute the farce of taking money out of your pocket, putting it right back in the same pocket, and claim-ing you had both paid a dividend and received some dividend revenue. Before Securities and Exchange Commission rules put an end to the charade, some companies were actually siphoning book dollars out of their "surplus" accounts to symbolize a dividend and were reflecting the very same dollars as "dividend income" in their income statements! In the absence of the prohibition, a company with $1,000,000 in its Retained Earnings account could show net earnings of nearly $1,000,-000 per year and not do a tap of work. It would merely declare a dividend, mostly payable to itself, recorded as follows:

(1)

Retained Earnings	1,000,000	
Dividends Payable		1,000,000
To record declaration of dividend.		

(2)

Dividends Payable	1,000,000	
Cash		100,000
Dividend Revenue		900,000
To record "payment" of dividend 10% of which is paid on stock held by outsiders and 90% on stock held in our treasury.		

In describing what treasury stock *is,* we should also understand what it *is not.* The investments that your company makes and holds in the form of securities issued by other companies are, without a doubt, *assets* (either current or noncurrent); the "investments" your company makes in its own stock, contrary to the implications of the headline quoted earlier, are not investments—shares of treasury stock are *not* an asset.

Certain companies doggedly persist in displaying their treasury stock on the asset side of their balance sheets. But that is ridiculous (even when it appears that the shares are held primarily for distribution under executive bonus plans). How can a company own all its assets and also own, and treat as an asset, *shares of stock that represent those same assets?* Beginning students of accounting often protest that the shares of treasury stock may be readily salable and thus be a ready source of cash. The answer, of course, is that the *possibility* of obtaining cash is not in itself an asset; if it were, we should then also list as an asset any capital stock which is authorized by our charter but which we have not yet issued (unissued stock), and we should list the notes payable that we have paid off, because we could, perhaps, reissue them for cash on a moment's notice.

Why corporations acquire treasury stock has not always been clear, but the leading reason cited in the WSJ article makes good sense. The article goes on to point out that business hadn't been so good lately; as a result, both the market price and the earnings per share of the company's outstanding common stock had dropped sharply while, in the meantime, the company's cash balances had risen in response to declines in inventories and receivables. If business is bad and you have a pile of idle cash, why not pull in your horns by retiring some of your outstanding stock at bargain prices? Of course, one important hoped-for effect will be a resulting rise in the amount of earnings per share of the stock that remains outstanding. Such rise in earnings per share, coupled with the impact of your purchases of the stock, may cause either a slackening of the decline or an upturn in the price of your stock in the market.

It is argued that it's fine to have some treasury stock around not only for management bonuses but for possible use in accomplishing a merger with another company. An important amount of stock may be involved in a merger transaction, and in such a case use of treasury stock, rather than unissued stock, limits the total number of shares outstanding and tends to avoid the dilution of the amount of earnings per share of stock.

It goes without saying that some companies acquire treasury stock at bargain prices when they are confident that the market price at which the stock can be reissued is going to rise. The gain in cash resulting from successful accomplishment of that aim is not classed as taxable income.

The accounting entries to record the acquisition and reissue of treasury shares are simple. The most widely used procedure consists in recording the acquired stock at cost. To illustrate, assume that our company buys 1,000 shares of its own $10 par common stock in the market for $25 per share. The entry is:

(1)

Treasury Stock—Cost	25,000	
Cash in Bank		25,000

To record purchase of 1,000 shares of our own stock at $25 per share, to be held in treasury as treasury stock.

To illustrate reissue of these shares, let's make three different assumptions, as follows: The shares are *(a)* reissued for cash at their purchase price of $25 per share, *(b)* reissued at $35, and *(c)* reissued at $15. The respective entries are:

(2a)

Cash in Bank	25,000	
Treasury Stock—Cost		25,000

(2b)

Cash in Bank	35,000	
Treasury Stock—Cost		25,000
Capital Arising from Treasury Stock Transactions		10,000

(2c)

Cash in Bank	15,000	
Retained Earnings	10,000	
Treasury Stock—Cost		25,000

Note that no operating gain is recognized when treasury shares are reissued above cost; however, when they are reissued at less than cost, it is apparent that a loss of some sort has been incurred. If at the time of reissue at a loss there is a balance in the account shown in (2b) as Capital Arising from Treasury Stock Transactions, that account should be used rather than Retained Earnings. Lacking such a balance, Retained Earnings would appear to be the inevitable recipient of the reissue loss.

On the balance sheet, any treasury stock should be displayed as a subtraction (negative item) in the owner's equity section. There is general agreement that the subtraction should be made from the total of the capital stock and retained earnings as follows:

```
Stockholders' equity (section of balance sheet):
  Capital stock (with details shown)          $1,000,000
  Retained earnings                              375,000
                                              $1,375,000
  Treasury shares (1,000 at cost, $25)            25,000   $1,350,000
```

Stock Splits—What, Why, and How?

Stock-splitting surgery is usually performed when the management believes that the stock would be more popular and have wider owner-ship if the market price were brought to a lower level. To make the change, the company may put in the hands of each existing stockholder two shares for each share now held, or five shares for each four, or some other ratio which increases the number of shares held, *without any additional investment* by the stockholders and *without any reduction of the retained earnings* of the corporation. Thus, if the current market price per share of the outstanding stock is $100, a two-for-one split should cause the market price to decline approximately to $50. The stockholder now owns twice as many shares but realizes no income and is not liable for any income tax directly as the result of the split.

A stock split has much in common with a stock dividend (which will be examined in the next chapter), since each is likely to have the same effect on the market price and neither is taxable. The only real differ-ence is that in the case of a stock dividend a certain amount of retained earnings disappears from the balance sheet and becomes embedded in the Capital Stock account.

To demonstrate the entry made for a stock split, assume that our company has 100,000 shares of $5 par common stock outstanding. Be-cause the stock is selling for $120 per share, the company decides upon a four-for-one split. Entries to reflect the action are made as follows:

```
Capital Stock Common—par $5                    500,000
  Capital Stock Common—par $1.25                          500,000
To record issue of 400,000 shares of $1.25 par com-
  mon in exchange for 100,000 shares of $5 par com-
  mon in the form of a stock split.
```

Stock Rights

The terms *rights, options,* and *warrants* tend to be used without dis-tinction by persons speaking about securities. Although there may be no established legal basis for precise distinctions, for our purposes it seems best to attempt them and to take the terms up one at a time.

In many jurisdictions, when a corporation undertakes to offer additional shares of a class of stock that is already outstanding, the existing holders of shares of that class must be given the opportunity to "preempt" the issue on a pro rata basis. That is, the existing holders have automatic, preemptive rights to buy the same fractions of the supplementary issue as they hold of the outstanding shares. Some states apparently require that preemptive rights go with any issue of stock; other states do not have such a requirement; and still others provide for waiver of the rights by a vote of the stockholders or by other appropriate action.

To illustrate, if a corporation has outstanding 100,000 shares of $10 par common with a current market value of $45 per share and it wishes to issue an additional 50,000 shares, it might offer the new shares to the holders of preemptive rights at a bargain price of any amount under $45, say, $39 per share. The offer would make the preemptive right attached to each old share worth $2, and the corporation would make provision for the rights to be separately traded on the market.

Because preemptive rights are embodied in the stock issue from its inception, the corporation makes no entry on its books when certificates evidencing ownership of rights are issued to present holders. After a month or so, the rights expire and the issue price of any leftover stock may be reset. In the meantime shares issued at $39 plus two rights are recorded exactly as are straight cash issues. Assume that all the 50,000 shares are issued; then the entry is:

Cash	1,950,000	
Capital Stock Common—Par $10		500,000
Capital Paid In in Excess of Par		1,450,000

Stock Options

An option also is a form of right, but commonly an option is acquired by some specific act or payment. Stockbrokers sell options which are known as *puts, calls,* and *straddles,* which respectively mean rights to sell, to buy, or to do either within a given period of time. They have no effect on the corporation's financial accounts, since they involve only deals among outsiders. On the other hand, during years with sky-high rates of personal income taxation and significantly lower tax rates on capital gains, corporations have made extensive use of stock option offers to present and potential executives of the corporation. In order to qualify for favorable tax treatment, a number of technical restrictions must be observed, but basically an executive stock option plan grants the executive the right (option) to purchase a specified number of shares of the company's common stock, at a set price, after specified intervals of continuous employment with the company. The expectation, of course, is that the market price of the stock will rise to a level which will make the purchase at the set price something of a bonanza for the officer. As history has shown, the bonanza is by no means guaranteed, and many option recipients have attached themselves to a company with exciting option grants only to see the stock tumble to so small a fraction of the initial value that the options become worthless. On the other hand, many corporate executives have realized spectacular gains through option programs—gains which far exceeded their basic salaries.

There is virtually no accounting for options of the type we are considering except to record receipt of cash and the issue of stock when an officer exercises his options. One might well theorize that the options are granted in lieu of a certain amount of cash salary (for the tax advantages), but most accountants have concluded that there is usually insufficient basis for determining a value for the options that are granted and that, accordingly, no entry is to be made on the corporate books until the shares of stock are actually sold to the executive.

With the recent significant reduction in the highest marginal tax rate for individuals and the virtual elimination of the difference between that rate and the capital gains rate, executive stock option plans have lost much of their appeal. Given Congress's penchant for altering the tax code, however, the rules could go back the other way, once again making stock option plans popular as a tax preference item.

Stock Warrants

Warrants commonly are detachable rights that are originally attached to bonds or to preferred stock when issued. The warrants are exercised (or detached and sold) by detaching and turning them, along with a specified amount of cash, in for shares of common stock. In other words, when a share of preferred stock, or a bond, is issued with a warrant attached, the investor is actually buying two things—the preferred stock or bond *and* a warrant which entitles him, at specified dates in the future, to buy a share of common stock at a fixed price or a schedule of prices varying with time in the future.

Because the warrants are separable, accountants have ruled that, when the preferred stock or bond is issued, recognition must be given to the amount of the purchase price allocable to the attached warrant.

Assume, thus, that our corporation issues 10,000 shares of $50 par preferred stock at $56 per share and that to each share is attached a warrant to buy one share of common at some future date at a specified price. Assume further that the market assigns a value of $3.50 to a warrant. In such case the entry for issue of the preferred stock and warrants is:

Cash in Bank	560,000	
Capital Paid In—Common Stock Warrants		35,000
Capital Stock Preferred—$50 Par		500,000
Capital Stock Preferred—Premium		25,000

In the future, as each warrant is exercised, a debit of $3.50 is made to the warrant account, a debit is made to Cash for the contractual price, and a credit is made to the common stock accounts for the total.

In this day of exotic types of securities, we find some companies issuing warrants that are not attached to anything. Such a warrant is simply a right to purchase (an option) a share of stock, sometime in the future, at a price which, we hope, will turn out to be a bargain. Warrants bear no interest, and no dividend is paid on them. If a corporation can issue them in exchange for income-producing assets, it would seem that the deal may be quite favorable from the corporation's point of view, unless the exercise price turns out to lead to excessive dilution of the value of the shares held by existing stockholders.

Convertible Preferred Stock

Somewhat akin to the various kinds of rights is the conversion privilege that attaches to convertible preferred stock. The essence can readily be explained by an example. Our corporation may issue shares of $100 par preferred stock with the understanding that for each $20 of par the investor can convert his preferred stock into one share of common stock which now is selling for $16 per share. At first glance that doesn't look like much of a bargain; but if the conversion privilege extends over a period of many months or years, the chances may be excellent that the common will rise in value above $20 and make conversion profitable for the investor. Quite commonly this preferred stock is also *callable,* which means that the corporation can demand that it be turned in for cash (usually at a significant premium over par) or be converted into common stock under existing market conditions.

Although, clearly, the conversion right that is embodied in the convertible preferred stock makes the preferred stock relatively more attractive, accountants have agreed that no attempt need be made to account for it separately, as is done with the detachable warrants described in the preceding section. In other words, when the convertible preferred stock is issued, the entries are the same as if no conversion privilege were present.

Common Stock Equivalents

In the preceding four sections we have been surveying not common stock itself, but some kinds of securities that have certain of the qualities of common stock as well as the potential for being exchanged for common stock. Stock rights, stock options, stock warrants, and convertible securities all benefit when the common stock for which they may be exchanged goes up in value; that is, these securities, or instruments, have the capacity to share in the speculative gyrations of the stock market. Rights, options, and warrants can be exchanged for common stock upon the payment of the required amounts of cash; convertibles can be exchanged for stock with no further cash payment. Each of these, then, represents a potential addition to the number of shares of common stock that a corporation already has outstanding. For purposes of determining EPS (earnings per share), these potential additions to the number of common shares outstanding may have to be treated as if they were the actual equivalent of shares of common stock.

Earnings per Share

Opinion No. 15 of the Accounting Principles Board, issued in May of 1969, has to do with setting equitable rules for computing, and reporting to investors, the amount which a corporation has earned per share (of common stock and equivalents) during the reporting period. This has been a difficult problem to solve. Little trouble exists in the case of the corporation with an elementary capital structure, that is, one with nothing but common stock and perhaps some old-fashioned bonds and preferred stock. But if the company also has one or more of the so-called *common stock equivalents* in its bag, those equivalents may have to be translated into their *equivalent number of common shares* and added to the pure common total, which is then to be divided into the earnings available to common, with the resulting amount labeled *earnings per share*.

Even the elementary structure may call for some second-grade arithmetic. The earnings for the year should be divided by the weighted average number of shares outstanding during the year rather than by the simple number outstanding at the end of the year. If there has been a stock split or a stock dividend during the year, the average number of shares outstanding last year must be adjusted as if the shares had been split if a comparison is to be made between this year's EPS and last year's.

When the structure becomes more complex, we must be on the lookout for the potentially "dilutive" effects of stock options, rights, etc. Opinion No. 15 is nearly 30 pages long and makes tough reading. We cannot possibly present its content here faithfully; however, one paragraph from the summary opinion may serve to indicate the objective. Paragraph 15 is as follows:

> Corporations with capital structure other than those described in the preceding paragraph should present two types of earnings per share data (dual presentation) with equal prominence on the face of the income statement. The first presentation is based on the outstanding common shares and those securities that are in substance equivalent to common shares and have a dilutive effect. The second is a pro-forma presentation which reflects the dilution of earnings per share that would have occurred if *all* contingent issuances of common stock that would individually reduce earnings per share had taken place at the beginning of the period (or time of issuance of the convertible security, etc., if later). For convenience in this Opinion, these two presentations are referred to as "primary earnings per share" and "fully diluted earnings per share," respectively, and would in certain circumstances discussed elsewhere in this Opinion be supplemented by other disclosures and other earnings per share data.

Organization Costs

Organization costs, commonly called *organization expense* by accountants, include the general costs of launching a business concern. This category consists of fees paid for legal services (such as the drafting of the corporate charter and bylaws), fees paid for accounting services, costs of issuing securities, printing costs, etc.

Possibly because organization services are in the main invisible and do not clearly attach to any tangible asset, businessmen and their accountants seem to be anxious to get such costs written off as soon as possible. Actually, the cost of launching an enterprise may well deserve to be maintained as a significant asset for so long as the organization exists.

Tax rules allow the amortization of some of the organization cost items over a period of 60 months or more, but this permission does not apply to the costs of issuing securities, costs of transfer of assets to the corporation, or costs of reorganization.

No one can seriously object to the accumulation of all the productive costs incurred to get an enterprise started in an account labeled Organization Costs. This account could then be properly listed permanently in the balance sheet of the corporation, although most corporations amortize this cost over the same period they use for tax purposes. It may be shown as an intangible, or it may be shown separately at the bottom of the noncurrent asset section.

TEST PROBLEM

The balance sheet of our corporation, at the end of a year, contains the following stock equity section:

Stockholders' equity:			
Capital stock, 5 percent, $100 par			
preferred			$ 1,000,000
Capital stock common, no par, stated			
value $2, authorized 2,000,000			
shares, issued 750,000 shares		$ 1,500,000	
Capital paid in in excess of stated			
value		8,500,000	
		$10,000,000	
Retained earnings		6,800,000	16,800,000
			$17,800,000

During the next year the following transactions occur:
(1) 250,000 shares of the unissued common stock are issued for cash at $45 per share.
(2) A two-for-one common stock split is performed. This is accomplished by reducing the stated value to $1 per share and by distributing 1,000,000 unissued shares to the present shareholders.
(3) A charter amendment is accomplished; it authorizes an additional 1,000,000 shares of no-par common (no entry required).
(4) We acquire 100,000 shares of common stock for cash at $30 per share, to be held as treasury stock.
(5) We sell 50,000 shares of treasury stock for cash at $35 per share.
(6) We call in the preferred stock, in accordance with the written provisions of the issue, at a cash call price of $110.
(7) We issue 10,000 shares of $100 par, 12 percent preferred stock.

To each share is attached a warrant to purchase one share of no-par common for $42. The warrants will expire in 5 years. The market value of a warrant is estimated to be $4. The shares, with warrants attached, are issued for cash at $105.

(8) Earnings retained during the year total $300,000 (no entry called for).

Required

Prepare journal entries to record the numbered transactions and, in the form provided, present the stockholders' equity section as it stands at the end of the year.

TEST PROBLEM Solution Space

	Debit	*Credit*
(1)		
(2)		
(3)		
(4)		
(5)		
(6)		
(7)		
(8)		

Stockholders' equity:
  Capital stock preferred—6 percent, $100 par $
  Capital paid in in excess of par
  Capital stock common, no par, stated value $1,
    authorized 3,000,000 shares issued 2,000,000
    shares $
  Capital paid in in excess of stated value
  Capital stock common—warrants
  Retained earnings
                                   $

  Less: Capital stock common in treasury at cost
    (50,000 shares)
                                   $

11
Dividends and Reserves

What Is a True Dividend?

If we were to prepare a catalog of business transactions and financial terms that are thoroughly misunderstood by laymen, "dividend" would appear high on the list.

Whereas a sole proprietorship and a partnership are made up of the individuals who contribute the capital, i.e., the owners, that is emphatically not so in the case of a corporation. The corporation has legally constituted existence as an entity in its own right, quite separate from its owner-investors. The earnings of the sole proprietorship and of the partnership are legally earnings of the proprietors (sole proprietor or the partners), but the earnings of a corporation are legally earnings *of the corporation;* they do not become earnings of the investor-owners *until a true dividend is rendered.* A true dividend is rendered only when something is detached from the corporation and presented to the stockholders, and this transaction does not qualify as a true dividend to the extent of any reduction in the stockholders' paid-in capital accounts.

In short, a true dividend (in double-entry style) has two facets: (1) The *stockholders are given something* (usually cash, but it can be in the form of other valuable assets such as merchandise or even a "promise to pay" cash sometime in the future) and (2) the *Retained Earnings* account is correspondingly *reduced.*

Thanks to the accounting method of depicting transactions, the accounting entries to record the declaration and payment of the classical cash dividend are as follows:

December 15

Retained Earnings or		
Dividend Charges	100,000	
Dividends Payable		100,000

On December 15 the directors of our corporation meet
and declare the regular quarterly cash dividend of
$.25 per share on the 400,000 shares of $10 par
common then outstanding; the dividend is payable on
January 15 next, to those who are listed holders of
shares (holders of record) on January 5.

January 15

Dividends Payable	100,000	
Cash in Bank		100,000

To record payment of cash dividend declared on December 15.

Note the two effects of the dividend in this example. First, an asset,
cash in bank, is reduced (and transferred to the stockholders); second,
retained earnings is reduced by the same amount. Also, take particular note of the fact that the directors, at the moment on December
15 that they declare the $100,000 dividend, create a current liabil-
ity.

In some cases a corporation may own shares of stock in another
corporation and, for a variety of reasons, the directors will elect to
distribute those shares, instead of cash, to the company's stockholders.
The entries are the same except that, instead of Cash in Bank being
credited on January 15, the credit is made to Investments or to Marketable Securities. This is a *true* property dividend.

On rare occasions, when it is short of cash but wishes to make a
dividend distribution which the stockholders will be able to convert
into cash, a corporation will mail promissory notes (scrip) to the stockholders for an amount of cash that is to be paid sometime later. Such
a distribution qualifies as a true dividend, since the corporation establishes a legal liability to pay the stockholders. Entries for such a declaration and ultimate payment are:

December 15

Retained Earnings	100,000	
Dividends Payable		100,000

To record declaration of dividend for which we will
issue, on January 15, in the form of promises to pay,
the cash sum of $.25 per share.

January 15

Dividends Payable	100,000	
Dividend Scrip Payable		100,000

To record distribution of interest-bearing (or noninterest-bearing) scrip (notes payable) to stockholders (scrip to bear interest at 12% and to become due in 30 days).

February 14

Dividend Scrip Payable	100,000	
Interest Expense	1,000	
Cash in Bank		101,000

Cash payment of maturing scrip plus 12% interest for 30 days.

Corporate Investment in Affiliated Company

Although in the preceding section the corporation was characterized as a distinctly separate entity and, as a corollary, it was pointed out that earnings of a corporation are not concurrently or automatically earnings of the owners, the principle is routinely violated in modern accounting practice in one situation. That is when one corporation holds a majority interest (more than 50 percent) of the common stock of another corporation and the resources of the two affiliated corporations are not reported in combined form in a "consolidated" balance sheet. We'll look at the techniques of preparing consolidated statements later, but for the present let's assume that our dominant, or "parent" corporation elects *not* to prepare fully consolidated statements. When such a choice is acceptable, the parent will merely publish its "legal" balance sheet and will show, *as a noncurrent asset,* its investment in the affiliate (known as a *subsidiary*).

To report the investment at its cost, however, is held to be inappropriate under the circumstances mentioned. Rather, it is preferred practice to accrue, as an increase (or decrease) in the investment account, the parent company's share of the earnings of the subsidiary, even though the subsidiary has not paid them in the form of dividends. When the earnings are then received from the subsidiary in the form of true dividends, the investment account is literally converted into cash to the extent of the dividend received. Assume, for example, that our corporation does the following: (1) It buys 70 percent of the outstanding common stock of Subsidiary Corp. for $95,000; (2) at the end of the year Subsidiary reports earnings of $20,000 since the date of our company's investment; (3) lastly, next year Subsidiary pays a cash dividend of $15,000 and our corporation recognizes receipt of its 70 percent share. The entries on our corporation's books under the method that we have been considering are:

(1)

Investment in Subsidiary Corp.	95,000	
Cash in Bank		95,000
Purchase of a 70% interest in the common stock of Subsidiary Corp. for cash.		

(2)

Investment in Subsidiary Corp.	14,000	
Earnings of Subsidiary Corp. (a revenue account)		14,000
To accrue as income our 70% share of the $20,000 of earnings recorded by Subsidiary Corp. this year since the date of our acquisition of Subsidiary Corp. common stock.		

(3)

Cash in Bank	10,500	
Investment in Subsidiary Corp.		10,500
To record receipt of cash dividend from Subsidiary Corp. and to treat this as conversion of part of our investment into cash since our share of Subsidiary Corp. earnings has already been accrued in entry (2).		

The reasoning in support of this violation of the entity convention is that (1) Subsidiary Corp. is in a field of activity so foreign to that which we are in that to consolidate the statements of the two companies might produce misleading results and (2) at the same time, the earnings strength of the affiliated companies may not be adequately disclosed unless the parent company's share of Subsidiary Corp. earnings is accrued on a current basis. This so-called equity procedure has become a generally accepted rule of accounting, even when ownership is less than 50 percent if the "investor" is able to exercise significant influence over affairs of the "investee."

Liquidating "Dividends"

The term *dividend* is commonly applied to two classes of transactions to which it is not fully applicable. The first is the return of capital to the owners; the second, considered in the next section, is the stock dividend.

If we are to make good use of terms in accounting, we should be able to rely on the meaning intended by the user. Certainly most people who give it any thought at all think that someone who receives a dividend earns some revenue or income—a return *on* investment. Clearly, though, there is no income when the corporation is undergoing partial or total dissolution and the stockholder is merely having his investment returned to him—a return *of* investment.

Entries on the books of the corporation when a liquidating dividend is paid fall in the following pattern:

(1)

Capital Paid In in Excess of Par	25,000	
Capital Stock—Par	75,000	
Cash in Bank		100,000

To record return of capital to stockholders, first by a reduction of "Excess of Par" to zero, then by a debit to Capital Stock—Par for the balance of the payout.

Payments in liquidation, improperly termed *liquidating dividends*, occur when the affairs of a corporation are being wound up and also in extractive industries that make an investment in a single venture with no intention of continuing actively when that venture (e.g., a mine of limited extent) is terminated.

Pseudo (Stock) Dividends

To illustrate what are known, misleadingly, as stock "dividends," let's start with an assumed stock equity section for our corporation as follows:

Capital stock, par $10, authorized 100,000 shares, issued 60,000	$600,000
Capital paid in in excess of par	120,000
Retained earnings	1,000,000
	$1,720,000

Now assume that our directors vote to "distribute" (what a poor word choice!) a 50 percent stock dividend. First, understand clearly that 50 percent means that we shall issue new shares in quantity equal to 50 percent of the number of shares now outstanding. (Many people think the 50 percent means we'll use up 50 percent of the retained earnings.) Second, with an issue in excess of 20 to 25 percent, the *amount* can be any amount that the directors choose to record so long as it is no less than the par value (in this case $10 per share). If the issue is less than 20 to 25 percent, as we'll note next, we encounter certain restrictions.

If we now assume that the directors vote to *capitalize,* for each new share issued, $10 representing par plus $2 per share to match the present "excess" account, or a total of $12 per share, the entry is:

```
Retained Earnings                                360,000
    Capital Stock—Par                                       300,000
    Capital Paid In in Excess of Par                         60,000
To record issuance of a 50% stock dividend, or 30,000
    shares, capitalized at $12 per share to match the $10
    par plus average $2 of excess over par from earlier
    issues.
```

If you analyze the above entry, you will recognize clearly that a stock dividend is in no sense of the word a true dividend. The corporation gives up absolutely nothing; the stockholders, individually and as a group, receive absolutely nothing but an additional piece of paper to represent exactly the same fractional ownership that they each held before the event. There are, however, two effects of stock dividends that may in some cases be quite significant. First, some retained earnings is wiped out as such and is established in a frozen state in the legal capital accounts. Since this eliminates the retained earnings (in our case $360,000) as a possible future basis for dividend appropriation, perhaps some of the stockholders may be worse off as the result of the so-called dividend. Second, the market value of the stock should drop, since we now have 90,000 rather than 60,000 shares representing exactly the same net assets. This second effect could improve the marketability of the stock because the price per share should drop about one-third.

In recent years it has become quite popular for certain "growth" companies to issue stock dividends of less than 10 percent; in fact, some companies started the practice of declaring "regular" stock dividends, even on a quarterly basis, of 2 percent or some similar amount. Undoubtedly the stockholders have believed that they are actually getting *paid* dividends of 2 percent per quarter while the corporation, at the same time, is enabled to retain its cash resources for expansion! These companies typically pay no cash dividend until they have attained their desired size (if ever). In some other companies, minor stock dividends are issued in order to accomplish a minor increase in cash dividend payout without having to change the traditional cash dividend per share. Thus, instead of increasing the cash dividend from $1 to $1.02 per share, the company presents each holder with two new shares of stock for each 100 held and continues to pay $1 per share.

It appears that the use of minor stock dividends may have been subject to abuse in view of the average stockholder's total ignorance of its significance. The trouble is that the market price of stock upon distribution of a 2 percent stock dividend should go down proportionately, but investor psychology (or ignorance) is such that the price is just about as likely to remain unchanged or even to rise. So in order to put a damper on the excessive use of such "distributions" (and, believe it or not, brokers, financial writers, and other experts even use the word "payout" for a stock dividend), the New York Stock Exchange, among others, has established the requirement (for the companies subject to their influence) that, when a stock dividend is under 20 to 25 percent, the corporation must capitalize an amount equal to the current market value per share. That, of course, can make a great difference in the amount of retained earnings that is frozen by the stock dividend action. Consider, for example, a corporation with a common stock par of $1.50 per share and a current market value of $75 per share.

A final word on stock dividends. Truly a stock dividend (particularly if it ranges above 25 percent in size) amounts to nothing more than a stock split with one added feature—the capitalization of retained earnings.

What Do Accountants Mean by "Reserves"?

One dictionary lists seven meanings for "reserve" used as a noun; of these, the one that addresses itself to financial matters says a reserve is "money or its equivalent kept in hand or set apart usually to meet liabilities." The first of the seven definitions leans in a similar direction, stating that a reserve is "something stored for future use." That is not what accountants have in mind.

For many decades accountants have made liberal use of "reserve," and for a comparable period of time the uninitiated reader has been totally confused. The upshot of all this is that now accountants have all but eliminated the confusing word from their vocabulary. In the next three sections we'll become acquainted with three different ways in which "reserve" formerly was used and will see what obedient accountants are now using in its place.

Contra Accounts Used to Be Called Reserves

As the annual reports from the companies whose stock you hold come rolling in, examine the balance sheets to see if any show a reserve for depreciation or a reserve for uncollectibles. A reserve for depreciation is an expression, a measure, of the amount by which depreciation has been recognized in the accounts with respect to the related assets. In other words, a reserve for depreciation is a *subtraction* from depreciable assets; it's a representation of services that have been removed from the asset's original bundle. Far from being anything that has been set aside, a reserve for depreciation is, figuratively, a hole in an asset.

Numerous times in this book we have mentioned contra accounts—accounts that are used as negatives or as offsets to other accounts. That is precisely what every reserve for depreciation is—a contra account. So also is the reserve for uncollectibles or bad debts.

It's not exactly easy to find a satisfactory substitute for "reserve" when a contra account is involved, but perhaps "allowance" is the best of the present candidates. Some companies show depreciable assets on the position statement followed by a subtraction simply labeled Accumulated Depreciation. That is not too bad, though some readers are bound to infer that the company has actually accumulated something. Can you "accumulate" a hole in the ground? In any case, it is perfectly acceptable to use Allowance for Depreciation and Allowance for Bad Debts to disclose the amounts that have been set up as offsets to depreciable assets or to accounts receivable.

Some Liabilities Used to Be Called Reserves

One still occasionally sees such titles as Reserve for Federal Income Taxes and Reserve for Product Warranties in present-day position statements. Why? What do they mean?

In these cases the word "reserve" is probably used solely because the dollar amount involved is an estimate, an approximation. The accounts are, clearly, liabilities. The first signifies that we owe "some" income taxes, but the final definite amount due for this year has not yet been established. Also, we undoubtedly have some outstanding customer claims under our warranty agreements, but the sum of those claims is, at best, an educated guess. Does the fact that the amount of a liability is uncertain justify dodging a true liability title? Obviously not. Let's be candid. Correctly, the two titles should be changed to Estimated Liability for Federal Income Taxes and Estimated Liability under Warranty Agreements.

Another situation in which the confusing terminology has been used is in the case of accrued pension obligations. Here we have a tangled skein of accounting preferences and theories and a variety of uncertain actuarial calculations sufficient to render the result quite speculative, but there is no justification for dodging the estimated liability label through use of the term *reserve.*

In short, when you're tempted, because of the uncertainties of the situation, to call a liability a reserve, don't.

Retained Earnings May Be Reserved

Before becoming simon-pure, many of us choose to use the word "reserve" to designate reservations of retained earnings. It's a bit hard to determine just what is accomplished by such reservations, but in order to attain the ultimate in shunning a misleading term, let's even restrict it here.

A couple of examples of retained earnings reservations may be worth mentioning. First, the corporation laws of many of our states specify that, if a corporation holds any treasury stock, the retained earnings of that corporation, in an amount equal to the cost of the treasury stock, must be reserved; that is, this amount of retained earnings stands unavailable for dividend charges so long as the treasury stock remains on hand. Some companies make no entries in the Retained Earnings account and merely state, parenthetically in their balance sheets, that so many dollars of retained earnings are restricted because of treasury stock holdings; other companies make explicit entries, somewhat as follows:

```
Retained Earnings                                          xxx
   Retained Earnings Reserved for Treasury Stock                  xxx
To record reservation of retained earnings in amount
   equal to the cost of stock now held in treasury.
```

Note that such an entry reserves retained earnings, but it still avoids the outright use of a reserve; there is no Reserve for Treasury Stock.

In summary, with respect to reserves in general, we may conclude that the title Reserve is a dead one. Don't use it at all under any conditions. If you have an account which nobody can explain, don't resort to the old dodge of calling it a reserve; get rid of it some way and stick to accounts that are clearly understood.

Deferred Credits when in Doubt

Accountants need a convenient receptacle or two into which they can deposit (dump or hide?) certain debits and credits which they don't clearly understand. One of the modern favorite dumping sites is under the caption, Deferred Credits. But let's back up a minute.

When you were introduced to the statement of financial condition, the balance sheet, you were quite willing to accept the proposition that the formal financial structure of any business enterprise consists of two coequal quantums—the aggregate of assets expressed as a dollar total and the aggregate of equities expressed as a dollar total, with the latter in turn made up of amounts due to creditors and the residual, or amount assigned to the owners. To cut through the verbiage, let's just say that one side of the financial coin consists of all the assets of the enterprise and the opposite side shows the allocation of the very same total as between amounts owed to outsiders and the amount left over, known as the *owner's equity.* "Assets" equal "equities."

Then what in the devil are deferred credits? They always appear on the equities side of the balance sheet, but do they then represent claims *other than those* of outsiders and insiders? Perhaps there's life on Mars after all!

Here are some typical deferred credits. The *Friday Monthly Post* collects subscriptions, running from 1 to 3 years in advance, totaling $100,000. Its accountant makes the following entry:

(1)

Cash in Bank	100,000	
Deferred Subscription Income		100,000
To record collections from subscriptions during month of June.		

How do you like that entry?

Well, the debit title is OK and we must assume the dollar amounts are correct (though most of us are suspicious of "round" numbers), but the accountant stumbles badly in coining the credit title. Now, in exchange for the $100,000 cash received, the company is obligated to deliver 12 monthly copies per year to each subscriber. As each monthly batch of magazines is sent out, the company "earns" one-twelfth of the amount it has collected on each annual subscription. So, as deliveries are made, the accountant will make the following entry:

(2)

Deferred Subscription Income	xxx	
Subscription Revenue		xxx
To recognize revenue earned by delivery of magazines against subscriptions collected in advance.		

Quite obviously the $100,000 collected and recorded in entry 1 is not yet revenue, but *it becomes revenue* as deliveries are made. Thus, the accountant reasons, the $100,000 initially is "deferred" revenue (surely not "income"). But then the accountant flunks the course by failing to recognize that, when trusting people have put a wad of money in your hands in the expectation of receiving future services, you have a simple, old-fashioned *liability*.

Most so-called *deferred credits* will turn out to be liabilities if properly analyzed. Think, for example, of advance collections of insurance premiums, club dues, telephone service charges, and a host of similar transactions.

Remember that the equity side of the balance sheet reflects where the assets came from, who made them available. Equities are the sources of the resources (assets) of the firm.

A few deferred credits, on the other hand, are actually asset contras. One large factoring company, in buying notes receivable from automobile dealers, recorded the purchase transaction essentially as follows. (The inserted percentage figures merely signify amounts.)

Notes Receivable—Face	100%
Cash in Bank	92%
Deferred Discount Revenue	8%

In this situation the finance company will collect 100 percent (plus interest) from the customer at maturity; and since the company paid only 92 percent face for the notes taken over, the balancing 8 percent becomes a gain, or revenue, from the factoring operation. But is there no better place than a Deferred Credits section of the balance sheet in which to report the unearned discount? Of course there is. The company paid 92 percent for this batch of notes because at the time the notes have a value of 92 percent of face. The proper conclusion, then, is to show the discount of 8 percent as a contra (subtraction) from the notes receivable on the balance sheet.

TEST PROBLEM

At its meeting on March 15, the directors of Our Company declare a 10 percent stock dividend which is distributed on April 15. Also at the meeting the directors ask the accountant to establish two retained earnings reserves of $100,000 each: a reserve for possible fire losses and a reserve for general contingencies. At the date of the directors' meeting, the stockholders' equity section of the position statement stands as shown below. At the time of the stock distribution, the current market value is $25 per share.

Stockholders' equity:
Capital stock common, par $5	$1,000,000
Capital in excess of par	500,000
Retained earnings	750,000
	$2,250,000

Required

Give journal entries to record the reservations of retained earnings and the issuance of the dividend shares.

TEST PROBLEM Solution Space

	Debit	*Credit*
March 15		
April 15		

12
Long-Term Debt

Why Go in Debt?

As individuals, most of us shun debt. We worry about the size of the national debt and fret over the charge accounts our spouses propagate. But, actually, if one really makes a science of it, isn't it possible for debt to be a thoroughly useful, profitable instrument of financial management?

One can readily think of at least four solid reasons for going into debt.

First, it is unbelievable that an enterprise of any size would pay cash on the spot for everything it buys; in fact, it would be virtually impossible to avoid getting in debt on a day-to-day basis with the employees of the company. Debt, particularly the short-term variety, is a great *convenience.*

Wages are paid at weekly intervals; vendors' invoices are accumulated and paid monthly; etc. But that is true primarily of interest-free short-term debt. Why does a company incur long-term debt?

Very often long-term debt is incurred to provide the company with more working capital. So often we find that when the business is growing—just as everything seems to be going well—we're short of cash. What has happened is that we've increased our sales and, at the same time, we've gone into the lending business ourselves by allowing our customers to open charge accounts. Also, with the growth of business we must carry more inventories (which earn no interest!). If we're running a family-owned corporation, we refuse to raise money by selling stock to outsiders, so we must either get long-term bank loans or issue bonds. In other words, long-term debt becomes a *necessity.* Even if our company is not closely held, we may not wish to increase the amount of common stock outstanding because market conditions are unfavorable.

Perhaps the most popular reason for long-term debt financing is covered by the word "leverage." This is the more modern term for what used to be called *trading on the equity,* and all it means is that you borrow somebody's money at an interest rate which is lower than the rate which you can earn on that money. If, for example, you can borrow a million dollars for a year at 12 percent and can employ the million dollars so that it produces a return of 14 percent, you should be a net gainer (before taxes) of 2 percent. That is the strategy used by many corporations to enhance the earnings rate on the common stock equity. Thus, if our company has assets of $2,000,000 which earn 14 percent and if half of our funds have come from a 12 percent bond issue, the earnings of our stockholders will amount to 14 percent on the $1,000,000 that they invested plus 2 percent leverage gain on the bond money, for a total of 16 percent.

One should not overdo a good thing, however. If, for instance, the financial structure of the company were made up of 10 percent equity ($200,000 of capital stock) and 90 percent debt ($1,800,000 of 12 percent bonds), the return on common stock would skyrocket to 14 percent of $200,000 (or $28,000) plus 2 percent of $1,800,000 (or $36,000) for a total of $64,000 divided by $200,000, or 32 percent. This would be known as a "thin" equity position. The net income before interest charges would be 14 percent of $2,000,000, or $280,000, which covers the $216,000 interest requirement, but the pretax $64,000 margin of coverage is not sufficient to assure the bondholders of being paid during hard times. In other words, the thinner the equity the more risky the situation, and the determination of how far to go with leverage requires exercise of managerial intelligence.

The final reason for the popularity of long-term debt is that interest charges are legitimate tax deductions. Thus, with a corporate tax rate of approximately 50 percent, the net cost of the interest payments is only half of the gross cost. That is, for every $1 of interest paid out, $.50 of income tax is saved (provided, of course, that we are operating at a profit). This fact alone accounts for a great deal of the long-term debt. Some banks, for example, issue bonds (debentures) on which they must pay 12 percent interest and invest the funds in tax-exempt municipal bonds on which they earn only 7 percent. Since the 12 percent interest has a net cost of about half that much and the 7 percent is nontaxable, the bank earns a net of approximately 1 percent on the borrowed funds.

Long-term debt takes many different forms, although the principles are basically the same. Since this is a book on accounting rather than corporation finance, let's take a look at some of the debt forms and examine them by the method of *accounting analysis*, i.e., by reducing them to journal entry form.

Installment Purchases

It seems quite unlikely that there is anybody old enough to read this material who hasn't at some time participated in an installment purchase. Because of the risk of running afoul of legal technicalities, let's not attempt to define our terms too precisely. Typically, when you buy something under an installment contract, you make periodic (monthly) payments of equal amount that apply first to accumulated interest and then to the principal of your debt, and you don't obtain legal title to the thing until you've made your final payment, unless there's some understanding to the contrary.

We can't afford much space on any of these forms of debt, so let's go directly to an example and journalize enough of it to be sure it is fully understood.

Our company buys a machine at a price of $12,000 under an installment contract which calls for a down payment of $2,000 and quarterly payments of $500 including interest at 15 percent per annum. The machine is delivered and the contract signed on September 1. The entries through the first three payments are as follows:

September 1, 19X1

Machinery	12,000	
Cash in Bank		2,000
Installment Contract Payable		10,000
(Explanation of terms)		

December 1, 19X1

Interest Expense	375	
Installment Contract Payable	125	
Cash in Bank		500

Payment of first quarterly installment of $500, of which $375 pays the interest up to date on $10,000 for 3 months, leaving $125 applicable to the debt itself.

December 31, 19X1

Interest Expense	123	
Interest Accrued Payable		123

To accrue unpaid interest, for purposes of end-of-year financial statements, at 15% on balance of debt

($9,875) for one month ($123.44 rounded to nearest dollar).

March 1, 19X2

Interest Accrued Payable	123	
Interest Expense	247	
Installment Contract Payable	130	
Cash in Bank		500

Payment of interest accrued on December 31, and interest for January and February, and balance of $130 on debt.

June 1, 19X2

Interest Expense	365	
Installment Contract Payable	135	
Cash in Bank		500

Payment of interest for 3 months on contract balance of $9,745 and payment of $135 on debt.

There's no point in continuing the journal entries through final payment. Needless to say, the debt would finally be paid off through the installments that include a bit less interest expense each quarter as the principal of the debt diminishes. The final payment would undoubtedly be some odd figure necessary to pay a very small amount of interest and the balance of the debt. Incidentally, you will occasionally hear someone say that when you are paying off a debt in installments, you are "amortizing" it.

Leases and Sale-and-Leaseback Transactions

We all know that to lease something is the equivalent of renting something—except that a lease implies the signing of a contract to pay the agreed-upon periodic rental for a minimum number of periods, usually a year or more. From the accounting standpoint the recording of the performance of such contracts would be easy were it not that the lawyers and others have figured out ways to complicate matters. In the absence of complications, our periodic entry is merely to debit Rent Expense and credit Cash in Bank for the contractual amount.

Actually, there are only two complications of importance. First, if the lease is noncancelable, it has some of the earmarks of a long-term debt; in fact, if we add certain other features, it becomes almost impossible to determine whether you are dealing with a lease or the transaction is in actuality an installment purchase.

Some accountants (a minority) argue that any noncancelable lease, because it is a promise to pay a periodic series of fixed amounts, is nothing less than a debt from the start. They want you to show the sum of the payments to be made in the future as a long-term liability and to show the same amount on the other side of the balance sheet as an asset. Note one important qualification: We aren't merely to use the sum of the future payments; rather, we find the *discounted, present value* of those payments and show it on both sides of the balance sheet. These accountants argue that you have a fixed obligation and a valuable right of occupancy that can be disclosed effectively only if they are entered in the balance sheet. At the risk of oversimplification, let's attack this position by asserting that, although you may have an obligation to pay the series of rents, you have no true liability for any one of them until you have received the service (the occupancy for one month, etc.). You are dealing with an "executory" contract, which essentially means you have agreed to buy a series of services one at a time; and in spite of your inflexible agreement, you don't actually owe for any one of the services until it is delivered to you. Conclusion: Treat the lease exactly as you would a common rental, but be sure to *disclose* any significant terms of the lease in a footnote to your statements.

Now, there are certain features that may be written into a lease which can make us believe the lease is actually an installment *purchase.* For instance, if the agreement includes an option to buy the item at much less than its fair value at the end of the lease, doesn't that imply pretty clearly that you will effectively purchase the asset during the initial term of the lease? Or if the agreement includes an option to extend or renew the lease after it first runs out and if the extended period covers the remaining useful life of the asset at a rental that is substantially less than the fair rental value, doesn't that also imply that you actually are *paying for the asset* during the initial term on the lease? The guiding rule nowadays is that we must interpret an agreement as an installment purchase, rather than as a lease, if either of those conditions is present.

An interesting complication appears when a company, by prior agreement, (1) buys or constructs a building or other asset, (2) sells the asset to another company (a subsidiary?), and (3) immediately leases the asset back. This is a *sale and leaseback.* The point of the whole thing is that whether the sale was made at a profit or at a loss, it is generally assumed that such gain or loss is part of the sale-and-leaseback plan and is really just a fiction because the parties to the contract are not likely to have an arm's-length relationship. This brings us to the conclusion that the gain or loss should not be recognized as such in the year of the sale but should be prorated over the life of the lease. Thus, if a lease calls for rental payments of $12,000 per year for 20 years and if the lessee (occupant) built the asset for $100,000 and sold it to the lessor for $120,000, then the $20,000 of gain would be recognized at the rate of $1,000 per year, which, in effect, produces a *net rental* cost of $11,000 per year. In journal form the entries to depict this deal are:

(1)

Building	100,000	
Cash, etc		100,000
To record cost of constructing (or buying) a building.		

(2)

Cash	120,000	
Building		100,000
Deferred Gain on Sale of Building		20,000
To record sale of building to subsidiary.		

(3)

Rent Expense	12,000	
Cash		12,000
Rent payment for first year.		

(4)

Deferred Gain on Sale of Building	1,000	
Rent Expense		1,000
Portion of gain recognized in first year.		

For a final subtopic on leases, note that some companies practice what has come to be known as *off-balance-sheet financing.* The major (parent) company establishes a satellite corporation (a subsidiary) and owns all its stock in exchange for cash or other assets. The subsidiary issues bonds or other debt and constructs or buys an asset which, by prearrangement, it will lease to the parent corporation. The subsidiary pledges the lease proceeds as security for the bonds or other form of debt so that, in a sense, the parent company is really the guarantor of the subsidiary's debt. By following this procedure, the parent has use of the asset but the debt incurred to buy the asset does not show on the parent's position statement—*unless the parent prepares a consolidated position statement.* The fact is that the preparation of a consolidated statement is called for under these circumstances. (We'll look at the subject of consolidations in Chapter 16, but for the present we will merely assume that a consolidated statement is essentially one that combines the statements of two or more affiliated companies.)

Long-Term Notes

Possibly the most common form of long-term (more than one year) debt consists of borrowing from banks, insurance companies, pension funds, and other institutional sources on the basis of a promissory note with a specified maturity date. A well-known variation of this is the so-called *line of credit* with a bank, whereby the borrower is extended the right to draw funds at will, up to an agreed-upon maximum, and to repay them at will. Under the line-of-credit plan the borrower will be charged a modest rate of interest on the unused portion of the available funds.

One cost-producing feature of borrowing from banks is the common requirement that if a company borrows, say, $100,000 at a stipulated interest rate, no more than $80,000 will actually be withdrawn; in other words, a "compensating balance" equal to a stated fraction of the loan must be left unused even though interest is paid on it. A typical fraction is 20 percent.

Accounting for long-term borrowing via promissory note presents no special problems. The interest costs of the loan should, of course, be recognized on an accrual basis.

Mortgage Loans

A mortgage loan, commonly referred to as a *mortgage payable,* consists simply of a long-term note which is backed by a legal instrument known as a mortgage on real or personal property. When the security is personal property, the mortgage is called a *chattel mortgage.* Essentially, the mortgage itself is a document that lists the provisions of the loan and what will happen in the event of default. If the borrower does fail to comply with the mortgage provisions, title to the property is transferred to the lender. However, the defaulting party may be entitled to recover the property (the so-called *equity in redemption* provision) if the repayment is made within a year. (See your lawyer for further information on this subject.) Mortgage notes are customarily paid off in regular monthly installments including interest.

Mortgage and Debenture Bonds

A bond is, again, a form of note payable with a definite maturity date except when callable "by lot." A *debenture bond* provides no collateral security; that is, the general credit of the company constitutes the security. A mortgage bond is backed by a mortgage on some or all of the real estate of the company.

Bonds commonly are issued in $1,000 denominations and are quoted in the bond market at prices which fluctuate with changes in the financial condition of the company and with changes in the bond market. The bond market responds continuously to fluctuations in market rates of interest. For example, if we issue a series of 14 percent, 20-year bonds at par (that is, in a 14 percent market) and later the prime interest rate (a mythical interest rate which big New York banks charge their "prime" customers for loans) rises to 16 percent, then our 14 percent bonds will be attractive only if they can be bought at a discount. To explain further, a 14 percent bond is a $1,000 bond which pays $70 of cash interest each 6 months, for a total of $140, or 14 percent, per year. Because the amount of cash interest cannot conveniently be varied from year to year as the market rate of interest fluctuates, the value of the bond itself fluctuates, with the result that a buyer will pay for the bond an amount above par (premium) or below par (discount) which will result in his earning whatever rate is necessary, provided he holds the bond until it matures.

Let's issue some bonds at par, some at a premium, and some at a discount. For an example, assume that our company issues $100,000 in 14 percent, 20-year, first-mortgage bonds (1) at par, (2) at a premium which will produce a true yield rate of 12 percent, and (3) at a discount which will produce a true yield rate of 16 percent. For each alternative the entries on our books through the first two years are as shown below. Assume in each case that we issue the bonds on January 1 and that interest is paid through the use of coupons.

(1) Issue at Par

January 1, 19X1

Cash	100,000	
Bonds Payable		100,000
To record issue at par.		

July 1, 19X1

Bond Interest Expense	7,000	
Cash		7,000
To record payment of first interest coupons. (14% for 6 months)		

December 31, 19X1

Bond Interest Expense	7,000	
Bond Interest Payable		7,000

To accrue interest from date of latest payment to
end of year.

January 1, 19X2

Bond Interest Payable	7,000	
Cash in Bank		7,000
Payment of second interest coupons.		

July 1, 19X2

Bond Interest Expense	7,000	
Cash in Bank		7,000
Payment of third interest coupons.		

December 31, 19X2

Bond Interest Expense	7,000	
Bond Interest Payable		7,000
Accrual of interest for fourth 6-month period.		

At maturity, we merely debit Bonds Payable and credit Cash in Bank
for repayment of the $100,000 borrowed initially.

(2) Issue at a Premium

January 1, 19X1

Cash	115,046	
Bonds Payable		100,000
Bonds Payable—Premium		15,046
To record issue of 14 percent, 20-year bonds at a price (premium) which will provide a true earning rate of 12 percent to holder to maturity.		

July 1, 19X1

Bond Interest Expense	7,000	
Cash in Bank		7,000
Payment of first interest coupons		
Bonds Payable—Premium	376	
Bond Interest Expense		376
To amortize one-fortieth of the initial bond premium as a reduction, or offset, to our interest expense, since we will repay only par to the lender at maturity.		

December 31, 19X1

Bond Interest Expense	7,000	
Bond Interest Payable		7,000
Accrual of interest to year-end.		

| Bonds Payable—Premium | 376 | |
| Bond Interest Expense | | 376 |

Same as entry on July 1.

January 1, 19X2

| Bond Interest Payable | 7,000 | |
| Cash in Bank | | 7,000 |

Payment of second coupons.

July 1, 19X2

| Bond Interest Expense | 7,000 | |
| Cash in Bank | | 7,000 |

Payment of coupon 3.

| Bonds Payable—Premium | 376 | |
| Bond Interest Expense | | 376 |

Amortization of one-fortieth of initial premium.

December 31, 19X2

Bonds Payable—Premium	376	
Bond Interest Expense	6,624	
Bond Interest Payable		7,000

Same as December 31, 19X1, with entries combined.

The logic of the entries for the bond issued at a premium should be clear to you. Because the bonds pay an excessively high *cash* interest, the lenders are willing to pay us a premium of $15,046 which they will never get back, and the result is that they effectively earn only 12 percent rather than the "nominal" 14 percent. We, in turn, spread the $15,046 evenly over the life of the bond as a sort of gain but, more accurately, as an offset to our cash interest cost.

(3) Issue at a Discount

January 1, 19X1

Cash	88,075	
Bonds Payable—Discount	11,925	
Bonds Payable		100,000

To record issue of 14 percent bonds at discount of $11,925, which will provide lender with a true earning rate of 16 percent if held to maturity when the full $100,000 is repaid.

July 1, 19X1

| Bond Interest Expense | 7,000 | |
| Cash in Bank | | 7,000 |

Payment of coupon 1.

Bond Interest Expense	298	
Bonds Payable—Discount		298

To accumulate one-fortieth of the original discount as an addition to interest expense, because at maturity lender must be paid amount borrowed ($88,075) plus the discount ($11,925) for a total of $100,000.

December 31, 19X1

Bond Interest Expense	7,000	
Bond Interest Accrued Payable		7,000

To accrue coupon 2.

Bond Interest Expense	298	
Bonds Payable—Discount		298

To accumulate one-fortieth of the discount to be paid at maturity.

January 1, 19X2

Bond Interest Accrued Payable	7,000	
Cash in Bank		7,000

Payment of coupon 2.

July 31, 19X2

Bond Interest Expense	7,000	
Cash in Bank		7,000

Payment of coupon 3.

Bond Interest Expense	298	
Bonds Payable—Discount		298

To accumulate one-fortieth of the discount.

December 31, 19X2

Bond Interest Expense	7,298	
Bond Interest Accrued Payable		7,000
Bonds Payable—Discount		298

To accrue coupon 4 and accumulate one-fortieth of the discount. (This again illustrates use of a combined journal entry.)

At the end of the second year, since we have recorded the bond issue and interest expense under three different assumptions, the bonds would be displayed in the balance sheet as follows:

(1) Par:		(2) Premium:		(3) Discount:	
Bonds payable— par	$100,000	Bonds payable— par	$100,000	Bonds payable— par	$100,000

Bonds payable— premium	13,542	Bonds payable— discount	10,733
	$113,542		$ 89,267

A couple of more comments should be made concerning bonds issued at odd prices. First, bond discount is a contra account. It measures the difference between the maturity value (par) and the present book value (initially, the amount borrowed) of the bonds. Some old-time accountants still believe bond discount is prepaid interest, a logical impossibility, and they insist on showing it as an asset. Second, bond premium is an "adjunct" to bonds payable—to show the effective amount of debt at any given time, it must be added to the face amount of the bonds. Some old-fashioned accountants classify bond premium as a *deferred credit*—a monstrosity.

Finally, we could use the true interest rate (also known as the *yield rate* or the *effective rate*) in recording the interest expense each period and our results would be more accurate. Instead, we have used the simpler straight-line procedure.

Convertible Bonds

When the market rate of interest for debenture bonds issued by a company with our credit standing is around 15 percent and our common stock is being traded in the market at around 35, we elect to issue 20-year *convertible* bonds with a 12 percent coupon and the proviso that the buyers can trade the bonds in for common stock at the exchange ratio of one share of common for each $40 of bond principal. The bonds can be "called" by us, after 5 years, at 105 per 100. (Bonds are always quoted at so much per 100 of par.)

Needless to say, people will not pay us par for 12 percent bonds if the market says we must pay 15 percent, but they might pay us par for 12 percent bonds if the bonds also carry the privilege of being converted into our common stock whenever the bondholders want to. In other words, we can get by with a significantly lower interest payment until the price of our stock rises to the point at which the bondholder would gain by exercising the option to convert. All this assumes, of course, that the market has real hope of a surge in the market value of our common stock.

From the investor point of view, a convertible bond has a certain attraction. The investors stand able to "get a piece of the action" if the value of our stock rises above 40; on the other hand, should the value of our stock tumble, they will not lose heavily because the market value of their bonds will fall only to the point at which the effective yield is approximately 15 percent. The convertible bond thus has an unlimited ceiling in value and, at the same time, a floor which limits the size of the possible loss.

Entries to record the issue of convertible bonds are made exactly like those to issue regular bonds. If and when some or all of the bonds are converted into common stock, the form of the entry is as follows:

Bonds Payable—Par	1,000	
Capital Stock—Common—Par $10		250
Capital Paid In in Excess of Par		750
To record conversion of bond into 25 shares of common stock on the basis of 1 share for each $40 of bond.		

It has been estimated that about one-third of the bond issues in recent years have been convertibles.

Bonds with Warrants Attached

In some cases a company may issue bonds which carry warrants that can be detached and turned in for common stock at a specified price. To illustrate, assume that we issue a series of 12 percent bonds, each with a warrant to buy one share of our stock at $40, and that our stock is currently trading at around $35. It has been widely argued that we are really issuing two securities rather than one; we're issuing a bond plus a warrant. If we issue the package at par, since part of the proceeds is attributable to the warrant, the bond itself is actually being issued at a discount. The question then is: How do we allocate the proceeds as between the two securities? Common sense suggests that we should attribute to the bond an amount which would give the bond a true yield commensurate with our credit standing, say, 15 percent, and attribute the remainder to the warrant. To illustrate, assume that the bond provisions are as just described and that the common stock is trading at $35. The entry to record this bond-and-warrant issue for $1,000 will then be:

Cash	1,000	
Bonds Payable—Discount	189	
Bonds Payable—Par		1,000
Common Stock Warrant Outstanding		189
To record 20-year 12% bond issued at discount to pro-		

vide 15% yield and to attribute remainder of $1,000 to the warrant. A 12% bond priced to yield 15% in 20 years is $811, or at a discount of $189, which we attribute to the warrant. (Were the package issued at more or less than $1,000, the procedure would be the same: assign a fair value to the bond and the balance to the warrant.)

In the balance sheet the common stock warrants should be shown in the stockholders' equity section.

TEST PROBLEM

Our Company issues $100,000 in $1,000 par, 20-year, 13 percent debenture bonds with warrants attached that provide for purchase of one share of our $10 par common stock at $5 per share. Each bond carries 10 warrants. Interest is paid semiannually. Without warrants, our bonds would have to carry 15 percent interest coupons to be salable at par, so the bond portion of the package is determined to amount to $87,406. The bonds and warrants are sold to a bank for $97,000.

Required

Journal entries (1) to issue the package, (2) to pay interest at the end of the first 6 months, and (3) to record exercise of all the warrants.

TEST PROBLEM Solution Space

	Debit	*Credit*

(1)

To record issue of 100 par $1,000 bonds, each with 10
warrants to buy one share of $10 par common stock for
$5.

(2)

To record payment of coupon 1.

(3)

To record issue of 1,000 shares of common stock at $5
cash plus one warrant per share.

13
Basic Cost Accounting

What Is Cost Accounting?

Actually, cost accounting is not a separate area of accounting; but because it employs a few technical words and procedures of its own, we often think of cost accountants as somewhat separate from the so-called *financial accountants.*

The cost accountants specialize in finding the "cost of" products that we make, or the "cost of" operating a department within the manufacturing area of the company. In more recent years the talents of the cost accountants have been applied more and more to finding the costs of nonmanufacturing departments as well. For example, cost accountants now do a lot more cost accounting in banks and insurance companies, where there is no product output in the physical sense, and they also work in the areas of selling and administrative expenses as well as in the manufacturing area.

What Are the Purposes of Cost Accounting?

There are three well-recognized purposes of cost accounting. The first, which is routine, is to help in the process of *determining the income* of any given accounting period. That consists primarily of determining the manufacturing costs and the amounts assignable to end-of-period inventories so that we can compute the cost of goods sold. When the company makes a variety of products, the determination of the manufacturing costs of each kind of product and the cost of goods sold for each class of product is no simple task.

A second and tremendously important responsibility of cost accounting (and, again a routine one) is to assist in *cost minimization*. By this, of course, we mean minimizing cost while still accomplishing the production and sales objectives of the company each period. The cost accounting devices that are specifically aimed at cost minimization are such things as standard costs, flexible budgets, and responsibility accounting. We'll look into them later.

The third major contribution of cost accounting is to assist management in *making decisions* when costs are a factor (aren't they always?). Most of these are ad hoc decisions—decisions which call for special studies and intelligent selection of cost factors relevant to the decision.

In the present chapter we'll concentrate mostly on the first purpose —the routine job of income determination. We're concerned here about assigning costs to departments, reassigning the costs of service departments to producing departments, and then applying those costs to the product output so that we can determine the cost of goods sold and its complement, the cost of goods remaining in inventory. This whole chapter will be devoted to what is usually called "historical" or "actual" cost accounting in contrast with "standard" cost accounting, which we'll investigate later.

Job-Order versus Process Cost Accounting

Although the distinction is not always clearly defined, it is customary to recognize two general kinds of "actual cost" accounting. One is known universally as *job-order* cost accounting and the other as *process* cost accounting. "Job order" means that the company makes things that are, usually, designed specially to a customer's order. A good example would be the construction of houses each of which is designed by an architect to comply with the wishes of the buyer. Here each job is a separate project and one would, of course, keep a separate cost account for each. There are many examples of job-order manufacture, although, obviously, they are not mass-production industries. On the other hand, an individual "job" may call for production of any number of identical products. The key feature of job-order cost accounting, then, is that we must keep a cost sheet for each job (a subsidiary record) and be sure to record on each cost sheet all the costs we incur that are chargeable to that job.

Process cost accounting is applied in situations in which one or more products are being manufactured on a more or less continuous schedule. Here, rather than find the cost of each unit separately, we accumulate our costs for a period of time (often for a month) and then divide the total cost for the period by the number of product units to get an average unit cost. In job-order situations the product is usually made to order and is not held in storage for future sale; in process situations we commonly manufacture finished goods that are stored for future sale.

Needless to say, many manufacturing situations represent a mixture of job-order and process activity, and hybrid accounting techniques are then applied to determine costs of manufacture, inventories, and costs of goods sold. In general, when there is room for choice, the simpler costing procedure seems to be in process cost accounting; when a choice exists, one should probably lean toward process rather than job-order cost accounting procedures.

In the sections that follow, we'll try to describe and illustrate the "actual" cost procedures in accounting for raw materials, direct labor, and, finally, manufacturing overhead under job-order and process cost conditions.

Use of Subsidiary Ledgers

In job-order cost accounting, raw materials are charged to a raw materials account in our general ledger as they are purchased. Because a manufacturing company may use a great number of raw material items, it is necessary to do some extremely detailed accounting in order to keep track of the raw materials purchased, used, and remaining in inventory at a given point in time. Suppose we consume 3,000 different raw material items, could we ever record them in a single ledger account and hope to tell later from that account how much we've bought of each? Used of each? And have left over of each? Clearly not, so we must use subsidiary ledger accounts, as we described in Chapter 3.

Let's systematically record *each* purchase of raw material on a card form (with a separate card for each kind of stuff we buy), and let's make entries on those cards the moment we receive and accept a batch of raw material. Therefore, if we stock 3,000 different kinds of raw materials, we'll have 3,000 such cards, and we'll call them our *subsidiary ledger* for raw materials (computerized, of course).

Each of the subsidiary ledger cards needs three columns: one to show debits for purchases, the second to show credits for materials issued as authorized by our requisition system, and the third to show our "running balance" of the item. Hence, at any time we should be able to go through our raw materials subsidiary ledger cards and find the complete story of each kind of material that we use. And, remember, when we need our total for financial statement purposes, we find it in our regular, general ledger control account.

Raw Materials Cost Accounting

When raw materials are purchased (have been received, examined, and found to be acceptable), the quantities and dollar amounts of each kind are immediately posted in the received (debit) columns of the raw materials subledger accounts. As each entry is made on a subledger card, the third (balance) column is also updated to show the revised quantity on hand and dollar balance. The entries are the same whether we are operating under a process or a job-order cost accounting system. The technical accounting can be depicted in the following journal entry:

```
Raw Materials—Control (end of month only)          xxx
    (also to subsidiary ledger cards in detail as
        each purchase is made)
    Accounts Payable—Control (end of month only)          xxx
        (also to subsidiary ledger accounts in detail as
            each purchase is made)
To record purchases of raw materials during a given
month.
```

An employee is allowed to draw raw materials from the storeroom upon presenting a "requisition," which has been signed by someone in authority and which identifies the job or department to be charged. As currently as feasible, the quantity of each raw material shown on each requisition is "priced" and entered in the issued (credit) column of the appropriate subsidiary ledger card. Pricing is done by looking at the appropriate subsidiary ledger card to see what the particular raw material cost per unit is. (This cost may be determined on an average-cost basis or on a FIFO basis.) Regardless of whether we are using job-order or process costing, the credit entries to withdraw raw materials from stores are the same. At the end of the month the requisitions are totaled and one aggregate credit entry is made to the general ledger control account.

The debit entries made to record consumption of raw materials do depend upon the type of cost accounting. If we are in a process cost situation, the debit is made against the department (which we may call simply the *process*) that called for the materials. Assume that we make a product which is homogeneous and which is manufactured in a continuous flow through processes known as Cooking, Decorating, and Packaging. Pro forma entries to depict a month's raw materials issuances would be as follows:

```
Cooking Process                xx
Decorating Process             xx
Packaging Process              xx
```

```
     Raw Materials—Control                              xx
     (and subledger accounts)
To record June consumption of raw materials by our
     three departments.
```

The three accounts debited in the entry shown above would also, in a sense, be control accounts, because we would surely want to maintain detailed information on the costs incurred by each process. Such detail is generally kept on what might be called *process cost sheets* which are specially designed for each company. At the least, a process cost sheet has three debit columns—one (or more) each for the costs of raw materials, labor, and manufacturing overhead costs.

Under job-order cost circumstances, raw materials are requisitioned for application to specific jobs. The monthly summary debits for materials used will go to a control account called Work in Process, which controls a very important subsidiary ledger consisting of a cost sheet for each job that we are working on. Thus a requisition for raw material gives rise to immediate credits to raw material subledger accounts and immediate debits to the cost sheets representing the various jobs; at the end of the month a summary entry is made (for total of all raw materials requisitions) crediting Raw Materials and debiting Work in Process. In journal form such an entry is as follows:

```
Work in Process—Control (end of month)              xxx
    (also to subsidiary job cost sheets in detail as materials
    are requisitioned)
        Raw Materials—Control (end of month)                xxx
        (Detail to subledger cards currently)
To record raw materials usage for month.
```

Needless to say, the great volume of repetitive entries makes accounting for raw materials inventories and usage a prime candidate for computerization.

Direct Labor Cost Accounting

Direct labor is labor cost that can (conveniently) be traced to a specific job and can readily be added to the cost of a specific job. The term is particularly appropriate in the case of job-order costing to distinguish direct labor from indirect labor which cannot be attached to a specific job but has to be prorated over all jobs that benefit from it. In the case of process accounting, in which costs are accumulated by departments rather than by jobs, any labor within a given process or department could be called direct, since the costing base in process accounting is the total output of the department for a month rather than a number of differentiated jobs. Even here, however, accountants are inclined to limit the term *direct labor* to that which actually works on the thing being made. Again, the term *productive* is common in practice to designate labor that really does something to the product versus the *nonproductive* (?) folks who do such things as boss and render ancillary services.

In any case, in this section we're concerned only with direct or productive labor. The whole trick here is to keep track of how much time each productive worker devotes to each job or task and feed the information to payroll clerks, who translate the time into money terms and then feed it on to the cost clerks, who copy the amounts onto the affected job cost sheets or process cost sheets. The secret here is time keeping via time clocks or timekeepers and code numbers for the jobs being worked on and for processing operations, all inscribed on time tickets. The fact is that so many variations in mechanics are possible that what is said here is intended only to convey the underlying aim of direct labor costing, which is to trace as much of your labor cost as feasible to the things which are produced by it so that your job cost sheets or process cost sheets will accumulate accurately, within tolerance limits, the "actual" raw materials and direct labor costs.

In journal entry form the direct labor costs, under a job-cost system, are recorded as depicted in the following journal entry.

```
Work in Process (end of month only)                    xxx
  (Also to subsidiary job cost sheets in detail currently
    from direct labor time tickets)
      Wages Payable (or Payroll)                               xxx
To record direct labor payroll for month.
```

In journal entry form the direct labor (productive labor) costs in a process manufacturing situation are:

```
Cooking Process                                        xx
Decorating Process                                     xx
Packaging Process                                      xx
      Wages Payable (or Payroll)                              xx
To record productive labor payroll for the month, all of
  which has currently also been recorded on process
  cost sheets. As with materials accounting, direct
  labor cost is an ideal target for computerization.
```

Manufacturing Overhead Cost Accounting—Process Costing

As we continue to explore actual cost accounting, we find that the handling of manufacturing overhead costs under job-order conditions differs sharply from that under process conditions. In process cost accounting you need only allocate your overhead costs to your producing departments. In job-order cost accounting you allocate your overhead costs to producing departments and *then* must *apply* them to the individual jobs that pass through the departments. Since the jobs are not homogeneous, we cannot simply apply the same amount of overhead cost to each job.

First, let's consider the simpler situation—process costing. What we seek to do, when we use "actual" costs, is find the overhead costs of operating each service department and each producing department. We might refer to this step as our primary overhead allocation. The allocation procedure is highly dependent on the exercise of judgment. Some overhead costs are quite surely and easily traceable to the various departments, fairly directly; others, however, need to be prorated—and proration very often is largely a matter of judgment. Let's make a few journal entries to illustrate the "primary" allocation of overhead costs (manufacturing costs).

(1)

Cooking	xx	
Decorating	xx	
Packaging	xx	
Power	xx	
Maintenance	xx	
Supplies		xx

To record supply costs incurred during the month by all departments, as determined by summation of requisitions for supplies.

(2)

Cooking	xx	
Decorating	xx	
Packaging	xx	
Power	xx	
Maintenance	xx	
Wages Payable		xx

To charge all departments with their indirect labor costs for the month, as determined by time and payroll records.

(3)

Cooking	xx	
Decorating	xx	
Packaging	xx	
Power	xx	
Maintenance	xx	
Machinery—Allowance for Depreciation		xx

To charge each department with one month's depreciation on machinery belonging to each department.

These first three entries illustrate manufacturing cost allocations that
are reasonably straightforward—the allocations are based on objective
measurements. The next group will depict some that are, at best, "reasonable."

(4)

Cooking	xx	
Decorating	xx	
Packaging	xx	
Power	xx	
Maintenance	xx	
Factory Building—Allowance for Depreciation		xx

To record depreciation of factory building for the month
and to allocate it to the various departments *on the
basis of the number of square feet occupied by each.*

(5)

Cooking	xx	
Decorating	xx	
Packaging	xx	
Power	xx	
Maintenance	xx	
Prepaid Insurance		xx

To record expiration of property insurance for the
month and *to allocate directly* that part which is attributable to machinery in each department and, *on the
basis of floor space,* to allocate the remainder.

As you recognize immediately, each of the two allocations reflected in
entries 4 and 5 must, of necessity, be judgmental. Let's call it *the
assessing* of each department with what we believe to be an equitable
share of the particular cost. The cost accountant has a whole bag of
tricks to be used in these primary allocations. What he always seeks is
a common denominator (floor space, value of machinery, direct labor
cost, etc.) which he can use to make the allocations with a semiclear
conscience. Let's add right here that allocations of this sort may stir up

ill will—particularly when some very cost-conscious department head does an excellent job of economizing only to be socked with heavy charges through a semiarbitrary allocation procedure. The result, understandably, is quite likely to be a loud squeal. That is why so-called *responsibility* accounting has been invented—a plan under which each department head is charged with, and held responsible for, only those manufacturing costs *which that person is able to control.* More of this later.

We've illustrated primary allocation. What should we do with the costs we've charged against Power and Maintenance? Since, obviously, we do not run those departments for their own sakes, we must now make a secondary allocation—their costs must be reallocated to the producing departments.

In our highly simplified situation, we have recognized only two service departments, and earlier we assumed that Maintenance not only serves the three producing departments but also serves Power. Thus, our first step should be to divide the maintenance total among the other four departments and then divide Power (including what it was charged from Maintenance). Did you ask what we do when some of the power is used by maintenance? A good question. When service departments serve each other reciprocally, it is known as *mutual service.* The more common solution is the allocation of them, one at a time, on a downstream basis. First allocate the service department that provides the most widely used (or, maybe, the most costly) services; then allocate the next most widely used; and so on, in each case ignoring all backwashes. Thus, if A serves B more than B serves A, allocate part of A to B but ignore the B-to-A backflow. Continue the procedure until all service department costs have been disgorged into producing department accounts.

An alternative procedure involves use of simple algebraic equations which work out very prettily but which leave you wondering, in view of the arbitrary allocation bases, if it's all worthwhile.

Manufacturing Overhead Cost Accounting—Job Order

It would complicate things beyond belief even to try to apply each manufacturing overhead cost separately to the various jobs produced under job-order conditions. Remember that we keep a separate job cost sheet for each job and that the direct raw materials and direct labor costs of each job are currently recorded on the cost sheets as the work progresses. But this can't be done with manufacturing overhead for three major reasons. First, by definition, manufacturing costs are the costs which simply cannot be traced directly to individual jobs; second, even if they could be so traced, we probably wouldn't make the effort because there are so many different items of overhead that the clerical cost would be exorbitant; and third, the overhead cost (unlike direct labor and direct materials) that happens to be incurred at the same time that specific jobs are being worked on is by no means likely to be the amount that is assignable to those jobs.

To get to the point: Under "actual" cost accounting (1) we *estimate* what the actual *total* manufacturing overhead will be for the coming year, (2) we *estimate* what our total direct labor hours, or total machine hours, will be during the coming year, (3) we then divide the estimated hours into the estimated overhead total to get an *overhead rate* per hour, and (4) as a given job progresses, we keep track of the hours spent on it and charge that job with the actual hours times the overhead rate. Thus is manufacturing overhead charged to jobs in a job-order system. Let's analyze this procedure.

The overhead rate is based upon an estimate of total manufacturing overhead and total hours (of machine use or of direct labor) *for the entire coming year,* because use of a year's average overhead per hour makes so much more sense than it would to charge a given job (or group of jobs) with the overhead costs that just happened to occur while they were being worked on. An obvious case in point would be maintenance costs. It is quite typical that important maintenance programs are scheduled for times when plant activity is at its lightest, and it would be totally inequitable to charge such cost to the few jobs that happened to be "in the works" at the time. Some factory costs do, of course, increase and decrease along with fluctuations in production activity (these we call *variable* overhead), but many occur simply with the passage of time (these tend to be the *fixed* overhead costs such as manager's and supervisor's salaries, property taxes, and depreciation). In short, the most equitable solution to finding an overhead rate appears to be to use the estimated total for the coming year divided by the estimated hours.

An important refinement of our discussion of overhead rates is the development of a separate overhead rate for each production department. Many companies use what we have just been describing—a single plant-wide rate. However, there's no doubt that improved accuracy results when a job is charged with high overhead during its stay in a high-overhead department and low overhead while it's in a low-overhead department. The development of departmental rates requires, first, estimating the overhead costs for all departments, including service departments, then allocating the estimated service department costs to the producing departments, and, finally, dividing each producing department total by its estimated labor or machine hours or whatever other application base may be used.

Now let's follow through hypothetical manufacturing overhead entries and assume use of departmental rates.

(1)

Manufacturing Overhead—Control	xx	
Service Department 1	xx	
Service Department 2	xx	
Producing Department 1	xx	
Producing Department 2	xx	
Producing Department 3	xx	
Credits to various accounts		xx

To record *actual* manufacturing overhead costs in general ledger control account and in subsidiary ledger department accounts.

(2)

Manufacturing Overhead—Control	xx	
Producing Department 1	xx	
Producing Department 2	xx	
Producing Department 3	xx	
Manufacturing Overhead—Control		xx
Service Department 1	xx	
Service Department 2	xx	

To transfer actual overhead costs from service departments to producing departments on the basis of actual services rendered.

(3)

Work in Process	xx	

(Also to subsidiary job-cost sheets in detail as jobs are finished; charges are based on hours worked on each job in each department multiplied by the overhead rate in each department.)

Manufacturing Overhead—Control		xx
Producing Department 1	xx	
Producing Department 2	xx	
Producing Department 3	xx	

To charge Work in Process and the individual jobs with overhead, at departmental hourly rates, as determined at the beginning of the year, and to credit the actual overhead accounts for the same amounts.

(4)

Income Summary	xx	
Producing Department 1	xx	
Manufacturing Overhead		xx
Producing Department 2	xx	
Producing Department 3	xx	

To transfer end-of-year leftover balances of overhead in each department to Income Summary.

Entry 4 illustrates end-of-year disposal of the overhead cost residuals in the various departments. As you have no doubt anticipated, we never assign to jobs, through use of our overhead rates that we set up at the beginning of the year, exactly the amount of overhead that is actually incurred in any given department through the year. Obviously, if, as the year progresses, we recognize we've made a significant error in setting our overhead rates, we simply change them to give us more realistic job-order costs. But because the application of overhead costs to jobs involves so much estimate and probability of errors, some companies are content to set departmental or plant-wide rates on the basis of an overhead cost study and leave them unchanged for several years.

Process Variations

In the illustrations of process accounting it was assumed that the company produces a single, homogeneous product. Surely this is only a special situation and there are many situations in which process cost techniques can be applied even though a lot of different products are turned out. Thus, in a canning plant different products are canned as the seasons change, and in a rubber-tire plant tires of various sizes and specifications are produced simultaneously. In short, wherever there are "runs" of products of standard specifications, or of varying mixes of standard operations and materials, process cost methods can be and should be applied. The techniques involve inventive modifications of the basic principles and procedures described earlier.

Internal Cost Statements

The reports which cost accountants prepare for management use are, of course, designed according to the ground rules of each situation. Two major reports tend to be widely used—the statement of costs of goods manufactured (and sold) and schedules of departmental overhead costs. In addition, there are unlimited varieties of reports on departmental labor and raw material usage. Following are pro forma examples of the two major reports:

OUR COMPANY
Cost of Goods Manufactured and Sold
Year Ended December 31, 19XX

Materials used:		
Inventory, January 1	$xxx	
Purchases	xxx	
	$xxx	
Inventory December 31	xxx	$xxx
Direct labor		xxx
Manufacturing overhead:		
(List actual items and amounts)—actual	$xxx	
Less: Amount not applied ("unapplied")	xxx	
Manufacturing overhead applied to production		xxx
Total manufacturing costs		$xxx
Add: Work in process on January 1		xxx
		$xxx
Less: Work unfinished on December 31		xxx
Cost of goods manufactured		$xxx
Add: Finished goods on hand on January 1		xxx
		$xxx
Less: Finished goods on inventory December 31		xxx
Cost of goods sold (see income statement)		$xxx

OUR COMPANY
Schedule of Departmental Overhead Costs and Variances
Year Ended December 31, 19XX

	Service 1	Service 2	Producing 1	Producing 2	Producing 3
Supplies	$xx	$xx	$ xx	$xx	$xx
Indirect labor	xx	xx	xx	xx	xx
Other expenses (detail)	xx	xx	xx	xx	xx
Totals	$xx	$xx	$ xx	$xx	$xx
Allocation of S1	xx	xx	xx	xx	xx
Totals		$xx	$ xx	$xx	$xx
Allocation of S2		xx	xx	xx	xx
Production totals			$ xx	$xx	$xx
Overhead applied to job (subtract)			xx	xx	xx
Unapplied overhead (overapplied)—Variances			$(xx)	$xx	$xx

TEST PROBLEM

Shown below are a number of spaces for making journal entries to record the flow of costs through a departmentalized job-order system. For each journal entry the explanation is given, but the accounts and amounts to be debited and credited have not been entered. On the basis of each explanation, it's up to you to fill in the debit and credit entries. Then prepare a statement of cost of goods manufactured. As usual, a solution is given in Appendix I.

	Debit	*Credit*

(1)

Record purchase of $100,000 of raw materials on account and indicate subledger record.

(2)

Record $97,000 of raw materials requisitions for materials going into work in process. Show subledger entries also.

(3)

Record $364,000 of direct labor and wages payable going to work in process. Show subledger notation for work in process. (Note for later use: $174,000 of direct labor was performed in Production 1 and $190,000 in Production 2.)

(4)

Record $643,000 of overhead to Factory Overhead—Control, charging $127,000 of this to Service 1; $94,000 to Service 2; $236,000 to Production 1; and $186,000 to Production 2. Make your credit to Various Accounts.

(5)

Transfer $127,000 from Service 1 as follows: to Service 2, $34,000; to Production 1, $63,000; to Production 2, $30,000. Make general ledger debit and credit to Factory Overhead for total.

(6)

Transfer balance in Service 2 ($128,000) to Production
1, $64,000, and Production 2, $64,000. Both debit
and credit Factory Overhead—Control for $128,000.

(7)

Charge Work in Process $614,000, and indicate posting
to subledger job cost sheets, for overhead applied in
Production 1 at the rate of 200% of direct labor in
Production 1, which was $174,000, and at the rate of
140% of direct labor in Production 2, which was
$190,000.

(8)

Cost of goods finished as shown on job cost sheets was
$960,000.

(9)

Close unapplied overhead remaining in Production 1 and
Production 2 to Income Summary.

OUR COMPANY
Statement of Cost of Goods Manufactured
Year Ended December 31, 19X1

Raw materials used		$
Direct labor		
Manufacturing overhead—actual	$	
Less: Unapplied overhead		
Total cost of manufacturing		$
Add: Work in process, January 1		100,000
		$
Less: Work in process, December 31		
Cost of goods finished		$

14
Cost
Standards

What's a Standard?

Now that we've spent an entire chapter exploring "actual" cost accounting, we're about to examine the proposition that actual cost accounting isn't as actual as it seems to be. Paradoxically, standard cost accounting is really more actual than actual cost accounting is.

Perhaps we can go directly to the point. Cost accounting focuses on finding the *cost of* an activity or a thing, such as a product. Certainly we'd like to avoid wild guesses and get as near to the *actual* cost of the activity or thing as we can (without wasting money in the effort). Now, standard cost accounting holds that when we set out to make or do something involving cost outlays, we may be less efficient than we should be; and if we're below par in efficiency, we are wasting time, money, or both. Under standard cost philosophy we assert that the *costs of* inefficiencies should be separated from the *costs of* the activity or thing we're working on. Actual cost accounting makes no real attempt to separate out those wastes, and they become incorporated indistinguishably as part of the actual cost of the product or activity. Under standard cost accounting the *actual* cost of a product can include *only the costs that are applied effectively* and all excesses are *costs of waste* rather than costs of product. Such excesses are called *variances,* and almost the whole aim of standard cost accounting is to sort out, to detect, variances (wastes) and report them to management *immediately* for remedial action. So "actual" costs are not actual costs, standard costs are actual costs!

Now, what's a standard? It is a scientific (engineered) *predetermination of what something should cost.* If you know in advance what something should cost, then that serves as the model, or standard, against which you compare your actual outlays; and your differences (materials, labor, overhead) are accounted for not as *cost of* the thing, but as variances (usually wastes). In short, under standard cost accounting, the total incurred costs are separated into two categories—the costs that are effectively incurred (the standard costs) and the costs that are wastefully incurred (the variances).

Illustration of Standards—Standard Cost per Unit

Because you're interested in concepts rather than bookkeeping complexities, we'll deal with a relatively simple situation. Assume that our company makes just one product and that all the work is done in a one-room, one-department plant. A committee of company personnel, including our cost accountant, our production manager, our engineer, our purchasing agent, and any other persons who can make a contribution, is set up to "figure" a standard cost per unit of our regular product. Here's what they finally develop:

OUR PRODUCT
Standard Cost per Unit

Raw material, 50 pounds of material A @ $1	$ 50.00
Direct labor, 10 hours @ $10	100.00
Manufacturing overhead, 10 hours @ $15	150.00
Total standard cost of one unit	$300.00

We'll refer to these figures repeatedly in the discussion that follows.

Raw Materials Standards

The standard cost specifications for our product allow us to consume 50 pounds of material A, no more and no less. The 50-pound quantity should be based on extremely careful analysis of all factors. First, the 50 pounds should be based on that *quality* of raw material that we'll buy. We might buy a cheaper material, but that would perhaps cause us to waste more and thus need to use more; use of a poorer quality of material might lead to more labor and more manufacturing overhead cost. Therefore, our engineers pick the raw material of quality that they believe will minimize our costs, and they determine how much (the standard quantities) we should use in producing one unit (or one batch) of our product.

The standard quantity of raw material to be used does not contemplate complete avoidance of scrap, but it does contemplate an allowance for scrap that aligns with other aspects of the work. You can't saw a board in two without producing some sawdust; you can't cut shoes out of a hide without some leftover, worthless clippings, and so on. But the important point is that the 50 pounds in our illustration should be "tight" enough to exclude needless (waste) scrap yet "loose" enough to allow our labor and machinery to work efficiently.

Thus, our engineers finally conclude that we should allow a standard quantity of 50 pounds of raw material per unit even though the final product may weigh only 45 pounds, since the standard must include a scrap allowance if called for under the circumstances.

In the meantime our purchasing expert has been making a thorough study of the market for our raw material (and has kept the engineer posted so his computation can incorporate purchase-price alternatives). For the quality selected, the price varies somewhat in relation to the quantity ordered. After taking into consideration the costs of storage, it is concluded that the price of $1 per unit is optimal and a *standard price* of $1 is agreed upon.

Needless to say, all prices fluctuate and a standard may soon become out of date. However, it is necessary to compromise here. We want our standard costs to be current, but to change them with every fluctuation in market price would be expensive and would actually sacrifice one major advantage of standard costs—the avoidance of varying prices for the same things as they flow through the factory. So it appears that most companies, even though they may avow that they employ *current* standards, do not adjust their standard prices more than once a year.

Raw Materials Accounting—Standard Costs

The big objective of standard cost accounting is cost minimization or cost control. Everybody realizes that the longer a leak goes untended the greater the loss. The rewards of a standard cost system are realized in proportion to the quality of the job of setting the standards and the speed with which variances from standard are reported to those in a position to stop the leaks. In many situations variances in materials and direct labor costs are reported daily. Contrast that with old-fashioned actual cost systems which claim victory if their relatively unhelpful reports reach management sooner than the second week after the end of each month.

To speed the disclosure of materials variances and, equally important, to relate the variances insofar as possible to the persons responsible for them, the favored practice is to recognize *variances in purchase prices* at the point of receipt of the materials and *variances in quantities* consumed at the point of requisitioning or as soon thereafter as possible. In other words, materials variances fall into two general types—price and quantity. Price variance on a purchase of materials is the amount paid above or below the standard price. It is recognized at the point of receipt as follows:

(1)

Raw Materials (at standard)	35,000	
Materials Price Variance	3,500	
Accounts Payable		38,500

To debit Raw Materials at the standard price of $1 per pound for purchase of 35,000 pounds of material A at $1.10 and to charge the variance of $.10 per pound to Materials Price Variance. This cleanses the price variances out of the recorded materials costs.

Note in entry 1 that material A will be inventoried at its *standard price* of $1; it will be carried through the accounts to its ultimate disposition as part of cost of goods sold at the same $1 price. If all purchases of material A throughout the year also are recorded at $1, this eliminates any need to use FIFO or average-cost schemes for pricing the requisitions; $1 is the *standard price on all requisitions.* This saves bookkeeping.

At the end of the year, whatever amount has been accumulated in the Materials Price Variance account may be closed out to our Income Summary account as an expense for the year or, if the amount is significant, a proportionate part of the variance may be added to the standard cost inventory for balance sheet purposes. Actually, materials price variances, whether on the debit or credit side, are not really losses and gains; they theoretically attach to the materials that have gone on out or have remained in the ending inventory.

The cost of raw materials used is, of course, two-dimensional—quantity times price. If we cleanse the materials for all price variances as we buy them and put them in the storeroom, the price dimension has been translated from actual to standard. This means that we need only look for quantity variances, the other dimension, as the materials are drawn from stores and pass on to work in process, finished goods, and, finally, cost of goods sold. Techniques for finding quantity variances on a "real-time" basis (i.e., as they occur) must be worked out by accountants and production men within each particular set of conditions. For our purposes of understanding the basics, let's assume that in our one-cylinder plant we requisition, at the beginning of each day, enough material A for the planned production of our product for that day. Pretend we set out to produce 1,000 units today. We might issue a requisition for 50,000 pounds of material A, which is the standard quantity for 1,000 units. But let's not let our standard cost system overpower our production system. We know, actually, that we'll produce somewhat more or, maybe, somewhat less, than 1,000 units; also, we've set our material quantity standard fairly tight, so we'll likely have a quantity variance of, say, 5 percent. Let's be on the safe side, to avoid running out of material a half hour before quitting time, and requisition an extra 10,-000 pounds. (We can always return the stuff to stores at the end of the day if necessary.)

Now we go to work and turn out as many of our product as we comfortably can, and we end up making 1,040 units during the day. We then find we have 4,000 pounds of unused material A, which we dutifully cart back to stores and get credit for (possibly an adjustment or correction on the original requisition). We're now ready to make an entry for the day's usage of raw materials, as follows:

(2)

Work in Process	52,000	
Materials Quantity Variances	4,000	
Raw Materials		56,000

To record consumption today of 56,000 pounds of material A at standard price of $1 per pound for production of 1,040 units of our product at 50 pounds per unit, or 52,000 pounds standard quantity for variance of 4,000 pounds at $1.

It is, of course, unlikely in practice that a journal entry would be made each day; but a simple three-column register could be used to keep track of the three elements of the entry, one line for each day, and at the end of the month one grand entry could be made for the totals. In the meantime, the daily output and daily variances would be reported to the appropriate persons.

Regretfully, we cannot explore the myriad of production situations under which materials quantity variations may be accounted for—this is what thick cost accounting textbooks are for. However, it should be appropriate for you to inquire about the accounting recognition of such variances in your company and learn *how the variances are analyzed* once they're disclosed. For example, in a multidepartment situation with more than one kind of material, the quantity variances may be broken down by departments (to "lay the blame"), by causes, and by kinds of material as well. Such data can be systematically produced in endless detail by computer, with resulting enhancement of managerial control.

Direct Labor Accounting—Standard Costs

Some of the same concepts that we have outlined in the section on raw materials apply equally to direct labor. Again, let's stick to basics.

Direct labor cost, like raw materials cost, is two-dimensional. We are again concerned with quantity (hours) and price (wages). The major difference is that we can't stock up on labor hours in our storeroom as we can materials, so we don't issue requisitions.

Assume continuation of our example in which, today, we produce 1,040 units with standard labor content of 10 hours each and standard wage rate of $10 per hour. This means our standard labor cost for today is 1,040 × 10 × $10, or $104,000. Actually, however, we used 10,730 hours of labor and the employee's earnings were $109,075. Right away you recognize that we missed our target by $109,075 minus $104,000, or $5,075. How do we analyze this "gross" variance into its quantity and price components?

First, let's find the wage (price) variance. For working 10,730 hours the employees earned $109,075. Is $109,075 more or less than the standard wage total for 10,730 hours? Merely multiply 10,730 by $10 and compare. We find 10,730 times $10 is $107,300, which shows that we are paying a wage variance of $109,075 minus $107,300, or $1,775.

Second, do we have a quantity variance? The answer is yes, and in the case of labor it's usually called an *efficiency variance.* Having cleansed all labor hours for the wage variance, we merely find the differences between actual and standard hours and multiply by the standard wage rate of $10. Thus, our labor efficiency variance is 10,730 actual hours minus 1,040 × 10 = 10,400 standard hours, or 330 hours, which at $10 per hour gives an efficiency variance of $3,300. Added together, the efficiency variance of $3,300 and the wage variance of $1,775 equals our gross labor variance of $5,075 for the day.

In journal entry form the recognition of gross labor liability, standard cost, and variances for the day is recorded as follows:

(3)

Work in Process	104,000	
Labor Wage Variance	1,775	
Labor Efficiency Variance	3,300	
Wages Payable		109,075

Again the techniques for determining the standard labor time (with scientific time-study methods), the standard wage (which can be an average wage for each type of labor in each department), and the real-time-efficiency variances must be developed by experts within your particular environment and cannot be elaborated upon here. It can only be added that in competitive industry it makes real sense to have a standard cost system for all aspects of manufacturing costs in order to operate profitably in an atmosphere of thin profit margins.

Manufacturing Overhead Accounting—Standard Costs

One of the better inventions in cost accounting in recent years is the *flexible overhead budget.* Sure, we take liberties with all budgets and the budgets become flexible in a certain sense, but this one works on an entirely different principle. What happens so sensibly under a flexible overhead budget is that at the end of each month (or other period) you determine what your output and manufacturing overhead costs *have been* for that month and then determine what your manufacturing overhead *should have been* for the production of that actual output.

For the moment let's assume that your manufacturing overhead is completely variable and that your scientific analysis of costs shows your overhead, at optimum level, to be $1 per standard direct labor hour. Then if your output for the month just ended was such as to justify 2,000 direct labor hours, your overhead cost *should have been* $2,000. In other words, the flexible budget doesn't tell you how much you should allow for overhead cost for the coming month in a given department; rather, it works entirely by hindsight. When the month is ended, you count your actual output, compute allowable overhead at that level, and compare allowable with actual.

Actually, as you well know, some overhead costs are quite variable, some are quite sticky, and some fall in between. So a flexible budget for a department is a list of all the overhead costs that department will incur and, in a series of columns representing various levels of activity for a month, the dollar amount of each overhead item at each activity level. The activity level can be designated as percentages of capacity, or direct labor or machine hours, units of output, or any other sensible measure of departmental activity. Commonly, the activity levels are within the normal operating range and at intervals of 10 percent, which

Figure 14.1 Flexible overhead budget for one month.

Expenses	Capacity, %					
	50	*60*	*70*	*80*	*90*	*100*
Variable (list them)	$ 60,000	$ 72,000	$ 84,000	$ 96,000	$108,000	$120,000
Nonvariable (list them)	60,000	60,000	60,000	60,000	60,000	60,000
Totals	$120,000	$132,000	$144,000	$156,000	$168,000	$180,000
Direct labor hours	6,000	7,200	8,400	9,600	10,800	12,000
Standard overhead rate per direct labor hour (180,000/12,000)						$15.00

means that if you operate at, say, 86 percent of capacity, you'll have to estimate the dollar allowance for each overhead cost because it falls between your 80 percent and 90 percent column. A highly condensed example of a flexible budget is shown in Figure 14.1.

Let's utilize the budget in Figure 14.1 as a continuation of the example of Our Company. Assume that the actual amount debited to Manufacturing Overhead this month turns out to be $170,000, made up of nonvariable expenses of $60,000 and variable expenses of $110,000. How do we evaluate these figures?

First, is the $170,000 total more or less than the amount justifiable by our actual activity for the month? To answer, we use hindsight to develop a budget. We note in the Figure 14.1 budget that the variable expenses regularly are scheduled at $10 per direct labor hour while the nonvariable expenses remain stable at a total of $60,000. We worked 10,730 direct labor hours, but we should have worked only 10,400 (which is the number of units produced—1,040—times the standard number of direct labor hours per unit). Should we expect our variable overhead actually to fluctuate with the *allowed* standard labor hours or with the *actual* direct labor hours? It would seem that one must acknowledge it as good performance if the production workers keep the variable overhead costs down to $10 per *actual labor hour,* because they could hardly be expected to avoid variable overhead costs that result from all labor hours, including those in excess of standard labor hours. So our overhead budget for 10,730 direct labor hours is $60,000 of nonvariable plus variable equal to $10 times 10,730 actual direct labor hours, or $167,300. The difference between the budget of $167,-300 and the actual variable overhead of $170,000 is $2,700, which we label our budget variance.

Let's examine the overhead variance further. If we turned out 1,040 units of product and have a standard overhead cost of $150 per unit, our standard overhead cost for the month is clearly $150 times 1,040, or $156,000, while our actual total was assumed to be $170,000. It would appear that we have a gross variance of $14,000. We have identified $2,700 as so-called *budget variance*. Can we pinpoint the remaining $11,300 of gross variance? Yes.

We worked 10,730 direct labor hours to produce what we should have attained with 10,400 hours, and in our budget we have allowed $15 per *actual* hour. So if we wasted 330 hours, we can ascribe $4,950 of overhead cost to inefficiency. We do, in fact, always calculate an overhead *efficiency variance* as the number of hours wasted (330) times the standard overhead rate ($15).

So now we have accounted for $2,700 plus $4,950, or $7,650 of our $14,000 gross variance. Where is the remaining $6,350? The answer is so-called *idle capacity variance*. This variance deals with nonvariable costs only, and it is easy to compute. We worked 10,730 hours as compared with capacity of 12,000—the plant was idle for 1,270 hours this month. Our cost of being ready to work (our plant, or nonvariable, costs) is exactly $5 per hour at capacity ($60,000 divided by 12,000 hours), and 1,270 wasted hours at $5 each equals our $6,350 of idle capacity variance.

The calculation of these overhead variances is summarized in Figure 14.2. It should be noted that many companies use partial standard costs and do not fully analyze their gross overhead variances.

Figure 14.2 Schedule of overhead variances.

Budget variance:			
Actual total overhead for month		$170,000	
Budget for 10,730 direct labor hours:			
Variable (10,730 × $10)	$107,300		
Nonvariable	60,000	167,300	$2,700
Efficiency variance:			
Actual labor hours at standard rate			
(10,730 × $15)		$160,950	
Standard labor hours at standard rate			
(10,400 × $15)		156,000	4,950
Idle capacity variance:			
Nonvariable overhead rate per hour at			
capacity ($60,000 ÷ 12,000) = $5			
Hours of unused (idle) capacity			
(12,000 − 10,730) = 1,270 @ $5			6,350
Gross overhead variance			
($170,000 − $150 × 1,040)			$14,000

Standard Cost Applications

The concept of standard costs can be applied in almost any spending situation, including administrative and selling departments. Of course, the setting of standards is likely to be most accurate when you are making only one simple product on a mass output basis and have loads of experience to rely on. Standards can always be set, no matter how great the uncertainty, but the greater the uncertainty the more careful you must be in your interpretation of the resulting variances. Quite obviously an inaccurate standard produces variances that are equally inaccurate, and management must simply adjust its reactions to the existing condition. When standards can be set with great accuracy, small variances have much more meaning than they have with standards that are based on rough estimates.

It follows that the bookkeeping for standard costs is a small part of the battle. The most important job is to analyze the variances as to their causes and to take remedial action before the leaks have become costly. The inventive construction of a standard cost system of accounting provides, insofar as possible, for the automatic assignment of variance *responsibilities* to departments and even to individuals within departments.

TEST PROBLEM

The problem that follows is quite similar to the one used for illustrative purposes in this chapter. You are given the standard cost specifications of a hypothetical product and a series of transactions, from which you will trace the flow of costs through a standard cost system in journal entry form.

The standard cost specifications for the Product, which is always manufactured in batches of 100 units, are as follows:

Standard Cost per Batch

Raw materials, 5,000 square feet @ $2	$10,000
Direct labor, 300 hours @ $12	3,600
Manufacturing overhead 300 (labor) hours @ $20	6,000
Standard cost, 100 units (one batch)	$19,600

The standard overhead rate was determined on the basis of budgeted overhead costs at capacity of 8,000 direct labor hours for a month, as follows:

Variable costs, 8,000 hours @ $12	$ 96,000
Nonvariable costs	64,000
Total at capacity, 8,000 hours @ $20	$160,000

Required

In the spaces which follow, make journal entries to record the information already shown in the explanation to each entry. Assume these to be summary entries for one month.

	Debit	*Credit*

(1)

To record purchase of 120,000 square feet of raw material at $2.04 per square foot. Raw material price variances are recorded at point of purchase and the materials are put in inventory at standard.

(2)

To record requisitions for 102,000 square feet of raw material used to produce 20 batches of finished product. (Make a debit, at standard cost, directly to Finished Goods.)

(3)

Finished Goods
Labor Wage Variance
Labor Efficiency Variance
    Wages Payable
To record $75,640 of wages payable for 6,100 hours of direct labor in the production of 20 batches. (Again, make a debit directly to Finished Goods for the standard cost of 20 batches.)

(4)

Manufacturing Overhead
    Various Accounts
To record all kinds of manufacturing overhead costs incurred during the month, $140,000, made up of variable costs of $76,000 and nonvariable costs of $64,-000.

(5)

Finished Goods
Overhead—Budget Variance
Overhead—Efficiency Variance
Overhead—Idle Plant Variance
    Factory Overhead
To charge Finished Goods with standard overhead cost of goods finished and to allocate the gross variance to three variance accounts.

15

Internal Management Accounting

The Concept of Management Accounting

Nobody is quite sure where accounting, in its narrowest sense, leaves off and where management, in the active sense, begins. First, we ought to agree that any accounting that is not helpful in some way should be scrapped. In all of its phases "useful" accounting is useful to some sort of management, whether it be the officers and subofficers of the company, the investors and potential investors, the creditors and potential creditors, or one or more government agencies. Each of these users of accounting data manages its relationships with the enterprise, in part at least, on the basis of accounting reports—all of which thereby qualify as management-serving.

For the purposes of this chapter we are limiting management to insiders only—the whole spectrum of persons on the corporate organization chart who have responsibilities for reaching decisions that will influence costs and revenues or be influenced by them. And we'll define as management accounting the accumulation, classification, storage, reporting, and interpreting of cost and revenue data to provide management with the optimum amount of useful information to help in the formulation of decisions.

Certain management accounting procedures are continuous in nature. The accounting documents and ledger accounts are so organized that the data are accumulated and reported continuously without any special call for help by the management who will receive the information. We'll consider these very briefly under the headings of responsibility accounting, standard costing, and direct costing.

Responsibility Accounting

In recent years a lot of fuss has been made over a very obvious, prosaic idea. The idea is this: Some costs are beyond a person's control, so let's not charge them to that person. If you agree with that proposition, you will next agree with the converse, that in making cost allocations we should examine each one, determine *who was responsible* for it, and then charge the cost against that person's department. *It is probable that almost every cost incurred by an enterprise can be traced to someone as the responsible party.* In general, operating costs are recurring, so it follows that a fixed pattern of cost assignments usually will be established—at least with respect to most costs.

An important accompaniment to "responsibility" cost assignments is a structure of departmental budgets, preferably flexible budgets, so that at the end of each quarter, or each month, the actual costs charged against each department can be viewed in comparison with the amount budgeted for the attained level of activity.

As a postscript to the definition of responsibility accounting, it must be added that the responsibility basis should be the guiding factor in the primary spreading of expenses. In many situations the expenses of service departments can, secondarily, be transferred to the producing departments on a responsibility basis. However, that will not always be true, and some costs may then remain in service departments. They also must be assigned to producing departments on a "best judgment" basis in order to complete the job of costing the goods manufactured in the producing departments; but such "judgmental" allocations, since they are beyond the control of the producing departments, should be excluded from any reckoning of the performance efficiencies of the producing departments.

The concept of responsibility accounting also works very well in the effort to control your selling and administrative expenses. What is needed is an organization chart clearly defining departmental responsibilities and identifying the responsible department heads so that one or more ledger accounts can be set up for each and the expenses can then be assigned and the departmental efficiencies evaluated. A budget may, again, be developed for each department; however, since it is quite difficult to measure performance when there is no objective unit of output, the budget in the case may simply be a forecast, planned expense allowance for each month in advance.

Standard Costing

Because Chapter 14 was devoted to it, standard costing is mentioned here only to have it prominently included among the internal management accounting devices.

As may not have been made fully evident, the management value in standard costing is found in the reporting and analysis of variances. The process reflects the principle of exceptions, one of the old, well-worn principles of managerial control. The principle holds that we report to busy management only the exceptions (variances from standard). If everything is "nominal," as the astronauts say, no report is necessary. Why flood the boss with "bed sheets" full of figures that merely show that nothing untoward has happened? A corollary is that, in any report to management, it may be possible for the accountant to underline or otherwise emphasize each item or figure that calls for action. The idea is to keep those reports condensed and put details in supporting schedules.

In standard cost accounting it is possible to devise an infinite number of variance accounts. For example, you could have a separate materials price variance account and a separate quantity variance account for each kind of material, and you could then subdivide each into departmental accounts. Probably that would be absurd in almost any situation, but the point is that the variances are worth recognizing and reporting *only if they're actionable.* In other words, it doesn't do much good to report month after month a variance which simply cannot be rectified.

Direct Costing

The last of the routine management accounting processes that we'll examine is direct costing. As in the case of standard costing and responsibility accounting, the ledger account system may be so structured that the routine accounting is conducted on a continuous rather than an ad hoc basis.

"Direct costing" is a misnomer. We have always reserved the term *direct cost* to identify a cost that can be traced directly (without apportionment) to some end product. What accountants now mean when they speak of direct costing is that in accounting for manufacturing costs they will feed into the inventory accounts (which are current assets) only *costs that vary with the amount produced.* The fixed (nonvariable) costs, because they will be incurred whether we produce anything or not, will be charged off against income in the period in which they are incurred. The fixed costs, under this scheme of things, are often referred to as *period* costs for that reason.

Direct costing is great for one important reason: If it is practiced, it means that the company has studied the behavior patterns of its various kinds of costs and is in a position to deal intelligently with them. As has been noted several times, costs may vary with the level of production or with some other activity measure, or they may remain relatively nonvariable. In between the costs that are completely variable and those that are completely fixed lie the behavior patterns of all other costs. Some rise, in a curved fashion, slower or faster than the activity measure to which they are related; they are commonly termed *semivariable costs.* Others rise in stair-step fashion as activity increases; they are commonly termed *semifixed costs.* Knowledge of cost behavior is of critical importance to the preparation of budgets, whether flexible or not, and it is also critical in the fashioning of some of the decisions we are about to discuss.

On the other hand, direct costing doesn't appear to fare well theoretically in the preparation of periodic financial statements. In other words, the very basic direct cost notion that the fixed costs are period costs is hard to defend. In short, in compiling the costs of goods manufactured, is it reasonable to assert that the manufacturing process causes no depreciation, no property taxes, no insurance, and no supervisory costs? To take an extreme example, assume that for a given year a company, for whatever reason, chooses to refrain from all selling activity and devote its full resources to the making and stockpiling of goods for sale in future periods. Would it make sense to suggest that the company has operated all year at a loss equal to its nonvariable manufacturing costs? Are those costs actually losses rather than costs of manufacturing? You should reject direct costing for annual statement purposes (it has not received the blessing of the income tax folks as of this date) and stick to its opposite form, which is universally known as *absorption* or *full absorption* costing.

Differential Costs and Related Decisions

Most of the remainder of this chapter will be devoted to cost aspects of decisions that may need to be faced from time to time in an ad hoc fashion—decisions which are not based on routine cost accumulation and reporting but rather call for selective cost groupings. In other words, we're now concerned with what is so often referred to as the need for different costs for different purposes.

The term *differential costs* has gained much prominence in recent years, and it will probably become increasingly recognized as a cost concept to be reckoned with.

Differential cost means the total addition to costs caused by any addition to output. It's that simple. If your total costs that would be incurred in a given period by producing, say, 20,000 units would be $100,000 and your total if you were to produce 25,000 would be

$115,000, then the differential output is 5,000 units, the corresponding differential cost is $15,000, and the unit differential cost for that particular set of assumptions is $3. Thus, differential cost is the *added cost of doing something extra*. The concept has numerous decision-making applications, but it should be applied with caution. Let's consider a few examples.

Our company in a given year produced and sold 100,000 units of its product. Total manufacturing costs were $1,000,000 (for an average unit cost of $10); total selling and administrative costs were $300,000. Our plant capacity for a year is 150,000 units, and we learn that next year the federal government will be in the market for 50,000 units, on which we are invited to bid. We immediately make a cost behavior study and determine that 30 percent of all our costs ($1,300,000) are nonvariable and the remainder are, for all practical purposes, variable. From this we conclude that our differential (you may prefer to call it *incremental*) cost of making and selling 50,000 incremental, or differential, units to the government would be 50 percent of the variable costs we incurred at the 100,000-unit level, or 50 percent of 70 percent of $1,300,000, which is $455,000, or $9.10 per unit (as compared with an average total cost of $13 per unit at the 100,000-unit level). Knowing this differential cost puts management in a position to increase total profits by supplying the 50,000 units to the government at any price above $9.10 (assuming, of course, that we can continue to sell the 100,000 through regular channels and at regular prices). In other words, the unit cost with which management should primarily be concerned in this case is the unit differential cost. It should always be borne in mind, in working from a differential cost base, that to seek volume increases by cutting prices invites price cuts by one's competitors, so the differential cost approach to pricing must be applied with great care.

Another interesting application of differential costs exists when a company, say the one we have just been considering, has made sales only for cash or has followed an ultraconservative policy in making credit sales. Assume that we produce 100,000 units as before and sell all of them for cash at $15 each for a before-tax profit of $200,000. Query: What percentage of bad debts could we afford if we were to allow customers to charge their purchases, assuming we continue to sell 100,000 for cash and, as the result of permitting credit sales, believe we can sell an additional 50,000 units? The answer lies in a differential cost calculation. If we produce and sell 50,000 more units, our total differential cost, as in the earlier example, will be $455,000; and this is the net amount we must receive to break even on the additional sales. The gross dollar amount of the additional sales will be 50,000 × $15, or

$750,000, which indicates that we could incur bad debts of $750,000 minus $455,000, or $295,000, and not be worse off. Our incremental bad debt loss could be as high as $295,000 divided by $750,000, or more than 39 percent! Needless to say, the temptation to begin selling on credit might be great under those circumstances; and similar calculations to test the wisdom of more generous extension of credit, when credit is already being granted on a limited basis, may encourage policy changes. Extreme care should most certainly be used in calculating the differential costs (and don't overlook increases in bookkeeping costs for accounts receivable) and the probable effects of any such policy changes.

In our next topic, the make-or-buy decision, we'll consider another possible differential cost situation.

Should We Make It or Buy It?

A great many articles have been published on the subject of "make or buy," and we surely cannot treat it exhaustively here. We're now concerned with questions such as these: Should we start making this particular part which up to now we have been buying ready-made from an outsider? Should we set up a garage for maintenance of our trucks and service cars, or should we continue to have the maintenance done outside? We're paying out a lot of money for printing and duplicating services; shouldn't we set up our own shop? We've been buying our tools and dies from specialty shops that seem to be making a good profit; why don't we make our own tools, dies, jigs, and fixtures? And a much more far-reaching make-or-buy type of question: Should we continue to sell through wholesalers; should we deal directly with retailers; or should we even set up our own retail outlets?

Underlying every make-or-buy survey is the belief, or maybe only the suspicion, that "our supplier is getting fat off us" and "we could just as well be making that profit ourselves."

Certainly a most fundamental question in approaching any make-or-buy decision is this: Which will be the more economical policy for us? And a most critical aspect of any economy study, of course, is the matter of costs.

In make-or-buy analysis, the adage, "use different costs for different purposes" seems to be most relevant. The fact that so many articles appear on the subject suggests a condition of uncertainty, which is no doubt the case. For our purposes two somewhat opposing schools of thought will be presented.

The first school recommends the differential cost approach to make-

or-buy. To illustrate it, let's assume we have been buying part X for $90 each and we feel that our earnings might be improved if we produced the thing ourselves. We call on our cost accountant to estimate our costs if we were to make part X. He presents the following condensed schedule:

PART X
Estimated Production Costs
(per 100 units)

Materials (including costs of ordering, receiving, storing, etc.)		$ 1,142
Direct labor (details in supporting schedule)		3,260
Variable overhead (at 120% of direct labor)	$3,912	
Fixed overhead	2,608	6,520
Estimated total cost of 100 units		$10,922

It takes but a moment to make a superficial, differential cost analysis of these data. Our *total* cost per 100 units is $10,922, which is higher than the total cost (100 × $90 = $9,000) of buying them; but our total cost includes $2,608 of fixed costs which are excluded in determining differential cost (i.e., the costs that would be incremental to our present total were we to make rather than buy). We determine our differential cost to be total cost of $10,922 minus fixed costs of $2,608, or $8,314, and this "clearly indicates a potential saving (earnings increase) of $9,000 minus $8,314, or $686, on every 100-unit batch of part X." Let's get busy and make those parts!

It is possible that many differential cost analyses go no farther than that, and it is equally possible that many of the decisions are faulty. Let's look at the full cost approach to the same question.

In general, the full cost approach to make-or-buy rests on the contention that fixed costs are a fact of life. The only basis for excluding them in make-or-buy decisions is that *you clearly have excess, unused capacity.* That is, you must feel that not only your plant assets but also your supervisor and managerial personnel are not fully occupied and, even more important, that in the foreseeable future the plant and managerial personnel *will continue to be inadequately occupied* unless you take on such activities as the manufacture of your own component parts. Stated differently, the only reason for excluding fixed costs is that you are clearly incurring them *and they're going to waste* and you see little or no prospect that you can step the volume of your regular activities up enough to soak up the reserve energies and reserve capacity of your personnel and plant.

The great risk of taking on the manufacture of something you've been buying—i.e., doing so on the basis that you can exclude fixed costs from your tally of costs to make—is that *new fixed costs* will "creep" into the picture. The creep effect is most likely to occur if you take on a sideline manufacturing or service operation and later increase your mainline activities. Then you won't have enough plant and personnel capacity to go around and the fixed costs will creep in. And you're likely to find that it's much more of a problem to disengage from an old activity than it is to add a new one.

The conclusion to be reached from the full cost approach to make-or-buy is that one should not take on (except, perhaps, temporarily to fill in short-term dips in activity) sideline activities unless the supplier's price exceeds your *total costs plus the rate of profit* that you make on your mainline activity.

Needless to say, a make-or-buy decision, even though it relies heavily upon cost analyses, must also take other noncost matters into consideration. For example, we might decide to make part X simply because that is the only way we can assure ourselves of a steady supply and good quality. On the other hand, it might be politically expedient to farm out as much as we can in order to maintain good public relations.

Thus, the make-or-buy question is not a simple one even in what may appear to be a simple situation. In general, one might very well lean in the "buy" direction and insist that any decision to "make" be rigorously documented.

Decisions to Acquire Plant Assets

How often is a new structure, a new unit of machinery, or other capital asset purchased or constructed on the recommendation of a wise old production manager with no objective analysis of the need and no concrete assurance that the capital outlay is a wise one? Admittedly some plant additions are made simply because they're unavoidable; they may even be required by legal action, as in the case of antipollution equipment. In many instances, however, financial management, equipped with relevant information, should be in a position to endorse or veto a capital outlay on the basis of logical analysis. The present custom is to refer to such analysis and planning of fixed asset acquisitions as *capital budgeting*.

Capital budgeting is not a precise tool; its employment does not assure the avoidance of mistakes, since estimates of future cash flows form a major portion of the analysis; but the chances are overwhelming that employment of systematic capital budgeting will reduce the number and cost of mistakes significantly.

Basically, the two major aspects of capital budgeting are (1) the ranking of capital outlay requests in the order of their probable value to the firm and (2) the determination of which outlays give promise of being worth making.

Underlying all capital budgeting techniques is our old friend, "net cash flow." Here's a quick review. If we invest $100 in a depreciable asset that will produce cash savings, or cash proceeds, of $50 per year, the gross cash flow is $50 annually. The net cash flow is the $50 minus any and all *cash expenditures* needed to produce the gross inflow. Let's assume cash outflows will amount to $10 per year; then the net cash flow is $40 per year. Note specifically that depreciation does not enter into this calculation. The $40 net flow hopefully will provide for "recovery" of depreciation, and any excess will be profit.

Three principal forms of analysis are applied in capital budgeting. The first of these is the so-called *payback period,* which is strictly a "no-go" check. What it does is rule that a particular capital asset shall *not* be acquired unless its payback period is less than a prescribed number of years. If, for example, we insist that every capital asset we buy must have a payback period no longer than 4 years, we aren't using the procedure to determine what assets should be acquired; we're merely ruling against all acquisitions that do not meet the payback schedule. The example in the preceding paragraph, with an annual cash flow estimated at $40, has a 2½-year payback period, so it would meet a 4-year test readily. However, a payback period under 4 years does not in itself constitute justification for the purchase of any asset. Quite obviously, if other things were equal, we might turn down a proposed 2½-year payback asset if we were short of funds and had alternative outlays with payback periods shorter than 2½ years. Again, a rule-of-thumb payback requirement is strictly a no-go tool—it rules that we *shall not* acquire an asset with a payback period of greater length, but it gives little help in choosing *which* assets with shorter payback periods should be chosen. In fact, it is doubtful that the payback method really has much to commend it for any part of the capital budgeting decision, because it overlooks so much that is of far greater importance. Nevertheless, the payback device is a popular one, and it should be well understood by executives.

Each of the two remaining tools depends on the use of compound interest arithmetic, and the two are closely related.

The great objection to the payback method is that it pays absolutely no attention to the "tail of the dog." Let's assume that we drill two wells, A and B, and both produce enough water, oil, or gas to pay back our full drilling cost in exactly 4 years. Are the wells of equal value? Certainly not if well A goes dry at the end of 4 years and well B continues to produce. In other words, the tail period (after payback is complete) is an important element in any capital budgeting decision. Of course, like most aspects of capital budgeting, the tail period will probably be a matter of estimate, but it certainly wouldn't make sense to choose well A, because of its 4-year payback, if it appeared probable that well B would pay back in 5 years and would then continue to flow for another 5 years.

Hence, we need some device for evaluating two factors at the same time—the *size* of the flow and the *persistence* of the flow. It should be added that the timing of peaks and valleys in the flow is also a matter of concern, though it is very difficult to predict with any assurance of reliability.

One method of evaluating both size and duration of flow is to reduce the estimated future net cash flow to a single present-value figure. This is the *present-value method.* To employ it with respect to a proposed acquisition requires estimating (1) the periodic net cash flow and (2) the number of periods that the flow will persist. For practical purposes it will probably be acceptable to assume that the flow is the same every year, although a more sophisticated (more certain?) prognostication may be employed. Also, finding the present value of something means that you "discount" the thing at an acceptable interest rate. When the estimates have been made and the net cash flow has been discounted to a single present-value figure, that amount must be larger than your proposed commitment (i.e., worth more than the amount you are proposing to commit in the fixed-asset investment).

To illustrate the present-value procedure, assume you are contemplating investment of $100,000 in an asset that you believe will produce net cash flow of $30,000 per year throughout a 5-year life. All that needs to be done is to refer to compound-interest tables to find the present value of the flow at your required rate per annum (say 12 percent) and then compare it with the $100,000 initial instrument. The effect of the discounting operation is to put the *series* of periodic payments on effectively the same time base (namely, the date of the initial investment) as the initial investment. The present value of $1 per period for 5 periods, discounted at 12 percent per period, is approximately $3.61. The present value of $30,000 per period, discounted at 12 percent, is 30,000 times $3.61, or $108,300. The fact that the present value of the cash flow annuity exceeds the amount of the proposed investment gives us a green light for this outlay, provided that it meets whatever other tests need to be considered.

A third test, which is something of a complement to the second, seeks to determine *what rate of return* is represented in the estimates we have made. In other words, if our $100,000 investment will return

$30,000 of net cash flow each year for 5 years, how good an investment is that in terms of rate of return? The solution again calls for use of compound interest tables. Now we are to determine what interest rate our asset earns per year over the assumed 5-year period based on the known $100,000 and the anticipated $30,000 of annual cash flow. Obviously, the answer is not simply 30 percent (30,000/100,000), since the basic $100,000 is presumed to depreciate down to zero during its 5-year life span. The answer, again, is determined by use of compound-interest tables somewhat as follows:

1. $100,000 is the present value of $30,000 per period for five annual periods at the unknown interest (discount) rate.

2. If (1) is true, then $100,000/30,000, or $3.33, is the present value of $1 per period for five annual periods at the same, unknown earning rate.

3. Compound-interest tables (the present value of $1 per period for n periods) show for each assumed interest rate the present value of $1 for a number of assumed periods ranging from one up to 50 or more. Since we know that we are dealing with five periods, we merely look in the various columns, at the amount shown for five periods, and find the one nearest our $3.33. The interest rate appearing at the top of the column is, then, approximately the sought-after rate —close enough for practical purposes.

4. Since compound-interest tables may not include high enough interest rates to include our required answer, a satisfactory treatment is to deal with, say, one-half of the annual $30,000 by assuming that $15,000 is earned semiannually. Thus, $100,000/15,000 = $6.667, which represents the present value of $1 per period for 10 periods at the unknown rate. In line 10 in the 7 percent column the amount is 7.024, which falls between the amounts shown for 8 percent and 10 percent. This indicates that our rate of return is a bit over 8 percent per half year, or around 17 percent per year, compounded semiannually.

To summarize this very abbreviated discussion of capital budgeting, any proposed capital addition may well be subjected to the three tests outlined in this section: (1) determination of the payback period, (2) determination of the estimated cash flow per period throughout the asset's life and comparison of the present value of the cash flow, discounted at our required interest rate, with the expected amount of the investment, and (3) determination of the actual rate of return that is implied in the cash flow that we have predicted. If the proposed investment meets all three of those tests and does it as well as, or better than, any competing opportunities to invest the funds, it should be safe to proceed with the investment.

Miscellaneous Topics

It is clearly impossible to outline, let alone describe exhaustively, all the devices that accountants and other quantitative information men have invented. Today's buzz words include MIS (management information systems), which is a very interesting computer-oriented story in itself. Also, the mathematicians have worked up many interesting business applications under the label "operations research." They include linear programming, Monte Carlo method, Bayesian analysis, simulation, PERT, economic order theory, and waiting line models. Much of this is in its infancy, although the third generation of computers seems to be stimulating the aging process to a point where reliability is greatly enhanced.

TEST PROBLEM

Here's a short one on capital budgeting. Our Company is considering purchase of a machine with a 10-year life which should reduce annual labor costs by $10,000. Operating costs of the machine, excluding depreciation, will be about $3,000 per year. List price of the machine is $41,000. Should we buy it? We require a maximum payback period of 6 years, and our minimum rate of return is 10 percent. Added information: The present value of an annuity of $1 for 10 periods at 10 percent is 6.144.

TEST PROBLEM Solution Space

Computation of payback period:

Computation of present value of machine at 10 percent discount:

16
Federal Income Tax Concepts

Everyone can appreciate the tremendous importance of the federal income tax. Some entities find the tax to be one of the largest single expenses of doing business. As significant as it is, we must recognize that it is but one segment of a total tax structure which includes other federal taxes, such as excise, employment, gift, and estate taxes, as well as state and local income, property, and sales taxes. This chapter deals only with the federal income tax.

The tax applies both to individuals and to corporations. Although the two applications are often thought of as separate taxes and are shown separately in government statistics, both are incorporated in the same Internal Revenue Code and in most respects are surprisingly similar. We will focus primarily on corporations, but we will also mention some aspects of the individual tax, primarily as that tax impacts on corporate employees (including executive-owners).

A chapter of this nature must be prefaced with an important caveat. In these few pages we cannot pretend to cover the many details that are essential to understanding the application of the tax law to specific situations. This discussion is intended to make you aware of some of the basic concepts in order that you can (1) recognize many of the important tax opportunities and pitfalls, (2) intelligently discuss the tax ramifications with your tax advisers, and (3) efficiently extend your tax study into some of the comprehensive tax volumes.

This chapter, revised and updated by the authors, was originally prepared by Donald H. Skadden when he was the Arthur Young Distinguished Professor of Accounting and Associate Dean of The Graduate School of Business Administration, The University of Michigan.

It is important to be aware that the tax is all-encompassing and that Congress has broad latitude in levying it. The constitutional authority derives from the Sixteenth Amendment, which grants Congress the "power to lay and collect taxes on incomes, from whatever source derived." In defining "gross income," Congress incorporated wording directly from the Sixteenth Amendment but at the same time reserved to itself the right to determine specifically what shall be taxed. The Internal Revenue Code (IRC or Code) states that "Except as otherwise provided in this subtitle, gross income means all income from whatever source derived. . . ." Thus, it is clear that Congress could base the tax on total income, with no income exempted and with no deductions allowed. However, since the initiation of the income tax in 1913, Congress has chosen to levy the tax on its version of "net" income and to exempt certain types of income from tax and make certain expenses deductible. In essence, that leads to the two most fundamental of all tax concepts: All income is taxable unless some authority to the contrary can be found, and nothing is deductible unless some authority so indicates.

Another set of broad concepts surrounds the doctrine of "business purpose." On several occasions the courts have held that the Internal Revenue Service may not substitute its judgment for the judgment of management or the taxpayer with regard to a transaction or other business activity, provided that some valid business purpose (other than simply reducing taxes) underlies that judgment. However, in the absence of a valid business purpose, the government has very broad authority to ignore "sham transactions," to reallocate income among related parties, to look through the "form to the substance" of a transaction, and to collapse two or more "steps" in a series of transactions to arrive at the actual substance of the action.

TAXPAYERS AND TAX RETURNS

There are three basic types of taxpayers: individuals, corporations, and fiduciaries. The fiduciary of each trust or estate files a Form 1041 and pays a tax on the income not distributed to the beneficiaries. However, this chapter will deal only with individuals and corporations. It is important to recognize the similarity in tax treatment of the two. Both are taxed according to the same Internal Revenue Code, and most sections of that code apply to all types of taxpayers. Exhibit I shows the route from total income to the final balance due and illustrates where the tax treatments are common and where they diverge. However, even within each of these major categories there are subgroups which are subject to different rules and, in some cases, different tax rates.

Individuals

All individuals file a Form 1040, an abbreviated Form 1040A, or Form 1040EZ. The tax on Form 1040 or Form 1040A is computed according to four different rate schedules:

- Unmarried individuals

- Married individuals filing jointly

- Married individuals filing separate returns

- Heads of households

Form 1040EZ can only be used by single filers with no dependents. For many years there was only one tax table for individuals, but a major inequity arose between married couples in community property states and those in common law states. A married couple with one income of $40,000 was taxed in community property states, such as California and Texas, as though the $40,000 were two separate $20,000 incomes. By use of graduated tables, the combined tax on two $20,000 incomes is less than the tax on one $40,000 income. In response to the difference in treatment, several states were in the process of shifting to community property laws when Congress agreed that the federal income tax law should not force such a major change on the states. To obviate the need for the change, the "joint return" was introduced; on it, the income, deductions, and credits of both spouses were combined. When the joint return was first adopted, the combined incomes paid exactly doubled the tax an unmarried person owed on one-half the income.

Several years later Congress recognized that an unmarried head of household (typically a single parent with dependent children living at home) has many of the same expenses and responsibilities as a married couple. The result was the third rate schedule, in which the tax was approximately halfway between the joint return tax and the separate return tax on the same income.

When the three rate schedules were in place, unmarried taxpayers complained that they were being taxed unfairly. Thus, after many years Congress reduced the rates, somewhat, for unmarried taxpayers. However, Congress did not want to encourage married taxpayers to file separate returns, so it left the old unmarried rates in place solely for married persons filing separate returns. Thus, today the tax break vis-à-vis married and unmarried individuals is completely reversed from the earliest situation. A married couple each of whom earns $20,000 will pay more tax on their $40,000 joint return than will two unmarried individuals who earn $20,000 each. There has been much publicity on

Exhibit I

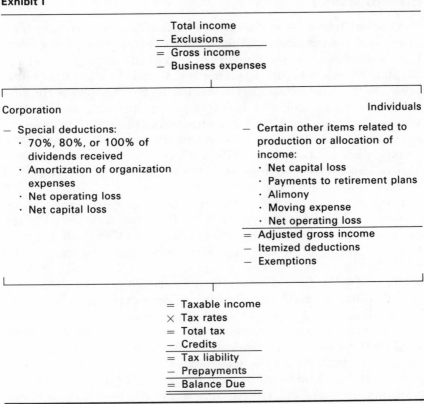

Total income
− Exclusions
= Gross income
− Business expenses

Corporation

− Special deductions:
 · 70%, 80%, or 100% of
  dividends received
 · Amortization of organization
  expenses
 · Net operating loss
 · Net capital loss

Individuals

− Certain other items related to
 production or allocation of
 income:
 · Net capital loss
 · Payments to retirement plans
 · Alimony
 · Moving expense
 · Net operating loss
= Adjusted gross income
− Itemized deductions
− Exemptions

= Taxable income
× Tax rates
= Total tax
− Credits
= Tax liability
− Prepayments
= Balance Due

this so-called "marriage tax." Congress will likely take some action, but no one has really come up with an acceptable, equitable solution to the dilemma.

Partnerships

A partnership is treated as a group of individual taxpayers, and not as a separate taxpaying entity. As a convenience for both the government and the partners, the partnership files a Form 1065 to report the incomes and deductions of the entity and the amounts allocated to each partner for such items as capital gains, charitable contributions, pension contributions, and ordinary income. The partners then report the allocated amounts on their respective 1040s. Thus, partnership income or loss flows through to the partners and is taxed (or deducted) only at the individual level.

Corporations

The tax law follows the concept of a corporation as a separate legal entity distinct from its shareholders. Thus, the corporation files a Form 1120 or 1120-A (short form) and pays a tax at the corporate level and the same income is taxable again to the shareholders when distributed as dividends. Dividends are not deductible by the distributing corporation. This separation of the taxable entities can be both a disadvantage and an advantage. Much has been written about the "double taxation" of corporate income. Special provisions discussed elsewhere in this chapter allow substantial relief (70 to 100 percent) when dividends are paid to another corporation. No relief is allowed for individuals to whom dividends are paid.

Tax planning opportunities can arise from the separateness of the entities. It is possible for a shareholder also to be an employee of the corporation. In that case salary payments are deductible by the corporation and taxable to the employee and various fringe benefits can be deductible even though they are not taxable to the employee-stockholder. Many closely held corporations manage to pay out substantially all of their income in salaries plus fringes. The income left in the corporation is taxed at the current percent corporate rates which, up to $75,000 of taxable income, are lower rates than for individuals. Starting at $75,000, however, the marginal tax rate for a corporation jumps to 34 percent, higher than the top marginal rate for individuals of 31 percent. It should be noted that the IRS has rather broad authority to disallow a portion of an "unreasonable salary" and treat it as a dividend —taxable to the recipient but not deductible to the payor. Within the past few years it has become possible for professional individuals or partnerships (accountants, attorneys, doctors, etc.) to incorporate as "professional corporations" and gain most of the tax benefits of a regular corporation.

Subchapter S Corporations

The sharp contrast in the tax treatment of corporations and partnerships quite logically meant that the tax law became one of the most critical factors in determining the form of business organization selected for many small businesses. Congress recognized that and enacted Subchapter S, which allows closely held corporations to elect not to pay the federal income tax. The corporation files a Form 1120S, but the shareholders report their allocated shares of income or loss on their 1040s. Thus Sub-S offers a "flow-through" characteristic similar to that of a partnership, but it also contains many limitations and restrictions that differ in several respects from those of a partnership. For example, in certain circumstances, capital gains will be taxed at the corporate level rather than passed through to the shareholders. While the technical label for such an entity is an "electing small business corporation," the only measure of size is the *number of shareholders.*

Multiple Corporations

Through a myriad of highly technical provisions, a group of related corporations is allowed to file a consolidated tax return. This is conceptually similar to the accounting consolidated income statement and provides for the elimination of intercompany transactions. Also, losses of some members of the group can offset incomes of other members. Affiliated corporations, for tax purposes, include the parent-subsidiary relationship (at least 80 percent control), and the "brother-sister" corporations in which five or fewer individuals own 80 percent control of two or more corporations.

Special Corporate Taxes

There are two provisions in the tax law to encourage closely held corporations to distribute earnings. The *personal holding company* (PHC) has sometimes been referred to as an incorporated investment portfolio. In greatly oversimplified terms, a PHC is a corporation (1) in which over 50 percent control (direct or indirect) is held by five or fewer shareholders and (2) which receives over 60 percent of its income from various passive sources such as interest, dividends, royalties, and rents. In addition to the regular tax, a PHC is subject to a heavy tax on its undistributed income.

Corporations other than personal holding companies are subject to a special *accumulated earnings tax.* The tax is a very heavy one and is based on the current year's undistributed income which is unnecessarily retained in the corporation for the purpose of avoiding the tax on dividends at the shareholder level. Income retained for expansion of the operations and for reasonable working capital needs is not subject to this tax.

Both taxes apply only to income after taxes, and both can be avoided by dividend distributions during the year or within 2½ months after the year-ends.

With the significant drop in 1986 in the highest marginal tax rates of individuals below the highest rates for corporations, these so-called "penalty" taxes have lost much of their significance. The problem now is not how to retain earnings in a corporation and avoid taxes but how to distribute them through salary, rental, and other payments and avoid double taxation.

ACCOUNTING PERIODS AND METHODS

Some of the basic tax concepts, some tax planning opportunities, and some interesting interrelationships with general corporate accounting are embodied in the areas of accounting periods and methods.

Tax Year

Most new taxable entities (e.g., a new corporation, trust, or estate) may elect almost any tax year that is desired. Partnerships have certain restrictions in this regard in order to coordinate the tax year of the business with that of the principal partners.

The tax law recognizes the calendar year, the fiscal year, and a 52–53-week year. The calendar year is assumed if no alternative is elected and is required if the taxpayer does not maintain an adequate set of accounting records. A fiscal year may end with any month, but it must end on the last day of the month. Many businesses prefer to account on the basis of thirteen 4-week periods. These are more standard and more comparable than 12 months of varying lengths. The tax law accommodates this preference by what is known as a 52–53-week year, which ends near the end of any month selected. Through the automatic action of the calendar, 4 or 5 years of exactly 52 weeks are followed by a 53-week year in which the thirteenth period has 5 weeks rather than 4 weeks. This is necessary in order for the end of the year to remain near the end of the same month and not move ever earlier in the year.

It is possible to change to a different tax year, although most changes require the approval of the Internal Revenue Service (IRS or Service). Such a change will create a short period between the old and the new, and usually the income for the short period must be annualized for tax reporting purposes. A short period which is the first or last period for a taxpayer need not be annualized.

Tax planning opportunities in this area relate primarily to the ability to effect a permanent deferral of tax by selecting a year which will end from 1 month to 11 months later than the year in which the income otherwise would have been reported. Also, this allows for filing tax returns at the end of a natural business year when inventories and other activity are at their lowest point. For the vast majority of taxpayers, the tax year is the same as the accounting year.

Cash Method

The tax law recognizes three distinct methods of accounting: the cash method, the accrual method, and a hybrid method. The cash method generally reports all income received in cash minus all expenses paid in cash. There are certain exceptions, most of which are intended to avoid either intentional or unintentional distortions of income. Capital expenditures must be capitalized and deducted over a period of years through depreciation or amortization. Income must be reported if it is "constructively received" even though cash is not actually received. A constructive receipt occurs when the income is unequivocally available to the taxpayer even though not actually in the taxpayer's possession; for example, interest credited to a savings account is income when credited, not when withdrawn in the form of cash. Also, to avoid distortion, the cash method is not allowed if inventories are significant in the calculation of income.

Most individuals, including most professionals and many other service businesses, report on the cash method even if they keep their own records on the accrual basis. This allows for some tax planning such as the timing of deductible expenditures and the delay or advancement of the billing-collecting cycle.

Accrual Method

With a few important exceptions, the tax version of the accrual method is essentially consistent with normal accrual accounting. The tax law embodies a concept that is known as the "wherewithal to pay taxes." In essence it provides that income should be taxed when the taxpaying capability exists even though the income is accrued during some other period. In some instances it is mandatory; in others it is optional. Income received in advance is taxable when received. If 5 years rent income is received in advance, all of it is taxable even though 4 years of it will be deferred for general accounting purposes.

Tax accrual accounting can also differ from financial accounting in the area of estimated expenses. For most expenses other than depreciation, the tax authorities will normally demand that a definite liability must exist and that its amount must be reasonably certain. Thus, estimated warranty or repair expenses that are accrued for book purposes will probably not be deductible until actually paid. Within the accrual method there are several instances in which the taxpayer may elect to treat things differently for tax purposes and book purposes. For example, different depreciation methods and lives and different methods of accounting for bad debts are allowed.

Whenever the tax treatment and financial reporting differ only as to the timing of an income or deduction (e.g., rent received in advance, depreciation), the consequence is a troublesome accounting problem often referred to as "tax allocation." The tax effect should be reflected in the income statement when the income or expense is so reflected even though the same item will be reported for tax purposes in a different period.

Hybrid Method

The cash method is not allowed if inventories are significant in the income calculation. In its place, primarily for the benefit of small businesses, is a hybrid of cash and accrual methods whereby sales and cost of goods sold are reflected on the accrual basis but the operating expenses may be reported on the cash basis.

Change of Accounting Method

A taxpayer must secure approval from the IRS to change the general accounting method, such as cash to accrual. In most instances permission also must be secured in order to change a specific accounting method such as methods of depreciation or inventory accounting. That is so even when sound accounting would dictate that the change is a substantial improvement.

INCOME

Inclusions

The Constitutional authority to tax "all incomes from whatever source derived" is extremely broad, yet it has certain basic limitations. "Income" is not a precise term, and the Constitution does not define it. Economists, lawyers, accountants, and the tax authorities have somewhat different views as to what should be included. All seem to agree, at least conceptually, that "income" must be distinguished from "return of capital," which is not taxable under an "income tax." Through the years Congress, the courts, and accountants have refined the concepts of income, and it is helpful to understand "realization," "recognition," and the "fruit-and-tree doctrine." The tree is the capital which produces the income (the fruit). Although income may be realized while the fruit is developing and ripening, it will not be recognized until the fruit is separated from the tree. Furthermore, for objectivity in valuation, the income tax will not be levied until the value of the fruit has been verified through sale to an outside party. Thus, an increase in value of land, shares of stock, or other assets is not recognized until the asset is sold.

However, it is neither reasonable nor correct to assume that income is recognized only when received in cash. Even cash basis taxpayers must recognize income whether received in cash or in property. Thus shares of stock issued to the promoter who formed the corporation constitute taxable compensation income. A bonus paid to a corporate executive in shares of stock may be compensation income. In certain "qualified" stock option or stock plans, Congress has intentionally deemed that such income may be deferred. Income received in property is measured by the fair market value. Thus, a cash basis taxpayer does not avoid income by "bartering" services for property or property for property. (That seems to be widely misunderstood or simply ignored by participants in the so-called "informal or underground economy.") In exchanges of property, the value will normally be established by whichever side of the transaction is more readily measured. Whether such a transaction results in income or return of capital depends upon the relationship of the value received to the cost or adjusted basis of the asset given up.

Exclusions

Congress has moderated its authority to tax "all income from whatever source derived" by mandating that a few types of income will be fully exempt from federal income tax, others will be partially exempt, and the tax on some types of income will be deferred. The more significant items which are fully exempt and not reported on the annual federal income tax returns are:

- State and local bond interest
- Life insurance proceeds

- Gifts

- Inheritances

- Social Security benefits

- Disability benefits

- Scholarships and fellowships

- Certain fringe benefits such as life insurance, health insurance, and employee discounts

The common application of the tax law to both individuals and corporations can be seen in the list of exclusions; these items are described in the Internal Revenue Code without reference to the type of taxpayer. Some of the items obviously apply only to individuals because of the nature of the income, but they are not differentiated by the tax code. Thus, interest on state and local bonds is exempt whether received by a corporation, a trust, or an individual. Similarly, life insurance proceeds are exempt whether received upon the death of a spouse or the death of the corporate president.

There are a few types of income which are only partially nontaxable:

1. Dividends received by one corporation from another corporation; 70 or 80 percent of the dividend received may be deducted (100 percent in the case of affiliated corporations)

2. A certain amount of gain on the sale of a residence by a taxpayer who is 55 or older

The present value of money plus the impact of inflation can make the deferral of tax highly advantageous. Some of the situations in which the tax is deferred are:

1. Sale and replacement (or exchange) of a personal residence

2. Exchanges of certain business assets

3. Certain types of installment sales

4. Deferred compensation contracts

5. Employer contributions (and in some circumstances employee contributions) to qualified pension plans

6. Contributions to individual retirement plans

The first two items will be discussed further in the section on property transactions.

DEDUCTIONS

As indicated earlier, Congress presumably could base the income on total income with no deductions allowed. However, substantial deductions have always been and are likely to continue to be allowed.

1. Business expenses. Both corporations and individuals are allowed, in general, to deduct expenses related to the production of income.

2. Individuals are allowed to itemize and deduct only a few personal expenses which further certain objectives:
   a. To encourage certain socially desirable activities:
      · Charitable contributions
      · Home ownership (property taxes and mortgage interest are deductible)
   b. To alleviate serious hardship:
      · Casualty losses
      · Medical expenses in excess of a substantial de minimis
   c. Expenses related to production of income, preservation of property, or tax compliance which are not deductible under the business expense category mentioned above.
   d. An individual has the option to deduct a flat amount in lieu of all itemized deductions.

Literally thousands of items may be deductible under these broad classifications. The Internal Revenue Code describes dozens of deductions in great detail (e.g., interest, taxes, depreciation, contributions, losses), but it also has several broad generic deduction sections such as "all the ordinary and necessary expenses paid or incurred during the taxable year in carrying on any trade or business."

However, there are several general concepts in the tax law that transcend all the deduction sections and identify types of expenditures that are *not* deductible even though they may appear to meet all the criteria of one or more specific deductions.

1. Capital expenditures are not deductible. Thus, otherwise deductible items, e.g., employee wages, must be capitalized

(that is, treated as additions to assets rather than as expenses) if the employee spends time constructing a new building.

2. Expenses related to the production of exempt income are not deductible. Business insurance premiums paid are a normal expense, but premiums on officer life insurance with the corporation as beneficiary are not deductible. Interest on loans the proceeds of which are used to purchase or carry tax-exempt bonds is not deductible.

3. Related party transactions. A loss on a sale to a related party is not deductible, but the loss may be used by the purchaser to offset gain on a subsequent sale. Interest or other expense paid by an accrual basis taxpayer to a related party who reports on the cash method is not deductible unless actually paid within 2½ months after the close of the year. "Related parties" include such entities as corporation and a controlling stockholder, or a partner and partnership, as well as family relationships.

4. Illegal expenses and expenditures contrary to public policy are not deductible. Thus, bribes and fines are not deductible. Some fines—such as those on overweight trucks—are often considered an ordinary cost of doing business, but they still are not deductible. It is interesting to note that although an illegal expense is disallowed, many expenses of an illegal business may well be allowed. This produces an interesting dichotomy between an "illegal expense of a legal business" (nondeductible) and a "legal expense of an illegal business" (deductible). Income from an illegal business is taxable, and the legitimate type of expense of producing that income would be deductible. Gambling may be illegal under local law, but it is not illegal under federal law. Thus, ordinary wages, rent, and utility bills are deductible. If, in order to stay in the gambling business, bribes are paid to local police or other officials, they are illegal expenditures and are not deductible.

5. Activities not entered into for profit. Normally, business profits are taxable and business losses are deductible—either from other forms of income or from profits of other years. However, income-producing activities such as some hobbies and the rental of vacation homes can be so structured that they produce losses every year or nearly every year. In such

a situation, an individual or a Subchapter S corporation may deduct only enough expenses to offset the income. A net loss is not deductible.

6. "Ordinary, necessary, reasonable." Several deduction sections in the Code include one or more of those adjectives. As a practical matter a disallowance on the ground that an expense violates any of the criteria is quite rare and arises only in related party situations. The courts have decreed that the IRS is not to substitute its judgment for that of the taxpayer or of corporate management in deciding whether or not an item is ordinary, necessary, and reasonable.

PROPERTY TRANSACTIONS

Some of the most important and more complex income tax rules relate to the acquisition, use, and disposal of property. Congress, for many years, has utilized the tax law to stimulate or dampen the economy or to encourage investments in specified types of property. One of the more popular devices for such manipulation has been the investment tax credit. The credit allows an amount, based on a percent of the cost of an asset, to be subtracted from the actual tax liability. The economic effect to the purchaser is essentially the same as a discount offered by the supplier of the asset.

Investment Tax Credit

Congress enacted the first general credit for the purchase of business equipment in 1961 to stimulate a lagging economy and encourage U.S. businesses to modernize their productive facilities. Since that time the credit has been suspended and reestablished, repealed and reenacted, increased, and made much broader in its application. In 1986 the investment tax credit was dropped, but we may well see it again when Congress feels it is needed to stimulate the economy.

Depreciation and Amortization

Probably no single area has ever created more controversy between taxpayers and tax authorities than depreciation. The tax law has always recognized that the taxpayer should be allowed to recover the cost of assets used for the production of income. However, tax as well as accounting has required that the cost of long-lived assets should be recoverable over their useful lives. This well-accepted concept has led to numerous controversies on three points: which expenditures should be capitalized, the useful life, and how rapidly the cost should be written off over the useful life.

Although the accounting notion of depreciation has been fundamental in the tax law, Congress has also used the cost write-off as one of its tools in attempting to bring about certain economic consequences. For example, a straight-line, 5-year (more specifically, 60-month) amortization was allowed on "emergency facilities" during World Wars I and II. Subsequently it was allowed for investments in "grain storage facilities" when there was a serious shortage of grain elevators. More recently, the 60-month amortization has been allowed for specified types of expenditures incurred during the specified periods; they include expenditures for railroad rolling stock, on-the-job training facilities, child-care facilities, rehabilitation of certain historic structures, rehabilitation of low-income rental housing, and certain pollution control devices.

Congress has modified the general depreciation rules several times in recent years to achieve two specified goals: (1) allow for more rapid recovery of capital expenditures and (2) reduce the level of controversy between the IRS and taxpayers. In very recent times the term "capital cost recovery" has been used frequently. "Depreciation" for tax purposes now differs markedly from the accounting concept, and perhaps it should be thought of as a capital cost recovery allowance rather than as depreciation.

An overview of the current provisions can be provided by a summary of the rules that apply to most tangible property, new or used.

1. Methods. For property acquired after 1986, taxpayers must use the Modified Accelerated Cost Recovery System (MACRS). MACRS rules classify property based on class life (3-year, 5-year, 7-year, etc. property) for purposes of determining the applicable depreciation method, the applicable recovery period, and the applicable convention (straight-line, 200 percent declining-balance, or 150 percent declining-balance methods). As long as a taxpayer uses the property class life, the decision will not be contested.

2. Salvage value. To alleviate another area of controversy, the law has specified that salvage value can be ignored in making the depreciation computation.

3. First-year bonus depreciation. This is a special first-year allowance which is of benefit primarily to small business, although it is available to all taxpayers. It allows for an immediate write-off of $10,000 for certain capital expenditures, with any remaining balance eligible for MACRS depreciation.

4. Recapture of depreciation. In general, any gain recognized upon the disposal of equipment must be reported as ordinary income up to the amount of any depreciation deducted after 1961, even if the transaction is one which otherwise would justify capital gain treatment. For all practical purposes this means that any gain on the sale or exchange of equipment will be ordinary income except in the relatively rare instance when the item is sold for a price which exceeds its original cost.

Disposition of Property

The treatment of gains and losses upon the sale or exchange of property is affected by both the nature of the asset and the type of the transaction. The rules in this area are numerous and complex. This brief discussion can cover only the more general situations, and it is important that it be used only as a base for further study or as an entree for consultation with a tax specialist. There are basically three steps in analyzing a property transaction: *determination, recognition,* and *taxation.*

First, the *determination* of the actual amount of gain or loss follows a format very similar to that of general accounting. The proceeds from the sale are compared to the "adjusted basis," which is similar in concept to the accounting net book value: cost (or other basis) plus capital additions minus depreciation and other capital recoveries. The tax "basis" of property, similarly to financial accounting, is usually cost, assuming the asset is purchased. When the asset is acquired other than by purchase, as by gift, inheritance, or any transaction in which gain or loss is postponed, the tax basis is subject to many complex rules.

The second step in considering property transactions is to learn how much of the determined gain or loss will be *recognized* for tax purposes in the current year. Generally, gains and losses are recognized except in a few very important situations such as:

1. A loss on the sale or exchange of a personal asset (e.g., personal residence) is not recognized.

2. A loss on a sale to a related party is not recognized.

3. For a taxpayer of age 55 or over, a significant amount of gain on a personal residence is not recognized in certain circumstances.

4. There are some transactions on which some or all of the gain or loss is not recognized but is deferred:
   a. On sale or exchange of a personal residence at a gain, the gain is deferred if the proceeds are reinvested in another personal residence. Gain must be recognized currently to the extent that the proceeds are not reinvested within a specified time period.
   b. Gain is not recognized on an involuntary conversion if the insurance or other proceeds are reinvested in a similar asset. Loss is recognized, and gain is recognized to the extent of any nonreinvestment proceeds.
   c. On exchanges of certain types of business assets for similar assets, loss is not recognized (i.e., is postponed) and gain is recognized only to the extent that cash or other "boot" is received. Note that this must be an exchange. The sale of a business asset accompanied by a purchase of a replacement asset does not qualify for deferral of gain or loss.
   d. A loss on the sale of stocks or bonds is not recognized if identical securities are acquired within 30 days before or after the loss transaction—the so-called "wash sale."

The third and final step, *taxation*, requires that all *recognized* gains and losses be classified as *capital* or *ordinary*. Inasmuch as long-term capital gains presently receive a slight preferential treatment for taxpayers in the 31 percent tax bracket, it is normally to those taxpayers' advantage to have *ordinary losses* and *capital gains*, since the excess of net long-term capital gains over net short-term capital losses are taxed at a maximum of 25 percent. However, once a transaction is consummated, the taxpayer has no choice; the tax rules dictate whether it is capital or ordinary. The taxpayer does have considerable planning opportunities in determining the form and the timing of the transactions, but it is essential that this planning take place in advance.

The tax law defines capital gain and loss quite narrowly, but it then allows capital treatment of other transactions in certain circumstances. A capital gain or loss arises only from the sale or exchange of a "capital asset," which is defined as all property except:

- Inventory or property held for resale in the ordinary course of business

- Real or depreciable property used in a trade or normal business

- Accounts or notes receivable

- Copyrights, compositions, letters, or memoranda created by or for the taxpayer

- And a few other relatively unimportant items.

It is evident that the definition excludes nearly all business assets except those held for investment. Thus, true capital gains or losses arise primarily from the sale or exchange of investment assets (e.g., stocks and bonds) or personal assets (e.g., personal residence).

A separate section of the Code grants capital treatment to a group of noncapital transactions, but only if gains exceed losses for the entire group. If losses exceed gains, then every transaction is treated as an ordinary gain or loss. Thus the timing of any one transaction has the potential to convert the entire group from capital to ordinary, or vice versa. The group includes all recognized gains and losses from the following transactions, but only for assets held more than one year:

- Sale or exchange of real or depreciable business assets (excluding ordinary income from the recapture of depreciation)

- Condemnation (government right of eminent domain) of business property or of capital assets

- Casualties (fire, flood, etc.) of business property or of capital assets, but only if gains from all such casualties exceed losses from all such casualties

All capital gains and losses and all items to be treated as though they were capital gains and losses are assembled and sorted into two categories: (1) short-term, items held one year or less, and (2) long-term, items held more than one year. The net gain or loss is computed for each of the two categories. The two net figures are then combined to produce either a "net capital loss" or a "net capital gain."

To this point, everything on acquisition, use, and disposition of property, including determination, recognition, and taxation, has applied in essentially the same fashion to both corporations and individuals. The treatment of the final net capital gain or net capital loss differs somewhat for individuals and corporations.

Net Capital Gain

If the comparison of the net short-term and net long-term figures results in a net capital gain, it is then necessary to look back at the two preceding figures to find if there is an "excess of net *long-term* capital gain over net short-term capital loss." It is the "excess," if any, which is given beneficial tax treatment. Here are some examples:

NSTCG	10,000 ⎱	NCG $ 7,000	No excess; $7,000 is taxed as
NLTCL	(3,000) ⎰		ordinary income.
NSTCL	(4,000) ⎱	NCG $ 9,000	Excess is $9,000 and is treated
NLTCG	13,000 ⎰		as described below.
NSTCG	5,000 ⎱	NCG $16,000	Excess is $11,000 (NSTCL is
NLTCG	11,000 ⎰		zero).

Corporations are not allowed any special advantage for net long-term capital gains.

Net Capital Loss

Corporations get no current deduction for net capital loss, but the loss can be carried back and forward several years to offset capital gains in those years. The carryover item is considered a short-term loss, regardless of the nature of the original loss transactions.

Individuals can deduct a limited amount from their ordinary income for net capital loss. In computing the deduction, the portion of the net capital loss which arose from the short-term transactions is used first. Individuals may carry all unused losses forward in the original short- or long-term category until they have been consumed.

CREDITS AGAINST TAX

Credits were relatively little known in the early years, but their use has increased appreciably since the early 1960s. Unlike a deduction, a credit gives a full dollar-for-dollar tax savings and provides the same amount of tax savings regardless of the taxpayers' marginal tax bracket.

Several credits are available to both corporations and individuals or only to individuals.

RATE STRUCTURE

One of the basic tenets of the U.S. income tax law has always been that the burden should be shared on the basis of "ability to pay." Thus, individuals have been taxed on a progressive rate basis; taxpayers with higher incomes have paid more tax. Sometimes it is assumed that each additional dollar of income will pay more tax than the preceding dollar. Some interpret a "progressive" rate schedule to mean that not only does the tax increase as incomes go up but the rates themselves increase. The latter two concepts would produce tax rates at or approaching 100 percent at the upper levels, and Congress has not viewed that as reasonable.

It can be argued that the "ability to pay" concept is relevant only to individuals. A corporation as an artificial entity really has no "ability to pay" per se. Any tax paid by a corporation is ultimately borne by people, e.g., stockholders, employees, customers, through lower dividends, lower wages, or higher prices. Economists have attempted for years, and unsuccessfully, to measure the true "incidence" of the corporate tax, i.e., how much is passed on to each group. The ultimate burden is shifted to someone, and it is not possible for it to be passed on to individuals in proportion to their ability to pay. Nevertheless, the corporate tax tables reflect considerable progression, more at present, in fact, than for individuals.

The "marginal rate" is the percent of tax that will be paid on the next dollar of income. This is the rate that is relevant in most tax planning decisions.

Earlier discussions have included several features of the tax law which modify the rate progressions, sometimes rather substantially. For example, the marginal federal tax rate on state and local bond interest is zero, whether the interest is received by an individual or a corporation.

Alternative Minimum Tax (Both Individuals and Corporations)

Congress, especially in recent years, has frequently used the tax law to motivate taxpayers to make certain investments or to influence economic behavior in some other way. When the taxpayer reacts as Congress wishes, some type of preferential tax treatment is granted. As Congress increased such preferences, it became apparent that some taxpayers—including some with very high incomes—were able to avail themselves of tax preferences sufficient to eliminate all tax liability. Congress decided the preferences were still needed but that no one should use them to avoid tax entirely. Therefore, Congress identified certain of the tax preferences and ruled that at least a minimum tax should be paid thereon. The more common preference items relate to depletion in excess of the adjusted basis of the interest, intangible drilling costs, depreciation in excess of the straight-line amount, and, for individuals, certain itemized deductions such as medical expenses, charitable contributions, and miscellaneous itemized deductions, among others.

TAX SHELTERS

In recent years, much has been written about "tax shelters," but with no real agreement on definitions and with a great deal of myth and misinformation. Some define shelters very broadly to include anything that allows any income to be free of income tax. That view of shelters would encompass such provisions as the personal exemption, the exemption of Social Security benefits, and the exemption of state and local bond interest, all of which are available to taxpayers at all levels of income.

A narrower, and more common, view of tax shelters relates to the various investment vehicles structured to take advantage of various benefits in the tax law which allow taxpayers to offset ordinary income from other sources. Certain basic features of tax shelters are fairly common:

· Maximum tax deductions are allowed in the first year or two.

· Income is deferred until later years.

· The income is realized as long-term capital gain when possible.

· The entity is usually a partnership (often a limited partnership) in order that the benefit of the deductions can flow through to the owners immediately.

It is not unusual for investors to receive tax deductions of 60 to 80 percent of their investments in the first year and 100 percent in the first two or three years. In certain circumstances it is still possible to deduct substantially more than the total investment, although an "at risk" rule was adopted to stop some of the more flagrant abuses. Typically, the shelter partnership uses substantial borrowed capital and thereby can generate deductions far in excess of the partners' investments. Under present rules each limited partner is allowed to deduct losses only to the extent of the actual investment, the amount for which the partner is at risk. When it has been determined that the loss is deductible under the at-risk rules, then the passive activity loss rules are then applied.

The passive activity loss rules were made significantly more detailed and complex in the 1986 tax code. Many new provisions were added, and considerable time, and litigation, will be required to determine what they all mean and how they ought to be applied. Any taxpayer involved in such passive activities is well advised to consult with a tax specialist. Here, therefore, we will consider, only briefly, the broad aspects of the tax law.

A passive activity is any activity which involves the conduct of a trade or business in which the taxpayer *does not* materially participate. Thus, a passive activity is not determined by the nature of the activity per se— any type of activity can be passive—but, rather, by the degree of participation in the activity by the taxpayer.

The basic rule is that losses from a passive activity are only deductible against income from a passive activity. You cannot, for example, deduct a passive loss against wages and salary income. Unused passive losses are not lost, however, but are suspended (carried over) until they can be offset by passive income in a future tax year, until the entire activity is disposed of in a fully taxable transaction, or until the taxpayer dies. As you can visualize, it might be years before a passive loss could be deductible, thereby postponing the reduction of taxes which have to be paid. This is a disincentive for investing in such activities.

There are several areas of concern or potential problems to be aware of:

- First, and foremost, a tax shelter should be examined on its merits as an investment, not merely as a means of tax savings.

- Income is usually deferred several years.

- The investor may not be able to sell out easily.

- Just as early deductions may exceed cash outflow, later taxable income may exceed cash inflow.

- There may be substantial gain or income on termination of the shelter with little or no cash received at that time with which to pay tax.

SUMMARY

Corporations and individuals are subject to the federal income tax as described in the Internal Revenue Code, which contains thousands of pages of complex and specific rules. Although most basic tax concepts and many of the rules relating to income, exclusions, deductions, and credits apply to both types of taxpayers, there are some important distinctions. Through proper economic and business planning, taxpayers often have an opportunity to reduce their tax liability. It is legal and ethical to structure one's affairs in such a way as to minimize taxes so long as one complies with the law. In these few pages we have examined the basic structure of the tax law and looked at some of the areas in which tax planning opportunities are available.

TEST PROBLEMS

1. In tax vocabulary one can see two similar sounding terms: "ability to pay" and "wherewithal to pay." Contrast the two terms and discuss their application to the tax law.

2. From time to time, bills have been introduced into Congress to grant tax relief for college expenses. Some have proposed a "deduction" of, say, $1,000; others have proposed a "credit" of, say, $300. *(a)* Contrast a tax deduction and a tax credit. (b) What is the principal argument in favor of each action?

3. We need to replace a piece of earthmoving equipment which cost $40,000 six years ago. Depreciation of $28,000 has been deducted during the 6 years. The manufacturer will sell us the new item we need for $50,000 cash or will allow us to trade in the old unit and pay a cash difference of $21,000. Alternatively, we can sell the old unit to a paving contractor in a neighboring city for $29,000. Thus, our net cash outlay will be $21,000 either way. (a) Discuss the tax considerations involved. (b) How would the tax considerations change if depreciation deducted in the past 6 years had been $7,000 rather than $28,000 and all other facts were unchanged? (c) If the market for used earthmoving equipment were very tight and we were able to sell our old unit for $43,000, describe the tax consequences. (Assume the $28,000 depreciation example.)

17
Personal Computers and Their Software

Background

Hundreds of firms produce personal computers and thousands develop software of every type and form, from fairly simple word-processing programs to very elaborate ones concerned with complex quantitative analysis. Of course, here we are concerned only with accounting software packages, but there are large numbers, even of those alone.

In this chapter we will not be concerned with trying to recommend hardware or software for you to buy, for one simple reason—*it would be impossible to do in any useful way!* It is impossible because you (the readers) are so diverse in your needs, and it is those needs which mainly determine the type of computer and the particular accounting software package required to fulfill those needs. What we can do, though, is discuss some of the basic guidelines for helping you to make the selections. These discussions are not intended to be exhaustive but only indicative of what needs to be done.

Personal Computers (Hardware)

The first question, of course, is, "Do you need a computerized system at all, or is a manual system better?" For most of you, this decision probably has been made by others in your firm, particularly if you are employed by medium- or large-sized businesses. Some of you, however, particularly owners, managers, and employees of small businesses, may still be grappling with this problem. The answer, of course, depends on weighing the costs of each system against the benefits of each system in making the selection—it is a cost/benefit analysis.

Two types of costs are involved. First, are the explicit, out-of-pocket costs associated with each alternative. These costs are relatively easy to estimate and compare. For example:

1. The costs of computer hardware and software must be compared with the costs of bookkeepers' wages and manual accounting records. Competent computer operators often can demand higher salaries than bookkeepers, but, on the other hand, fewer individuals are needed, in many cases, to run a computer system.

2. Microcomputers must be repaired and maintained. The operators must be trained and then retrained as new technologies come into existence. These can cause downtime and delays unless there is a backup system.

The second type of costs to consider in making the decision are the "implicit" costs, often difficult to codify, of choosing one alternative versus the other. Stated another way, these are the costs associated with benefits lost if one alternative is chosen rather than the other. Such costs ultimately find their way into the income statement and reduce profits; they simply are not so obvious, they are more difficult to measure, and they are easier to overlook. For example, computerized systems can process data much more rapidly than a manual system, particularly if real time processing is used, and therefore are at a distinct advantage in situations (1) where the number of transactions is large; e.g., large numbers of accounts receivable or accounts payable, significant numbers of different types of inventory items, large numbers of employees, and/or (2) where relatively complex analyses of data are needed.

As an illustration, businesses strive to maintain an optimum inventory level. In simplest terms, inventory must be sufficient to take care of customer and production needs, including a reasonable margin of safety for unexpected events, but not larger than that. If a customer comes in for an item normally carried by a retailer and is told none is on hand but that the retailer would be pleased to order the item, the customer is likely to go to a competitor and may never return. Or, if a component is not on hand when needed on the assembly line, production has to be halted. In either case, these situations translate into reduced sales and/or increased costs, reducing the profits of the firm.

However, maintaining excess inventories is costly and wasteful.

Profit is earned when inventories are used or sold. If funds are used to acquire and carry excess inventories, the firm loses the income that could have been earned by investing those funds productively, again reducing the bottom-line profits. With proper programs, microcomputers can aid in maintaining optimum inventory levels and thereby preventing such problems.

Numerous other examples could be cited, such as paying bills on time to ensure discounts are taken when available and to maintain a good credit rating or collecting receivables as soon as possible to ensure that excess funds are not unnecessarily, and unproductively, tied up in accounts receivable.

On the other side, problems can arise when personal computers are improperly programmed or errors are made by the operator when inputing data. You all know the term "GIGO"—garbage-in, garbage-out. Many who have received a bill containing an error know the difficulty often involved in getting such errors corrected.

Take, for example, errors in credit reports as reported on TV and in newspapers. The scenario often runs like this: A customer applies for a loan at the bank, the money needed quickly for business or personal reasons, only to be turned down because of an input error on his or her credit report. It is not the error which is so devastating—most people recognize that we all make mistakes and are reasonably tolerant when they are made—it is the time and effort involved to get it corrected, often spanning many months. Meanwhile, approval of the loan is delayed, and the money isn't available when needed for the business or personal use. The firm creating the error ends up with a public relations problem, which, again, can result in reduced sales and/or increased costs and fewer profits. Usually, such errors are more quickly corrected in a manual system because you can deal with the person directly responsible for the error and the one, often, who has the authority to correct the error.

If a general conclusion is appropriate, it is this. The *net* advantage usually rests on the side of using computerized accounting systems, if management is to be efficient and effective, even in relatively small businesses. More timely, complex data are needed in this era of increased complexities in the business environment. These complexities include environmental concerns, more complex tax laws, increased consumer demands, greater need for cost containment in a highly competitive business world, and increased local and national regulations. As we have said in other places in this text, the best advice is to obtain the services of an expert in both computer accounting software and accounting systems to help you decide. And this advice is sound, also, when selecting a personal computer.

Computer Programs (Software)

"Selecting accounting software is tricky business, demanding plenty of time and careful research—even for the relatively inexpensive PC-based packages available."[1] The fundamental objectives in selecting a computer program is to get one compatible with your microcomputer, one that fulfills your needs, and one that is "failsafe." The first is easy to accomplish, the second and third are more difficult. Let's discuss a few of the more basic guidelines to help in the selection.

First, numerous software catalogues list accounting software packages, briefly describe what the software will do, indicate the personal computers with which the program is compatible, and list the price. The software packages range all the way from relatively simple programs for the preparation of individual tax returns to highly complex, sophisticated, and integrated programs which will bill customers, keep track of all needed payroll data, pay vendors, and prepare financial statements and analyze them. Even if you have little technical knowledge about accounting software packages, and assuming your needs are relatively simple (such as a bookkeeping program to help you take care of your personal accounting requirements), you may be able to use the software catalogues to choose a software package. However, you should try out the software in-house, using your data, to make sure it provides the information you desire.

Second, many good computer magazines contain articles describing and rating accounting computer software, including some of the more complex integrated systems. These can be very helpful in providing information regarding the software packages and generating questions for you to discuss with a professional in making the correct decision. But again, the overriding guideline, before purchasing a program, is to try it out in-house to determine whether it accomplishes what you need it to do and to establish that it doesn't have any bugs and deficiencies. The following quotes advice from *Datamation:*

A good start on the road to locating potential software vendors may be three products from Computer Training Services Inc., of Rockville, Md. CTS publishes an annual survey of microcomputer accounting product evaluations; a 250-page guide to selecting accounting software; and a Lotus 1-2-3 template ("A Do-It-Yourself Software-Rating System"), which automates your own product evaluation.

The 1992 survey, the company's fifth annual, presents scores and comments from 160 CPAs and consultants who install and recommend

[1] Ned Snell, "Top Accountants Rate Accounting Software," *Datamation,* June 1, 1992, p. 80.

accounting software. They rate nine of the leading MS-DOS-based integrated accounting packages. . . .

CTS also includes comments, but not ratings, for five more packages: AccountMate from SourceMate Information Systems Inc., BusinessWorks from Manzanita Software Systems, CYMA Professional Accounting Series from Cyma Systems Inc., Libra from Libra Corp. and SBT Database Accounting Library from SBT Corp.[2]

In any case, you should not ask advice from hardware vendors, since they often have little knowledge about accounting and accounting systems. Choosing the top-selling package is not a good approach either, since it may not fulfill your specific needs.

Again, the best advice is to retain the services of a professional who is competent and knowledgeable in both accounting and computer software to analyze your needs and help you select a package specific to those needs. Initially taking the easy, quick, least costly approach could well create serious impacts on your business later on, if the package turns out not to fit your needs. As the *Datamation* article says, ". . . the price of a bad decision—including lost productivity and the cost of migrating to and retraining for a replacement accounting package—grows."[3]

[2]Ibid., p. 81.
[3]Ibid., p. 81.

18
Consolidated Statements

What Is a Consolidated Statement?

Basically a consolidated balance sheet, or income statement, is one in which we have combined the financial data of two or more affiliated companies in accordance with certain rules of the game.

But why in the world should we combine the data of two or more companies? Answer: Under appropriate circumstances a combined (consolidated) statement of two or more companies conveys financial information better than if our financial report presented the statements of each company separately.

For example, if our company, in addition to its cash, inventories, machinery, buildings, etc., owns as a long-term investment all of the outstanding capital stock of another company, we could present our company's own (legal) balance sheet and it would show, among the noncurrent assets, its investment in the other company. That investment would probably be shown at cost, as noncurrent assets are customarily shown. Then, for us to analyze the financial position of our company, we would need to "look behind" the investment; that is, we would also want to see the current balance sheet of the other company, particularly if the cost of our company's investment in the other company constituted a significant element among our company's assets.

The task of examining our company's legal balance sheet and also the legal statement of the other company might be relatively easy. Because our company owns 100 percent of the stock of the other company (i.e., we own the whole works), we would probably add together, mentally or on paper, the cash of our company and that of the other (subsidiary) company to determine our overall cash position. We would also add together the assets of each other category and then add together the liabilities. In other words, ownership of stock in our company at the same time effectively constitutes ownership in the other (subsidiary) company. Now, if the officers and directors of our company, through our company's ownership of all the stock of the other company, can control all the affairs of the other company, just as if that company were a mere branch of our company, why don't we save the reader a lot of bother and combine the statements for him? That's just what we do; only instead of calling the result a combined statement, we call it a *consolidated statement.*

You should now be ready for a definition. A consolidated balance sheet is one which presents the assets, liabilities, and owners' equities of two or more affiliated companies in a single balance sheet *as if the affiliated companies were a single legal entity.* Let's face it. We're not really dealing with a single legal entity, we're dealing with two or more entities. So please observe now, and remember, that every consolidated statement contains an element of fiction: The statements are drawn up *as if* they represented a single entity even though they truly consolidate the data of a parent company and its subsidiary companies.

Once again let's remember that a balance sheet lists (1) the assets owned by the corporate entity, (2) the liabilities owed to outsiders by the corporate entity, and (3) the (residual) equity of the owners.

Why Isn't a Consolidated Statement a Combined Statement?

To prepare a simple, *combined* balance sheet for two or more companies would involve nothing more than listing all the cash, all the receivables, and all the "everything else," but then you would not have a consolidated statement. So please hold on tight as we travel through the next sentences. If we present the separate, legal balance sheets of two companies, we'll show *all* the assets and *all* the liabilities of each. If we consolidate the two, any debts that one owes to the other will be canceled out (for consolidation purposes only) because when the two are hypothetically brought together *as a single entity,* such debts cease to be owed to or by outsiders.

The key to the preparation of consolidated statements lies in recognizing the need for eliminating mirror items. By *mirror items* we mean items that, figuratively, bridge the space between two separate but affiliated corporations. If you consolidate their statements, you eliminate the space between them and, in so doing, eliminate the bridges. Such a bridge, or pair of mirror items, is the $100 debt that the other company owes our company. On our legal balance sheet it shows as a $100 account receivable, while on their legal balance sheet it shows as a $100 account payable. If, then, we consolidate and make up a single balance sheet, the $100 item is eliminated because it becomes, for this purpose only, strictly an internal debt (within the family). Thus, in the case of your own company, when an employee signs out a tool from the toolroom, he owes something to the toolroom and the toolroom has a claim against him, but since this liability-receivable relationship is all intramural, it would not show up on your balance sheet.

A consolidated statement is in a true sense a fiction. It brings together what would otherwise be the separate, legal statements of two or more affiliated companies, and, in so doing, it shaves off all mirrored items so as to avoid duplication.

Consolidation Buzz Words

The accountant's vocabulary includes a bunch of words that relate primarily to consolidated statement matters. A preview of them will save our stopping for definitions when we look into the actual process of making consolidated statements. Here are some, but certainly not all, of the buzz words. The definitions are loosely presented, since few formal definitions exist.

AFFILIATES: Companies are said to be affiliated when they have more or less permanent relationships, usually through stock ownership. For our purposes, when Company A owns an influential portion of the total voting stock of Company B, we will refer to A and B as affiliated companies, or simply as affiliates.

PARENT COMPANY: When one affiliate owns a "controlling interest" in the stock of another company (also an affiliate), the owner company is the parent company. Technically, to be a parent company requires more than 50 percent ownership interest in the affiliate's stock, but this requirement is subject to relaxation when the owner company, as a practical matter, controls the affairs of the other company.

SUBSIDIARY COMPANY: The affiliate whose stock is owned by a parent company is the subsidiary company. It is, of course, possible for Company A to exercise overwhelming influence over Company B while holding less than 50 percent of B stock, and consolidated statements may be required in that case.

MAJORITY INTEREST: A majority interest refers to the stockholding of the parent company; it must be more than 50 percent of the stock which the subsidiary has outstanding.

MINORITY INTEREST: A minority interest refers to shares of subsidiary stock held by persons, corporations, etc., other than the parent corporation. Thus, if the parent holds a 51 percent majority interest, the minority shareholder, or shareholders altogether, hold the remaining 49 percent, which could be held by any number of minority stockholders from one to many.

CONTROLLING INTEREST: If a corporation (or a person) owns more than 50 percent of the outstanding voting (usually common) stock of another corporation, it has considerable power to control the decisions of that corporation, including the determination of who shall be its officers and directors and the determination of dividend declarations. In fact, when ownership of the balance of the voting stock is widely scattered, such decision control can be exercised through holdings of much less than 50 percent of the total shares. On the other hand, serious obstacles to the exercise of such control sometimes exist, as when the company the majority of the stock of which is owned is located in a foreign country which is sustaining internal upheaval such as severe economic crisis or armed revolt.

In short, a controlling interest exists only when supported in fact by exercisable power to control the subsidiary company. The presumption is that when control exists in both the technical (over 50 percent) and effective sense, the financial statements are to be consolidated. When control exists in the practical sense but with holdings under 50 percent, the general opinion is that a substitute concept should be employed to depict the fact of control. That concept is referred to as the "equity" method of recording investments in another company. It consists of accruing, as an addition to the reported amount of the investment, the investor company's percent share of the earnings or losses of the investee company with corresponding credit or debit to a revenue account which might be labeled "Equity in Earnings of Affiliated Company." As a rule, the allowed minimum holding in instances such as this is 20 percent of the outstanding voting stock of the investee company.

INTERCOMPANY ITEMS: These are the mirror items referred to earlier. The major examples are:

1. Parent makes a loan (advance) of $100,000 to Subsidiary. On Parent's books the loan is a receivable; on Subsidiary's books

(and on Subsidiary's legal statement) the same loan is a liability. As a group, these cases are referred to as intercompany debt. It shows as debit items on lender's books and credit (liability) items on borrower's books. Both disappear upon consolidation.

2. Parent owns 51 percent of Subsidiary common stock. On Parent's *legal* statement this stock is shown as a single figure labeled Investment in Subsidiary. On Subsidiary's *legal* statement this stock doesn't show separately but is included as part of the total stock outstanding. (Let's refresh our memories here. Each corporation, even though an affiliate, remains a separate legal entity, and its "legal" statement is its own balance sheet or income statement, not a consolidated one. A consolidated statement combines the legal statements of two or more affiliated companies.)

3. Parent sells merchandise to Subsidiary. On their respective legal statements the sales by Parent are shown in their entirety, as are the purchases by Subsidiary. In effecting a consolidated statement, with the companies' statements combined, these intercompany sales and purchases fade out since, *as a family,* the transactions are the same as if they were mere movements of goods from one department to another within a single enterprise.

4. When one affiliate sells something to a subsidiary at a profit, the price (cost) of the thing to be recorded on the buyer's books is higher than it was on the seller's books. This markup is reflected *(a)* in a higher price (cost) on the buyer's books and *(b)* in retained earnings on the seller's books. Thus, "intercompany profits," so long as the marked-up item remains in the family, constitutes an intercompany item. There are numerous other forms of intercompany items, but these should suffice for your understanding of their nature.

Elimination Entries

So-called *elimination entries* must be made for *all intercompany items.* Thank goodness, they all fit neatly into our basic debit-credit structure. Let's introduce them by an example. In the preceding section, the example given for what was there listed as group 1 items had Parent lending $100,000 cash to Subsidiary. You know that on Parent's books making the loan would be recorded by the following entry:

(1)

Advance to Subsidiary	100,000	
Cash in Bank		100,000

To record loan of $100,000 to our affiliate, Subsidiary Co.

On the books of Subsidiary, the receipt of the cash from Parent would be recorded as follows:

(2)

Cash	100,000	
Advance from Parent		100,000

To record receipt of cash advance from our affiliate, Parent Co.

In these entries you should clearly recognize the intercompany items (Advance to Subsidiary and Advance from Parent). Now, when the position statements of Parent and Subsidiary are to be consolidated, we must first make the following eliminating entry. (Later, we'll note that the eliminating entries are made only on the work sheet—not on actual books.)

(3)

Advance from Parent	100,000	
Advance to Subsidiary		100,000

To eliminate intercompany items resulting from advance from Parent to Subsidiary.

The second group of intercompany items listed in the preceding section consisted of intercompany stockholdings; Parent owns more than 50 percent of the outstanding voting stock of Subsidiary. Assume that Parent had bought 90 percent of Subsidiary common stock from the present stockholders of Subsidiary for $1,170,000 cash, at a time when the stockholders' equity section of Subsidiary's legal position statement stood as follows:

SUBSIDIARY CO.
Stockholders' Equity, December 31, 19XX

Capital stock, common, $10 par	$1,000,000
Retained earnings	300,000
	$1,300,000

The entry to record this acquisition on Parent's books is:

(4)

Investment in Subsidiary Stock	1,170,000	
Cash in Bank		1,170,000

To record purchase of 90% of Subsidiary common
stock for cash.

What entry would be made on Subsidiary's books? Of course, there
would be none. Subsidiary's stock outstanding merely changed hands,
and there is no direct effect on Subsidiary's assets or equities. However,
the mirror item is already on Subsidiary's books in the form of existing
stockholders' equity, and we'll again have to do some eliminating in the
process of consolidating. Here's the way it's done:

(5)

Capital Stock Common, $10 par (90%)	900,000	
Retained Earnings (90%)	270,000	
Investment in Subsidiary Stock		1,170,000

To eliminate intercompany 90% stock ownership as of
date of acquisition.

Entry 5 needs more clarification. When Parent bought up 90 percent
of the outstanding stock of Subsidiary, it acquired 90 percent of the
Subsidiary stockholders' equity. In a sense, 90 percent of the $1,300,000
stock equity (or $1,170,000) is now "owed" to Parent (and Parent has
a sort of claim of the same amount against Subsidiary). This intercompany item is made up of 90 percent of the stock and 90 percent of the
retained earnings (at date of the stock purchase by Parent—at "acquisition" date). Before we proceed to the next group, note that the $1,170,-
000 cost of shares assumed in our example exactly matched 90 percent
of the stock equity as it stood on the books of Subsidiary. Such perfect
matching will rarely occur in real life, and we'll run into problems of
accounting for the disparities. Entries shown later will demonstrate the
handling of these cases.

The third group of intercompany items consists of intercompany
sales of merchandise. Assume that Parent, during a given year, makes
cash sales totaling $500,000 to Subsidiary. The entries on both sets of
books are:

(6)

On Parent's Books

Cash	500,000	
Sales		500,000

(7)

On Subsidiary's Books

Purchases	500,000	
Cash in Bank		500,000

The intercompany, or duplicating, items in entries 6 and 7 are Sales and Purchases. The obvious eliminating entries for purposes of consolidation are:

(8)

Sales	500,000	
Purchases		500,000

The fourth group of intercompany items includes the "unrealized profit" (the markup) on assets, of whatever kind, sold by one affiliate to another *and remaining in the hands of the purchaser* affiliate as of the date of our consolidated statement. Please bear in mind that the profit is truly realized so far as the selling and buying entities are concerned, but when the balance sheets (and income statements) of the affiliates are *consolidated,* the profit lodged in any assets is strictly "in house" profit and must be treated as unrealized. If we didn't eliminate it, the profit would make room for some first-class shenanigans. For instance, Parent could buy a ping-pong ball for $.25 and sell it to Subsidiary (on account) for $1; without elimination entries, the consolidated position statement would show the ball at "cost" of $1 and would include a $.75 gain in the Retained Earnings account of Parent. For real fun, bounce the ping-pong ball back and forth between Parent and Subsidiary, with each buying it at one price and immediately reselling it at a higher price to the other. We might end up with the world's first million-dollar ping-pong ball!

Now for an illustration refer again to entries 6 and 7, where Parent sold merchandise to Subsidiary for $500,000. We then made an elimination entry 8 to cancel the mirrored sales/purchases of $500,000. Next assume that Subsidiary has resold 80 percent of these goods to outsiders before the end of the accounting period. Subsidiary's position statement will still include 20 percent of the $500,000, or $100,000, priced at the intercompany sales price. Now assume that the goods include a markup by Parent of 40 percent of selling price. Clearly, then, the goods remaining on Subsidiary's shelves had a cost *to the family* of only $60,000, and $40,000 of *unrealized profit* must be eliminated by the following entry:

(9)

Retained Earnings (Parent)	40,000	
Inventories (Subsidiary)		40,000

To eliminate the $40,000 of unrealized profit in Subsidiary inventory.

You might wonder why we don't also eliminate the intercompany profit on the remaining $400,000 of sales from Parent to Subsidiary. The answer is that, to the degree that Subsidiary resells goods bought from Parent, Subsidiary's expenses (cost of goods sold) will be inflated by an amount which matches the profit we allowed Parent to claim. That is, Subsidiary resold $400,000 of the goods which had been marked up by $160,000, so Subsidiary's cost of goods sold is inflated by that amount, which exactly offsets the $160,000 profit that we allowed Parent to claim when we eliminated only $40,000 of the $200,000 gain that Parent booked from the sales. We'll do some further tinkering with this subject in illustrating consolidated income statements.

Where Are Elimination Entries Recorded?

By now you must be wondering how it is possible to record a journal entry in which a debit is made to an account on one entity's books and the related credit is made to an account on another entity's books. For instance, in entry 8 we debited Sales to eliminate intercompany sales from Parent's financial data and we credited Purchases for the same amount to eliminate the mirrored item from Subsidiary's financial data —all to match the data ready for consolidation. (We might insert here that a consolidated statement can properly be called a *combined* statement of the financial data of affiliated entities *after* the effects of intercompany transactions have been eliminated.)

The answer to our pending question is that the elimination journal entries *are not made in any set of books.* The *legal* accounting records of Parent and the legal accounting records of Subsidiary are not touched in the consolidation process. Each entity may, if desirable, issue its legal financial statements. The entries are entirely hypothetical and need not actually be written down anywhere just so long as you see to it that you do eliminate all the intercompany items before you combine the statements.

In actual practice the preparation of consolidated statements is usually done on a multicolumn work sheet. What you do is list the legal balance sheet data of Parent in the first pair of columns; list the data of

Subsidiary in the next pair of columns; make all necessary debit and credit elimination entries in the third pair of columns; and then combine (consolidate) what's left. If your company has one or more subsidiaries, you might ask the accountant in charge of preparing consolidated statements to show you his consolidated working papers and explain them to you.

Because in this book we're concerned with the understanding rather than the mechanics of accounting, in our consolidation examples, coming up next, we will not utilize work sheets. Instead, we will employ a journal entry procedure because it is more flexible and useful for our particular purposes.

Consolidation of Balance Sheets at Acquisition Date

Assume that Parent Co. buys 80 percent of the outstanding common stock of Subsidiary Co. on January 1, 19XX, for $120,000 and that the legal balance sheet data of the two companies, in condensed form, stand as follows on that date just after Parent Co. buys the stock:

	Parent Co.	*Subsidiary Co.*
Assets		
Current	$100,000	$ 50,000
Investment in S Co. (cost)	120,000	—
Plant (net)	80,000	100,000
	$300,000	$150,000
Equities		
Current liabilities	$ 40,000	$ 20,000
Capital stock	150,000	100,000
Retained earnings	110,000	30,000
	$300,000	$150,000

If we wish to prepare a consolidated balance sheet immediately after the stock acquisition, what elimination entries must we make before we combine the data? For the sake of simplicity, assume that the two companies have had no dealings with each other. Then the only elimination items are the investment account on Parent's books and 80 percent of the stockholders' equity on Subsidiary's books. The needed elimination entry (with one item temporarily omitted) is:

(9)

Capital Stock—Subsidiary (80%)	80,000	
Retained Earnings (at date of acquisition)—Subsidiary (80%)	24,000	
Balance	16,000	
Investment in Subsidiary		120,000

To eliminate intercompany investment and corresponding capital stock and "purchased" retained earnings.

What do we do about the $16,000 tentatively labeled "balance"? The traditional answer is that it must represent a mix of two things: (1) unrecognized appreciation (or inflation) assignable to the various assets owned by Subsidiary Co. and (2) goodwill. The accepted rule is to replace the balance with debits to *Subsidiary asset accounts,* insofar as such write-ups are justified, and charge only any leftover balance to *consolidated goodwill.* So if we assume that Subsidiary's current assets are up to date but that the plant has a current appraised value of $110,000, we replace "balance" by a debit to Plant of $10,000 and to Goodwill of $6,000 and revise the entry as follows:

(9a)

Capital Stock—Subsidiary	80,000	
Retained Earnings—Subsidiary	24,000	
Plant	10,000	
Goodwill	6,000	
Investment in Subsidiary		120,000

Preparation of a consolidated balance sheet now requires only that we combine the original data, as modified by our "eliminating" entry. Our consolidated statement (with helpful notations) becomes as shown in Figure 18.1.

Figure 18.1 Consolidated position statement, January 1, 19X1

PARENT CO. AND SUBSIDIARY CO.
Consolidated Position Statement, January 1, 19X1

Assets		Equities		
Current (sum)	$150,000	Current liabilities (sum)		$ 60,000
Plant (sum plus $10,000)	190,000	Minority interest (20% of Subsidiary equity)		26,000
Goodwill (new item)	6,000	Stockholders' equity:		
		Capital stock	$150,000	
		Retained earnings	110,000	260,000
	$346,000			$346,000

Consolidated Balance Sheet Sometime Later

Ten years have passed since Parent acquired its 80 percent interest in Subsidiary, and we are now expected to prepare the annual consolidated balance sheet. The statement data at this moment stand as follows in the books of the two affiliates:

	Parent Co.	Subsidiary Co.
Assets		
Current	$150,000	$ 75,000
Investment in S Co. (cost)	120,000	—
Plant (net)	120,000	150,000
	$390,000	$225,000
Equities		
Current liabilities	$ 60,000	$ 30,000
Capital stock	150,000	100,000
Retained earnings	180,000	95,000
	$390,000	$225,000

Assume that (1) Parent now owes Subsidiary $10,000, (2) the current assets of Parent include merchandise inventory purchased from Subsidiary on which Subsidiary recorded profit of $5,000, (3) the plant adjustment in entry 9a must be reduced to reflect depreciation of $8,000, and (4) the goodwill adjustment in entry 9a must be reduced to reflect amortization of $1,500. As before, our first step is to prepare the necessary elimination (and adjusting) entries. They are:

(10)

Capital Stock	80,000	
Retained Earnings (80% of amount at acquisition, as before)	24,000	
Plant	10,000	
Goodwill	6,000	
Investment in Subsidiary		120,000

To eliminate intercompany investment, corresponding capital stock, and "purchased" retained earnings and to recognize the $16,000 amount paid in excess of book value as an adjustment of Plant and Goodwill of Subsidiary.

(11)

Retained Earnings (Parent)	9,500	
Plant		8,000
Goodwill		1,500

To charge off against consolidated retained earnings the amounts indicated as accumulated depreciation and amortization, respectively, of plant and goodwill adjustments made at date of acquisition.

(12)

Current Liabilities	10,000	
Current Assets		10,000

To eliminate intercompany debt.

(13)

Retained Earnings (Subsidiary)	5,000	
Current Assets		5,000

To eliminate unrealized Subsidiary profits from inventories of Parent.

Our final "elimination" entry is not actually an elimination. Rather, it consists of splitting the retained earnings of Subsidiary between the minority and the parent company majority interests. We have already reduced Subsidiary's retained earnings by $5,000 in entry 13, leaving a balance of $90,000. Of this, 20 percent belongs to the minority and the rest (less the $24,000 "purchased" at acquisition date) goes to consolidated retained earnings. This may all be put in journal entry form as follows:

(14)

Retained Earnings (Subsidiary) (95,000–5,000 in entry 13)	90,000	
Minority Interest (20%)		18,000
Investment Account (already entered in 9*a*)		24,000
Consolidated Retained Earnings		48,000

To allocate retained earnings of Subsidiary between minority and consolidated (majority) interests.

We are now ready to combine the leftovers in a consolidated balance sheet, which is shown as Figure 18.2.

Figure 18.2   Consolidated position statement, ten years later.

PARENT CO. AND SUBSIDIARY CO.
Consolidated Position Statement, Ten Years Later

Assets		Equities		
Current (sum minus $10,000 and $5,000)	$210,000	Current liabilities (sum less $10,000)		$ 80,000
Plant (sum plus $10,000 less $8,000)	272,000	Minority interest (20% of $195,000 less $5,000)		38,000
Goodwill ($6,000 less $1,500)	4,500	Stockholders' equity: Capital stock	$150,000	
		Retained earnings ($180,000 minus $9,500, plus $48,000)	218,500	368,500
	$486,500			$486,500

Consolidation of Income Statements

To illustrate the preparation of a consolidated income statement, assume the following income statement data for the tenth year of affiliation:

	Parent Co.	Subsidiary Co.
Sales	$200,000	$100,000
Cost of goods sold	$120,000	$ 60,000
Other expenses and taxes	60,000	30,000
	$180,000	$ 90,000
Net income	$ 20,000	$ 10,000

Assume as before that Parent owns 80 percent of the outstanding common stock of Subsidiary, that $90,000 of the sales of Subsidiary were
shipments to Parent, and that by year-end Parent had resold $40,000
of those goods to outsiders (leaving $50,000 in Parent's end-of-year
inventory). The requirement is to prepare a consolidated income statement. For this purpose assume that all goods sold by Subsidiary Co.
provide the same rate of profit.

There are several ways in which this problem and other problems
like it can be handled, and each has its supporters. No doubt all would
agree that we should eliminate the $90,000 of sales shown on Subsidi-
ary's books as going to Parent. From here on practices differ, but we'll
follow through only one plan and assume that you will discuss it and its
alternatives with your accountants if the matter is of interest to you.

If, as the assumption states, the profit margin is the same on all of

Subsidiary's sales, then total profit on sales to Parent this year was 90 percent of $10,000, or $9,000. This profit, as we've noted before, represents within-the-family markup, and we should trace its impacts on the legal statements and eliminate them in a logical manner. The tip-off is the statement that Parent has resold $40,000 of the goods to outsiders. This means that $4,000 of the $9,000 profits has been carried into the Parent cost-of-goods-sold account, and the remainder, $5,000, must still be lodged in Parent's inventory. Next, if we eliminate part ($90,000) of Subsidiary's sales, don't we then have to eliminate the same proportion (nine-tenths) of Subsidiary's cost of goods sold? Yes. And if the other expenses of Subsidiary were proportionately related to the sales made to Parent, the same share (nine-tenths) of them will also be eliminated. Now we have all the necessary elements of our elimination entry, which comes out as follows:

(15)

Sales (of Subsidiary, 90%)	90,000	
Cost of Goods Sold (of Subsidiary, 90%)		54,000
Other Expenses and Taxes (of Subsidiary, 90%)		27,000
Cost of Goods Sold (of Parent, 4/9 of $9,000)		4,000
Merchandise Inventory (of Parent, 5/9 of $9,000)		5,000
To eliminate intercompany sales and related expenses,		
as well as related profit.		

The resulting consolidated income statement may now be prepared. It is shown as Figure 18.3, with informal notations added for purposes of clarification.

Figure 18.3 Consolidated income statement, tenth year of affiliation.

PARENT CO. AND SUBSIDIARY CO.
Consolidated Income Statement, Tenth Year of Affiliation

Sales (sum minus $90,000 eliminated)		$210,000
Expenses:		
Cost of goods sold (sum minus $54,000 and $4,000)	$122,000	
Other expenses and taxes (sum minus $27,000)	63,000	185,000
Total net income (sum less $5,000 unrealized)		$ 25,000
Minority interest (20% of $10,000 less $5,000		
unrealized)		1,000
Consolidated net income		$ 24,000
Proof of consolidated net income:		
Earnings of Parent		$ 20,000
Parent's share of Subsidiary earnings (80% of		
$10,000 less $5,000)		4,000
		$ 24,000

Consolidated Statements—Conclusion

We have only scratched the surface of the world of consolidated statements. The mere mention of consolidated statement problems to anyone who is about to take CPA exams will usually bring on a cold sweat. The student has practiced doing consolidations of horrendous complexity and fully expects the worst. CPA examiners delight in setting problems involving a flock of, rather than only two, affiliates or problems involving subsidiaries and sub-subsidiaries. Sometimes when only a couple of affiliates are involved, each owns some of the capital stock of the other (mutual holdings), ownership interests may change in mid-year, bonds are issued at a discount by one affiliate and are purchased in the open market at a different price by another affiliate, etc.

One nice thing about the consolidation problems of a given company is that, once consolidated statements have successfully been prepared, their repetitive preparation in future years, or months, becomes pure routine.

All we've attempted to accomplish here, of course, is to present an outline of some of the typical problems along with one pattern of solution. From this point on you should be able to think along with your accountants in terms of consolidated data as well as the data of the individual affiliates.

TEST PROBLEM

On January 1, 19XX, Our Company acquires 90 percent of the outstanding common stock of Their Company for $82,000 cash. On this date the position statement data of the two companies (condensed) stand as follows after the stock purchase:

	Our Company	*Their Company*
Current assets	$ 50,000	$ 30,000
Investment in Their Company (at cost)	82,000	
Plant assets (net)	118,000	70,000
	$250,000	$100,000
Current liabilities	$ 20,000	$ 20,000
Capital stock	180,000	50,000
Retained earnings	50,000	30,000
	$250,000	$100,000

Required

1. Assume that there have been no intercompany transactions and that the payment in excess of book value represents goodwill. Prepare elimination entries and a consolidated position statement as of January 1, 19XX.

2. Next, assume that each company earns $20,000 during 19XX, that Their Company pays cash dividends of $12,000 (of which 90 percent is added to Our Company's earnings), and that at year-end Their Company owes Our Company $5,000. Assume also that $500 of consolidated goodwill must be amortized. The position statements at the end of 19XX contain the following:

	Our Company	Their Company
Current assets	$ 83,800	$ 41,000
Investment in Their Company (at cost)	82,000	
Plant assets (net)	115,000	67,000
	$280,800	$108,000
Current liabilities	$ 20,000	$ 20,000
Capital stock	180,000	50,000
Retained earnings	80,800	38,000
	$280,800	$108,000

Prepare elimination entries and a consolidated position statement as of the end of 19XX.

TEST PROBLEM Solution Space

(1) Elimination entries on January 1, 19XX:

	Debit	*Credit*
Capital Stock		
Retained Earnings		
Goodwill		
Investment in Their Company		

OUR COMPANY AND THEIR COMPANY
Consolidated Position Statement
January 1, 19XX

Assets		Equities		
Current	$	Current liabilities		$
Plant		Minority interest		
Goodwill		Stockholders' equity:		
		Capital stock	$	
		Retained earnings	_____	
	$			$

(2) Elimination entry on December 31, 19XX:

	Debit	*Credit*

(1)

Capital Stock		
Retained Earnings		
Goodwill		
Investment in Their Company		

(2)

Retained Earnings		
Goodwill		

(3)

Current Liabilities		
Current Assets		

OUR COMPANY AND THEIR COMPANY
Consolidated Position Statement
December 31, 19XX

Assets		Equities		
Current		Current liabilities		
$				
Plant		Minority interest		
Goodwill		Stock equity:		
		Capital stock	$	
		Retained earnings	_____	
	$			$

19
Income
Tax
Allocation

Why Bother?

It's a tough enough job just to determine how much income tax your company owes at the end of any year—why complicate things by attempting to "allocate" your taxes to periods other than the ones in which they become due?

This question has led to countless arguments among accountants and nonaccountants, and it has, in general, helped to keep the profession of accounting from becoming deadly dull.

The answer to the question, why bother? can be reduced to a brief statement which will require elaboration, but here it is: The determination of periodic enterprise income rests upon the process of matching costs with revenues on a logical basis. Such matching is virtually synonymous with *accrual basis,* rather than *cash basis,* accounting. Income tax allocation is synonymous with accrual accounting; nonallocation is synonymous with cash basis accounting. Therefore, we must allocate. To summarize, the question is: Why isn't the income tax that we actually have to pay the amount of income tax that we should show as our current income tax expense in our income statement? The answer is that the income tax burden must be matched (accrued) with the items of revenue and expense which generate it. To treat the tax as an expense in a given year only because we pay it, or owe it, makes no sense at all.

What Conditions Make Interperiod Allocation Necessary?

We would have almost no tax allocation problems at all if the rules for measuring taxable income were made to conform to the "generally accepted principles" of accounting or if the principles governing accounting were made to conform to the tax rules. Either change, however, is only a creature of the dream world. The tax folks are too anxious to get their hands on the taxpayers' hard cash to allow them full exercise of sound accounting principles; at the same time, the taxpayers would be most reluctant to give up certain tax-deferring opportunities which do not fit well into their accounting records and reports. So tax allocation is needed when either the revenues or the expenses that we record in our books and financial statements differ from the amounts that we report (honestly) on our tax return. It should be added that we're not concerned with accounting or reporting errors, nor are we concerned with possible tax evasion. The differences are almost entirely the result of timing. Thus, a particular $10,-000 may be recognized as revenue in our books in one year and may be shown on our tax return as revenue in either an earlier or a later year, and the same may be true of certain expense outlays. For purposes of completeness, we'll divide this part of the discussion into four segments, as follows:

1. Cases in which *revenues* show up in our books and financial statements *before* they are subject to tax (that is, before they are reported on our tax returns).

2. Cases in which *expenses* show up in our books and financial statements *before* they are used as tax deductions (that is, before they are reported on our tax returns).

3. Cases in which *revenues* show up in our books and financial statements *after* they have been taxed (that is, after they have been reported on our tax returns).

4. Cases in which *expenses* show up in our books and financial statements *after* they have been used as tax deductions (that is, after they have been reported on our tax returns).

General Principles of Interperiod Allocation

The all-encompassing principle of tax allocation requires that we employ the accrual method (not the cash method) of recognizing income taxes as an expense. Corollaries, or subprinciples to this general principle, with more detail added, may be phrased as follows:

1. If income is recorded in the books and financial statements before it has been subjected to income tax, we must accrue an appropriate amount of tax in order to avoid overstatement of income.

2. If taxes are paid on "income" before being properly recognized in the books and financial statements, the tax charges, from the standpoint of our books, have actually been "prepaid" and should be so shown in our financial statements pending recognition of the income.

Revenue Recognized before It Is Taxed

The weight of accounting opinion nowadays favors comprehensive use of accrual accounting; more specifically, it favors the recognition of sales revenue at the time a sale is made, even though it may be an installment sale, so long as collection of the sales price is reasonably assured. On the other hand, the government allows the cash basis of accounting for certain types of installment sales in determining *taxable* income (subject, of course, to meeting technical tax rules). The installment method of accounting is presently allowed for tax purposes only for reporting gains from *nondealer* sales of property other than inventory. In other words, sales of real or personal property in the ordinary course of a taxpayer's trade or business may no longer be reported on the cash basis. However, it is still a good example for income tax allocation problems, so let's assume the property sold qualifies for following the installment sales method for tax purposes. What this means is that on an installment gain you are able to defer the actual payout of tax money beyond the point of sale by taking advantage of the tax provision which says your income may be taxable in proportion to the fraction of the sales price that you actually collect each year.

Let's take a fairly clear-cut example. Assume that we sell for $20,000 an asset which cost $5,000, and assume that the buyer pays 10 percent down (and no more during the year of sale). Our entry at the time of sale, using accrual accounting, is:

(1)

Installment Account Receivable	18,000	
Cash	2,000	
Asset—Cost		5,000
Gain on Sale of Asset		15,000

Assume that the tax rate on this kind of gain is 25 percent; however, since we've collected only 10 percent of the selling price, only 10 percent of the gain is taxed this year, for a total tax of $375. When we recognize this tax liability, our entry is:

(2)

Income Tax Expense	375	
Income Tax Payable (or Cash)		375

Now the question is, would it be "fair" reporting to show this portion of our income statement as follows?

Gross gain on sale of asset	$15,000
Less: Tax on collected portion	375
Net income from sale of asset	$14,625

Quite obviously this is a misleading presentation, because we have claimed the entire gross gain in this accounting period but have charged against it only the "cash" portion of the income tax that presumably will have to be paid. This situation clearly calls for a tax allocation (accrual) entry to charge against the gain recognized this period the tax that will become payable on the total gain. The obvious solution is to *accrue* the 25 percent tax on the remaining 90 percent of the gain in the year of sale. Such an entry is made as follows:

(3)

Income Tax Expense	3,375	
Accrued Future Tax Liability		3,375

To accrue 25% tax on $13,500 of installment gain recognized in the accounts but subject to tax only in the future as cash installments are collected.

With entry 3 on the books, the income statement will now show the following:

Gross gain on sale of asset	$15,000
Less: Income tax expense (including $3,375 deferred on installment basis)	3,750
Net income	$11,250

This discussion is necessarily abbreviated. Its aim, however, is to introduce you to the concept of tax allocation. Upon further reading, and discussion with your accountants, you will find that the tax allocation entry requires a credit to a "deferred tax liability" account. The conclusion would appear logical since whenever revenue that will sometime be taxed is recognized in the accounts as earned before the period in which it actually becomes subjected to tax, a charge should be made to the tax expense account to accrue the future tax so that the current period's statement will not be distorted. The related credit, therefore, is an accrued liability.

Other cases in which revenue may be booked before it is taxed occur in connection with accounting for long-term construction contracts, in the technical handling of leaseholds on the books of the lessor, and in connection with current earnings of foreign subsidiaries under certain circumstances.

Expenses Recognized before They Become Tax Deductions

The Internal Revenue decision makers have steadfastly refused to allow businesses to deduct expenses of a conjectural or strictly estimated nature, such as estimated future inventory losses and estimated outlays for product warranties, but the accrual of such expenses is thoroughly logical and necessary on a timely basis in order to avoid overstatements of income. What this boils down to is that such expenses are shown on the income statement as reductions of earnings but income taxes, in fact, are not correspondingly saved. Again the question: Do we show on our income statement only the income taxes we actually pay (or owe), or do we allocate the taxes to make them match up with the revenues and expenses that we have booked, knowing that the differences are almost entirely matters of timing and will eventually wash out? The answer, again, would appear to be that when we pay a tax in one year that really should be matched against the income of the next, or later, period, we should hold the tax charge in abeyance until its proper time for appearance in the income statement. This is done by treating the tax as being "prepaid" or, as the practitioners prefer to call it, "deferred."

For an example, assume that Our Company accrues $100,000 of product warranty expense in the year in which the sales of these products are recorded as revenues, and assume also that our income tax rate is 30 percent. The warranty entry and the tax entries are:

(1)

Product Warranty Expense	100,000	
Accrued Liability for Product Warranty		100,000

To accrue as warranty expense and liability the percentage of sales that has been found by experience to be reasonable.

(2)

Prepaid (Deferred) Income Tax Charge	30,000	
Income Tax Expense		30,000

To reduce the cash tax expense account, and treat as prepaid, 30% of the amount accrued as warranty expense which is not currently tax deductible.

Other examples of expenses booked before they become tax deductible could easily be cited. However, the conclusion would appear to be sound that under circumstances in which expenses are recognized in the books before they are deductible, the tax payment made as the result of such nondeductibility should be set up as a prepayment or deferred charge to be transferred to tax expense as the accrued expenses materialize in the form of actual outlays.

Revenue Taxed before It Is Recognized

Apparently under many circumstances the government assesses income taxes on collections of cash that a business firm may make in advance of rendering a service. Thus, rents collected in advance, dues in advance, subscriptions in advance, payments for correspondence lessons in advance, etc., may be taxable in the period of receipt (i.e., on a cash basis), rather than in the period when the services are rendered and the revenue is recognized in accordance with sound accounting principles.

Needless to say, the accountant resists showing advance cash collections as revenue. The entry to record these takes the following general form:

(1)

Cash	xxx	
Liability for Amounts Collected in Advance from Customers		xxx

As the services are rendered, whether in later periods or the current one, the earning (realization) of revenues is recorded as follows. (Assume that we're dealing with rents collected in advance.)

(2)

Liability for Amounts Collected in Advance from Customers   xxx
    Rent Revenue   xxx

If entry 1 occurs in one year and entry 2 in the second, then the income tax will be payable in year 1 on revenue that is not recognized until year 2.

Fortunately, again, we can resort to the accrual methods of accounting. To do so, the tax which we pay in year 1 (on the revenues to be earned in year 2) is debited to a prepaid (or deferred) tax account; like any other prepayment, it is treated as an asset to be written off as it is used up. In the second year, when the rent revenue is recognized, the amount in the prepaid tax account is transferred to the tax expense account so that it will become matched with the rent revenue in the second year's income statement.

The general conclusion, thus, for all cases in which income taxes must be paid prematurely on cash advances from customers or clients is to hold the tax in a prepaid expense (or deferred charge) account as an asset to be written off in the period or periods in which the services are rendered to the customers and the advances are transferred from liability to revenue accounts.

Expenses as Tax Deductions before They Are Recognized

This final category of interperiod tax allocation cases has created much more controversy than the others. The circumstances are these: We own a depreciable asset which has an assumed 5-year life. On our books we use the straight-line depreciation method, whereas we use the accelerated cost recovery system (ACRS) or modified cost recovery system (MACRS) (depending on when the property was placed into service) method for tax purposes. The result is that our tax deduction for depreciation during the first 2 years is greater than our book depreciation and during the final 2 years it is less. (In the third year the two are identical.) Over the full 5 years, the depreciation totals are, of course, alike. The timing, however, differs as between book and tax depreciation. The respective annual depreciation charges are shown in Figure 19.1 for an asset assumed to have cost $900.

If we assume that our company has net revenue (after deducting everything except depreciation and tax) of $300 per year and an effective tax rate of 25 percent, its actual income tax liabilities for the 5-year period will be as shown in Figure 19.2.

Were our company to present its income statements without allocation of taxes, it would, of course, show a relatively high net income in the first two years and a relatively low net income in the final two years. The customary buzz words for a presentation of this sort are "flow through"; that is, we ignore the inconsistent relationships between the taxes we pay, as compared with the revenues and expenses that we record, and merely let the cash tax consequences flow through. In Figure 19.3 are shown the income statement data for the 5 years on a flow-through basis.

Figure 19.1   Book and tax depreciation.

Year	Book (straight-line)	Tax (ACRS)	Differences
1	$180	$300	$+120
2	180	240	+ 60
3	180	180	—
4	180	120	− 60
5	180	60	−120
Total	$900	$900	$ —

Figure 19.2   Our company's tax liabilities.

Year	Revenue before depreciation	Tax depreciation	Taxable income	25% tax
1	$ 300	$300	—	—
2	300	240	$ 60	$ 15
3	300	180	120	30
4	300	120	180	45
5	300	60	240	60
Total	$1,500	$900	$600	$150

Figure 19.3 Comparative income statements on flow-through basis.

OUR COMPANY
Comparative Income Statements on Flow-through Basis

	\multicolumn{6}{c}{Years}
	1	*2*	*3*	*4*	*5*	*All*
Net revenue (before depreciation and tax)	$300	$300	$300	$300	$300	$1,500
Depreciation per books	180	180	180	180	180	900
Net before tax	$120	$120	$120	$120	$120	$ 600
Tax (actual)	—	15	30	45	60	150
Net income	$120	$105	$ 90	$ 75	$ 60	$ 450

Surely anybody making an analysis of Our Company's progress as reflected in its net income trend would be quite pessimistic because of the persistent decline. That is exactly what is wrong with flow through; again, it consists of an unfortunate mix of accrual accounting for all data except taxes, which are naïvely recognized on a cash basis. One of the more popular inequities which regulatory commissions throughout the country have imposed upon our public utility companies has been to require the companies (1) to use one of the rapid depreciation methods for tax purposes, (2) to use straight-line depreciation in their books, and (3) to use the flow-through scheme for determining income subject to regulation. The early effects of such requirements are, of course, an apparently inflated amount of earnings, which the commissions then proceed to chisel down with no promise of compensatory adjustment as the tide reverses itself in later years.

Next, let's apply tax allocation techniques to these same data. In year 1, $300 of the asset's cost was written off as a tax deduction (leaving only $600 for future write-offs in the next 4 years). On the other hand, only $180 of cost was written off in the accounting records. If we present a flow-through income statement (as in Figure 19.3), do we properly disclose the fact that in this first year we have, in a sense, borrowed some $120 of depreciation deductions from our future? Does it put the reader on notice that our remarkably low tax bill was achieved at the expense of higher tax bills in the future? Wouldn't it be more honest to accrue an appropriate amount of income tax charge against the $120 of apparent earnings, on the ground that because we are using up $300 of depreciation deduction now we'll be obligated to pay commensurately more taxes in future years? All those questions would appear to point in the direction of tax allocation. Stated most simply, our *cash* tax has, indeed, been delayed (deferred), but it has not been evaded or *avoided;* our tax burden should be accrued on the basis of our pretax book income. In the present instance the tax charge has been only temporarily reduced, and the amount of this temporary reduction is found by multiplying our tax rate (25 percent) by the amount of *extra* depreciation taken for tax purposes ($120). We should accrue against this year's earnings 25 percent of $120, or $30, as deferred income tax. The entry is:

(1)

Income Tax Expense	30	
Deferred (or Accrued) Income Tax Payable		30

In year 2 the amount deferred is 25 percent of $60 (which is tax depreciation of $240 minus book depreciation of $180), or $15. In year 3 no allocation entry is needed. Then, in the final two years the situation turns around. The difference between tax depreciation and book depreciation becomes negative, so our allocation entries are the reverse of those made in the first two years, or as follows:

Year 4
(2)

Income Tax Expense	45	
Cash (or Tax Payable)		45
To record tax liability for year 4.		

(3)

Deferred (or Accrued) Income Tax Payable	15	
Income Tax Expense		15
To reverse deferral of 25% of $120 — 180.		

Year 5
(4)

Income Tax Expense	60	
Cash (or Tax Payable)		60
To record tax liability for year 5.		
Deferred Income Tax Payable	30	
Income Tax Expense		30
To reverse deferral of 25% of $60 — 180.		

If tax allocation entries are recorded in the fashion illustrated, the income statements for the 5 years should produce the same amount of net income each year, since all other things were unchanged. In Figure 19.4 the income statements are presented again with the effects of the tax allocation entries clearly disclosed (as they should be).

Figure 19.4 Comparative income statements on full accrual basis.

OUR COMPANY
Comparative Income Statements (on full accrual basis)

	Years					
	1	*2*	*3*	*4*	*5*	*All*
Net revenue (before depreciation and tax)	$300	$300	$300	$300	$300	$1,500
Depreciation, straight-line ($900/5)	180	180	180	180	180	900
Net revenue before tax	$120	$120	$120	$120	$120	$ 600
Income tax:						
Cash	$ 0	$ 15	$ 30	$ 45	$ 60	$ 150
Accrual	30	15	0	(15)	(30)	0
	$ 30	$ 30	$ 30	$ 30	$ 30	$ 150
Net Income	$ 90	$ 90	$ 90	$ 90	$ 90	$ 450

There are those who believe that the same allocation results could be obtained more logically if the amounts of additional tax accrued in the first two years and the tax reductions of the last two years were treated instead as adjustments of the straight-line depreciation accruals. The theory is that, in consuming $300 worth of tax depreciation in the first year, we "sapped" the asset of some of its future cash flow power and this should be reflected as additional depreciation. Were this plan adopted, our income statements would show as tax expense the amounts actually owed each year and the periodic depreciation would be the $180 of straight-line charge increased by $30 and $15, respectively, in the first two years and decreased by $15 and $30, respectively, in the last two years; net income would be the same—$90 for each year.

We have gone through the alternatives to gain a better understanding of the issues involved; remember, however, that the flow-through method is not allowed for purposes of presenting external financial statements.

Tax Allocation and Permanent Differences

So far we have looked at tax allocation procedures when differences between the books and the tax returns are only differences in timing; in other words, the cumulative difference eventually reduces to zero for all practical purposes. There are some situations, however, in which certain items of income or expense recorded in the books are never to be included in the income tax determination. Quite obviously we here have no problem of allocation; no allocation entries are to be made because the two (books and tax returns) never catch up with each other. That is the case with all permanent differences.

Arguments against Tax Allocation

Some persons feel that no tax allocation entry should be made in the case of depreciation differences because the company could, by continually expanding at a uniform or accelerating rate, permanently delay part of its tax payments. Flow through, so they argue, is then the only proper course. Accountants have strongly rejected that view; they point out that it would be much like arguing that a growing company should treat its current liabilities as part of retained earnings because the total is never likely to be reduced below a certain level.

Tax Allocation within a Period

Even within a single year taxes may require allocation. That happens in the relatively unusual cases when income determination items are shown partly in one part of a statement and partly in another. If, for example, your income statement reports an extraordinary gain, the gain will be shown at the bottom of the statement. Quite logically, the gain should carry with it its full share of operating expenses and income taxes; so just as income may be shown in two different places in the income statement, taxes also may be split.

Also, on rare occasions we may make charges or credits directly to Retained Earnings to record corrections of earnings carried forward from prior years. To the degree that such entries enter into the income tax determination, a portion of the tax (sometimes a negative portion) should be allocated to them. One obvious result of such allocations is that the tax remaining in the income statement approximates the amount chargeable against the income reported therein (by excluding the amount attributable to the entry in retained earnings).

TEST PROBLEMS

1. Assume that our tax rate is 30 percent. If Our Company uses the accrual method to record installment sales, with a resulting net income (before taxes) of $100,000, and we use the cash (install-

ment) method for tax purposes, with a resulting taxable income of $40,000, we should make the following tax allocation entry:

Debit
    Credit

2. If we accrue product warranty expenses of $100,000 that are not allowable tax deductions until we actually incur the expenses, we should make the following tax allocation entry:

Debit
    Credit

3. If we collect $100,000 in rents and earn only $60,000 of that amount this year, we should make the following tax allocation entry at year-end:

Debit
    Credit

4. If we record total straight-line depreciation of $100,000, while reporting $250,000 for tax purposes, we should make the following entry:

Debit
    Credit

20
Business Combinations: Mergers, Acquisitions, and Consolidations

How Business Combinations Are Achieved

Nothing has created more interest, for those who enjoy a good fight, than the battle during recent years among accountants and financiers, low and high, over the manner in which we should account for various types of business combinations. It has been said repeatedly that many mergers simply would not be carried out if the companies were not permitted to account for them the way they want to. This is sad! In any case, let's apply accounting analysis to the major patterns of combinations so we can see what the argument was all about.

The heart of the ruckus can be boiled down to two words—pooling and purchase. For years and years, given the requisite arrangements, companies have been allowed to decide how they will account for a combination, whether as a purchase or as a pooling, and, depending on the choice of method, the resulting financial reports could be vastly different. Then the Accounting Principles Board of the American Institute of Certified Public Accountants set out to narrow the range of choice to the point at which some people cried that poolings, for all practical purposes, would be choked off entirely. The end result was a compromise which throws the doors wide open for poolings *if the combining transactions qualify* but which insists that there shall be no freedom of choice in the accounting once the transaction has been consummated in a given form.

In the process of developing its principles, the Board adopted the word "acquisition" to replace "purchase"; from now on, we'll employ the terms *acquisitions* and *poolings*.

The Physiology of an Acquisition

The management of A Co. has an excess of working capital and wants to employ it by acquiring the business (the net assets) of B Co. There are several ways in which it can do so. For purposes of discussion we'll assume that the balance sheet data of the two companies stand, at the moment of decision, as shown in Figure 20.1.

Figure 20.1   Balance sheet data at time of acquisition.

	A Co.	B Co.
Assets		
Current	$ 700,000	$100,000
Plant	500,000	500,000
Total	$1,200,000	$600,000
Equities		
Current liabilities	$ 100,000	$ 50,000
Bonds payable	400,000	—
Capital stock, par $1	500,000	450,000
Retained earnings	200,000	100,000
Total	$1,200,000	$600,000

For our first variation, assume that A Co. bargains directly with B Co. and the two agree that A Co. is to pay B Co. cash, in the amount of $650,000, for the net assets of B Co. (which consist of the asset total of $600,000 minus the liability total of $50,000).

On the books of A Co. we can delay the difficult part of the acquisition entry a few minutes by making the following initial entry:

(1)

Investment in Net Assets of B Co.—Cost	650,000	
Cash in Bank		650,000

To record purchase of B Co. net assets, with book value of $550,000, for $650,000 cash.

We could now leave B Co. to its own devices if we wanted to, since it will have no subsequent effect on A Co. Just for the sake of this excursion, though, let's assume that B Co., now flooded with cash and nothing else, elects to dissolve. The entries, including the sellout, are:

(1a)

Cash	650,000	
Current Liabilities	50,000	
Current Assets		100,000
Plant		500,000
Gain on Sale of Net Assets (or Retained Earnings)		100,000
To record sale of all net assets to A Co. for cash.		

(2a)

Capital Stock	450,000	
Retained Earnings (with $100,000 added)	200,000	
Cash in Bank		650,000
To record distribution of cash to stockholders in liquidation.		

In the meantime, A Co. must face the problem of recognizing on its books and statements the net assets acquired from B Co. The easy way out would be simply to debit the various asset accounts for the same amounts at which they were carried on the books of B Co., credit liability accounts also for the amounts formerly owed by B Co., and then credit the investment account with the amount of its $650,000 balance and make a "plug" entry to Goodwill to make the entry balance. Such an entry would appear as follows:

(2)

Current Assets (in detail)	100,000	
Plant (in detail)	500,000	
Goodwill (plug to balance)	100,000	
Current Liabilities (in detail)		50,000
Investment in Net Assets of B Co.—Cost		650,000
To replace investment account with accounts for specific assets and liabilities acquired from B Co., at B Co. book values, and to charge Goodwill for the amount paid ($100,000) in excess of the book value of the net assets.		

Needless to point out, entry 2 balances because we *made* it balance with the goodwill plug, but the entry makes no sense whatsoever. There is not the slightest reason (other than indolence or stupidity) for continuing the book values of B Co. on the books of A Co. following their purchase for cash. It would make equal sense, if you were to buy your neighbor's car for $2,000, for you to record it on your books at $3,500 with an allowance for depreciation of $2,000 (a net of $1,500) and charge the $500 difference (2,000 − 1,500) to Goodwill simply because the neighbor had originally paid $3,500 for the car and had, to date, recorded $2,000 of depreciation.

The point is that we should, at least initially, record assets at cost. When we buy a basket of assets (cum liabilities) for $650,000, it should mean that we have appraised the lot and can allocate the purchase price to them on a reasonable basis including, perhaps, a lump sum for goodwill (which is often simply debited with the amount that is left over).

For a more sensible solution, assume that the current assets are found to be worth approximately their B Co. book values, the plant assets are appraised at $530,000, and Goodwill is valued at $70,000. Now the entry to clear the Investment account becomes:

(2)

Current Assets (in detail)	100,000	
Plant (in detail)	530,000	
Goodwill	70,000	
Current Liabilities (in detail)		50,000
Investment in Net Assets of B Co.—Cost		650,000

To replace the investment account with specific asset and liability accounts at their current values.

For another variation, assume that A Co. issues bonds payable to B Co. for $650,000 instead of paying cash. The acquisition and investment-clearing entries (assuming the same values as before) then become:

(1)

Investment in Net Assets of B Co.	650,000	
Bonds Payable		650,000

(2)

Current Assets	100,000	
Plant	530,000	
Goodwill	70,000	
Current Liabilities		50,000
Investment in Net Assets of B Co		650,000

The same end results can be obtained if the acquisition is made through the purchase of the outstanding capital stock of B Co. and the company is then liquidated. Alternatively, B Co., after purchase, can be "kept alive" as a subsidiary, and the combining of assets and liabilities then is accomplished only in consolidated statements. The first entry, in either case, records purchase of the capital stock. Assume that a total of $650,000 cash (or it could be in bonds) is paid. The purchase entry is:

(1)

Investment in B Co. Common Stock	650,000	
Cash in Bank		650,000
Purchase of 100% of B Co. common for $650,000.		

(2)

Current Assets	100,000	
Plant	530,000	
Goodwill	70,000	
Current Liabilities		50,000
Investment in B Co. Common Stock		650,000
Dissolution of B Co.		

Under the new rules of the game, a business combination must be recorded as a purchase, or acquisition, in all cases except when the merging is accomplished by the issuance of voting common stock in exchange for the common stock of the other company. In the examples that we have examined so far, A Co. might have accomplished an acquisition by issuing preferred stock or consideration of any other form except common stock, instead of cash or bonds, and the entries would follow the pattern shown. When preferred stock instead of cash or bonds is issued, it may be necessary to find a "fair market value" for the stock so that the resulting valuations of current and noncurrent assets will be the same as if cash had been paid.

Impact of Acquisition Transaction on Income

The accounting for a business combination by the "acquisition" route may have a very drastic effect on net income. Prior to acquisition, B Co. might be reporting annual earnings of, say, $60,000 per year, or a rate of return of 10 percent on total assets; however, this amount is based on book values at historical cost. If, as we assumed, the price paid for the assets places them at a total valuation of $700,000, the rate of return drops to $60,000 divided by $700,000, or 8.6 percent, as the result of increasing the "rate base." But that is not all. If the depreciable asset valuations are stepped up and the useful lives are assumed to be unchanged, then the periodic depreciation charges are increased and this causes the net income to decline by the amount of the depreciation increase less the related reduction in income taxes. Furthermore, and this could be the real hitch, we came up with goodwill in the amount of $70,000. Accounting logic requires that this asset be amortized over a reasonable (10- to 40-year) period. In our example, 10-year amortization of the $70,000 of goodwill would reduce the net income by $7,000 per year (with no income tax relief). Thus, from a 10 percent return before acquisition, the purchased business might provide less than 8 percent on the basis of revised asset valuations, depreciation, and amortization. For that reason businessmen and a lot of accountants have argued stoutly for the continued privilege of recording business combinations by what is known as the *pooling-of-interests,* or *pooling,* method whenever certain prerequisites are met.

Before moving on to the subject of poolings, we should stop to ask whether the apparent undesirable consequences of the acquisition method of recording a combination are in any way undeserved. The answer would appear to be that acquisition, or purchase, accounting rules are entirely realistic. In a nutshell, if one pays a high price for an enterprise, whether the payment is made in the form of cash, bonds, or some other type of security, it is only realistic to reflect the high cost in the accounts and in the subsequent financial statements. Any accounting device that actually obscures the cost or other sacrifice made to acquire the enterprise is subject to severe condemnation.

The Physiology of a Pooling of Interests

If in the process of effecting a business combination one company acquires the outstanding voting common stock of another by a payment of cash or by exchanging preferred stock, bonds, or anything at all other than voting common stock, just forget any pooling of interests; you can't do it that way. But you can pool by issuing your *common stock* in exchange for the common of the other company, and that is then the only way you can do it.

What do we mean by pooling? It means that we don't put up-to-date values on the assets acquired (we don't attempt to determine what they cost us); we bring them onto our books and statements at their old book values. To use the current expression, when the assets of one company are pooled with those of another, "they do not have a new basis of accountability." This is to say that when our company issues common stock to the stockholders of your company in exchange for all your common stock, the assets of your company end up in the pool at their present book values per your books.

The underlying theory of pooling is that, in a sense, two or more companies simply elect to join forces—to pool their resources. To do so, the stockholders of one company give up their stock in exchange for stock of the other company; they continue to be stockholders, but now in the expanded entity.

In order to emphasize the very important differences between the treatment of a combination as an acquisition and as a pooling of interests, we'll use the same initial position statements that we used in the purchase examples. For your convenience they are repeated in Figure 20.2.

Figure 20.2 Balance sheet data at time of pooling.

	A Co.	B Co.
Assets		
Current	$ 700,000	$ 100,000
Plant	500,000	500,000
Total	$ 1,200,000	$ 600,000
Equities		
Current liabilities	$ 100,000	$ 50,000
Bonds payable	400,000	—
Capital stock, par $ 1	500,000	450,000
Retained earnings	200,000	100,000
Total	$ 1,200,000	$ 600,000

To bring B Co. into the family, A Co. now persuades the stockholders of B Co. to accept 1⅑ shares of A Co. common for each share of B Co. stock they now hold. In other words, A Co. issues 500,000 shares of $1 par stock in exchange for 450,000 shares of B Co. stock. It matters not what is the value of A Co. stock in the market (or what is the apparent "opportunity cost" incurred by A Co. upon trading its shares for those of B Co.). The easiest way to visualize the accounting treatment of the transaction is, as before, to record it in two successive entries, as follows:

(1)

Investment in B Co. Stock (book value)	550,000	
Capital Stock, par (500,000 shares)		500,000
Retained Earnings (plug, maximum $ 100,000)		50,000
To record acquisition of all outstanding common stock of B Co. by exchange of our common stock, treated as a pooling of interests.		

Entry 1 requires further explanation. We now hold all the B Co. stock; and we've recorded it at $550,000, which is the book value of the stockholders' equity on B Co.'s position statement. We could have picked up all of B Co.'s retained earnings if we had issued only $450,000 in our stock. What we did, however, is substitute $500,000 par of our stock for $500,000 of the B Co. stock equity, leaving another $50,000 of B Co. equity to be carried into our accounts as retained earnings.

So we see that a pooling of interests has two unique characteristics. First, regardless of how much stock we give for the stock of B Co., we record the investment at $550,000—the book value of the stock received; second, to the extent that the par or stated value of the stock which we issue amounts to less than the total stock equity of B Co., we pick up B Co. retained earnings for the difference. The limit on the second point is that we cannot pick up more retained earnings than the amount shown on B Co.'s balance sheet; if we have to fill a still larger gap, we do it with capital surplus, i.e., Capital in Excess of Par (or Stated Value).

The next step may be to dissolve B Co. now that we hold all the stock (or we may keep B Co. alive and report periodically by means of consolidated statements). The entries to record dissolution are simple because the B Co. values are already represented in our investment account. To record liquidation, the following entry is made:

(2)

Current Assets (at book value)	100,000	
Plant (at book value)	500,000	
Current Liabilities		50,000
Investment in B Co. Stock		550,000
To record dissolution of B Co. and recognition of B Co. assets and liabilities on our books at their B Co. book values.		

Impact of Pooling Transaction on Income

No goodwill and no new or higher asset values! With those handicaps eluded, we avoid subsequent shrinkage in the earnings of the B Co. assets that we've taken over; we don't change the amount of depreciation, nor do we have any goodwill to amortize.

In order to gain some notion of the effects of the two kinds of combinations, we can compare the postcombination balance sheets resulting from our assumed acquisition and pooling transactions. Shown side-by-side, the balance sheets are displayed in Figure 20.3.

Figure 20.3 Comparative balance sheets.

A CO.
Comparative Balance Sheets Immediately
Following Combination with B Co.

| | Combination treated as: | |
	Purchase	Pooling
Assets		
Current	$ 150,000	$ 800,000
Plant	1,030,000	1,000,000
Goodwill	70,000	—
Total	$1,250,000	$1,800,000
Equities		
Current liabilities	$ 150,000	$ 150,000
Bonds payable	400,000	400,000
Capital stock, par $1	500,000	1,000,000
Retained earnings	200,000	250,000
Total	$1,250,000	$1,800,000

Some of the differences that result from following one course of action as compared with the other are fairly obvious upon examining Figure 20.3. First, the pooling procedure caused no significant drain on working capital, which in our example amounts to $650,000 (the sum of the precombination working capital of A Co., $600,000, and B Co., $50,000). Combination via acquisition, on the other hand, required an outlay of $650,000, which directly reduced the combined working capital. This apparent advantage of pooling may not be especially attractive when the acquiring company (A Co.) enters the transaction primarily as a means of investing idle funds. Also, many acquisition-type combinations are financed with freshly borrowed funds or by issuing various types of securities, other than voting common stock, directly in exchange for the voting stock of the acquired company.

The second major difference, of course, lies in the effects upon earnings after combination. The expenses of A Co. with the net assets of B Co. taken in at cost will be higher than the sum of each prior to acquisition, and the increase will result directly from the fact of purchase rather than pooling. As demonstrated in Figure 20.3, under acquisition treatment the very same assets are marked up by $30,000; also, goodwill appears. If we assume future revenues to be the same under either treatment, then net income will be lower under purchase treatment by the amount of the increased depreciation (less income tax saving) and goodwill amortization (not deductible for tax purposes). The downward influence of purchase on recorded net income is further evidenced in relating the earnings to the earnings' base. If we exclude working capital from the reckoning, we find in Figure 20.3 that the rate of return under acquisition accounting must be related to noncurrent assets totaling $1,100,000 as compared with $1,000,000 under pooling treatment.

Finally, businessmen seem to have an almost emotional objection to listing goodwill on the balance sheet. There is no logical basis for their objection when the acquiring company has clearly expended funds for goodwill. To submerge the cost of goodwill in such a case is tantamount to telling an untruth.

Pool versus Purchase Accounting

In earlier years the accounting rules for recording transactions involving business combinations were, to put it mildly, permissive. A large segment of the membership on the Institute's Accounting Principles Board have struggled for years to outlaw pooling entirely; but under heavy pressure from the minority, which was aided and abetted by the Financial Executives Institute, the Board compromised and agreed to *require* use of pooling accounting in all cases when, as in our example, A Co. issues voting common stock (only) in exchange for the voting common of B Co.

Prior to the issuance of rules on the subject, the accounting was an unhappy gallimaufry of permissiveness, abuse of freedom of choice, and fancy-dan accounting. The value of securities issued in exchange for assets was not reflected in the recording of the assets on the acquirer's books. There have been many cases of "instant profits" in which such assets were almost immediately resold at large (but perhaps unreal) gains. Thus, A Co. issues valuable common stock in exchange for the common of B Co.; next, B Co. is dissolved so that its assets become assets of A Co. at the amounts at which they were carried on the books of B Co. (in no way reflecting the worth of what A Co. exchanged for them); then A Co. immediately sells them and reports a fat gain in its current income statement! The one feature which appears to have caused the most serious objections to the pooling procedure is, as it is commonly stated, "under pooling, the assets of the absorbed companies have *no new basis of accountability.*"

TEST PROBLEM

The condensed balance sheet data of Our Company and Your Company stand as follows:

	Our Company	Your Company
Assets		
Current	$100,000	$ 80,000
Noncurrent	400,000	320,000
	$500,000	$400,000
Equities		
Current liabilities	$ 50,000	$ 40,000
Capital stock, par $10	300,000	200,000
Retained earnings	150,000	160,000
	$500,000	$400,000

The current market value of the common stock of Our Company is $40 per share, and of Your Company is $19 per share. Management of Our Company believes that the stockholders of Your Company would be willing (a) to exchange all their common stock in the ratio of two shares for one share of Our Company (which is better than the market ratio) or (b) to exchange all their common for 12 percent 20-year, convertible debenture bonds of Our Company on the basis of a $1,000 par bond for each 50 shares of stock. The debentures would be convertible into Our Company common at the rate of 22 shares for each bond, and the bonds would not be subject to call until after 10 years. The bonds would probably have a market value of par. Assume that the current assets of Your Company are worth approximately the amount of their book value and plant is appraised at $350,000.

Required

Assume, first, that the combination is effected by the offer described in (a), on a pooling-of-interests basis. (1) Prepare a journal entry to record, on the books of Our Company, the issue of 1,000 shares of common stock in exchange for the 2,000 outstanding shares of Your Company. (2) Next, prepare a journal entry to record the dissolution of Your Company.

Assume that method (b) is followed. (3) Prepare an entry to record the initial investment. (4) Then prepare an entry to record the dissolution of Your Company. Assume that the bonds are worth par.

Finally, in comparative form, present the balance sheet data of Our Company resulting from each of the two combination procedures.

TEST PROBLEM Solution Space

	Debit	*Credit*

(1)
Pooling

Investment in Your Company Common Stock
    Capital Stock, Par $10
    Retained Earnings
    Capital Paid In in Excess of Par Value
To record exchange of 1,000 shares of Our Company
  common for 2,000 shares of Your Company common,
  with pooling-of-interests treatment.

(2)

Current Assets
Noncurrent Assets
    Current Liabilities
    Investment in Your Company Common Stock
To record dissolution of Your Company with assets re-
  corded with "no new basis of accountability."

(3)
Acquisition

Investment in Your Company Common Stock
    Convertible Bonds Payable
To record purchase of Your Company common in exchange for our 12% convertible bonds with par and
  market value of $400,000.

(4)

Current Assets (appraised)
Noncurrent Assets (appraised)
Goodwill (to balance—cost)
    Current Liabilities (per books)
    Investment in Your Company Common Stock
To record dissolution of Your Company and recognition
  of assets at current value, including goodwill.

OUR COMPANY
Balance Sheets after Combination

	Recorded as	
	Pooling	*Acquisition*
Assets		
Current	$	$
Noncurrent		
Goodwill	—	
	$	$
Equities		
Current liabilities	$	$
Bonds payable	—	
Capital stock, par $10		
Capital in excess of par		—
Retained earnings		
	$	$

21
Recognition
of Effects
# of Inflation

First Let's Set the Scene

We all know, as surely as anything, that with each passing year our dollar buys less and less. In short, we're all conscious of inflation. Accountants and businesspeople have begun to realize that the accounting data which are being ground out may be deficient if they are not modified or adjusted to compensate for the effects inflation has upon them.

In fact, in the late 1970s and early 1980, with an inflation rate that went as high as 14 percent, certain large, publicly held companies, were required to present certain types of *supplemental* price-adjusted data in footnote disclosures to their financial statements. After a few years, when the inflation rate dropped to the low to middle single digits, these requirements were dropped. The problem had eased significantly, and many concluded that such data were not only not very useful, they were also very expensive to produce. Nevertheless, inflation does often significantly influence accounting data and the decisions users of those data make. So it is important that we spend some time to gain at least a basic understanding of the problems created by inflation and its impact on accounting data.

The problem with respect to accounting data, as represented in accounting reports, is twofold. First, the only dollars with which everyone is thoroughly familiar are those which we handle today, i.e., "current dollars." If we quote the price of something, we are presumed to be specifying the amount that we would have to pay *in the kind of dollars currently circulating* in order to buy that thing. In other words, it would be quite misleading for us to quote a price and then, when a customer accepted it, say that it was actually the price 10 years ago and the customer must now pay us double or more because all prices have risen. In our accounting reports we commit virtually this same sin whenever we list the amount we paid for some asset (its "cost") and fail to point out that the price we're quoting is actually the price we paid some 10 or more years ago! Second, we compound our misbehavior by the manner in which we indiscriminately fuse together the costs of things purchased at various times.

For a simple example, assume that we buy one unit of equipment for $500; later, when prices in general have doubled, we buy an identical second unit for $1,000. There are at least three ways that we could represent the two pieces of equipment in our position statement. First, we could merely add $500 and $1,000 and report the cost of equipment as $1,500. In effect, we are saying that the cost price of our equipment total is $1,500 when, in reality, it consists of $1,000 in today's prices plus $500 in yesterday's prices. Surely that is misleading; yet it has been *the* traditional accounting procedure.

Second, we might show the equipment in a schedule such as the following, which includes dates of acquisition and an index of prices at each date:

OUR EQUIPMENT ACCOUNT
Explanation of $1,500 Cost
Shown in Our Balance Sheet

Date of purchase	Cost	Price index
Jan. 1, 19X1	$ 500	100
Dec. 31, 19X9	1,000	200
	$1,500	

This is a pretty good method. If the reader understands price indexes, he will interpret the schedule somewhat as follows: "Because the price index measures the purchasing power of money, I would assume that the second piece is not twice as elaborate as the first but rather that it took twice as much money to buy about the same thing." Unfortunately the method suffers from two major drawbacks. It would be too clumsy and impractical if there were more than a half-dozen or so pieces of equipment. Also, it tends to imply that the price of this particular kind of equipment has doubled when, in fact, it is the prices of "things in general" that have doubled; that is, the general purchasing power of the dollar has deteriorated one-half during the period in question.

A third, entirely practical and far superior, method consists simply of listing all the equipment in terms of current dollars. The purchase on December 31, 19X9, is already in current dollars (if we are presenting a balance sheet as of December 31, 19X9); the cost on January 1, 19X1, can be translated into current dollars by adjusting it for the 100 percent change in general price level. In other words, we are saying that we have invested 1,000 current dollars in a piece of equipment today and we also have a second piece in which we invested *the equivalent of* 1,000 current dollars. In the third form of presentation we have translated the dollars of two different years into dollars of common purchasing power equivalent, or common dollars. Since each 19X1 dollar had twice as much purchasing power as each 19X9 dollar, we had to multiply the 500 dollars of 19X1 by 2 to translate them into the equivalent of 19X9 dollars.

The act of translation into common dollars is not much of a feat. You merely multiply the raw dollar amount by a fraction which consists of the *current price index over the old price index,* i.e., the current index over the index that *prevailed* at the time of the original transaction. Thus, to translate the $500 cost, we multiply by current index (200) over the prevailing index (100), or 200/100, to arrive at $1,000. The $1,000 then is the number of dollars of today's purchasing power needed to be the equivalent of the $500 spent on equipment in 19X1, and our total, now in homogeneous dollars, becomes $2,000. We'll be using this technique throughout the remainder of the chapter.

A Simple Example

On December 31, 1969, the Consumer Price Index stood at 112.9. Ten years later, December 31, 1979, it registered 230! This was an increase of 103.7%. Between 1969 and 1979 the general cost-of-living index rose an average of over 10 percent per year. Assume that you had loaned the government $750 at the end of 1969; to do so, assume you purchased, for $750, a $1,000 bond to be repaid at maturity value of $1,000 some 10 years later. What was the *real* effect on your economic well-being of your investing $750 in 1969 for a return of $1,000 in 1979? Let's make a series of computations and see which is the most logical.

First, if you invest $750 and later receive $1,000 in return, historical cost accounting reckons your *gain* as the difference between $750 and $1,000, or $250 (to be reduced, of course, by income tax on the "gain").

Second, you might argue that the $250 is really an exaggeration of your true gain since, during the earning period, your cost of living almost doubled. Might we not, therefore, cut the $250 in half as a measure of our real gain? In other words, you didn't really have clear gain of $250 but, rather, only the equivalent of half that much, or $125.

On further thought, you realize that the very subtraction of $750 from $1,000 violates the rules of arithmetic because the 750 dollars of 1969 vintage were quite different from the 1,000 dollars of 1979 vintage, and it's just as incorrect to subtract unlike things from each other as it is to add unlike things together. So you proceed to translate the 1,000 dollars of 1979 vintage into their 1969 equivalent. To do so, you divide by the prevailing index (230) and multiply by the index to be used for common dollar purposes (112.9). Your 1,000 dollars in 1979 dollars translate into 491 dollars in 1969 dollars, and you then realize that you really didn't earn $250, and you didn't really earn half that amount—you actually *lost* $250 of the 1969 kind of dollars.

Then you think a bit more and conclude that your reckoning should be in terms of up-to-date current dollars; therefore, you decide to translate the 750 dollars of 1969 vintage into their 1979 counterpart. To do so, you divide by the prevailing index (112.9) and multiply by the current index (230). Now you realize that in 1969 you loaned the government the equivalent of 1,528 dollars in 1979 dollars and you got back only 1,000 dollars in 1979 dollars! You didn't earn $250, you didn't earn $125, and you didn't lose $259; you effectively lost $528, and to crown your investment success you paid income tax on your "gain"!

How Do You Translate Old Dollars into Current Dollars?

The process of translating dollars of years past into equivalent dollars of current vintage is extremely easy. Failure to perform such translation whenever dollars of different vintage are to be mixed together leads to serious distortions, as our example in the preceding section illustrates. The Bureau of Labor Statistics prepares a monthly index of the cost of urban living in the United States. This index should rate as the best for our translation purposes because it is based on the proposition that we can compare the purchasing power of the dollar at two different points in time simply by finding how much it cost on each date to purchase a wide variety of consumer items ranging from recreation to housing. What we're concerned with in our financial reports are "people" dollars —dollars that people saved from their earnings and entrusted to our stewardship. It follows that we should render our reports to them in people dollars—dollars that we are employing in our efforts to generate earnings with which to pay people dividends. For this purpose neither the widely heralded gross national product price deflator nor the wholesale price index seems appropriate, though each has a respectable number of supporters. In any case, almost any index is better than none.

As some accountant has said, "If you don't take steps to translate the dollar amounts in your statements, you're as much as contending that the index always remains at 100!"

To translate, merely divide the dollar quantum by the cost-of-living index that prevailed when the particular quantum came into existence and then multiply by the current index (presuming you're aiming for a homogeneous dollar statement in terms of today's dollars).

The Consumer Price Index is based on an average of prices in the base year, which let's assume is 19X7, to which is assigned the base number 100. In a dozen years assume this index rose to over 230. If we had purchased a piece of equipment in 19X7 for $10,000 and wanted to determine how many consumer dollars we would have to get out of it at the end of 19X9 in order to break even (i.e., to recover our invest- ment in real cost terms), we would use a translation factor consisting of denominator 100, representing the *prevailing* index at date of acquisi- tion, and numerator 230, representing the current index at end of 19X9. The $10,000 of translated cost becomes more than $23,000.

You might recognize the translation process as very similar to the translation of foreign currencies into the local equivalent, and the prin- ciple is indeed the same. Dollars of yesteryear should be just as foreign to income and balance sheets carrying today's date as would be dollars of Australian, Canadian, or Hong Kong domicile. Few people would be foolish enough to add together raw dollars from Australia, Canada, Hong Kong, and the United States indiscriminately.

The Particulars of Translation Technique

Above all, bear in mind that the translation of raw, heterogeneous United States dollars of different vintages into their homogeneous cur- rent equivalent has nothing to do with the actual record keeping. The *records continue to be kept in original, raw dollars with all entries properly dated.* Each translation then involves going back to the index that *prevailed* on the original date of the transaction, and the original dollar amount is then translated each year into the up-to-date level of prices. Thus, the dated raw dollar data must remain in the accounts.

Now let's scan the major statement elements to observe the transla- tion requirements. Assume that we are looking at a balance sheet dated December 31 of the current year but made up of the traditional mess of heterogeneous dollars. What do we do to improve it?

CASH AND CLAIMS TO CASH: If our current balance sheet shows that we now have $50,000 of cash and claims to cash on hand, we'll not tamper with that figure, because dollars now on hand are automatically current dollars. Also, if we have accounts receivable now of $50,000, we don't modify that figure because, again, the amount is automatically stated in terms of today's money (even though it originated at an earlier date). On the other hand, if we want to compare the $50,000 of cash and $50,000 of receivables that we now possess with the corresponding asset holdings of a year ago or at any other date, the old balances do require translation because they were claims to dollars of their own time period. Thus, assume that our comparative balance sheet shows the following monetary current assets at the beginning and end of a given year in which the price index rose from 118 to 124. Before translating, the raw comparative amounts are:

	Monetary current assets	
	January 1	*December 31*
Cash in banks	$ 59,000	$ 61,000
Accounts receivable	177,000	185,000
Total	$236,000	$246,000

As traditionally reported, our liquid asset position shows $10,000 of improvement. Now, let's make the two totals more comparable. The amounts on December 31 need no adjustment; the amounts on January 1 are multiplied by the fraction $124/118$ to produce the following results:

	Monetary current assets			
	January 1 *raw*	*Translation* *factor*	*Translated*	*December 31* *raw*
Cash in banks	$ 59,000	124/118	$ 62,000	$ 61,000
Accounts receivable	177,000	124/118	186,000	185,000
	$ 236,000	$ 248,000	$ 246,000	

Under the assumption that we have made, the misleading signs of progress disappear and we see that our liquid asset position has actually worsened by $2,000 in terms of its ability to buy things:

NONMONETARY ASSETS: All other assets require translation both in "today's balance sheet" (unless they were acquired today) and in the comparative balance sheet. Consider the cost of a long-lived asset, such as a building. Suppose we purchased a building for 1,000,000 dollars in 19XX dollars. Each year thereafter, so long as the building remains our property, its 19XX dollar cost should be translated into dollars of the date of the statement in which the building's cost is reported. Thus, if the general price index was 80 at time of acquisition of the building, and if the index rose in the next 4 years in the pattern of 83, 87, 92, and 95, the building's cost would be reported in the following amounts in the 4 years following acquisition:

Year	Ledger cost	Translation factor	Cost in current dollars
0	$1,000,000	80/80	$1,000,000
1	1,000,000	83/80	1,037,500
2	1,000,000	87/80	1,087,500
3	1,000,000	92/80	1,150,000
4	1,000,000	95/80	1,187,500

Needless to point out, the translation process must be applied to all assets and the cost of each building (or of all buildings acquired on a given date) must be translated on the basis of the price index that prevailed when the particular building was acquired. That is not as complicated as it appears, provided that the price index that prevails at the time of each asset acquisition is duly recorded in that asset's ledger account so that it can readily be used as the denominator for each subsequent translation.

LIABILITIES: Liabilities that appear in the *current* balance sheet require no translation because they automatically represent the number of dollars in today's currency that are needed to pay off the indicated debts; however, for proper comparison of today's liabilities with the liabilities of a year ago or of some other earlier date, the liabilities of earlier dates must be translated into their today equivalent. Thus, if we owed $1,000,000 a year ago when the index stood at 100 and we owe $1,050,000 today at index 110, our debt position, viewed by itself, has actually improved because the year-ago debt is the equivalent of a debt of $1,100,000 in today's dollars.

STOCKHOLDERS' EQUITY: The capital stock account, unlike a true liability account, must be translated from the date of origin to today's date because we must show in it the amount needed in current dollars just to break even. If investors contributed $1,000,000 when the cost-of-living index stood at 80, then 15 years later at index 120 the original investment must be shown at $1,500,000, because that is the number of today's dollars the stockholders would have to be paid in order for them to break even in terms of purchasing power.

RETAINED EARNINGS: The retained earnings figures developed from untranslated data will differ radically from the homogeneous dollar amount. Since retained earnings is actually a pool or a series of layers of earnings retained through time, the amount each year will consist of the preceding year's amount modified by the increment resulting from the operations of the current year and by the losses or gains resulting from the company's monetary working capital and noncurrent liability changes. This will be elaborated upon in the comprehensive illustration to follow.

CURRENT REVENUES AND EXPENSES: Revenues and expenses of the current year, unless they are clearly bunched in some one or two seasons of the year, for all practical purposes can be translated into year-end, homogeneous (common) dollars by using the year's average, or midpoint, index as the denominator and the end-of-year index as the numerator. This does not hold true, however, for at least two items—depreciation and cost of goods sold. The numerator for both of them, as always, is the current index, but the denominators must be those which prevailed in the cases of the assets being depreciated and those which prevailed with respect to the opening and closing inventories in the case of the cost of goods sold. Both will be illustrated.

Common Dollar Reporting— Comparative Data

As we'll see later, an income statement covering a period of a year or less in raw dollars may not be seriously misleading *provided* that the depreciation of assets acquired some years ago is not significant in amount relative to the net income. On the other hand, when raw net income after all charges is, say, $1,000,000 and the amount of depreciation that is included in the expenses also is $1,000,000, quite obviously a 20 percent price-level adjustment upward for depreciation causes an equal 20 percent decline in reported earnings. It is not at all unusual for the depreciation charge for the period to be considerably larger (double or more) than the net income, so the leverage effect can be very serious.

Even if we are presenting data that do not include depreciation, we must not overlook the fact that any such data when reported in comparative form can be mighty misleading. To illustrate this point, just examine the data in Figure 21.1. Here we will use actual data for the decade between 1970 and 1979, since the CPI increased fairly dramatically during that period. In column 1 Our Company reports its sales revenue for each of the past 10 years, and in column 2 it gives the reader assistance in interpreting the sales data by showing the cumulative percentages of growth throughout the 10-year period. In column 4 you'll find inserted the factor needed to translate the sales for each year into homogeneous dollars as of the end of 1979. Column 5 then shows

Figure 21.1 Our Company Comparative sales revenue for 1970 to 1979.

Year	Sales (1)	Index of apparent growth (2)	CPI* yearly average (3)	Translation factor (4)	Translated sales (5)	Index of common $ growth (6)
1970	$100,000	100	116	1.98	$198,000	100.0
1971	102,000	102	121	1.90	193,800	97.9
1972	105,000	105	125	1.84	193,200	97.6
1973	108,000	108	133	1.73	186,840	94.1
1974	112,000	112	148	1.55	173,600	87.7
1975	117,000	117	161	1.43	167,310	84.5
1976	120,000	120	171	1.35	162,000	81.8
1977	124,000	124	182	1.26	156,240	78.9
1978	130,000	130	195	1.18	153,420	77.5
1979	138,000	138	218	1.06	146,280	73.9

CPI = Consumer Price Index

the translated data, and column 6 lists the percentages of growth in uniform dollars. Needless to say, the translated data significantly change the growth pattern. Rather than 38 percent growth, the table shows an absolute decline of some 26 percent over the 10-year period! It is common practice to present 10-year comparisons in raw dollars for purposes of showing growth. It seems perfectly amazing that such data have gone unchallenged all these years! Some companies have followed the practice of issuing a small, say, 3 percent, stock dividend each year while keeping the cash dividend per share unchanged. Pity the poor stockholder who believes in such circumstances that his fortunes are improving by 3 percent each year when, in actuality, over the past 10 years he would have required an increase of approximately 65 percent just to break even. As an aside, note that interest rates of over 12 percent per annum take on quite a different complexion when they are properly adjusted for price-level increases in the neighborhood of 12 percent or more per year.

Common Dollar Reporting—Comprehensive Illustration

Let us repeat that common dollar reporting adds little if any to the burdens of accounting. All account data are kept in their original raw form, since each year they must be retranslated for statement purposes in terms of the general price index at the end of the year.

Our illustration will utilize a pair of assumed comparative balance sheets as of the beginning and end of a given year and an income statement for the same year. The purposes of the illustration are, first, to demonstrate the technique and, second, to show again how important it is that modern accounting statements be supplemented, if not replaced, by statements that are in homogeneous or common dollars of the kind in current circulation. The raw data are presented in Figure 21.2.

The first schedule that should be prepared is the one for determining monetary working-capital inflation loss, since the amount as determined must be appended to the income statement to account for the whole change in retained earnings during the year. The necessary schedule is shown as Figure 21.3. Remember that monetary working capital is the net balance of cash and receivables less current liabilities.

Next we prepare the common dollar income statement as shown in Figure 21.4.

Finally, the comparative position statements are prepared as demonstrated in Figure 21.5. Note that the retained earnings balance in common dollars at the end of 19X8 is a "plug" figure, since it represents the net result of all past earnings, dividends, etc.

Figure 21.2 Problem data.

PROBLEM DATA
OUR COMPANY
Comparative Balance Sheets as of December 31

	19X8	19X9
Assets		
Cash	$ 20,000	$ 25,000
Receivables (net)	30,000	35,000
Inventories	10,000	15,000
Land	10,000	10,000
Buildings and equipment	50,000	50,000
Allowance for depreciation	(20,000)	(25,000)
	$100,000	$110,000
Equities		
Accounts and notes payable	$ 10,000	$ 15,000
Capital stock	70,000	70,000
Retained earnings	20,000	25,000
	$100,000	$110,000

Income statement, year ended December 31, 19X9

Sales and miscellaneous revenues		$ 60,000
Expenses and taxes:		
Merchandise cost of sales	$ 40,000	
Salaries and wages	8,000	
Depreciation (19XX assets, $2,000;		
19X5 assets, $3,000)	5,000	
Taxes	2,000	55,000
Net income (all retained)		$ 5,000

Notes to statements:

(1) Our Company was established in 19XX and all the capital stock was issued then at par.

(2) Merchandise purchases in 19X9 were $45,000.

(3) Depreciation of $5,000 in 19X9 came $2,000 from 19XX assets and $3,000 from 19X5 equipment.

(4) Relevant consumer price index data are:

Date or Event	Prevailing Index
Company started in 19XX	100
Land purchased for $10,000	100
Building and equipment purchased, 19XX, $40,000	100
Equipment purchased, 19X5, $10,000	110
Depreciation of 19XX assets to December 31, 19X8, $15,000	100
Depreciation of 19X5 assets to December 31, 19X8, $5,000	110
Inventory held on December 31, 19X8, FIFO	123
Index on January 1, 19X9	124
Average index for revenues and expenses in 19X9	128
Inventory held on December 31, 19X9, FIFO	130
Index on December 31, 19X9	131

Figure 21.3 Working capital.

OUR COMPANY
Working Capital in Raw and Common Dollars to Determine Inflation Loss

	Raw	Translation* factor	Common dollars
Monetary working capital, 1/1/X9	$ 40,000	124	$ 42,258
Add: Sales and other revenues	60,000	128	61,406
	$100,000		$103,664
Less:			
Merchandise purchases	$ 45,000	128	$ 46,055
Salaries and wages	8,000	128	8,188
Taxes	2,000	128	2,047
	$ 55,000	xx	$ 56,290
Computed balance, 12/31/X9	$ 45,000		$ 47,374
Actual balance, 12/31/X9	45,000		45,000
Inflation loss	—		$ (2,374)

*The numerator is 131, the December 31, 19X9 index, throughout the solution to the problem.

Figure 21.4 Income statement.

OUR COMPANY
Income Statement for Year Ended December 31, 19X9 in Raw and Common Dollars

	Raw	T/F*	Common
Sales and other revenues	$60,000	128	$61,406
Cost of goods sold:			
Inventory, Jan. 1, 19X9	$10,000	123	$10,650
Purchases	45,000	128	46,055
Total	$55,000		$56,705
Inventory, Dec. 31, 19X9	15,000	130	15,115
	$40,000		$41,590
Salaries and wages	8,000	128	8,188
Depreciation—19XX—$2,000	2,000	100	2,620
—19X5—$3,000	3,000	110	3,572
Taxes	2,000	128	2,047
	$55,000		$58,017
Net income before inflation	$ 5,000		$ 3,389
Inflation loss	—		(2,374)
Net income	$ 5,000		$ 1,015

*Translation factor numerator is 131 throughout.

Figure 21.5 Comparative balance sheets.

OUR COMPANY

Comparative Balance Sheets in Raw and Common Dollars as of December 31

	19X8			19X9		
	Raw	*T/F**	*Common*	*Raw*	*T/F**	*Common*
Assets						
Cash	$ 20,000	124	$ 21,129	$ 25,000	131	$ 25,000
Receivables (net)	30,000	124	31,694	35,000	131	35,000
Inventories	10,000	123	10,650	15,000	130	15,115
Land	10,000	100	13,100	10,000	100	13,100
Buildings and equipment						
—19XX	40,000	100	52,400	40,000	100	52,400
—19X5	10,000	110	11,909	10,000	110	11,909
Allowance for depreciation						
—19XX	(15,000)	100	(19,650)	(17,000)	100	(22,270)
—19X5	(5,000)	110	(5,955)	(8,000)	110	(9,527)
	$100,000		$115,277	$110,000		$120,727
Equities						
Accounts and notes payable	$ 10,000	124	$ 10,565	$ 15,000	131	$ 15,000
Capital stock	70,000	100	91,700	70,000	100	91,700
Retained earnings	20,000	xx	13,012	25,000	var.	14,027
	$100,000		$115,277	$110,000		$120,727

*Translation factor numerator is 131 throughout.

22
Accounting for Foreign Operations

Our Foreign Relations

Financial involvement in foreign countries has the capability of generating interesting, even exciting, accounting ramifications. At the outset it may be worthwhile to review, briefly, some of the various forms that such involvement can take. They may range from relatively simple purchases of raw materials from abroad to complex multinational situations encompassing foreign branches and subsidiaries around the world.

Accounts Receivable

For the least complicated cases, assume that we, located in America, advertise our products for shipment to Canadian customers at prices quoted in Canadian dollars and that our terms of sale stipulate that payment is due in Canadian dollars 30 days from date of our invoice. Under those circumstances we would record accounts receivable, as usual, in American dollars. The amounts, however, would have to be in harmony with the specified Canadian dollar amounts, which would be translated into their U.S. dollar equivalents as of the dates of sale. The United States–Canadian dollar relationship is a variable one; and when we receive the customer remittance in a check drawn on a Canadian bank, we are likely to end up with an amount of U.S. dollars that differs from our original debit to Accounts Receivable. Differences of that sort are known as "exchange gains and losses," and they are properly treated as elements in our current income determination.

In addition to the exchange gains and losses realized at the time of collection, there is also implied (or accrued) gain or loss in the accounts receivable that have not been collected and remain on the books at the end of the accounting period.

Accounts Payable

If we make purchases from foreign suppliers and are obligated to remit specified amounts of foreign funds, the American dollar equivalents of our accounts payable are subject to fluctuation in the same manner as the accounts receivable. If we receive invoices priced in Canadian dollars and we elect to delay payment in accordance with the suppliers' terms, we must translate the stated prices into U.S. equivalents at the time of our recognizing them as accounts payable. The amounts of U.S. dollars ultimately expended to make the required Canadian dollar remittances, perhaps 30 to 60 days later, are likely to vary (often significantly) from those recorded at the dates of purchases. Also, the amounts remaining unpaid at the end of an accounting period will usually require adjustment to reflect accrued translation differences. Such adjustments, at time of remittance or at time of financial statement preparation, are, again, exchange gains or losses and should be interpreted as an element in our current income determination. Note that our discussion so far has been related to current "monetary assets" (accounts receivable) and current "monetary liabilities." Note also that when we hold receivables denominated in Canadian dollars, we have an exchange gain when the Canadian dollar "gains" (i.e., goes from 90 to 91 cents) but an exchange loss on any Canadian-denominated payables.

Foreign Branches

In order to maintain continuity, a U.S. corporation may establish "branch" sales offices in one or more foreign countries. Sooner or later it may broaden the scope of the branch's activities to include not only sales but also warehousing, the assembly of components shipped from the United States, and, ultimately, the manufacture of parts or complete products designed either for overseas consumption or for shipment back to the United States. Such foreign operations may be continued in the form of unincorporated branches.

Branch accounting has its interesting aspects, and they are amplified when the branches are maintained in foreign countries. The connecting link between the foreign branch and the "home office," insofar as the accounting is concerned, is likely to be one or more pairs of "reciprocal" accounts. On the books of the home office an account may be labeled Due from Branch, and its counterpart at the foreign branch would naturally be labeled, in the opposite sense, Due to Home Office. Then, as long as the respective sets of accounting records are accurately maintained and are up to date, the debit balance shown as due *from* branch should be a mirror match of the credit balance, on branch books, shown as due to home office. There is one complication: the ever-varying difference in the monetary units employed in the two countries. Each country has what is variously termed its "domestic," "local," or "functional" currency. Unfortunately, the domestic currencies of two countries cannot be added together without prior harmonization of their respective values even though (as in the case of Canada, Australia, Hong Kong, Singapore, and others) the countries use the "dollar" as their official monetary unit.

Foreign Subsidiaries

Large-scale business activity usually is most conveniently carried on in the form of corporations. That is true not only in the United States but in practically all of the noncommunist countries in the world. Most accounting problems are the same whether the foreign activities are or are not carried on through corporate form, and there would appear to be little reason for variation in the manner of valuing assets, for example, as between noncorporate and corporate entities. The principal connecting link between the U.S. "parent" corporation and the foreign branch, whether incorporated or not, is the set of reciprocal accounts. Thus, a portion of the outstanding capital stock and retained earnings in the balance sheet of the branch is reflected (but not necessarily in identical amount) in the "investments" section of the domestic parent corporation's balance sheet. Apart from that linkage, the remaining interrelationships are the same whether the foreign branch is or is not incorporated.

Accounting for Receivables and Payables

If we assume that sales and purchases of goods are made in various foreign countries directly with the buyers and sellers, rather than through branches, the accounting entries are not different from those made to record similar transactions domestically. Sales are recorded by debits to Accounts Receivable and credits to Sales; purchases are recorded by debits to Merchandise, Raw Materials, etc., and credits to

Accounts Payable. If those transactions are carried on in U.S. dollars (domestic currency), no special accounting problems arise.

On the other hand, purchases and sales are often denominated in foreign currency; that is, they call for remittance in the monetary unit of the foreign country. And there's the rub. The amount of U.S. dollars implied to be paid or to be received changes with each change in the value relationship between the U.S. and the foreign currency, and the amount of any change constitutes what is commonly termed "Foreign Exchange Gain and Loss," an element in current income determination. For example, assume that on date 1 we sell merchandise to a Canadian company for $1,000, to be paid in 60 days in Canadian funds; on the same date we purchase raw materials from another Canadian company for $1,000, also payable in 60 days, and calling for remittance in Canadian dollars. Assume that the Canadian dollar is quoted at 85 cents on date 1, the transaction date, at 95 cents on date 2, when our next balance sheet is prepared, and at par on the remittance date. The following entries may be appropriate to reflect all those facts:

Date 1
(1)

Accounts Receivable—Foreign	850	
Sales—Foreign		850

To record sales in Canada for $1,000 Canadian now worth 85 cents.

(2)

Raw Materials	850	
Accounts Payable—Foreign		850

Purchase to be paid in 1,000 Canadian dollars currently available @ 85 cents, or $850 U.S.A.

Date 2
(3)

Accounts Receivable—Foreign	100	
Foreign Exchange Gain and Loss		100

The current exchange value of our $1,000 of Canadian receivables is now 1,000 × .95, or $950 U.S.A., an increase of $100.

(4)

Foreign Exchange Gain and Loss	100	
Accounts Payable—Foreign		100

Liability increase from Canadian dollar

Date 3
(5)

Cash	1,000	
Accounts Receivable—Foreign		950
Foreign Exchange Gain and Loss		50
Collection of Canadian receivables at par for exchange gain of $50 since last revaluation		

(6)

Accounts Payable—Foreign	950	
Foreign Exchange Gain and Loss	50	
Bank		1,000
Payment of Canadian account payable at par with exchange loss of $100 since last revaluation		

From the journal entries, and their explanations, that have just been presented you should observe that an underlying principle is being employed. The principle is that when an enterprise accumulates either assets or liabilities that must be liquidated in terms of the currency of another country (i.e., monetary assets or liabilities) and such monetary items are required to be reported in (translated into) the monetary units of the former country, the translation should be performed at the most current rate of exchange. Resulting gains or losses are properly treated as elements in *current income* determination. In short, exchange gains or losses with respect to current monetary items (such as cash, receivables, and payables) arising from changes in exchange rates are to be recognized as they accrue, and they become an element in current income determination.

Foreign Branch Accounting

Assume that USCAN Corporation, in Chicago, establishes a semiautonomous branch in Toronto for the purpose of manufacturing and selling complete products. The activities for the first year are depicted in the following journal entries with their explanations. When the events to be recorded affect the accounting records of both Chicago and Toronto, entries for each are shown.

Date 1
Chicago books

Investment in Branch	850,000	
Cash in Bank		850,000

Chicago office sends funds to Toronto for purchase of manufacturing plant, $510,000, and equipment, $340,000. On this date the Canadian dollar is valued at 85 cents, for a total of $C1,000,000.

Toronto books
(Canadian dollars)

Cash in Bank	1,000,000	
Home Office Capital		1,000,000

Receipt of funds from Home Office for purchase of building and equipment

Building	600,000	
Equipment	400,000	
Cash in Bank		1,000,000

Purchase of plant as indicated.

Date 2
Chicago books

Investment in Branch	87,000	
Cash in Bank		87,000

Cash sent to branch for use as current working capital (exchange rate now 87).

Toronto books

Cash in Bank	100,000	
Home Office Capital		100,000

Cash received from Chicago, converted into $1.1494 Canadian per U.S. dollar

Date 3
Toronto books

Finished Goods	350,000	
Cash in Bank		100,000
Accounts Payable		200,000
Allowance for Depreciation		50,000

Summarization of all factory costs of production of finished products for the year. (No home office entry needed.)

Cash in Bank	400,000	
Sales		400,000

Branch sales for the year

Cost of Goods Sold	250,000	
Finished Goods		250,000

Factory cost of goods sold for the year

Selling and Administrative Expenses	60,000	
Cash in Bank		60,000

Branch expenses for the year

Date 4
Branch Trial Balance before Closing

	Debit	Credit
Cash in Bank	$ 340,000	$
Finished Goods	100,000	
Building	600,000	
Equipment	400,000	
Allowance for Depreciation		50,000
Accounts Payable		200,000
Home Office Capital		1,100,000
Sales		400,000
Cost of Goods Sold	250,000	
Selling and Administrative Expenses	60,000	
	$1,750,000	$1,750,000
Sales	400,000	
Cost of Goods Sold		250,000
Selling and Administrative Exp.		60,000
Income Summary		90,000
Income Summary	90,000	
Home Office Current		90,000
Branch office closing entries		

Branch Trial Balance after Closing

	Debit	Credit
Cash in Bank	$ 340,000	$
Finished Goods	100,000	
Building	600,000	
Equipment	400,000	
Allowance for Depreciation		50,000
Accounts Payable		200,000
Home Office Capital		1,100,000
Home Office Current		90,000
	$1,440,000	$1,440,000

Chicago Entries (Optional)

Cash in Bank (340,000 × .90)	306,000	
Finished Goods (100,000 × .90)	90,000	
Building (600,000 × .90)	540,000	
Equipment (400,000 × .90)	360,000	
Allowance for Depreciation (50,000 × .90)		45,000
Accounts Payable (200,000 × .90)		180,000
Branch Income (90,000 × .88)		79,200
Investment in Branch		937,000
Equity Adjustment—Exchange Gain		54,800

These entries will bring the branch assets and liabilities onto the Home Office books as of the end of the year for accounting statement purposes. Alternatively, this complex entry can be made on a work sheet to combine the branch and home office accounts with the same resultant balance sheet. The sales and expenses of the branch should also be combined with their counterpart items on the home office books, which will lead to a consolidated (combined) income statement to be submitted along with the combined balance sheet.

Foreign Currency Translation

The entries made at home office (Chicago) under date 4 include parenthetical notations showing how the amounts are derived. Actually, there's little to explain. We have assumed that at the end of the year (date 4) the exchange rate for the Canadian dollar is 90 cents, and we have multiplied most of the balances that are recorded in Canadian dollars by .90 to attain their U.S. equivalents. Also, it was assumed that the average exchange rate for the year was 88 cents, and that provided the best translation rate for the reported net income (which was assumed to have accrued evenly throughout the year.)

Clearly, if we have 340,000 Canadian dollars in a Canadian bank account and are presenting a report in U.S. dollars, we must translate the Canadian amounts into their current U.S. equivalents. If the exchange value of the Canadian dollar, for purposes of conversion into U.S. money, is 90 cents, then our 340,000 Canadian dollars have current, translated value of 340,000 × .90, or 306,000 U.S. dollars. Translation of cash at the current rate of exchange is a very widely accepted accounting practice. The same rule applies to translation of other monetary items—accounts receivable, accounts payable, and the like. The basic reason for use of the current rate here is that the resultant, translated amount is the amount *most likely* to be available when the monetary items mature.

In certain situations exchange rates have lapsed into wildly fluctuating conditions requiring special consideration. Translation of a foreign currency at the current rate in the belief that you are depicting the real worth when it shows every likelihood of as much as, say, 50 percent deterioration in value before realization is, obviously, not a useful exercise *unless* such translation is accompanied by a special provision, similar to the allowance for bad debts, which charges off against current earnings as much of the item as is likely to be lost overall from deterioration of the foreign currency.

The foreign currency representation of nonmonetary assets may also be translated at current exchange rates (as was done in the example above), but the justification for that treatment is far less popularly supported. As you may recognize, application of a single rate (e.g., .90) to all balance sheet items of the foreign subsidiary does maintain the relationships that exist in their untranslated state. But just what benefits are derived from that particular rigidity are not easily visualized, especially if use of the current rate can be proved to be a defective choice with respect to any prominent members of the asset family of a given subsidiary. The much more popular translator of nonmonetary assets is, for each, the rate that prevailed at its date of acquisition.

As things now stand, under certain circumstances, published financial statements must continue to report noncurrent assets at historical cost. At the same time, they must supply, in the form of supplementary information, estimates of current cost of replacement and/or historical costs restated to reflect change in the purchasing power of the dollar. However, the historical costs traditionally displayed in the body of the balance sheet are retained without change. Results would appear to be inconsistent if companies with foreign subsidiaries were required to translate the foreign currency costs of foreign assets at rates other than the historical exchange rates—the rates that prevailed at the time the assets were acquired. To translate those assets at current rates would constitute a departure from the historical cost principle when the current rates of exchange were different from those that prevailed at date of acquisition.

Needless to say, a strong case can be advanced in favor of reporting asset costs in terms of current purchasing power of our currency (as was recommended in Chapter 19). However, use of current foreign exchange rates, while modifying the historical costs, can by no means be relied upon to perform the task of adjusting for inflation in a consistent, rational fashion.

Translation and Inflation

In conclusion, let us briefly look at the translation process under the assumption that historical costs are to be modified to reflect the changes in the purchasing power of the U.S. dollar. With respect to foreign assets recorded in terms of foreign currency, two alternatives appear to be available. First, the valuation of a particular foreign asset may be restated to reflect changes in the purchasing power of the functional (foreign) currency, or it may be restated on the basis of an appraisal. If either of those steps were taken, the final step would be to translate the revised (up-to-date) foreign currency valuation at the *current* (up-to-date) exchange rate. We would thus be reporting to our U.S. stockholders the present-day representation of the asset's historical cost as influenced by inflation in the foreign country.

The alternative route would be, first, to translate the unmodified historical cost of the asset at the historic, date-of-acquisition/exchange rate to arrive at the U.S. dollar representation of the asset's historical cost. Then the historical cost would be translated into up-to-date terms by use of the appropriate index representing change in purchasing power of the dollar. By that procedure we would be reporting to our U.S. stockholders the present-day representation of the asset's historical cost as influenced by inflation in the United States.

The choice between those two options is not easy to make, and both options are hypothetical under present accounting rules. However, the first scheme might be given a slight edge on the grounds that the original cost of the asset typically is expressed in foreign currency, translated to U.S. dollars, by using the historic exchange rates. To apply similar procedure as the first step in arriving at a defensible "current cost" appears to have the merit of consistency.

CHAPTER 1

DENTON BREAD CO.
Balance Sheet as of December 31, 19XX

Assets

Current:			
Cash		$ 9,200	
Accounts receivable (less $500 allowance for uncollectibles)		11,500	
Raw materials inventory (at cost)		5,000	
Miscellaneous supplies		1,000	
Prepayments		500	$ 27,200
Noncurrent:			
Land (cost)		$ 5,000	
Buildings (cost)	$ 50,000		
Machinery and equipment (cost)	60,000		
	$110,000		
Less: Accumulated depreciation	3,400	106,600	111,600
			$138,800

Equities

Current liabilities:			
Wages payable		$ 1,600	
Taxes payable		3,000	
Interest payable		200	$ 4,800
Mortgage payable			30,000
Total liabilities			$ 34,800
Stockholders' equity:			
Capital stock, par $10		$100,000	
Retained earnings		4,000	104,000
			$138,800

CHAPTER 2

TARRANT CO.
Income Statement for the Year 19XX

Revenues		
Sales (Less: Uncollectibles of $24,000)		$5,603,483
Other income		13,680
		$5,617,163
Revenue deductions:		
Expenses:		
Cost of goods sold	$3,980,000	
Selling	592,000	
Administrative	614,250	$5,186,250
Income taxes		154,000
		$5,340,250
Income before extraordinary item		$ 276,913
Uninsured flood loss		125,000
Net income		$ 151,913
Retained earnings at beginning of year:		
As previously reported		$1,500,000
Adjustment for litigation losses of prior years		75,000
As restated		$1,425,000
		$1,576,913
Cash dividends on common stock, $1 per share		100,000
Retained earnings at end of year		$1,476,913
Per share of common stock:		
Income before extraordinary item		$2.71
Extraordinary item (flood loss)		(1.22)
Net income		$1.49

COMMENT: Technically the income taxes in this problem should be "allocated" in relation to the extraordinary charges for flood and litigation losses. Tax allocation is examined in a special chapter on that subject (Chapter 17).

CHAPTER 3

EMPIRE CORP.
Ledger

Cash in Bank				Capital Stock			
(1)	100,000	(2)	1,000			(1)	100,000
		(3)	30,000				
		(6)	10,000				

Accounts Receivable				Retained Earnings			
(5)	60,000					(12d)	13,875

Merchandise				Sales			
(4)	50,000	(7)	35,000	(12a)	60,000	(5)	60,000

Store Equipment				Merchandise Cost of Sales			
(3)	30,000	(8)	125	(7)	35,000	(12b)	35,000

Accounts Payable				Miscellaneous Expenses			
		(4)	50,000	(2)	1,000	(12c)	11,125
				(6)	10,000		
				(8)	125		

Income Summary			
(12b)	35,000	(12a)	60,000
(12c)	11,125		
(12d)	13,875		

(9) EMPIRE CORP.
Trial Balance (before closing), July 31, 19XX

	Balances	
Account Title	*Left*	*Right*
Cash in bank	$ 59,000	
Accounts receivable	60,000	
Merchandise	15,000	
Store equipment	29,875	
Accounts payable		$ 50,000
Capital stock		100,000
Retained earnings		
Sales		60,000
Merchandise cost of sales	35,000	
Miscellaneous expenses	11,125	
	$210,000	$210,000

(10) EMPIRE CORP.
Income Statement for July, 19XX

Sales		$60,000
Expenses:		
Merchandise cost of sales	$35,000	
Miscellaneous	11,125	46,125
Net income (and earnings retained)		$13,875

(11) EMPIRE CORP.
Balance Sheet, July 31, 19XX

Assets			Equities		
Current:			Current liabilities:		
Cash in bank	$59,000		Accounts		
Accounts			payable		$ 50,000
receivable	60,000		Stock equity:		
Merchandise			Capital stock	$100,000	
inventory	15,000	$134,000	Retained		
Store			earnings	13,875	113,875
equipment		29,875			
		$163,875			$163,875

CHAPTER 4

BLITZ CO.
Work Sheet for the Year Ended December 31, 19XX

	Trial balance		Adjusting entries		Income statement		Balance sheet	
	Debit	Credit	Debit	Credit	Debit	Credit	Debit	Credit
Cash in bank	2,500			(1) 25			2,475	
Accounts receivable	40,000						40,000	
Allowance for bad debts		100		(2) 600				700
Merchandise	40,000			(3) 30,000			10,000	
Plant	100,000						100,000	
Allowance for depreciation		35,000		(4) 4,000				39,000
Accounts payable		20,000						20,000
Interest accrued payable				(5) 1,000				1,000
Income tax accrued payable				(6) 650				650
Bonds payable		25,000						25,000
Capital stock		50,000						50,000
Retained earnings		13,400						13,400
Sales		60,000				60,000		
Bad debts			(2) 600		600			
Cost of goods sold			(3) 30,000		30,000			
Selling expenses	10,000		(4) 3,600		13,600			
Administrative expenses	11,000		(1) 25		11,425			
			(4) 400					
Interest expense			(5) 1,000		1,000			
Income taxes			(6) 650		650			
Net income for year					2,725			2,725
Totals	203,500	203,500	36,275	36,275	60,000	60,000	152,475	152,475

BLITZ CO.
Income Statement, Year Ended December 31, 19XX

Sales		$60,000
Less: Bad debts		600
Net sales		$59,400
Expenses:		
Cost of goods sold	$30,000	
Selling expenses	13,600	
Administrative expenses	11,425	
	$55,025	
Interest expense	1,000	
Income taxes	650	56,675
Net income (and earnings retained)		$ 2,725

BLITZ CO.
Balance Sheet, December 31, 19XX

Assets

Current:			
Cash in bank		$ 2,475	
Accounts receivable	$40,000		
Less: Allowance for bad debts	700	39,300	
Merchandise		10,000	$ 51,775
Plant (cost)		$100,000	
Less: Allowance for depreciation		39,000	61,000
			$112,775

Equities

Current liabilities:			
Accounts payable		$ 20,000	
Interest accrued payable		1,000	
Income taxes accrued payable		650	$ 21,650
Bonds payable			25,000
Total liabilities			$ 46,650
Stockholders' equity			
Capital stock		$ 50,000	
Retained earnings, January 1	$13,400		
Earnings retained, 19XX	2,725	16,125	66,125
			$112,775

CHAPTER 5

(1)	Cash	500	
	Sales		500
(2)	Accounts Receivable	600	
	Sales		600
(3)	Cash	196	
	Sales Discounts	4	
	Accounts Receivable		200
(4)	Cash in Bank	5,000	
	Notes Payable		5,000
(5)	Interest Expense	100	
	Notes Payable	5,000	
	Cash in Bank		5,100
(6)	Cash	800	
	Allowance for Depreciation	1,100	
	Retirement Loss	100	
	Machinery		2,000
(7)	Sales—Bad Debts	500	
	Accounts Receivable—Allowance for Bad Debts		500
(8)	Accounts Receivable—Allowance for Bad Debts	120	
	Accounts Receivable		120
(9)	Cost of Goods Sold	9,000	
	Merchandise		9,000
(10)	Insurance Expense	300	
	Prepaid Insurance		300

CHAPTER 6

DECATUR CO.
Statement of Changes in Working Capital, Year Ended December 31, 19X2

Sources of working capital:		
Net income	$30,000	
Add back: Depreciation	10,000	
Working capital flow		
from operations		$ 40,000
Sale of land		15,000
Issue of capital stock		50,000
		$105,000
Applications of working capital:		
Cash dividends		$ 25,000
Purchase of plant		50,000
Payment on Mortgage		10,000
Net increase in working		
capital (schedule)		20,000
		$105,000

Schedule of Working Capital Changes

	19X1	*19X2*	*Increase (Decrease)*
Current assets	$80,000	$100,000	$20,000
Current liabilities	40,000	40,000	—
Working capital	$40,000	$ 60,000	$20,000

CHAPTER 7

TIPTON CO.
Statement of Changes in Cash, Year Ended December 31, 19x2

Sources of cash:		
Net income		$ 63,000
Add: decrease in accounts receivable (net)	$ 5,000	
Increase in accounts payable	10,000	
Depreciation	10,000	25,000
Deduct: Increase in inventories	$ 48,000	
Decrease in wages payable	5,000	(53,000)
Cash flow from operations		$ 35,000
Sale of land		15,000
Issuance of capital stock		50,000
		$ 100,000
Uses of cash:		
Cash dividends		$ 25,000
Purchase of plant		50,000
Payment of mortgage		10,000
Net increase in cash		15,000
		$ 100,000

CHAPTER 8

January 10

Raw Materials	19,600	
Accounts Payable		19,600

Purchase of 25,000 pounds @ 80 cents, terms 2/10, n/30.

January 19

Accounts Payable	19,600	
Cash in Bank		19,600

January 20

Raw Materials	17,640	
Accounts Payable		17,640

January 31

Accounts Payable	17,640	
Loss from Lapsed Discounts	360	
Cash in Bank		18,000
	30,032	

Work in Process		
Raw Materials		30,032

Consumption of all but 22,000 pounds with FIFO cost of $17,640 plus $1,568 (which is 2,000 units of the first purchase at 80 cents less 2%).

CHAPTER 9

Straight-line procedure:

Year 1

Depreciation	1,700	
Allowance for Depreciation		1,700

Year 2

Depreciation	1,700	
Allowance for Depreciation		1,700

Year 3

Depreciation	1,700	
Allowance for Depreciation		1,700

Year 4

Allowance for Depreciation	5,100	
Cash	3,000	
Retirement Loss	1,900	
Machinery		10,000

Sum-of-years' digits procedure:

Year 1

Depreciation	2,833	
Allowance for Depreciation		2,833

COMPUTATION: $1 + 2 + 3 + 4 + 5 = 15$. Depreciation for first year is then $5/15$ of $8,500. Second year will be $4/15$ of $8,500, or $567 less. The amount declines by $567 each year, leaving a salvage of $1,500 at the end of year 5 if the asset is not retired earlier.

Year 2

Depreciation	2,266	
Allowance for Depreciation		2,266

Year 3

Depreciation	1,700	
Allowance for Depreciation		1,700

Year 4

Allowance for Depreciation	6,799	
Cash	3,000	
Retirement Loss	201	
Machinery		10,000

CHAPTER 10

(1)

Cash in Bank	11,250,000	
Capital Stock Common—Stated Value $2		500,000
Capital Paid In in Excess of Stated Value		10,750,000

(2)

Capital Stock Common—Stated Value $2	2,000,000	
Capital Stock Common—Stated Value $1		2,000,000

(3)

No entry. Unissued stock has no effective financial significance and no basis for entry.

(4)

Treasury Stock Common—Cost	3,000,000	
Cash in Bank		3,000,000

(5)

Cash in Bank	1,750,000	
Treasury Stock Common—Cost		1,500,000
Capital Paid In in Excess of Stated Value		250,000

(6)

Capital Stock Preferred	1,000,000	
Retained Earnings	100,000	
Cash in Bank		1,100,000

(7)

Cash in bank	1,050,000	
Capital Stock Preferred—Par		1,000,000
Capital Stock Common—Warrants		40,000
Capital Paid In in Excess of Par		10,000

(8)

No entry called for.

Stockholders' Equity:	
Capital stock preferred—12%, $100 par	$ 1,000,000
Capital Paid In in Excess of Par	10,000

Capital stock common, no par, stated value $1, authorized 3,000,000 shares, issued 2,000,000	$ 2,000,000	
Capital Paid In in Excess of Stated Value	19,500,000	
Capital stock common—warrants	40,000	
Retained earnings	7,000,000	
	$28,540,000	
Less: Capital stock common in treasury at cost (50,000 shares)	1,500,000	27,040,000
		$28,050,000

CHAPTER 11

March 15

Retained Earnings	200,000	
Retained Earnings Reserved for Possible Fire Loss		100,000
Retained Earnings Reserved for General Contingencies		100,000

April 15

Retained Earnings	500,000	
Capital Stock, Par $5		100,000
Capital in Excess of Par		400,000

To record 10% stock dividend or 20,000 shares at market value of $25 per share.

CHAPTER 12

(1)

Cash	97,000	
Bonds Payable—Discount	12,594	
Bonds Payable—Par		100,000
Common Stock Warrants		9,594

Issue of 100 bonds with warrants attached, each to buy 10 shares of common stock at $5.

(2)

Bond Interest Expense	6,500	
Cash		6,500

Payment of coupon 1 at 13%.

Bond Interest Expense	315	
Bonds Payable—Discount		315

To accumulate one-fortieth of the original bond discount.

(3)

Common Stock Warrants	9,594	
Cash	5,000	
Capital Stock—Par		10,000
Capital Paid In in Excess of Par		4,594

To record issue of 1,000 shares of common stock at
$5 cash plus one warrant per share.

CHAPTER 13

(1)

Raw Materials—Control	100,000	
(Also subledger cards, received col- umn, for each kind of material)		
Accounts Payable—Control		100,000

(2)

Work in Process—Control	97,000	
(Also individual subledger job-cost sheets)		
Raw Materials—Control		97,000
(also subledger cards, issued column, for each kind)		

(3)

Work in Process—Control	364,000	
(Also subledger job-cost sheets)		
Wages Payable		364,000
(and individual employee earn- ings records)		

(4)

Manufacturing Overhead—Control	643,000	
Service 1	127,000	
Service 2	94,000	
Production 1	236,000	
Production 2	186,000	
Various Accounts	643,000	643,000

(5)

Manufacturing Overhead—Control	127,000	
Service 2	34,000	
Production 1	63,000	
Production 2	30,000	
Manufacturing Overhead—Control		127,000
Service 1	127,000	

(6)

Manufacturing Overhead—Control	128,000	
Production 1	64,000	
Production 2	64,000	
Manufacturing Overhead—Control		128,000
Service 2	128,000	

(7)

Work in Process—Control	614,000	
(also, subledger job-cost sheets)		
Manufacturing Overhead—Control		614,000
Production 1	348,000	
Production 2	266,000	
	614,000	

(8)

Finished Goods	960,000	
Work in Process—Control		960,000

(9)

Income Summary	29,000	
Manufacturing Overhead—Control		29,000
Production 1	15,000	
Production 2	14,000	
	29,000	

OUR COMPANY
Statement of Cost of Goods Manufactured
Year Ended December 31, 19X1

Raw materials used		$ 97,000
Direct labor		364,000
Manufacturing overhead—actual	$643,000	
Less: Unapplied	29,000	614,000
Total manufacturing costs		$1,075,000
Add: Work in process, January 1		100,000
		$1,175,000
Less: Work in process, December 31		215,000
Cost of goods manufactured		$ 960,000

CHAPTER 14

(1)

Raw Materials	240,000	
Materials Price Variance	4,800	
Accounts Payable		244,800

(2)

Finished Goods	200,000	
Materials Quantity Variance	4,000	
Raw Materials		204,000 .

(3)

Finished Goods	72,000	
Labor Wage Variance	2,440	
Labor Efficiency Variance	1,200	
Wages Payable		75,640

(4)

| Manufacturing Overhead | 140,000 | |
| Various Accounts | | 140,000 |

(5)

Finished Goods ($6,000 × 20 batches)	120,000	
Budget Variance 140,000 − (73,200 + 64,000)	2,800	
Efficiency Variance $20 × (6,100 − 6,000)	2,000	
Idle Plant Variance $8 × 1,900 hours	15,200	
Manufacturing Overhead		140,000

CHAPTER 15

Payback Period: Cost, $41,000, divided by annual net cash flow of $7,000 equals 5⁵/₇ years payback period.

Present value at 10%: $7,000 times present value at 10% of 10-year annuity of $1, or 6.144, is $43,008, which is favorable.

CHAPTER 16

Question 1

Ability to pay relates to a taxable entity's general capacity to bear a tax burden. The concept of marginal utility of money states that, above a modest income level, each additional dollar of revenue has less utility than the preceding dollar. Therefore, the recipient can afford to pay more taxes with each additional dollar of revenue. This concept underlies the graduated tax tables. In essence, higher incomes should pay a higher percentage of tax.

Wherewithal to pay relates to whether cash (or an asset readily convertible to cash) with which to pay the tax is received this year. An installment sale or a trade-in of an old truck for a new truck may give rise to an economic or accounting gain, but any taxable income may be postponed until cash (or the equivalent) with which to pay the tax is received.

Question 2

a. A *deduction* reduces taxable income and thereby produces a tax benefit related to the marginal tax rate. The $1,000 deduction might reduce taxes by $170 or by $500 for different taxpayers. A *credit* is subtracted from the tax liability and gives essentially equal tax benefit to all affected taxpayers.

b. A deduction is used when Congress wants the benefit to be graduated in the same fashion as the tax is graduated. Congress uses a credit when it wants the dollar benefit to be the same at all income levels.

Question 3

Analysis:

Cost of old unit	$ 40,000
− Depreciation	28,000
= Adjusted basis	$ 12,000
Fair market value of new unit	$ 50,000
− Cash to be paid	21,000
= Value of old unit	$ 29,000
Value received for old unit	$ 29,000
− Adjusted basis	12,000
= Gain realized	$ 17,000

a. If the old unit is traded in, the gain of $17,000 will be deferred by reducing the basis of the new unit to $33,000. If the old unit is sold, the $17,000 of gain will be recognized currently. The gain will be taxed as ordinary income inasmuch as it represents the recapture of prior depreciation deductions. The basis of the new asset will then be $50,000.

b. The adjusted basis would be $33,000 and there would be a loss of $4,000 rather than a gain of $17,000. If the unit were exchanged, the $4,000 loss would be deferred by increasing the basis of the new unit to $54,000. If the old unit were sold, the loss would be recognized currently. Technically, it would be an ordinary loss (business equipment is not a capital asset), but it might be treated as a capital loss depending on certain other gains and losses that were recognized during the year.

c. The gain would be $31,000 (43,000 − 12,000), and all would be recognized this year. $28,000 would be ordinary income (depreciation recapture). The remaining $3,000 of gain would be treated as capital gain or as ordinary income depending upon the nature of the other recognized gains and losses.

CHAPTER 18

(1) Elimination entries on January 1, 19XX:

Capital Stock (90% of Their Company)	45,000	
Retained Earnings (90% of Their Company at date of acquisition)	27,000	
Goodwill	10,000	
Investment in Their Company (at cost)		82,000

OUR COMPANY AND THEIR COMPANY
Consolidated Position Statement
January 1, 19XX

Assets		Equities		
Current (sum)	$ 80,000	Current liabilities (sum)		$ 40,000
Plant (sum, net)	188,000	Minority interests:		
Goodwill (per		Capital stock (10%)	$ 5,000	
journal)	10,000	Retained earnings (10%)	3,000	8,000
		Stock equity:		
		Capital stock	$180,000	
		Retained earnings	50,000	230,000
	$278,000			$278,000

(2) Elimination entries on December 31, 19XX:

(1)

Capital Stock (90% of Their Company)	45,000	
Retained Earnings (90% of Their Company at date of acquisition)	27,000	
Goodwill	10,000	
Investment in Their Company (at cost)		82,000

(2)

Retained Earnings (consolidated)	500	
Goodwill		500

To amortize $500 of consolidated goodwill against consolidated retained earnings.

(3) (not required)

Retained Earnings (Their Company—since acquisition)	8,000	
Minority Interest (10%)		800
Consolidated Retained Earnings (90%)		7,200

To divide new retained earnings between minority and majority.

(4)

Current Liabilities	5,000	
Current Assets		5,000
To eliminate intercompany debt.		

OUR COMPANY AND THEIR COMPANY
Consolidated Position Statement
December 31, 19XX

Assets		Equities		
Current (sum less $5,000)	$119,800	Current liabilities (sum less $5,000)		$ 35,000
Plant assets (net sum)	182,000	Minority interests:		
Goodwill ($10,000 less $500)	9,500	Capital stock (10%)	$ 5,000	
		Retained earnings (10%)	3,800	8,800
		Stock equity:		
		Capital stock	$180,000	
		Retained earnings ($80,800 plus $7,200 less $500)	87,500	267,500
	$311,300			$311,300

CHAPTER 19

(1)

Income Tax Expense	$18,000	
Deferred (or Accrued) Income Tax Credit		$18,000
The amount is 30% of $60,000.		

(2)

Deferred Income Tax Charge	30,000	
Income Tax Expense		30,000
The amount is 30% of the $100,000 expense that won't be allowed as a deduction until a later period.		

(3)

Deferred Income Tax Charge	12,000	
Income Tax Expense		12,000
The amount is 30% of the $40,000 of rent which we have not yet earned but on which we must pay (prepay) tax.		

(4)

Income Tax Expense	45,000	
Deferred Income Tax Credit		45,000

The amount is 30% of the $150,000 of extra depreciation deducted in the tax return.

CHAPTER 20

(1)
Pooling

Investment in Your Company Common Stock	360,000	
Capital Stock, par $10		100,000
Retained Earnings (maximum permissible)		160,000
Capital Paid In in Excess of Par Value (to balance)		100,000

To record investment in Your Company stock at its total book value ($360,000) in exchange of $100,000 par value of Our Company common, with resulting carry-forward of entire balance of Your Company retained earnings plus "capital excess" sufficient to balance the transaction.

(2)

Current Assets	80,000	
Noncurrent Assets	320,000	
Current Liabilities		40,000
Investment in Your Company Common Stock		360,000

To record dissolution of Your Company and recognition of assets and liabilities at unchanged book values on Our Company books.

(3)
Acquisition

Investment in Your Company Common Stock	400,000	
Convertible Bonds Payable		400,000

To record issue of 40 bonds, par $1,000 each, in exchange for 2,000 shares of Your Company Common, recorded at market value of bonds which coincides with par value.

(4)

Current Assets (appraised)	80,000	
Noncurrent Assets (appraised)	350,000	
Goodwill (plug)	10,000	
Current Liabilities		40,000
Investment in Your Company Common Stock		400,000

To record dissolution of Your Company and recognition of assets at current values plus goodwill, at assumed cost, to balance.

OUR COMPANY
Balance Sheets after Combination

	Recorded as	
	Pooling	*Acquisition*
Assets		
Current assets	$180,000	$180,000
Noncurrent assets	720,000	750,000
Goodwill	—	10,000
	$900,000	$940,000
Equities		
Current liabilities	$ 90,000	$ 90,000
Bonds payable		400,000
Capital stock, par $10	400,000	300,000
Capital in excess of par	100,000	
Retained earnings	310,000	150,000
	$900,000	$940,000

Supplementary Problems

CHAPTER 1

1-1

A. Company begins business on January 1 with 1,000 shares of capital stock. Andrus and Payton invest $7,500 each, in cash, and 500 shares of stock are issued to each. On December 31, after one year of activity, the records show assets and liabilities as follows:

Cash	$ 3,000
Coal inventory	12,000
Taxes payable	1,000
Equipment	5,000
Wages accrued payable	400
Notes payable (short term)	2,500
Due from customers	3,500
Due to suppliers	2,000
Unexpired insurance	250
Rent payable	250
Advances from customers	500
Dividends paid	750

Directions

a. Prepare a balance sheet as of December 31.
b. Determine the amount of net earnings for the year.

1-2

As of December 31, 19XX, the accounts of Another Company show the following balances:

Cash in Office	$ 700
Retained Earnings	14,000
Accounts Receivable	25,000
Unexpired Insurance	1,000
Cash in Bank	5,800
Dividends Payable	1,000
Office Equipment	1,000
Interest Payable on Notes	150
Advances by Customers	1,100
Taxes Payable	2,500
Accounts Payable	20,000
Office Supplies	300
Payroll Payable	750
Store Equipment	14,800
Merchandise	45,000
Store Equipment Contract (1)	2,000
Delivery Equipment	2,500
Capital Stock	50,000
Note Payable (due Jan. 1, 19X3)	5,000
Store Supplies	400

(1) Payable in four quarterly installments.

Directions

a. Prepare a balance sheet.
b. Compute the current ratio and the equity ratio.

CHAPTER 2

2-1

On December 31 the accounts of Kelly Corp. show the following balances after one year of operation:

Cash in Bank	$ 1,000
Accounts Receivable	3,000
Land	1,200
Equipment	6,000
Building	12,000
Accounts Payable	1,400
Notes Payable (6 months)	1,200
Capital Stock	24,000
Sales	14,000
Merchandise	13,600
Selling Expenses	1,800
General Expenses	2,000

The merchandise remaining on hand on this date cost $6,500.

Directions

Prepare an income statement and a balance sheet.

2-2

On December 31, after one year of operation, the accounts of Laing Corp. show the following amounts:

Cash in Bank	$ 2,000
Accounts Receivable	6,000
Merchandise	27,200
Land	2,400
Building	24,000
Furniture	12,000
Accounts Payable	2,800
Notes Payable (2-year)	2,400
Capital Stock	48,000
Sales	28,000
Selling Expenses	3,600
General Expenses	4,000

The amount of merchandise represents the total purchased this year; the present inventory amounts to $13,000. Depreciation of building was $1,000, and that of furniture was $1,200. The depreciation has not been recognized in the amounts above.

Directions

Prepare an income statement and a balance sheet.

2-3

The accounts of Tidy Service Co. show the following contents at the end of the year:

Cash on Hand	$ 600
Cash in Bank	5,050
Accounts Receivable	15,500
Estimated Uncollectibles	2,100
Prepaid Insurance	1,000
Land	10,000
Buildings	30,000
Machinery	45,000
Delivery Equipment	6,500
Depreciation to date	15,000
Accounts Payable	6,500
Mortgage Payable	15,000
Capital Stock	60,000
Retained Earnings (Jan. 1)	8,050
Sales	27,500

Office Wages	4,000
Plant Maintenance	2,000
Heat, Light, Power	10,000
Advertising	1,000
Taxes	2,000
Miscellaneous expenses	1,500

Of the total depreciation to date ($15,000), $1,000 has been recorded this year; it is included in the $1,500 of "miscellaneous expenses."

Directions

Prepare an income statement for the present year and a balance sheet as of the end of the year.

CHAPTER 3

3-1

Ann and Alice are granted a charter to operate a cash-and-carry grocery under the name Ann & Alice, Inc. The following data summarize the events of June:
(1) Each of the organizers invests $5,000 cash, and 500 shares of stock are issued to each. This money is deposited in the State Bank.
(2) Showcases and other fixtures are purchased by check, $1,000.
(3) Merchandise is purchased by check, $6,000.
(4) Merchandise is received from the Essex Co. on account, $1,000.
(5) Freight on merchandise is paid by check, $100.
(6) A check for $120 is issued to pay for the installation of the fixtures.
(7) The cost of labor used in unpacking and placing the merchandise on the shelves, $50, is paid by check.
(8) June rent is paid by check, $150.
(9) Wrapping paper and other selling supplies are purchased by check, $50.
(10) Flowers are purchased by check, $50, and are given away during the opening.
(11) Sales for the month are $4,000, cash, and all receipts are deposited in the bank immediately.
(12) Selling and delivery wages are paid by check, $400.

(13) The Essex Co. account is paid by check.

(14) The cost of merchandise on hand on June 30, including freight and labor applicable, totals $4,450.

(15) Selling supplies on hand June 30 total $15.

(16) Depreciation of the store fixtures is estimated at $10.

Directions

a. Record in skeleton T accounts with the following titles: State Bank, Merchandise, Supplies, Equipment, Essex Co., Capital Stock, Retained Earnings, Sales, Cost of Goods Sold, Selling and Delivery Wages, Misc. Selling Expense, Supplies Expense, Depreciation Expense, Rent Expense, and Income Summary. Make proper entries to summarize Expense and Revenue. Allow 15 lines for State Bank, 10 for Income Summary, and 5 for each of the others.

b. Prepare an income statement and a balance sheet.

3-2

At the beginning of the year the accounts of Della, Inc. have the following titles and balances:

Left (debit) balances

Cash in Bank	$ 2,500
Accounts Receivable	22,000
Merchandise	31,000
Supplies	1,300
Prepaid Insurance	1,450
Land	15,500
Building	30,500
Equipment	10,500
	$114,750

Right (credit) balances

Accounts Payable	$ 27,000
Payroll Payable	2,500
Capital Stock	76,000
Retained Earnings	9,250
	$114,750

In summary form the transactions for the year are shown below:

(1) Insurance premiums paid, $1,200.

(2) Merchandise purchased on account, $200,000.

(3) Supplies purchased on account, $2,000.

(4) Sales of merchandise on account, $250,000.

(5) Collections on account, $245,000.

(6) Payments on account, $205,000.

(7) Property taxes for the year paid, $900.

(8) Salesmen's services received on a credit basis, $7,000.

(9) Payments to salesmen, $6,800.

(10) Delivery expenses paid, $5,000.

(11) Public utility expenses incurred on a credit basis, $3,200.

(12) Maintenance costs paid, $3,000.

(13) Depreciation for the year: building, $915; equipment, $1,050.

(14) Insurance expired during year, $850.

(15) Inventory of supplies at end of year, $3,000.

(16) Inventory of merchandise at year-end, $30,000.

(17) Income tax due at year-end, $10,000.

Directions

a. Record the transactions of Della, Inc. for the year in skeleton T accounts labeled as follows: All of the titles in the listing above and Delivery Expense, Depreciation Expense, Income Tax, Insurance Expense, Maintenance Expense, Merchandise Cost of Sales, Property Tax, Public Utility Expense, Sales, Salesmen's Services, Supplies Expense, Taxes Payable, and Income Summary. Allow 10 lines for Cash in Bank and 15 for Income Summary. Enter the balances shown in the tabulation as of the beginning of the year, and record the transactions for the year in those accounts. Number the entries.

b. Make entries in the T accounts to close them.

c. Prepare financial statements.

CHAPTER 4

4-1

At end of the first year of operation the trial balance of the general ledger of Molly's Restaurant stands as follows:

	Debit	Credit
Cash in bank	$ 1,000	
Accounts receivable	4,000	
Land	2,500	
Building	65,000	
Equipment	5,000	
Accounts payable		$ 8,500
Notes payable (5-year, 12%)		2,500
Capital stock		70,000
Sales		50,000
Food costs	40,000	
Selling expenses	7,500	
General expenses	6,000	
	$131,000	$131,000

Additional data: (1) Specific accounts amounting to $500 are presumably uncollectible. (2) Estimated life of the building is 40 years; equipment life, 8 years. It is assumed that there will be no net salvage in either case. (3) A year's interest is due on the notes. (4) Food on hand, priced at cost, totals $10,000. (5) Accrued salaries: selling, $500; general, $1,000. (6) Estimated accrued tax liabilities, $1,500.

Directions

Prepare work sheet, income statement, and balance sheet.

4-2

After one year of operation, the general ledger of Brown Co. shows account balances as follows before adjusting and closing entries:

	Debit	Credit
Cash in Bank	$ 4,000	
Accounts Receivable	12,000	
Merchandise	54,400	
Land	6,800	
Building	48,000	
Equipment	24,000	
Accounts Payable		$ 5,600
Notes Payable (5-year, 12%)		20,000
Capital Stock		80,000

Sales		58,800
Selling Expenses	7,200	
General Expenses	8,000	
	$164,400	$164,400

Other data: (1) Merchandise on hand December 31, at cost, $26,000; (2) depreciation of building, $1,200, and equipment, $2,400; (3) interest accrued for one half year on notes; (4) accrued selling salaries, $500, and accrued general salaries, $1,000; (5) estimated taxes accrued, $2,000.

Directions

Prepare a work sheet and financial statements.

CHAPTER 5

5-1

For the first 6 months of 19X2 the Milan Co. has planned as follows:

	Jan.	*Feb.*	*Mar.*	*April*	*May*	*June*
Sales	$30,000	110%	120%	150%	200%	220%
Purchases	30,000	110%	115%	140%	150%	110%
Miscellaneous						
expenses	10,000	$10,600	$12,000	$12,000	$14,000	$10,000

January is treated as the base month, and sales and purchases for the other months are expressed as percents of January figures. On January 1 the cash balance is $15,000. Past experience shows that sales will probably be 50 percent cash and 50 percent credit. Accounts receivable, on the average, are collected 80 percent in the month following sale, 10 percent the following month, and 9 percent in the next month, with an average of 1 percent uncollectible. Credit sales made in October, November, and December of 19X1 were $15,000 in each month. Purchases require a 10 percent down payment with the balance paid in the next month. December purchases require a payment of $10,000 in January. Payments for miscellaneous expenses are paid in the month when the expenses are incurred. When the cash balance falls below $14,000, $10,000 will be borrowed; when the cash balance exceeds $25,000, $10,000 will be repaid.

Directions

Prepare a cash budget for the first six months of 19X2.

5-2

Toledo Co. has regularly followed the practice of recording sales at net prices, using terms 2/10, n/30. A change to use of the "gross" method is now contemplated. The accountant is asked to present in journal and ledger form a series of typical transactions recorded under each of the two procedures for purposes of comparison. Following are the transactions chosen; all amounts shown are "gross" amounts:

(1) Sales on account, $100,000.

(2) Collections within discount period, $70,000.

(3) Collections too late for discount, $20,000.

(4) Sales returns from customers whose accounts are unpaid, $500.

(5) Sales returns from customers whose accounts have been collected, $500; of these, $400 had been collected at net. (Use Customer Advances for amount of credit granted.)

(6) Of the uncollected accounts at the end of the period it is anticipated that $9,000 will be collected within the discount period. The discount period has expired with respect to the remainder.

(7) The collections are made during the next period as anticipated.

Directions

Journalize and post to T accounts (a) assuming use of net prices throughout and (b) using gross prices.

5-3

The Small Co. begins business January 1, 19X1. Sales on account during the year total $100,000, and collections on account are $85,000. On December 31 one account of $750, that of Jane Doe, is written off as uncollectible. During 19X2, sales on account total $140,000 and collections total $135,000; in addition, $100 is recovered from Jane Doe. At the end of 19X2 it is decided to establish an allowance for uncollectibles on 19X2 business of 2.5 percent, to write off certain accounts of 19X1 not yet collected, $2,900, and to write off against the allowance several charges originating in 19X2 in the total amount of $1,925.

Directions

Make journal entries for 19X1 and 19X2.

CHAPTER 6

6-1

MARIE E. CO.
Comparative Balance Sheets, December 31

	19XX	19X1
Cash in bank	$ 40,000	$ 50,000
Marketable securities	20,000	90,000
Accounts receivable (net)	100,000	300,000
Inventories	500,000	900,000
Current prepayments	3,000	10,000
Land	30,000	40,000
Buildings	100,000	100,000
Equipment	150,000	200,000
Goodwill	70,000	50,000
	$1,013,000	$1,740,000
Accounts payable	$ 180,000	$ 467,000
Other current liabilities	10,000	34,000
Bonds payable	—	200,000
Allowance for depreciation	20,000	33,000
Capital stock	800,000	1,000,000
Retained earnings	3,000	6,000
	$1,013,000	$1,740,000
Income statement data for 19X1		
Net sales	$ 300,000	
Cost of goods sold	180,000	
Selling expenses	20,000	
General expenses (includes depreciation of		
$23,000)	40,000	
Bond interest	6,000	
Federal and state taxes	30,000	
Gain on equipment sale (cost, 15,000;		
depreciation to date, $10,000)	10,000	
Write-down of goodwill	20,000	
Dividends paid	11,000	

Directions

Prepare a funds working capital statement for 19X1

6-2

From the reports of Amy Enne Co.:

Balance Sheet Data

	19XX	19X1
Cash in bank	$ 15,000	$ 30,000
Receivables	55,000	100,000
Inventories	100,000	260,000
Equipment	30,000	60,000
Buildings	20,000	40,000
Land	10,000	40,000
	$230,000	$530,000
Accounts payable	$100,000	$190,000
Mortgage payable	—	40,000
Allowance for bad debts	1,000	3,000
Allowance for depreciation	20,000	15,000
Capital stock	80,000	230,000
Retained earnings	29,000	52,000
	$230,000	$530,000

Income Statement Data for 19X1

Net sales	$400,000
Expenses	330,000
Taxes	38,000
Total expenses	368,000
Net income	$ 32,000
Dividends paid	$ 4,000

OTHER DATA: Equipment which cost $30,000, and had been depreciated down to $14,000, was sold for $9,000 cash. The loss was debited to Retained Earnings.

Directions

Prepare a funds working capital statement for 19X1.

CHAPTER 7

For Problems 7-1 and 7-2 we will use the data used for Problems 6-1 and 6-2 respectively. This will provide the opportunity to compare funds statements on a working capital basis with those on a cash flow basis. We will discuss the differences at the end of the solution for Problem 7-2, but give some thought to it as you work the problems.

Problem 7-1

MARIE E. CO.
Comparative Balance Sheets, December 31

	19XX	*19X1*
Cash in bank	$ 40,000	$ 50,000
Marketable securities	20,000	90,000
Accounts receivable (net)	100,000	300,000
Inventories	500,000	900,000
Current prepayments	3,000	10,000
Land	30,000	40,000
Buildings	100,000	100,000
Equipment	150,000	200,000
Goodwill	70,000	50,000
	$1,013,000	$1,740,000
Accounts payable	$ 180,000	$ 467,000
Other current liabilities	10,000	34,000
Bonds payable	—	200,000
Allowance for depreciation	20,000	33,000
Capital stock	800,000	1,000,000
Retained earnings	3,000	6,000
	$1,013,000	$1,740,000

Income statement data for 19X1	
Net sales	$ 300,000
Cost of goods sold	180,000
Selling expenses	20,000
General expenses (includes depreciation of $23,000)	40,000
Bond interest	6,000
Federal and state taxes	30,000
Gain on equipment sale (cost, 15,000; depreciation to date, $10,000)	10,000
Write-down of goodwill	20,000
Dividends paid	11,000

Directions

Prepare a cash flow funds statement for 19X1

7-2

From the reports of Amy Enne Co.:

Balance Sheet Data

	19XX	19X1
Cash in bank	$ 15,000	$ 30,000
Receivables	55,000	100,000
Inventories	100,000	260,000
Equipment	30,000	60,000
Buildings	20,000	40,000
Land	10,000	40,000
	$230,000	$530,000
Accounts payable	$100,000	$190,000
Mortgage payable	—	40,000
Allowance for bad debts	1,000	3,000
Allowance for depreciation	20,000	15,000
Capital stock	80,000	230,000
Retained earnings	29,000	52,000
	$230,000	$530,000

Income Statement Data for 19X1

Net sales	$400,000
Expenses	330,000
Taxes	38,000
Total expenses	368,000
Net income	$ 32,000
Dividends paid	$ 4,000

OTHER DATA: Equipment which cost $30,000, and had been depreciated down to $14,000, was sold for $9,000 cash. The loss was debited to Retained Earnings.

Directions

Prepare a cash flow funds statement for 19X1.

CHAPTER 8

8-1

On January 1, Megansett Inc. has on hand 1,400 ounces of X inventories at $3 per ounce. During the year the purchases are as follows:

Date	Quantity, ounces	Cost
Feb. 15	1,200	$3,720
Apr. 20	2,000	6,400
July 10	1,800	5,940
Oct. 15	1,750	6,125
Dec. 30	1,500	5,400
Dec. 31 inventory	3,400	

Directions

Determine the cost of X on hand on December 31 and cost of X sold (1) by weighted-average method, (2) by the FIFO method, and (3) by the LIFO method.

8-2

Priscilla's Variety Store uses the retail method of computing inventory and cost of goods sold. It does so by, first, determining the average markup percentage for the period, second, determining the final inventory at retail prices, and, third, subtracting the average markup percentage from the final inventory at retail. Step 1 consists of determining the retail value of the initial inventory (carried over from last period), plus the retail value of all purchases (determined at the time of receipt of each purchase order), plus all subsequent markups. This total (at retail), compared with the cost of initial inventory plus purchases, provides the markup percentage. The final inventory at retail is found by adding purchases, at retail, to initial inventory, at retail, *minus sales* and, for the sake of conservatism, all markdowns. Now, try this out on the accompanying problem.

Priscilla's merchandising data for the year are:

	At cost	At retail
Inventory, Jan. 1	$ 73,465	$ 105,000
Purchases during year	896,546	1,280,780
Additional markups		247,120
Markdowns		362,140
Sales		1,142,960

Directions

Prepare journal entries to record the merchandising data for the year, including cost of goods sold and final inventory.

8-3

Brewster Stores Corp. records merchandise purchases at net invoice prices and sales at gross prices, although the latter are subject to cash discounts. The merchandise inventory on December 1, including freight costs, is $70,000. On that date accounts receivable total $80,-000 and the allowance for sales discounts is $1,800. During December the following transactions involving merchandise accounts occur:

(1) Merchandise purchases, at invoice prices, $150,000, terms 2/10, n/30.

(2) Transportation and other handling costs paid by check and all applicable to December purchases, $10,100.

(3) Sales on account, $180,000.

(4) Collections on account, $185,000 less discounts of $5,000.

(5) Payments on account, $140,000 net; actual amount paid, $140,900.

(6) Merchandise returned to vendors, at gross invoice prices, $5,000, of which $4,000 had been paid for at net prices and $1,000 at gross. The corporation was required to pay freight charges on this return amounting to $680.

(7) Sales returns, at invoice prices, $4,000.

(8) Purchase allowances, at gross invoice prices, granted by vendors, $1,000.

(9) Estimated sales discounts to be taken by customers with respect to account balances on December 31, $2,000.

(10) Merchandise inventory on December 31, at net invoice prices and before assigning transportation and handling charges, $35,280. (Free advice: Did you notice that the net $35,280 price of the final inventory is exactly one-fourth of the net cost of purchases for the period?)

Directions

Journalize the above transactions, including entries reflecting a reasonable assignment of transportation charges to the final inventory and to merchandise cost of sales.

CHAPTER 9

9-1

Dunfey Co. purchased a parcel of land, a vacant store building thereon, and some delivery equipment from Strong Co. for a lump-sum price of $125,000; terms, 25 percent in cash and the balance in 6 months with interest at the annual rate of 12 percent. A qualified appraiser estimated the market values of the assets as follows: land, $22,000; building, $104,500; equipment, $11,000. On the books of Strong Co., just prior to the transfer, the property sold was represented by the following accounts and balances:

Land	$15,000
Building	95,000
Delivery Equipment	28,888
Building—Allowance for Depreciation	31,000
Delivery Equipment—Allowance for Depreciation	18,500

Directions

Make an apportionment of the total cost of the property acquired by Dunfey Co. on the basis of relative appraised values and, using the apportionment, record the acquisition on the buyer's books. Also, give the entries when the balance of the purchase price is paid, assuming the entire transaction falls within one accounting period.

9-2

On April 25, year 1, Spring Co. purchased a secondhand delivery truck for $11,000, cash. On April 29, Auto Repair Service submitted a bill for repairs on the truck for $2,500. The truck was placed in service on May 1. Service life was estimated at 2½ years (30 months) and salvage value at $1,500. The buyer's accounting period is the calendar year.

On February 1, year 2, the old truck was exchanged for a new truck with a list price of $32,000. The vendor granted a trade-in allowance of $7,500 for the old equipment, and the balance of the invoice was paid in cash. At that time the old truck could have been sold on the used-car market for $5,000, cash. Depreciation is recorded by the straight-line method.

Directions

a. Record all entries relating to the delivery truck during year 1, including accrual of depreciation for the year.

b. Record the exchange occurring on February 1, year 2, under each of the following: (1) "fused-transaction" interpretation, (value of new asset is net book value of old plus cash boot paid); (2) acceptance of list price as cost of new equipment; (3) defining cost of new unit on a cash or equivalent basis.

9-3

On July 1, 19XX, Bickford Co. purchased a machine which cost $5,000 cash. It was estimated that the machine would have a salvage value of $500 after a useful life of 10 years. Installation costs of $300 were charged to machine repairs expense as of July 1, 19XX. Entries recognizing depreciation were made on December 31, 19XX, and on December 31, 19X1. When the accountant was adjusting the books at the end of 19X1, she discovered the error concerning the installation charge, and at that time it was agreed by the accountant and the management that the probable remaining useful life of the machine, from December 31, 19X2, would be 10 years, with salvage unchanged at $500.

Directions

Make journal entries correcting the machine account and the allowance for depreciation as of January 1, 19X2, taking into account both the error with respect to installation and the useful life. Record depreciation on December 31 for the year 19X2.

CHAPTER 10

10-1

At the close of business December 31, 19XX, the general ledger of Black and White, equal partners, showed the following balances (000's omitted):

Debits		Credits	
Cash	$ 10,000	Accounts Payable	$ 20,000
Accounts		Allowance for	
Receivable	10,000	Bad Debts	1,000
Merchandise	45,000	Allowance for	
Land	10,000	Depreciation	9,000
Buildings	20,000	Black, Capital	40,000
Equipment	10,000	White, Capital	35,000
	$105,000		$105,000

At this time White retired from the firm and sold his equity to Blue. The new partner agreed to assign to the firm patent rights with an estimated value of $5,000,000. The book values of the assets and liabilities as shown above were not revised except that the allowance for depreciation was reduced to $4,000,000, land appreciation in the amount of $5,000,000 was recognized, and the value of patents contributed by Blue was recorded.

Immediately after the reorganization of the firm, a corporation was formed, the Black & Blue Co., with an authorized capital of 20,000,000 shares of no-par common stock. Subscriptions were received from various parties covering 1,000,000 shares at $10 each, to be paid in cash. Subscriptions were received from Black and Blue for 9,000,000 shares (4,500,000 each), to be settled by transferring to the corporation all the assets of the partnership and the assumption by the corporation of the accounts payable of the firm as shown on the books. These capital-raising transactions were carried through as agreed, and stock certificates were issued.

Directions

a. Prepare entries to cover the reorganization of the partnership as outlined.

b. Present entries covering the organization of Black & Blue Co., assuming new books to be employed. Prepare a balance sheet.

10-2

In June, Montrose Corp. offers 15,000 shares of 15 percent par $100, preferred stock. Each share of stock carries the right to subscribe for three shares of no-par common stock at $8 per share; the rights are exercisable at any time prior to August 1. The offering price of the investment unit (one share of preferred plus rights to acquire three shares of common) is $110. Summarized transaction data for the period of June to August 1 are as follows: (1) 14,000 investment units are issued for cash at $110 per unit, and subsequent transactions between investors indicate a value of $101 per share for the preferred shares and $3 each for a right to subscribe for one common share; (2) amount invested on exercise of rights is $333,600.

Directions

a. Make entries to record the activities of the June to August 1 period.

b. Compute the amount of lapsed rights. What treatment should be accorded this element in the statements?

10-3

Johnson Co. enters into negotiations with John Goodyear with the objective of obtaining Goodyear's services for a period of years as an executive of the corporation. The cash value of Goodyear's services, on the basis of a careful determination, is found to be $60,000 per year. A 5-year contract is finally agreed upon. Under it Johnson pays Goodyear $50,000 in cash per year and grants him an option to acquire 2,000 shares of unissued common stock of the company at the end of each year of employment, or within 3 months thereafter, for a cash investment of $95 per share. The market value of the company's stock at the time of the agreement is made is $100 per share.

Directions

Make summary entries for Johnson Co. for the first year of the contract, assuming Goodyear exercises his option for all 2,000 shares at the end of the year.

CHAPTER 11

11-1

A corporation has outstanding 2,000 shares of preferred stock and 35,000 shares of common stock. Par value in each case is $100 per share, and both classes of stock were issued at par. Successful operation has resulted in retention of earnings in the amount of $550,000.

During a year the following transactions relating to the two stock issues occurred:

January 25. Declared a dividend of $1.50 on the 2,000 shares of preferred.

February 5. Paid the preferred dividend.

February 14. Declared a dividend of $5 per share on common stock in the form of notes due in 60 days without interest.

April 15. Paid the note dividend.

June 5. Declared a stock dividend on common stock of 4 percent of par value of outstanding common stock.

June 30. Issued the dividend shares (1,400).

October 6. Declared a dividend payable in one-half share of Boston Co. stock for every share of common stock outstanding. The stock cost $5 per share and now has a market value of $15 per share.

October 10. Paid dividend declared on October 6.

November 5. Split common stock two for one with a reduction of par to $50 per share. (Three other quarterly dividends were declared and paid on the preferred shares, but the data are omitted from the above list.

Directions

Journalize.

11-2

A corporation has retained earnings of $500,000 on December 31, and on that date the directors approve:

(1) Declaration of a cash dividend of $100,000.

(2) Appropriation of $20,000 to the reserve for bond sinking fund.

(3) Issuance of a check for $20,000 to the trustee of the sinking fund.

(4) Establishment of a reserve for contingencies, $100,000.

(5) Calling and retiring 500 shares of preferred stock (par 100) at the call price of $105.

(6) Establishment of a special fund (in a separate bank account) of $50,000 to be used to replace old equipment.

Directions

Give general journal entries to record the transactions. In each case, state the effect upon Retained Earnings, if any.

11-3

The following items were reported between the liabilities and the stockholders' equity section in a recent balance sheet:

Reserves:

Reserve for insurance	$ 5,500
Reserve for contingencies	4,000
Reserve for federal income tax	15,000
Reserve for loss on bad debts	3,000
Reserve for building expansion	10,000
Reserve for depreciation	35,000
Reserve for depletion	10,000
Total reserves	$82,500

Deferred credits:

Unearned receipts from customers	$25,000
Refundable advances from subsidiary	10,000
Total deferred credits	$35,000

Directions

Classify the above "reserves" and "deferred credits" as (1) contra asset, (2) retained earnings, or (3) liability.

CHAPTER 12

12-1

On January 1 a company issues $800,000 maturity amount of 20-year, 12 percent debenture bonds at a price which produces an effective yield of 14 percent. Interest is payable July 1 and January 1.

Directions

Make entries for the following dates:

   a. January 1 (date on which the bonds are sold)

   b. July 1

   c. December 31

   d. January 1 of second year

NOTE: The present value of $1 per period for 40 periods at 7 percent per period is 13.33171.

12-2

On January 1 a company issues $2,000,000 maturity amount of 20-year notes bearing coupon interest of 12 percent, payable semiannually, and priced to yield 11 percent compounded semiannually.

Directions

Journalize the history of these notes through January 1 of the second year. Note that the present value of $1 per period for 40 periods at 5½ percent is 16.04612.

CHAPTER 13

13-1

Manufacturing costs in process II during a given month consisted of raw materials, $8,600, labor, $25,800, and overhead, $17,200, in addition to product received from process I consisting of 8,600 units with an average cost of $2 per unit. At the beginning of the month in process II there were 400 units of work in process and these were complete as to process I and raw materials costs and three-fourths complete as to labor and overhead. At the end of the month 500 units remained unfinished in Process II. These were complete as to process I and raw materials costs, and were 80 percent complete as to labor and overhead costs.

Directions

Prepare a schedule showing computation of unit costs of materials, labor, and overhead for the month as well as work in process at the end of the month and cost of product transferred to the next process, process III.

13-2

Following is a summary of the manufacturing activities for a year. The company employs process cost accounting methods with three processes recognized: foundry, grinding, and finishing.

Open the following ledger accounts: Materials and Supplies, Foundry, Grinding, Finishing, Finished Goods. To the extent that these accounts are affected, enter the following transactions directly in the accounts. Number your entries to correspond with the transaction numbers.

(1) Materials and supplies purchased on account, $35,000.

(2) Materials and supplies issued: foundry, $30,000; finishing, $2,000.

(3) Wages accrued: foundry, $22,000; grinding, $10,000; finishing, $14,000.

(4) Company-owned machinery consists of units costing $55,-000. Depreciation, at the rate of 10 percent, is charged one-half to foundry and one-fourth each to grinding and finishing. No salvage is anticipated.

(5) Insurance expired, $660, is assignable in the same ratio as depreciation.

(6) Miscellaneous manufacturing costs incurred all for cash, are foundry, $12,000; grinding, $8,000; finishing, $6,000.

(7) All production passes directly from foundry to grinding and on to finishing. At year-end there is no unfinished product in foundry and finishing; the inventory of unfinished product in grinding has a computed cost of $3,000. There were no inventories at the beginning of the year.

Directions

a. Open ledger accounts for Materials and Supplies, Foundry, Grinding, Finishing, and Finished Goods. Enter the numbered transaction data insofar as they affect these four accounts.

b. Prepare a statement of cost of goods manufactured.

CHAPTER 14

14-1

A company records materials at standard costs in the accounts, and it uses a process cost system. Materials records for April show the following information:

Material	Quantity purchased	Quantity used Actual	Quantity used Standard	Process	Price Actual	Price Standard
1	2,100	2,300	2,200	A	$ .52	$ .50
2	4,200	3,500	3,200	A	1.05	1.00
3	1,800	1,500	1,600	B	2.06	2.00
4	2,000	1,800	1,700	C	.74	.75

Directions

Construct ledger accounts for Raw Materials, Raw Materials Price Variances, Accounts Payable, Process A, Process A Quantity Variance, Process B, Process B Quantity Variance, Process C, Process C Quantity Variance. Enter the data of the problem.

14-2

A company uses standard costs in accounting for direct labor and employs a job-order plan of accounts. Records provide the following information for September:

	Labor hours		Wage rates	
Department	Actual	Standard	Actual	Standard
1	4,200	4,150	$2.75	$2.50
2	3,758	3,800	3.10	3.00
3	5,640	5,600	2.90	3.00

Directions

Construct ledger accounts for Payroll, Work in Process, Department 1 Wage Variance, Department 1 Efficiency Variance, Department 2 Wage Variance, Department 2 Efficiency Variance, Department 3 Wage Variance, Department 3 Efficiency Variance. Enter the data of the problem.

14-3

At the end of the first year of operations certain accounts of a company stand as follows:

	Totals	
	Debit	Credit
Materials	$210,000	$180,000
Work in Process	540,000	500,000
Finished Goods	500,000	470,000
Manufacturing Overhead	120,000	120,000
Payroll—Direct Labor	—	285,000
Payroll—Indirect Labor	—	40,000
Accounts Payable	—	215,000
Materials Price Variances	12,000	7,000
Materials Quantity Variances	14,000	4,000
Labor Wage Variances	8,000	$ 3,000
Labor Efficiency Variances	13,000	3,000
Manufacturing Overhead Variances	25,000	5,000
Miscellaneous Accounts		80,000
Cost of Goods Sold	470,000	

Directions

In journal form present summary entries to record the transactions during the year which gave rise to the amounts shown above.

CHAPTER 15

15-1

We offer two income options to a prospective executive for our corporation. Option 1 provides that, in addition to annual salary, the officer will be given a bonus in shares of treasury stock at the end of each year. The bonus will amount to $100,000 worth of stock at current market value at the end of year 1. It will be increased by 20 percent in terms of market value each year for 10 years, and it will culminate in retirement with a special bonus of $500,000 in the form of a paid-up annuity (in addition to the regular stock bonus). Option 2 provides the same annual salary, but the bonus will be $150,000 worth of treasury stock each year-end. There will be a special bonus, at the 10-year terminal date, in the form of a paid-up annuity of such amount as will make option 2 have the same present value as option 1.

Directions

Determine the amount needed at end of 10 years under option 2 to make option 2 equal to option 1 in present value. (NOTE: The present value of $1, discounted at 20 percent per period for 10 periods, is .1615. The present value of an annuity of $1 per period for 10 periods, at 20 percent, is $4.19247. One dollar invested now at 20 percent per annum will grow to "future value" of $6.1917 in 10 years.

15-2

A company is considering purchase of equipment for $60,000, which should produce an increase of $18,000 in annual revenue, an increase in operating costs annually of $9,000, and a reduction of annual labor costs of $4,000. Estimated useful life, with no salvage, is 10 years. Straight-line depreciation will be used for tax purposes, and the company's average income tax rate is 40 percent.

Directions

a. Determine the approximate payback period.

b. Determine present value of prospective annual net cash flow, using 15 percent rate. Is purchase justified? (NOTE:

Present worth of annuity of $1 per period for 10 periods at 15 percent is $5.019.)

15-3

The estimated costs of in-house production of a component part are:

Materials (all costs of order, receive, store)	$1,250
Direct labor	1,750
Variable overhead (200 percent of direct labor)	3,500
Fixed overhead	2,000
	$8,500

A reliable manufacturer offers to supply this item, F.O.B. our plant, for $7,000 each.

Directions

Present your recommendation and reasons. (NOTE: Our ratio of profit to sales is approximately 10 percent.)

CHAPTER 18

18-1

The ledger balances of Parent Co. and Sub Co., after closing entries have been made, stand as follows at year-end:

	End of year	
	Parent Co.	*Sub Co.*
Cash in bank	$ 30,000	$ 8,000
Customers (Includes Sub Co. $2,000)	55,000	19,000
Merchandise	62,000	30,000
Investment B Co. stock, cost	60,000	
Land	20,000	6,000
Plant (net)	70,000	33,000
	$297,000	$96,000
Current liabilities	$ 52,000	$23,000
Capital stock	160,000	60,000
Retained earnings	85,000	13,000
	$297,000	$96,000

Parent Co. bought 80 percent of $60,000 outstanding capital stock of Sub Co. at beginning of this year when Sub Co. retained earnings balance was $5,000. At year-end, merchandise on Parent Co. books includes goods which Sub Co. bought for $8,000 and sold to Parent Co. for $10,000, of which Parent Co. at year-end owes $2,000 to Sub Co. During the year, Sub Co. sold land to Parent Co for $10,000 cash. This land originally cost Sub Co. $6,000.

Directions

Prepare consolidated balance sheet as of year-end for Parent Co. and its subsidiary, Sub Co. Assume any excess of investment cost over book value represents goodwill.

18-2

Papaco acquired 100 percent of the voting stock of Babaco when the latter was organized and, during the following year, all sales of Babaco were made to Papaco. At the end of the year, Papaco inventories included 25 percent of all goods purchased during the year from Babaco. Condensed income statement data for the year are as follows:

| | End of year | |
	Papaco	Babaco
Sales	$600,000	$240,000
Cost of goods sold	$360,000	$160,000
Other expenses and taxes	120,000	40,000
Total deductions	$480,000	$200,000
Net income	$120,000	$ 40,000

Directions

Prepare a consolidated income statement for Papaco and Babaco.

18-3

Use the same income-statement amounts as shown in 16-2. Assume Papaco acquired only 80 percent of Babaco stock, that 75 percent of Babaco sales go to Papaco, and 20 percent of the goods remain in Papaco inventory at year-end.

Directions

Prepare a consolidated income statement.

CHAPTER 19

19-1

a. Our Company uses the "allowance for bad debts" procedure in its financial statements and recognizes uncollectibles for income tax purposes only when specific accounts are clearly worthless. At the end of a given year, with credit sales of $500,000, the company makes an adjusting entry to provide 1 percent of gross sales as an addition to the "allowance." During that year, a total of $3,800 in specific accounts receivable were recognized as uncollectible and were charged off (and reported as bad debt "expense") on the tax return. The tax rate amounted to an average of 30 percent.

What provision should the company make in its accounts so that the statements will properly reflect the disparity in accounting versus tax treatments? Journalize.

b. Assume that we make cash collections which, for accounting purposes, we consider and treat as "advances" from the remitters but are required to report in full as taxable income. Assume the amount of collections is $100,000.

Make the indicated tax allocation journal entry (with 30 percent tax rate).

c. We use the sum-of-years' digits depreciation method for tax purposes and the straight-line method for book purposes. In a given year this difference results in taxable income (at 30 percent) of $50,000 less than the pretax income per books.

Make the required tax-allocation entry.

CHAPTER 21

21-1

For year 20 the reported earnings retained, after deducting dividends of $30,000, are $20,000. Depreciation for the year is reported at $40,-000. Analysis of the depreciation charge shows it to be made up as follows:

Year asset acquired	General price index	Dollar cost	Depreciation charged in year 20
1	80	$400,000	$18,000
4	100	10,000	1,000
8	130	50,000	5,000
12	150	50,000	5,000
16	180	30,000	2,000
20	198	100,000	9,000

At the end of year 20 the price index stands at 200.

Directions

In tabular form translate the depreciation charge from dollars of the year of origin to dollars at end of year 20. Determine the corrected earnings of stockholders and corrected change in retained earnings.

21-2

In its stockholder report a company regularly presents a comparative schedule showing the composition and amounts of "working capital" for each of the past 5 years. A sample schedule is as follows (000's omitted):

	Years ending December 31				
	1	2	3	4	5
Current Assets:					
Cash	$ 600	$ 620	$ 630	$ 650	$ 690
Receivables (net)	1,200	1,240	1,270	1,300	1,320
Inventories	800	820	850	900	920
Prepayments	10	12	14	14	16
Totals	$2,610	$2,692	$2,764	$2,864	$2,946
Current Liabilities	$1,200	$1,220	$1,264	$1,300	$1,346
Working Capital	$1,410	$1,472	$1,500	$1,564	$1,600
General price index on December 31	100	105	113	117	130

Directions

Prepare a similar schedule in uniform dollars as of end of year 5. Assume that the price level changes occurred evenly throughout each year (including a 4-point increase in year 1). Assume also the inventories and the prepayment balances were acquired throughout the final 6 months in each year.

21-3

NEW WORLD CO.
Income Statement, Year Ended December 31, 19XX

Sales		$250,000
Expenses and taxes:		
Merchandise cost of sales	$150,000	
Salaries and wages	37,500	
Depreciation	30,000	
Miscellaneous	15,000	
Taxes	7,000	239,500
Earnings of stockholders		$ 10,500
Dividends		8,000
Earnings retained		$ 2,500

Date or period	*Consumer price index*
End of present year	100
Average for year	105
Acquisition date, depreciable assets	150
Average dates for cost of merchandise sold	107

Assume that the revenue and deductions (except merchandise cost of sales and depreciation) accrued evenly throughout the year.

Directions

Prepare an income statement with all amounts stated in dollars of uniform purchasing power.

CHAPTER 22

22-1

In the Republic of ZO all foreign exchange is controlled by the Central Bank, where the officers, Roz and Jim, decide from day to day the prices for which the Zodiaks can buy whatever foreign currency they need (at the foreign currency "selling" rates). The officers also decide the prices which the Central Bank will pay the Zodiaks, in Phegns (#), for any foreign currencies they may have received (the foreign currency "buying" rates).

Parent Co., in U.S.A., established a subsidiary (TXYPCO) years ago in ZO by investing $1,500,000 when the buying rate was #1=$1.50. Other rates of significance for our exercise are:

Date	Relevant rate
Land acquired	$1.70
Building and equipment acquired	1.65
Initial inventory acquired	1.52
Ending inventory acquired	1.48
January 1	1.50
December 31	1.40
Average for year	1.45

At the beginning of business on January 1, the trial balance of TXYPCO, stated in Phegns, is as follows (with 000's omitted):

	Debit	Credit
Cash	# 50	#
Receivables	120	
Inventories	240	
Land	100	
Building	400	
Equipment	500	
Allowance for depreciation		180
Accounts payable		230
Capital stock (all held by Parent Co.)		1,000
	#1,410	#1,410

Transaction data for one year, all stated in Phegns, and with 000's omitted, are as follows:

· Sales of merchandise, #1,250, all on account.

· Purchases of merchandise, on account, #1,000.

· Payments to creditors, #950.

· Collections from customers, #1,100.

· Selling, general, and administrative expenses incurred, on account, #360.

· Depreciation: building, #12; equipment, #50.

· Merchandise inventory on December 31, #440.

· End-of-year liability for local income tax, #15.

Directions

a. Prepare a trial balance for TXYPCO in Phegns at the end of the year. To do so, you may wish to enter the transaction data in T accounts along with their initial balances in order to determine the amounts to be shown in the trial balance.

b. Prepare journal entries for the parent's consolidating work sheet to combine the TXYPCO accounts with those of the parent for purposes of preparing (1) a consolidated income statement and (2) a consolidated balance sheet.

Solutions to Supplementary Problems

CHAPTER 1

1-1

A. COMPANY
Balance Sheet, December 31, 19XX

Assets			Equities		
Current:			Current liabilities:		
Cash	$ 3,000		Taxes payable	$ 1,000	
Due from			Wages accrued		
customers	3,500		payable	400	
Coal inventory	12,000		Notes payable	2,500	
Unexpired			Advances by		
insurance	250	$18,750	customers	500	
Noncurrent:			Due to suppliers	2,000	
Equipment		5,000	Rent payable	250	$ 6,650
			Stockholders' equity		
			Capital stock	$15,000	
			Retained earnings	2,100	17,100
		$23,750			$23,750

Earnings for the year: Paid out in dividends, $750 + retained, $2,100 = $2,850.

1-2

ANOTHER COMPANY
Balance Sheet, December 31, 19X1

Assets			Equities		
Current:			Current liabilities:		
Cash in office	$ 700		Dividends payable	$ 1,000	
Cash in bank	5,800		Interest on notes	150	
Accounts			Customer		
receivable	25,000		advances	1,100	
Merchandise	45,000		Taxes payable	2,500	
Store supplies	400		Accounts payable	20,000	
Office supplies	300		Payroll payable	750	
Unexpired			Equipment		
insurance	1,000	$78,200	contract	2,000	$27,500
Noncurrent:			Noncurrent notes		
Office			Payable		5,000
equipment	$ 1,000		Total liabilities		$32,500
Store			Stockholders' equity:		
equipment	14,800		Capital stock	$50,000	
Delivery			Retained earnings	14,000	64,000
equipment	2,500	18,300			
		$96,500			$96,500

Current ratio is 78,200/27,500 = 2.8 to 1; equity ratio is 64,000/96,500 = 66 percent.

CHAPTER 2

2-1

KELLY CORP.
Balance Sheet, December 31, 19XX

Assets			Equities		
Current:			Current liabilities:		
Cash in bank	$ 1,000		Accounts		
Accounts			payable		$ 1,400
receivable	3,000		Notes payable		1,200
Merchandise	6,500	$10,500			$ 2,600
Noncurrent:			Stockholders'		
Land	$ 1,200		equity:		
Equipment (net)	6,000		Capital stock	$24,000	
Building (net)	12,000	19,200	Retained		
			earnings	3,100	$27,100
		$29,700			$29,700

KELLY CORP.
Income Statement, Year Ended December 31, 19XX

Sales		$14,000
Expenses:		
Cost of goods sold	$7,100	
Selling	1,800	
General	2,000	10,900
Net Income		$ 3,100

2-2

LAING CORP.
Balance Sheet, December 31, 19XX

Assets			Equities		
Current:			Current liabilities:		
Cash in bank	$ 2,000		Accounts payable		$ 2,800
Accounts			Noncurrent liabilities:		
receivable	6,000		Notes payable		2,400
Merchandise					$ 5,200
inventory	$13,000	$21,000	Stockholders' equity:		
Noncurrent:			Capital stock	$48,000	
Land	$ 2,400		Retained earnings	4,000	52,000
Building	23,000				
Furniture	10,800	36,200			
		$57,200			$57,200

LAING CORP
Income Statement, Year Ended Dec. 31, 19XX

Sales		$28,000
Expenses:		
Cost of goods sold	$14,200	
Selling	3,600	
General	4,000	
Depreciation	2,200	24,000
Net income and earnings retained		$ 4,000

2.3

TIDY SERVICE CO.
Balance Sheet, December 31, 19XX

Assets			
Current:			
Cash on hand		$ 600	
Cash in bank		5,050	
Accounts rec.	$15,500		
Less uncoll.	2,100	13,400	
Prepaid insurance		1,000	$20,050
Noncurrent:			
Land		$10,000	
Buildings	$30,000		
Machinery	45,000		
Equipment	6,500		
	$81,500		
Allow. for			
deprec.	15,000	66,500	76,500
			$96,550

Equities			
Liabilities:			
Current:			
Accounts payable		$ 6,500	
Noncurrent:			
Mortgage payable		15,000	
Total liabilities			$21,500
Stockholders' equity:			
Capital stock		$60,000	
Retained earnings		15,050	75,050
			$96,550

TIDY SERVICE CO.
Income Statement, Year Ended December 31, 19XX

Sales		$27,500
Expenses:		
Office wages	$ 4,000	
Plant maintenance	2,000	
Heat, light, power	10,000	
Advertising	1,000	
Taxes	2,000	
Miscellaneous	1,500	20,500
Net income		$ 7,000
Retained earnings, Jan. 1		8,050
Retained earnings, Dec. 31		$15,050

CHAPTER 3

3-1

NOTE: To save space, the contents of the T accounts are listed rather than being presented in T form. The account for *State Bank* has the following left-hand (debit) entries: (1) 10,000, (11) 4,000. The right-hand (credit) entries are (2) 1,000, (3) 6,000, (5) 100, (6) 120, (7) 50, (8) 150, (9) 50, (10) 50, (12) 400, (13) 1,000. *Merchandise* debits: (3) 6,000, (4) 1,000, (5) 100, (7) 50. *Merchandise* credit: (14) 2,700. *Supplies* debit: (9) 50. Credit: (15) 35. *Equipment* debits: (2) 1,000, (6) 120. Credit: (10) 10. *Essex Co.* debit: (4) 1,000. Credit: (3) 1,000. *Capital Stock* credit: (1) 10,000. *Retained Earnings* credit: *(h)* 655. *Sales* credit: (11). Debit: *(a)* for 4,000. *Cost of Goods Sold* debit: (14). Credit: *(b)* for 2,700. Selling Expense debit: (10). Credit: *(e)* 50. *Selling and Delivery Wages* debit: (12). Credit: *(d)* for 400. *Supplies Expense* debit: (15). Credit: *(e)* for 35. *Depreciation Expense* debit: (16). Credit: *(f)* for 10. *Rent Expense* debit: (8). Credit: *(g)* for 150. *Income Summary* credit: *(a)* with 4,000. Debits: *(b)* 2,700, *(c)* 50, *(d)* 400, *(e)* 35, *(f)* 10, *(g)* 150, and *(h)* 655. The *income statement* shows Sales, $4,000, from which are subtracted the list of expenses: Cost of Goods Sold, 2,700; Selling Expenses, 50; Selling and Delivery Wages, 400; Supplies, 35; Depreciation, 10; and Rent, 150, for a total of 3,345, leaving Net Income, $655. The *balance sheet* shows current assets: State Bank, 5,080; Merchandise, 4,450; and Supplies, 15. To the total of 9,545 is added the Equipment, 1,110, to make Total Assets, $10,655. The equities consist of no liabilities and Stockholders' Equity made up of Capital Stock, 10,000, and Retained Earnings, 655, for a total (also) of $10,655, Total Equities.

3-2

NOTE: To save space, the contents of the T accounts are listed rather than being presented in T form. The account for *Cash in Bank* has the following left-hand (debit) entries: Bal. 2,500, (5) 245,000. The right-hand (credit) entries are (1) 1,200, (6) 205,000, (7) 900, (9) 6,800, (10) 5,000, (12) 3,000. *Accounts Receivable* debits: Bal. 22,000, (4) 250,000. Credit: (5) 245,000. *Merchandise* debits: Bal. 31,000, (2) 200,000. Credit: (16) 201,000. *Supplies* debits: Bal. 1,300, (3) 2,000. Credit: (15) 300. *Prepaid Insurance* debits: Bal. 1,450, (1) 1,200. Credit: (14) 850. *Land* debit: Bal. 15,500. *Building* debit: Bal. 30,500. Credit: (13) 915. *Equipment* debit: Bal. 10,500. Credit: (13) 1,050. *Accounts Payable* debit: (6) 205,000. Credits: Bal. 27,000, (2) 200,000, (3) 2,000, (11) 3,200. *Payroll Payable* debit: (9) 6,800. Credits: Bal. 2,500, (8) 7,000. *Taxes Payable* credit: (17) 10,000. *Capital Stock:* Bal. credit, 76,000. *Retained Earnings* credits: Bal. 9,250, (c) 16,785. *Sales* debit (a) and credit (4) for 250,000. *Merchandise Cost of Sales,* debit (16) and credit (b) for 201,-000. *Delivery Expense,* debit (10) and credit (b) for 5,000. *Salesmen's Services,* debit (8) and credit (b) for 7,000. *Depreciation Expense,* debit (13) and credit (b) for 1,965. *Insurance Expense,* debit (14) and credit (b) for 850. *Maintenance Expense,* debit (12) and credit (b) for 3,000. *Public Utility Expense,* debit (11) and credit (b) for 3,200. *Supplies Expense,* debit (15) and credit (b) for 300. *Property Tax,* debit (7) and credit (b) with 900. *Income Tax,* debit (17) and credit (b) for 10,000. *Income Summary* debits [all labeled (b)] 201,000, 5,000, 7,000, 1,965, 850, 3,000, 3,200, 300, 900, 10,000, and (c) 16,785. Credit: (a) 250,000.

The income statement lists *Sales,* $250,000, followed by the list of expenses shown as debit items in the Income Summary account and Net Income of $16,785.

The balance sheet lists, as current assets, Cash, 25,600; Accounts Receivable, 27,000; Merchandise, 30,000; Supplies, 3,000, and Prepaid Insurance, 1,800. As noncurrent assets: Land, 15,500; Building, 29,585; and Equipment, 9,450. The total for all assets is $141,935. Under Equities, the current liabilities are Accounts Payable, 27,200; Payroll Payable, 2,700; and Taxes Payable, 10,000, totaling $39,900. The Stockholders' Equity consists of Capital Stock, 76,000, and Retained Earnings, 26,035, a total of 102,035. And Equities total is $141,935.

CHAPTER 4

4-1

	Trial balance		Adjusting entries		Income statement		Balance sheet	
	Debit	Credit	Debit	Credit	Debit	Credit	Debit	Credit
Cash	1,000						1,000	
Accounts receivable	4,000			(1) 500			3,500	
Land	2,500						2,500	
Building	65,000						65,000	
Equipment	5,000						5,000	
Accounts payable		8,500						8,500
Notes payable		2,500						2,500
Capital stock		70,000						70,000
Sales		50,000				50,000		
Food inventory	40,000			(4) 30,000			10,000	
Selling expense	7,500		(5) 500		8,000			
General expense	6,000		(5) 1,000		7,000			
Sales—bad debts			(1) 500		500			
Depreciation			(2) 2,250		2,250			
Allowance for depreciation				(2) 2,250				2,250
Interest			(3) 300		300			
Interest payable				(3) 300				300
Food cost of sales			(4) 30,000		30,000			
Salaries accrued				(5) 1,500				1,500
Taxes			(6) 1,500		1,500			
Taxes accrued				(6) 1,500				1,500
Earnings of stockholders					450			450
Totals	131,000	131,000	36,050	36,050	50,000	50,000	87,000	87,000

4-2

BROWN CO.
Work Sheet, Year Ended December 31, 19XX

	Trial balance		Adjusting entries		Income statement		Balance sheet	
	Debit	Credit	Debit	Credit	Debit	Credit	Debit	Credit
Cash	4,000						4,000	
Accounts receivable	12,000						12,000	
Merchandise	54,400			(1) 28,400			26,000	
Land	6,800						6,800	
Building	48,000						48,000	
Equipment	24,000						24,000	
Accounts payable		5,600						5,600
Notes payable		20,000						20,000
Capital stock		80,000						80,000
Sales		58,800				58,800		
Selling expense	7,200		(4) 500		7,700			
General expense	8,000		(4) 1,000		9,000			
Cost of goods sold			(1) 28,400		28,400			
Depreciation			(2) 3,600		3,600			
Allowance for depreciation				(2) 3,600				3,600
Interest			(3) 1,200		1,200			
Accrued liabilities				(3) 1,200				4,700
				(4) 1,500				
				(5) 2,000				
Taxes			(5) 2,000		2,000			
Earnings of stockholders					6,900			6,900
	164,400	164,400	36,700	36,700	58,800	58,800	120,800	120,800

CHAPTER 5

5-1

MILAN CO.
Cash Budget, First Six Months, 19X2

	January	February	March	April	May	June
Cash balance	$15,000	$21,850	$22,300	$21,200	$23,850	$18,835
Receipts (see schedule)	29,850	31,350	34,050	39,900	51,285	60,870
Total cost	$44,850	$53,200	$56,350	$61,100	$75,135	$79,705
Disbursements:						
Purchases of last month	$10,000	$27,000	$29,700	$31,050	$37,800	$40,500
Down payments	3,000	3,300	3,450	4,200	4,500	3,300
Miscellaneous expenses	10,000	10,600	12,000	12,000	14,000	10,000
Total disbursements	$23,000	$40,900	$45,150	$47,250	$56,300	$53,800
Cash balance	$21,850	$12,300	$11,200	$13,850	$18,835	$25,905
Borrowed		10,000	10,000	10,000		
Repaid						10,000
Balance forward	$21,850	$22,300	$21,200	$23,850	$18,835	$15,905

Receipts:

Month	Sales	January	February	March	April	May	June
October	$30,000	$ 1,350					
November	30,000	1,500	$ 1,350				
December	30,000	12,000	1,500	$ 1,350			
January	30,000	15,000	12,000	1,500	$ 1,350		
February	33,000		16,500	13,200	1,650	$ 1,485	
March	36,000			18,000	14,400	1,800	$ 1,620
April	45,000				22,500	18,000	2,250
May	60,000					30,000	24,000
June	66,000						33,000
Collections		$29,850	$31,350	$34,050	$39,900	$51,285	$60,870

5-2

a. Net prices

Cash

(2)	68,600		
(3)	20,000		
(7)	9,320		

Accounts Receivable

(1)	98,000	(2)	68,600
(6)	10	(3)	19,600
		(4)	490
		(7)	9,320

Customer Advances

		(5)	492

Sales

		(1)	98,000

Lapsed Sales Discounts

(5)	2	(3)	400
		(6)	10

Sales Returns

(4)	490		
(5)	490		

b. Gross prices
   Cash—same as in (a)

Accounts Receivable

(1)	100,000	(2)	70,000
		(3)	20,000
		(4)	500
		(7)	9,500

Allowance for Outstanding Discounts

(7)	180	(6)	180

Customer Advances

		(5)	492

Sales

		(1)	100,000

Sales—Discounts

(2)	1,400	(5)	8
(6)	180		

Sales Returns

(4)	500	
(5)	500	

5-3

19X1

(1)

Accounts Receivable	100,000	
Sales		100,000

(2)

Cash	85,000	
Accounts Receivable		85,000

(3) December 31

Bad Debt Loss	750	
Accounts Receivable		750

19X2

(1)

Accounts Receivable	140,000	
Sales		140,000

(2)

Cash	135,000	
Accounts Receivable		135,000

(3)

Cash	100	
Bad Debts Recovered		100

(4) December 31

Sales Adjustment—Bad Debts	3,500	
Accounts Receivable—Allowance for Bad Debts		3,500
Loss from Bad Accounts of Prior Periods	2,900	
Accounts Receivable		2,900
Accounts Receivable—Allowance for Bad Debts	1,925	
Accounts Receivable		1,925

CHAPTER 6

6-1

MARIE E. CO.
Working Capital Funds Statement, Year Ended
December 31, 19X1 (000 omitted)

Sources of working capital:	
Net income [300 − (180 + 20 + 40 + 6 + 30 − 23)]	$ 47
Bonds issued	200
Capital stock issued	200
Sale of equipment (15 − 10 + 10)	15
	$462
Disposition of working capital:	
Purchase of land (net change)	$ 10
Purchase of equipment (net change + 15)	65
Dividends	11
Increase in working capital (473 to 849)	376
	$462

6-2

AMY ENNE CO.
Working Capital Funds Statement, Year Ended
December 31, 19X1 (000 omitted)

Sources of working capital:	
Net income (400 − (330 + 38 − depreciation 11)	$ 43
Equipment sold (loss, 5,000)	9
Mortgage issue	40
Capital stock issue	150
	$242
Disposition of working capital:	
Dividends	$ 4
Equipment purchase (increase + 30)	60
Buildings (increase)	20
Land (increase)	30
Working capital (increase 69 to 197)	128
	$242

CHAPTER 7

7-1

MARIE E. CO.
Cash Flow Funds Statement, Year Ended December 31, 19x (000 omitted)

Sources of cash:		
Net income [300−(180+20+40+6+30+20−10)]		$ 14
Add: Increase in accounts payable	$ 287	
Increase in other current liabilities	24	
Depreciation	23	
Amortization of goodwill	20	354
Deduct: Gain on sale of equipment	$ 10	
Increase in accounts receivable (net)	200	
Increase in inventories	400	
Increase in current prepayments	7	(617)
Net cash used by operations		($249)
Bonds issued		200
Capital stock issued		200
Sale of equipment (15 − 10 + 10)		15
		$ 166
Uses of cash:		
Purchase of land (net change)		$ 10
Purchase of marketable securities		70
Purchase of equipment (net change + 15)		65
Dividends		11
Increase in cash in bank		10
		$ 166

Notice in problem 6-1 that operations provided net working capital of $47, which may appear to be pretty good. However, problem 7-1 shows that operations used $249 more cash than was generated by operating activity. This is not good, and any business finding itself in this position must turn the situation around quickly, or face insolvency and, perhaps, bankruptcy.

Cash is the asset *par excellence,* and, over the long haul, a business must generate enough net cash flow from operations to pay off creditors, pay dividends to shareholders, and pay operating costs such as wages, salaries, rents, and a whole array of others. So how well (or badly) a business is doing this is useful information, and the reason a cash flow statement is now required in the annual report.

Note that the remainders of the two statements in problems 6-1 and 7-1 are nearly identical.

7-2

AMY ENNE CO.		
Cash Flow Statement, Year Ended December 31, 19x1 (000 omitted)		
Sources of cash:		
Net income [400−(330+38)]		$ 32
Add: Depreciation	$ 11	
Increase in accounts payable	90	101
Deduct: Increase in receivables (net)	$ 43	
Increase in inventories	160	(203)
Net cash used in operations		($70)
Equipment sold		9
Mortgage issue		40
Capital stock issue		150
		$ 129
Uses of Cash:		
Dividends		$ 4
Equipment purchase (increase + 30)		60
Buildings (increase)		20
Land (increase)		30
Increase in cash in bank		15
		$ 129

The same comments are appropriate here as with problem 7-1.

CHAPTER 8

8-1

1. Average cost method:

Inventory, Jan. 1, 1,400 oz.		$ 4,200
Purchases, 8,250 oz.		27,585
Total cost to be accounted for, 9,650 oz.		$31,785
Average cost per ton ($31,785 9,650)	$3.2938	
Inventory, Dec. 31, 3,400 oz. @ $3.2938		11,199
		$20,586

2. FIFO method:

Total cost to be accounted for (see 1)		$31,785
Inventory, Dec. 31:		
Purchase on Dec. 30, 1,500 oz.	$5,400	
Purchase on Oct. 15, 1,750 oz.	6,125	
From purchase July 10, 150 oz.		
@ $3.30	495	12,020
		$19,765

3. LIFO method:

Total cost (as above)		$31,785
Inventory, Dec. 31:		
On hand Jan. 1, 1,400 oz.	$4,200	
Purchase on Feb. 15, 1,200 oz.	3,720	
From purchase Apr. 20, 800 oz.		
@ $3.20	2,560	10,480
		$21,305

8-2

Merchandise	896,546	
Accounts Payable (and Bank)		896,546
Accounts Receivable	1,142,960	
Sales		1,142,960
Merchandise	73,465	
Merchandise Inventory		73,465
Merchandise Inventory	75,913	
Merchandise Cost of Sales	894,098	
Merchandise		970,011

	Cost	Retail
Inventory, Jan. 1	$ 73,465	$ 105,000
Purchases	896,546	1,280,780
Additional markups		247,120
Totals (markup percentage, 40.6%)	$970,011	$1,632,900

Sales		$1,142,960
Markdowns		362,140
Total of sales and markdowns		$1,505,100
Closing inventory at retail		$ 127,800
Less markup of 40.6%		51,877
Closing inventory at estimated cost	75,913	
Cost of goods sold	$894,098	

8-3

(1)

Merchandise	147,000	
Accounts Payable		147,000

Purchases on account, at net, Gross = 150,000.

(2)

Transportation Costs	10,100	
Bank		10,100

(3)

Accounts Receivable	180,000	
Sales		180,000

Sales recorded at gross

(4)

Bank	180,000	
Allowance for Sales Discounts	1800	
Sales Discounts	3200	
Accounts Receivable		185,000

Collections, including prior period accounts.

(5)

Accounts Payable	140,000	
Loss from Lapsed Discounts	900	
Bank		140,900

Payments on account, including $900 in late-payment penalties.

(6)

Accounts Payable (or Due from Vendors)	4,920	
Loss from Lapsed Discounts		20
Merchandise—Returns and Allowances		4,900

Returns, including $980 on which $20 penalty was paid.

(7)

Sales—Returns	4,000	
Accounts Receivable		4,000

(8)

Accounts Payable	980	
Merchandise—Returns and Allowances		980

(9) End of period

Sales—Discounts	2,000	
Accounts Receivable—Allowance for Sales		
Discounts		2,000

(NOTE: This is a valid entry under accrual accounting—like Allowance for Bad Debts.)

(10)

Merchandise—Returns and Allowances	5,880	
Merchandise		5,880

To close returns and allowances (a contra account) to Merchandise, which now has a net balance of (147,000 − 5,880 = 141,120).

(11)

Merchandise Cost of Sales	70,000	
Merchandise Inventory		70,000

To close out old inventory (FIFO) under first-in, first-out.

(12)

Merchandise Inventory (35,280 net)	37,975	
Merchandise Cost of Sales (105,840 net)	113,925	
Merchandise		141,120
Transportation Costs (one fourth to Inventory)		10,780

To set up end-of-period inventory as $35,280 plus share of transportation cost which is 10,780/141,120 = 7.639%, or $2,695 for a total of $37,975. The remainder represents an addition to the cost of goods sold.

CHAPTER 9

9-1

	Appraised value	%	Apportioned cost
Land	$ 22,000	16	$ 20,000
Building	104,500	76	95,000
Delivery Equipment	11,000	8	10,000
	$137,500	100	$125,000

Since the total appraised value is 110 percent of cost, each of such values is 110 percent of its respective cost figure.

Land	20,000	
Building—Cost	95,000	
Delivery Equipment—Cost	10,000	
Bank		25,000
Strong Co., Contract Payable		100,000
Interest Charges	6,000	
Strong Co., Contract Payable	100,000	
Bank		106,000

9-2

Year 1, April 25

Delivery Equipment—Cost	11,000	
Bank		11,000

April 29

Delivery Equipment—Cost	2,500	
Accounts Payable		2,500

December 31

Delivery Expense	3,200	
Delivery Equipment—Allow. for Deprec.		3,200

Year 2 February 1

Delivery Expense	400	
Delivery Equipment—Allow. for Deprec.		400

$(13,500 - 1,500) \times 1/30 = \$400$, depreciation for one month.

(1)

Delivery Equipment—Cost	34,400	
Delivery Equipment—Allow. for Deprec.	3,600	
Bank		24,500
Delivery Equipment—Cost		13,500

Fused transaction treatment.

(2)

Delivery Equipment—Cost	32,000	
Delivery Equipment—Allow. for Deprec.	3,600	
Retirement Loss	2,400	
Bank (32,000 − 7,500)		24,500
Delivery Equipment—Cost		13,500

List price treatment.

(3)

Delivery Equipment—Cost (5,000 + 24,500)	29,500	
Delivery Equipment—Allow. for Deprec.	3,600	
Retirement Loss	4,900	
Bank		24,500
Delivery Equipment—Cost		13,500

9-3

January 1, 19X2

Machinery	300	
Retained Earnings		300

To charge Machinery with installation cost erroneously expensed in 19XX.

Retained Earnings	45	
Machinery—Allowance for Depreciation		45

Correction of depreciation for 1½ years.

Depreciation	408	
Machinery—Allowance for Depreciation		408

To recognize depreciation for one-tenth of the estimated remaining life on $4,800 - 720 = \$4,080, \times 10\% = \$408$.

CHAPTER 10

10-1

a. On partnership books:

Allowance for Depreciation	5,000,000	
Land	5,000,000	
Black, Capital		5,000,000
White, Capital		5,000,000
Patents	5,000,000	
White Capital	40,000,000	
Blue, Capital		45,000,000

b. Entries on corporation books:

Cash	20,000,000	
Accounts Receivable	10,000,000	
Merchandise	45,000,000	
Land	15,000,000	
Buildings and Equipment	26,000,000	
Patents	5,000,000	
Allowance for Bad Debts		1,000,000
Accounts Payable		20,000,000
Capital Stock		100,000,000

10-2

(1)

a.	Cash	1,540,000	
	Capital Stock—Preferred		1,400,000
	Capital Stock—Preferred, Pre-mium		14,000
	Common Stock Rights		126,000
	To record issuance of 14,000 shares preferred and 42,000 rights to buy one common for $8		

(2)

Common Stock Rights (41,700 × 3)	125,100	
Cash (333,600/8 = 41,700)	333,600	
Common Stock		458,700

b. Total rights are three for each of the 14,000 units, or 42,000. Each right grants purchase of one common for $8; so if $333,600 is collected, it must represent 333,600/8 = 41,700 rights, leaving 300 lapsed, at $3 each. This amounts to $900, which can be treated simply as additional capital paid in (458,700 + 900) for the common stock.

10-3

(1)

Administrative Services	60,000	
Salaries Payable		50,000
Stock Options Outstanding (2,000 @ $5)		10,000

(2)

Salaries Payable	50,000	
Bank		50,000

(3)

Cash (2,000 × 95)	190,000	
Stock Options Outstanding	10,000	
Capital Stock Outstanding		200,000

CHAPTER 11

11-1

January 25

Retained Earnings (or Dividends)	3,000	
Dividends Payable—Preferred		3,000

February 5

Dividends Payable—Preferred	3,000	
Cash		3,000

February 14

Retained Earnings	175,000	
Note Dividend Payable		175,000

April 15

Note Dividend Payable	175,000	
Cash		175,000

June 5

Retained Earnings	140,000	
Capitalized Earnings		140,000

June 30

Capitalized Earnings	140,000	
Capital Stock		140,000

October 6

Retained Earnings	91,000	
Dividend Payable in Boston Stock		91,000
(36,400 common @ $2.50)		

October 10

Dividend Payable in Boston Stock	91,000	
Boston Stock		91,000

November 6

Capital Stock Common—Par $100	3,640,000	
Capital Stock Common—Par $50		3,640,000

11-2

(1)

Retained Earnings	100,000	
Dividend Payable		100,000
Decreases Retained Earnings by $100,000.		

(2)

Retained Earnings	20,000	
Reserve for Bond Sinking Fund		20,000
Earmarks Retained Earnings but has no effect on total.		

(3)

Sinking Fund Trustee	20,000	
Bank		20,000

No effect on Retained Earnings.

(4)

Retained Earnings	100,000	
Reserve for Contingencies		100,000

No effect on total.

(5)

Preferred Stock	50,000	
Retained Earnings	2,500	
Bank		52,500

Decreases Retained Earnings by amount of call premium.

(6)

Bank—Equipment Replacement Fund	50,000	
Bank (General banking account)		50,000

No effect on Retained Earning.

11-3

Reserve for federal income tax	An estimated current liability
Reserve for loss on bad debts	Contra asset account
Reserve for depreciation	Same
Reserve for depletion	Same
Reserve for insurance	Segregated retained earnings
Reserve for contingencies	Same
Reserve for building expansion	Same
Unearned receipts from customers	Liability (customer advance)
Refundable advances from subsidiary	Liability

COMMENT: There is no excuse for a "reserve" section in the balance sheet—accounts typically listed there should all be reclassified and properly located.

CHAPTER 12

12-1

Bond price to yield 14 percent is computed as follows:

Par of bond		$1,000.00
Coupon, 12%/2 =	60.00	
Coupon needed to make bonds		
worth par, 14%/2 =	70.00	

Semiannual discount factor (shortage)	− 10.00	
P.V. of $1 for 40 pds. @ 7% =	13.33171	
P.V. of $10 =	× 10 =	− 133.32
Price yielding 14% =		$ 866.68

January 1

a.
Cash (866.68 × 800 bonds)	693,344	
Bond Discount (133.32 × 800)	106,656	
Bonds Payable—Par		800,000

July 1

b.
Interest on Bonds (693,344 × .07)	48,534.08	
Bank (800,000 × .06)		48,000.00
Bond Discount (to balance—plug)		534.08

To record payment, and true interest cost, of first coupons—using compound interest procedure for amortizing the bond discount. Bond base becomes 693,344 + 534.08, or 693,878.08. (it will grow to $800,000 in 40 periods). See (bl) for traditional, straight-line procedure.

bl. Straight-line handling of the same entries (same amounts every 6 months):

Interest on Bonds (48,000 + 106,656/40	50,666	
Bank		48,000
Bond Discount (106,656/40)		2,666

December 31

c.
Interest on Bonds (693,878 × .07)	48,571	
Bond Coupon Interest Payable		48,000
Bond Discount (plug)		571

cl. Straight-line entry; same as bl except no Bank credit. Credit Bond Coupon Interest Payable, $48,000.

January 1

d. Debit Bond Coupon Interest Payable and credit Bank, $48,000.

12-2

Bond price computation:

Par of bond		$1,000.00
Coupon, 6%	60.00	
Need for par, 5½%	55.00	
Premium factor	+ 5.00	
P.V. $1 per pd., 40 pds. @ 5½% =	16.04612	
P.V. $5 per pd.		80.23
Bond price to yield 11%		$1,080.23

January 1

Cash (2,000,000 + 80.23 × 2,000 bonds)	2,160,460	
Bonds Payable—Par		2,000,000
Bonds Payable—Premium		160,460

July 1 (compound interest solution)

Interest on Bonds (2,160,460 × .0550)	118,825	
Bond Premium (plug)	1,175	
Bank (2,000,000 × .06)		120,000
Base for next period will be (2,160,460 − 955)		

July 1 (Straight-Line Solution)

Interest on Bonds (120,000 − 164,060/40)	115,899	
Bond Premium (160,460/40)	4,101	
Bank		120,000

December 31 (Compound Interest)

InterestonBonds(2,160,460− 1,175) × .055)	118,761	
Bond Premium (plug)	1,239	
Bond Interest Payable		120,000

December 31 (Straight Line)

Same as July 1 except that credit is to Bond Interest Payable.

January 1 (Same for Both Methods)

Bond Interest Payable	120,000	
Bank		120,000

CHAPTER 13

13-1

| | | Finished equivalents | | | | Cost |
	Number	Process I	Materials	Labor	Overhead	totals
Started and finished	8,100	8,100	8,100	8,100	8,100	
In process, finished (¼)	400	—	—	100	100	
Started, 80% finished	500	500	500	400	400	
Totals	9,000	8,600	8,600	8,600	8,600	
Costs		$17,200	$8,600	$25,800	$17,200	$68,800
Cost per equivalent unit		$ 2	$ 1	$ 3	$ 2	
In process equivalents (units)		500	500	400	400	
Work in process		$ 1,000	$ 500	$ 1,200	$ 800	3,500
Cost of product transferred						$65,300
Process III	65,300					
Process II		65,300				

13-2

a.

Materials and Supplies

(1)	35,000	(2)	32,000

Foundry

(2)	30,000	(7)	67,080
(3)	22,000		
(4)	2,750		
(5)	330		
(6)	12,000		
	67,080		67,080

Grinding

(3)	10,000	(7)	83,620
(4)	1,375		
(5)	165		
(6)	8,000		
(7)	67,080	v	3,000
	86,620		86,620
v	3,000		

Finishing

(2)	2,000	(7)	107,160
(3)	14,000		
(4)	1,375		
(5)	165		
(6)	6,000		
(7)	83,620		
	107,160		107,160

Finished Goods

(7)	107,160

b.

Statement of Cost of Goods Manufactured
Year Ended December 31, 19xx

Materials and supplies		$ 32,000
Labor		46,000
Overhead:		
Depreciation	$ 5,500	
Insurance	660	
Miscellaneous	26,000	32,160
Total factory costs		$110,160
Work in process, Dec. 31		3,000
Cost of goods manufactured		$107,160

CHAPTER 14

14-1

Raw Materials

(1)	1,050	(1)	1,150
(2)	4,200	(2)	3,500
(3)	3,600	(3)	3,000
(4)	1,500	(4)	1,350

Raw Materials Price Variances

(1)	42	(4)	20
(2)	210		
(3)	108		

Accounts Payable

	(1)	1,092
	(2)	4,410
	(3)	3,708
	(4)	1,480

Process A

| (1) | 1,100 |
| (2) | 3,200 |

Process A Quantity Variance

| (1) | 50 |
| (2) | 300 |

Process B

| (3) | 3,200 |

Process B Quantity Variance

| | (3) | 200 |

Process C

| (4) | 1,275 |

Process C Quantity Variance

| (4) | 75 |

14-2

Payroll

	Dept. 1	11,550.00
	Dept. 2	11,649.80
	Dept. 3	16,356.00

Work in Process

Dept. 1	10,375.00
Dept. 2	11,400.00
Dept. 3	16,800.00

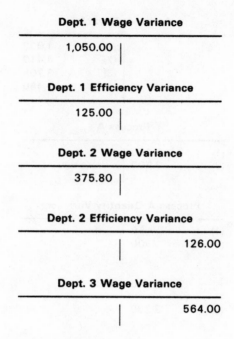

Dept. 1 Wage Variance

1,050.00	

Dept. 1 Efficiency Variance

125.00	

Dept. 2 Wage Variance

375.80	

Dept. 2 Efficiency Variance

	126.00

Dept. 3 Wage Variance

	564.00

Dept. 3 Efficiency Variance is $120 dr.

14-3

Materials	210,000	
Materials Price Variance	12,000	
Materials Price Variance		7,000
Accounts Payable		215,000

To summarize purchases of materials for the period, resulting in loss variance of $12,000 and gain variance of $7,000.

Manufacturing Overhead	120,000	
Payroll—Indirect Labor		40,000
Miscellaneous Accounts		80,000

To summarize entries for the period to record "actual" factory overhead costs incurred.

Work in Process	270,000	
Labor Wage Variance	8,000	
Labor Efficiency Variance	13,000	
Labor Efficiency Variance		3,000
Labor Wage Variance		3,000
Payroll—Direct Labor		285,000

To charge standard direct-labor cost to Work in Process and recognize resultant gain and loss variances in wage rates and labor efficiency.

Work in Process	170,000	
Materials Quantity Variance	14,000	
Materials Quantity Variance		4,000
Materials		180,000

To summarize materials requisitions at standard cost, charging standard quantity to Work in Process and quantity excesses and savings to quantity variance account.

Work in Process	100,000	
Manufacturing Overhead Variances	25,000	
Manufacturing Overhead		120,000
Manufacturing Overhead Variances		5,000

To charge Work in Process with standard overhead cost and to show amounts in excess, and savings from, standard to variance accounts.

CHAPTER 15

15-1

PLAN OF SOLUTION: Find present value of option 1 payments, including special bonus at retirement date; find present value of option 2 annual bonus; subtract the latter from the former to find present value of necessary terminal bonus under option 2; finally, convert present into future value of option 2 terminal bonus. Use 20 percent as the discount rate to neutralize growth of annual bonus in option 1.

1. Present value of option 1 annual payments: Since these payments increase at the rate of 20 percent per annum, each such payment will be reduced to the same $100,000 present value (as of *end* of first year) if a 20 percent *discount* rate is used and the present value, end year 1, is $1,000,000

But we need present value at the start, at the beginning of year 1, so we discount the $1,000,-000 for one year by dividing by 1.20, or $ 833,333

To the 833,333 we now add the present value of the terminal $500,000 lump sum. To do so, we multiply by .1615 and get   80,753

The sum gives total present value of option 1 excluding the annual salary (which is same under both plans): $914,086

2. Present value of option 2 annual payments is calculated as the present value of a $1, 10-payment annuity at 20 percent multiplied by 150,-000, or $150,000 × 4.19247 = 628,870

3. The difference (914,086 − 628,870) = $285,215

4. The difference as of 10 years later, 285,215 × $(1.20)^{10}$, or 285,215 × 6.1917 = 1,765,976

15-2

a. Payback period is cost of asset divided by average (or other determination of) cash flow: $60,000/10,200 = *5.88 years.* The 10,200 is 18,000 + 4,000 − 9,000 = 13,000, less 40 percent tax on 13,000 minus depreciation of 6,000, or .4 × $7,000 = $2,800.

b. 10,200 × present worth of 10-period annuity of $1 at 15 percent, or 10,200 × 5.019 = 51,193. Acquisition appears unwise, since present value of future proceeds is less than the amount that would have to be expended now to obtain those proceeds.

15-3

Our variable (differential) cost of manufacture is $8,500 − 2,000, or $6,500, for a component element in our product. The best bid from suppliers is $7,000. This relationship appears to favor in-house production. However, our apparent gain of $500 is 500/7,000, or 7.1 percent, which compares unfavorably with our overall 10 percent profit ratio. This suggests that we might better undertake to expand our regular product output to soak up idle capacity if demand exists at present prices. If not, in-house production on a temporary basis can be justified, assuming no other, more profitable, alternative.

CHAPTER 18

18-1

Consolidating Journal Entries

---

(1)

Capital Stock—Sub Co. (100%)	60,000	
Retained Earnings—Sub Co. (100%)	5,000	
Goodwill	8,000	
Investment—B Co. Stock—Cost (80%)		60,000
Minority Interest (20%)		13,000

To eliminate intercompany stock equity items as of
date of acquisition.

(2)

Retained Earnings—Sub Co.	6,000	
Merchandise—Parent Co.		2,000
Land—Parent Co.		4,000

To eliminate intercompany profit in assets remaining
"in the family," referred to as "unrealized."

(3)

Retained Earnings—Sub Co. (13,000 − 5,000 − 6,000)	2,000	
Minority Interest (20%)		400
Consolidated Retained Earnings (80%)		1,600

To allocate realized earnings of subsidiary to minority
and majority interests.

(4)

Current Liabilities	2,000	
Customers		2,000

18-2

a.	Sales (100% of Babaco)	240,000	
	Merchandise Cost of Sales (100% of Babaco)		160,000
	Other Expenses and Taxes (100% of Babaco)		40,000
	Merchandise Cost of Sales (Large Co., 75% of Small Co. income)		30,000
	Inventory (Large Co, 25% of Babaco income)		10,000

b.

Consolidated Income Statement

Sales		$600,000
Merchandise Cost of Sales	$330,000	
Other Expenses	120,000	450,000
Consolidated Net Income		$150,000

18-3

a. Consolidating journal entries (work sheet only):

Sales (75% of Babaco)	180,000	
Merchandise Cost of Sales (75% of B)		120,000
Other Expenses and Taxes (75% of B)		30,000
Merchandise Cost of Sales—Papaco (80% of 75% of Babaco profit)		24,000
Inventory—Papaco (20% of 75% of Babaco profit)		6,000

b. Consolidated income statement after entries above (000's omitted):

Sales (840 − 180)		$660
Merchandise cost of sales (520 − 144)	$376	
Other expenses and taxes (160 − 30)	130	506
Total net income		$154
Minority interest 25% of (40 − 6)		8.5
Consolidated net income*		$145.5

CHAPTER 19

19-1

a. Deferred Income Tax Charge	360	
Income Tax Expense		360

The amount is 30% of (5,000 − 3,800), deferred because, from the standpoint of the "books" method of recognizing bad debts, the amount reported for tax purposes is understated by $1,200, resulting in $1,200 × 30%, or $360, apparent overpayment of taxes.

*PROOF OF CONSOLIDATED NET: It should be equal to the net income of the parent (120) plus 75 percent of the net income of the subsidiary after subtracting "unrealized" profit of $6 = 145.5.

b. Deferred Income Tax Charge   30,000
      Income Tax Expense   30,000

c. Income Tax Expense   15,000
      Deferred Income Tax Credit   15,000
      (See text for explanation)

CHAPTER 21

21-1

Year	Nominal depreciation	Translation factor	Common $ depreciation
1	$18,000	200/80	$45,000
4	1,000	200/100	2,000
8	5,000	200/130	7,692
12	5,000	200/150	6,667
16	2,000	200/180	2,222
20	9,000	200/198	9,091
Total corrected depreciation			$72,672
Total uncorrected depreciation			40,000
Increase in depreciation charge			$32,672
Reported earnings of stockholders			$50,000
Less depreciation adjustment			32,672
Corrected earnings			$17,328
Dividends paid			30,000
Retained earnings change, corrected—decrease			$12,672

21-2

	1	2	3	4	5
Current Assets:					
Cash	$ 780	$ 768	$ 725	$ 722	$ 690
Receivables (net)	1,560	1,535	1,461	1,443	1,320
Inventories	1,051	1,027	996	1,009	944
Prepayments	13	15	16	16	16
Total	$3,404	$3,345	$3,198	$3,190	$2,970
Current liabilities	$1,560	$1,510	$1,455	$1,444	$1,346
Net working capital	$1,844	$1,835	$1,743	$1,746	$1,624

Translation factors used:

Year	For inventories and prepayments	For other items
1	130/99	130/100
2	130/103.75	130/105
3	130/111	130/113
4	130/116	130/117
5	130/126.75	130/130

21-3

NEW WORLD CO.
Income Statement, Year Ended December 31, 19XX
Stated in Uniform Dollars as of December 31, 19XX

	Translation factor		
Sales	100/105		$238,095
Expenses and taxes:			
Merchandise cost of sales	100/107	$140,187	
Salaries and wages	100/105	35,714	
Depreciation	100/150	20,000	
Miscellaneous	100/105	14,286	
Taxes	100/105	6,667	216,854
Earnings of stockholders			$ 21,241
Dividends	100/105		7,619
Earnings retained			$ 13,622

CHAPTER 22

22-1

a.

TXYPCO
Trial Balance as of December 31

	Debit	Credit
Cash (50 + 1,100 − 950)	# 200	#
Receivables (120 + 1250 − 1,100)	270	
Inventories (240 + 1,000 − 800)	440	
Land	100	
Building	400	
Equipment	500	
Allowance for depreciation (180 + 62)		242
Accounts payable (230 + 1,000 − 950 + 360 + 15)		655
Capital stock		1,000
Sales		1,250
Expenses, selling, general, and admin.	360	
Depreciation	62	
Cost of goods sold	800	
Income tax	15	
	#3,147	#3,147

b. Parent Co. work sheet entries for preparation of consolidated income statement:

Selling, general, and administrative (360 × 1.45)	522	
Cost of goods sold (365 + 1,450 − 651)	1,164*	
Depreciation (62 × 1.65)	102	
Taxes (15 × 1.45)	22	
Due from subsidiary (plug)	2	
Sales (1,250 × 1.45)		1,812

Entries for consolidated balance sheet:

Capital stock (1,000 × 1.50)	1,500	
Cash (200 × 1.40)	280	
Receivables (270 × 1.40)	378	
Inventory (440 × 1.48)	651	
Land	170	
Building and equipment (900 × 1.65)	1,485	
Allowance for depreciation (242 × 1.65)		400
Investment in ZO (given)		1,500
Net income		2
Gain on foreign exchange—equity adjustment		2,562

*Calculation of cost of goods sold:

	#'s	Rate	$'s
Initial inventory	240	1.52	365
Purchases	1,000	1.45	1,450
	1,240		1,815
Final inventory	440	1.48	651
Cost of goods sold	# 800		$1,164

Index

Final Examination

The McGraw-Hill 36-Hour Accounting Course

If you have completed your study of *The McGraw-Hill 36-Hour Accounting Course,* you should be prepared to take this final examination. It is a comprehensive test, consisting of 100 questions.

Instructions

1. You may treat this as an "open-book" exam by consulting this and any other textbook. Or, you can reassure yourself that you have gained superior knowledge by taking the exam without reference to any other material.

2. Answer each of the test questions on the answer sheet provided at the end of the exam. For each question, write the letter of your choice on the answer blank that corresponds to the number of the question you are answering.

3. All questions are multiple-choice, with two to four alternative answers from which to choose. Always select the answer that represents in your mind the *best* among the choices.

4. Each correct answer is worth one point. A passing grade of 70 percent (70 correct answers) entitles you to receive a Certificate of Achievement. This handsome certificate, suitable for framing, attests to your proven knowledge of the contents of this course.

5. Carefully fill in your name and address in the spaces provided at the top of the answer sheet, remove the answer sheet from the book, and send to:

Allison Collier
The McGraw-Hill 36-Hour Accounting Course
Professional Books Group
McGraw-Hill, Inc.
11 West 19th Street
New York, NY 10011

---

1. A company whose balance sheet shows total assets $100,000 and total liabilities $40,000 is worth:
   a. $100,000
   b. $160,000
   c. $60,000
   d. Probably none of these

2. If Company A has an accounting net worth of $500,000 with 100,000 shares of common stock outstanding and Company B has a net worth of the same amount but with only 50,000 shares outstanding, the market value of a share of Company B stock will be twice that of a Company A share.
   a. True
   b. Very unlikely

3. The current ratio is the ratio of current liabilities to current assets.
   a. True
   b. False

4. The equity ratio is the ratio of stockholders' equity to total assets.
   a. True
   b. False

5. In most situations a company's revenues for the period, its net income for the period, and its cash inflow for the period are likely to be three entirely different amounts.
   a. True
   b. False

6. The accountant's concept of the accrual basis of accounting represents a practical compromise between, on the one hand, the cash basis of accounting and, on the other hand, the economist's theory that income accrues as production proceeds.
   a. True
   b. False

7. Under the accrual basis of accounting, revenue (and result-ing income) is recognized in the period when:
   a. Cash is collected if the customer pays in advance of delivery of the product
   b. Cash is collected if the customer pays after product delivery
   c. Cash is collected
   d. The goods or services are delivered to new owners

8. An expense is:
   a. Any loss
   b. Any amount spent for an asset
   c. Any item of factory overhead
   d. A cost incurred to produce rev-enue

9. The operating ratio is the ratio of total expenses to total revenues.
   a. True
   b. False

10. Bad debts are an operating expense.
    a. True
    b. False

11. Working capital (or net working capital) is the arithmetic excess of cash over bank loan.
    a. True
    b. False

12. Working capital increases when we borrow money from a bank on a short-term loan.
    a. True
    b. False

13.

ESSEX PRODUCTS CO.
Income Statement, Year Ended December 31, 19XX

Sales and other revenues		$320,000
Cost of product sold	$180,000	
Selling expenses	41,000	
General expenses	62,000	
Income taxes	10,000	293,000
Net income		$ 27,000
Dividends on common stock		20,000
Earnings retained		$ 7,000

NOTE: Depreciation total of $15,000 is included in the expenses listed above.

The "working capital flow" of Essex Products Co. for 19XX, as evidenced by the income statement, was:

a. $320,000   c. $22,000

b. $27,000   d. $42,000

14. Increases in assets are recorded by:
    a. Debits
    b. Credits

15. Increases in expenses are recorded by:
    a. Debits
    b. Credits

16. Increases in liabilities are recorded by:
    a. Debits
    b. Credits

17. Increases in owners' equity are recorded by:
    a. Debits
    b. Credits

18. Increases in revenues are recorded by:
    a. Debits
    b. Credits

19. A discount which you are allowed to take upon paying a bill before a certain date is properly classified as:
    a. Income
    b. Adjustment of cost of item purchased

20. From the managerial point of view, the more important of the following items of information is the amount:
    a. Of discounts you have "earned"
    b. Of discounts you have "lost"

21. Assume:

Date	Item	Units	Cost
Jan. 1	Initial inventory	10,000	$100,000
Jan. 12	Purchase	12,000	150,000
Jan. 24	Purchase	8,000	120,000
Jan. 31	Inventory	15,000	?

The cost of the January 31 inventory, using FIFO, is:

a. $162,500   c. $207,500

b. $185,000   d. None of these

22. See question 21. The cost of inventory using LIFO is:

a. $162,500   c. $207,500

b. $185,000   d. None of these

23. See question 21. The cost of the January 31 inventory at average cost is:
    - a. $162,500
    - c. $207,500
    - b. $185,000
    - d. None of these

24. During a given year our sales total $250,000, our cost of goods sold is $150,000, and our ending inventory (at FIFO cost) is $10,000. Our inventory turnover approximates:
    - a. 25 times
    - b. 15 times

25. See question 24. Our ending inventory amounts to approximately:
    - a. 24 days' supply
    - b. 17 days' supply

26. We trade in an automobile that cost $10,000 originally and on which we have, so far, recorded depreciation of $7,000. We have been offered a fair cash price of $3,500 for our car, but we elect to give the car, plus $8,600 in cash, for a new car which has a list price of $13,000. The new car should be put on our books at the following valuation:
    - a. $11,600
    - c. $13,000
    - b. $12,100
    - d. $18,600

27. The straight-line method of recording depreciation has merit when the depreciable asset renders approximately the same amount of service in each month, year, or other uniform time period.
    - a. True
    - b. False

28. Because most depreciable assets render more valuable (or less costly) services per period in the earlier periods of useful life than they do in the later periods, some form of increasing-charges depreciation method is generally to be preferred.
    - a. True
    - b. False

29. If an asset which cost $1,000 has an estimated useful life of 5 years and probable salvage value of $400, the amount of annual depreciation charge by the straight-line method is:
    - a. $280
    - c. $120
    - b. $200
    - d. $110

30. See question 29. The annual depreciation for the second year will be the following amount if the sum-of-years' digits method is used:
    a. $200   c. $120
    b. $160   d. $80

31. If we were to use the declining-balance method for the asset in question 29, the amount of depreciation in year 1 would be:
    a. $400   c. $200
    b. $240   d. $120

32. Depreciation is a source of funds.
    a. True
    b. False

33. See question 26. Assume that instead of trading the automobile in, we accept the cash offer. One element in the entry to record the sale would be:
    a. Credit Gain on Sale, $500
    b. Credit Gain on Sale, $1,400

34. Depreciation must be recorded in order to provide for replacement of the asset.
    a. True
    b. False

35. In a balance sheet the account, Allowance (or Reserve) for Depreciation, denotes that the company has reserved funds in an amount at least as great as the balance of that account.
    a. True
    b. False

36. A stock split automatically increases the value of the common stock held by a stockholder.
    a. True
    b. False

37. A stock dividend distributes corporate earnings.
    a. True
    b. False

38. Because of the ambiguity of the term *reserve,* use of the term as the title of an item in the balance sheet is generally discouraged by professional accountants.
    a. True
    b. False

39. When long-term notes (or bonds) are issued at a price above par value, they are said to be issued at a:
    a. Discount
    b. Premium

40. Bond premium represents income to the debtor company at the time of issuance.
    a. True
    b. False

41. Bond discount should be amortized (accumulated) over the life term of the bond issue and thus shown as an addition to the periodic interest expense.
    a. True
    b. False

42. Under so-called "actual" cost accounting procedures, the actual overhead costs of manufactured goods are approximated by use of applied overhead rates that are established on the basis of estimates made at the beginning of the period.
    a. True
    b. False

43. Of the two objectives of cost accounting, (1) the determination of the cost of goods manufactured and (2) the minimization of costs, the latter is likely to be the much more significant to the welfare of the business.
    a. True
    b. False

44. Under a system of standard cost accounting, if we purchase 10,000 pounds of material for $11,000 during a period when our standard cost for that material is $1 per pound, we should record a materials price variance of $1,000 as a credit.
    a. True
    b. False

45. If we consume 8,500 pounds of the material referred to in question 44 to produce 100 units of product with a standard raw material content of 80 pounds per unit, we should record a materials quantity (usage) variance of:
    a. $150 debit   c. $500 debit
    b. $550 credit   d. $500 credit

46. If we turn out 1,000 units of product today in a department which has a standard direct labor allowance of 5 hours per unit and a standard wage rate of $10 per hour, the standard cost of the day's output, as far as direct labor is concerned, is $50,000.
    a. True
    b. False

47. See question 46. If we actually use 5,500 direct labor hours to produce the 1,000 units and if the actual wage rate is $11.00 per hour, our direct labor efficiency variance is:
    a. $5,500 debit   c. $5,000 debit
    b. $5,500 credit   d. $5,000 credit

48. In a given department the capacity level of operation for a 4-week period is considered to be 6,000 machine hours, with departmental fixed overhead of $6,000 and variable overhead of $2 per hour. In the 4 weeks just past, this department operated for 4,500 machine hours and had fixed overhead of $6,000 and variable overhead of $10,000. The overhead budget variance for the period was:
    a. $2,000 debit   c. $1,000 debit
    b. $2,000 credit   d. $1,000 credit

49. See question 48. The cost standards for this department provide for 4,300 machine hours for the amount of product actually turned out. The overhead efficiency variance for the period was:
    a. $1,700 debit   c. $600 debit
    b. $3,400 credit   d. $600 credit

50. See questions 48 and 49. The idle capacity variance for the 4-week period was:
    a. $1,500 debit   c. $4,500 credit
    b. $4,500 debit   d. Zero

51. The essential element of "responsibility" accounting is the assigning of responsibility for costs, as they are incurred, to the persons most immediately in a position to control them.
    a. True
    b. False

52. Under a system of responsibility accounting, costs that have once been assigned as the responsibility of one individual are never subsequently transferred to another department.
    a. True
    b. False

53. The term "direct costing" denotes a system in which only the direct costs of material and labor are charged to products.
    a. True
    b. False

54. Under a system of direct costing, fixed costs are known as "period" costs, and they are assigned to products on the basis of predetermined allocation rates.
    a. True
    b. False

55. If the fixed costs for a given period amount to $20,000 and the variable costs are $5 per unit of product, the differential cost of production at 80 percent of capacity (8,000 units) versus production at 60 percent of capacity is:
    a. $10,000   c. $20,000
    b. $14,000   d. Zero

56. See question 55. If we sell our products for cash only, at $10 each, and are able to sell only 6,000 units per period, what percent of bad-debt losses could we afford to incur (and break even on the added sales) if we were to increase our sales to 8,000 units by allowing the new customers to charge their purchases?
    a. 20 percent   c. 50 percent
    b. 30 percent

57. Your accountant presents the following analysis of cost and profit data with respect to a component part:

Comparative Costs

	To make	To buy
Direct materials	$ 50	$ —
Direct labor	30	—
Variable factory overhead	30	—
Nonvariable factory overhead	20	—
General administrative overhead	10	2
Purchasing overhead, nonvariable	10	15
Normal profit margin	50	—
Invoice cost of complete part	—	120
	$200	$137

If your make-or-buy decision is to be resolved on the basis of incremental (differential) costs, the decision should be to:
a. Buy
b. Make

58. See question 57. The unit differential cost of producing the part internally appears to be approximately:
a. $100   c. $50
b. $110   d. $120

59. See question 57. If your make-or-buy decision is to be resolved on the basis of full, or total, costs, the decision should be:
a. Buy
b. Make

60. See question 57. The numbers to be compared in arriving at the decision in question 59 are:
a. $130 and $120   c. $150 and $137
b. $140 and $120   d. $200 and $137

61. You are contemplating purchase of an item of machinery and your accountant provides you with the following data:
Invoice cost of machine, $25,000; installation cost, $5,000; probable useful life, 10 years, with no salvage value.
Benefits from machine: labor cost saving of $10,000 per year.
Operating costs of machine per year: power, $2,000; maintenance, $1,000; depreciation, $3,000; sundry cash costs, $1,000. The estimated approximate payback period for this machine on the basis of the available data is:
a. 10 years   c. 5 years
b. 6 years   d. 4 years

62. Would acquisition of the machine of question 61 be justified if you decide it must produce a 15 percent (before-tax) rate of return over its lifetime? (NOTE: the present value of $1 per year for 10 years, discounted at 15 percent per period, is approximately $5.02).
a. Yes, by a considerable margin (more than $2,000)
b. Yes, by a narrow margin
c. No, by a considerable margin (more than $2,000)
b. No, by a very narrow margin.

63. See question 62. In order to estimate the probable rate of return to be earned by a new machine, we assume that our cost (assume $30,000) represents the present value, at our

effective earning rate, of the future periodic cash flow (assume $6,000 per period). Thus, for each $1 of cash flow we will have to invest $30,000/$6,000 = $5. By reference to compound-interest tables for 10-year periods, we find the present value of $1 per period that most nearly approximates $5. The column in which this amount appears will be headed by the sought-for interest rate. In the present case the rate is approximately:

a. 5 percent   c. 20 percent
b. 10 percent   d. 15 percent

64. Consolidated statements automatically contain at least some element of fiction.
   a. True
   b. False

65. The terms "consolidated" and "combined" statements have the same meaning for accounting purposes.
   a. True
   b. False

66. When one company owns sufficient voting stock of another company to be able to exercise a major influence upon the decisions of the other company, the two companies are properly referred to as:
   a. Affiliated companies
   b. Consolidated companies

67. One of the principal tasks to be performed in the preparation of consolidated statements is that of eliminating intercompany items.
   a. True
   b. False

68. Entries for eliminations referred to in question 67 are not made on the books of either the parent or its subsidiaries— they are, essentially, worksheet entries.
   a. True
   b. False

69. The stockholders' equity of Sub Co. stands as follows on the date when Parent Co. acquires 80 percent of Sub Co. common stock for $2,000,000, cash:

Capital stock, common, par $10	$1,000,000
Retained earnings	500,000

If the other assets of Sub Co. are already reasonably valued in their balance sheet, preparation of a consolidated balance sheet at date of acquisition would probably call for recognition of goodwill amounting to:

    a. $500,000   c. $800,000

    b. $1,000,000   d. Zero

70. To reflect acquisition of the Sub Co. stock (see question 69), Parent Co. would record a credit to cash and debit(s) to:

    a. The various assets held by Sub Co. plus goodwill

    b. Intercompany liabilities

    c. Investment in Subsidiary

71. See question 70. On Sub Co. books, entries must be made to mirror those made by Parent Co. at date of acquisition.

    a. True

    b. False

72. The preparation of a consolidated balance sheet commonly requires elimination from Inventories, and correspondingly from Retained Earnings, of the amount of profits (booked by any of the affiliates) resulting from sales among affiliates and upon which the profits have not yet been "realized" through sale to outsiders.

    a. True

    b. False

73. In the preparation of consolidated income statements the key principle is that sales and expenses representing strictly transactions between affiliates must be eliminated.

    a. True

    b. False

74. The term *deferred debit,* or *deferred charge,* refers to account balances that now show on the asset side of the balance sheet and will later show up in the income statement as expenses (charges against income).

    a. True

    b. False

75. The term *deferred credit* refers to account balances that are now shown on the right-hand side of the balance sheet and will later show up in the income statement as credits (additions to income).

    a. True

    b. False

76. Income taxes have characteristics similar to the various classes of operating expenses and accordingly should be matched, as realistically as is feasible, against the income to which they pertain.
    a. True
    b. False

77. If we, as lessors of machinery, collect rentals in advance for the next year, our accountant should record the receipts as a debit to Cash and should make a credit to:
    a. A revenue account (such as Lease Revenue)
    b. A deferred credit account (such as Deferred Lease Income)

78. See question 77. If we are required to pay income tax this year on the advance leasehold collections, our accountant should record the payment (or accrual) as a credit to Cash (or Taxes Payable) and a debit to:
    a. Income Tax Expense
    b. Deferred Income Tax

79. In the case of certain types of installment sales, the income of which is fully recognized in the books at date of sale but is deferred for income tax purposes until collections are made, tax allocation is accomplished in the period of sale by:
    a. Making credits to a deferred credit account
    b. Making credits to an accrued tax liability account

80. If the depreciation that we record on our books is less than that reported on our tax return and we fail to make tax allocation entries, then our current income will be:
    a. Overstated
    b. Understated

81. The tax allocation entry appropriate for question 80 consists of a debit to tax expense accounts and a credit to:
    a. Deferred income tax credit
    b. Accrued income tax liability

82. If in a given period we record expenses which are not allowable as tax deductions until a later period, we must make appropriate tax allocation entries so that our net income will not be:
    a. Overstated
    b. Understated

83. The term *net assets* means:
    a. Total assets minus total liabilities
    b. Plant assets minus allowances for depreciation
    c. Receivables minus allowance for uncollectibles
    d. The sum of (b) and (c)

84. If our company takes over another company by buying all of the net assets or all of the common stock of the other company for cash, the transaction is properly termed:
    a. An acquisition (purchase)
    b. A pooling of interests

85. If our company issues common stock to another company in exchange for all of the other's net assets or to the other's stockholders in exchange for all of the common stock, the transaction is properly treated as:
    a. An acquisition (purchase)
    b. A pooling of interests

86. In the case of an acquisition (purchase), good accounting requires that the acquired assets be recorded at reasonably current (appraised) values and that goodwill (or other intangibles) be recognized in the event that the purchase price exceeds the aggregate appraised values of the tangible assets minus liabilities.
    a. True
    b. False

87. If the transaction whereby Company A takes over the business of Company B is interpreted and accounted for as an acquisition, the probabilities are that the reported income for the ensuing period will be somewhat different than if the transaction is handled as a pooling of interests. How different?
    a. Larger
    b. Smaller

88. If Company A and Company B have $100,000 each in properly recognized goodwill and the companies are joined through a pooling of interests, the new initial balance sheet must show goodwill of $200,000.
    a. True
    b. False

89. An alleged advantage of pooling of interests, as compared with purchase acquisitions, is that:

   a. No newly recognized goodwill is created
   b. All existing goodwill must be recognized

90. Another alleged advantage of poolings of interests is that the net assets of all of the pooled companies:
   a. Are recognized at their current (appraised) values
   b. Are carried forward at their existing book values

91. Goodwill recognized in the process of an acquisition:
   a. Must be kept on the books permanently
   b. Must be amortized over a period of reasonable length
   c. Must immediately be charged off to Retained Earnings

92. It is not proper to account for a business combination by the acquisition method if the combination was effected by the giving of preferred stock, or bonds payable, of Company A for the common stock outstanding of Company B.
   a. True
   b. False

93. Assume an employee earned $500 per week in the base period and is still earning the same wage when the cost-of-living index has risen 100 percent. What fraction of the base-period purchasing power does the employee now retain?
   a. 100 percent
   b. 50 percent
   c. 33 percent

94. See question 93. Assume the consumer price index rises from 100 to 300. Same question as in question 93.
   a. 100 percent
   b. 50 percent
   c. 33 percent

95. See question 94. In terms of "now" dollars, what was the employee earning per week in the base period?
   a. $500
   b. $1,000
   c. $1,500

96. Assume our employee had debts of $10,000 at the end of the base period and that they remain unpaid (and unchanged) now that the index is at 300. The employee now

owes $10,000. What was the employee's base period debt in terms of current ("now") dollars?
a. $10,000
b. $20,000
c. $30,000

97. Our corporation invested $100,000 in land when the general price index stood at 120. Currently the same index stands at 150. What is the amount of our investment in land, stated in terms of current dollars?
a. $150,000
b. $120,000
c. $125,000

98. Our sales for the year total $1,500, and they were spread evenly throughout the year. The consumer price index rose at an even rate from 120 on January 1 to 130 on December 31, for an average of 125 during the year. What is the amount of our sales for the year as stated in end-of-year dollars?
a. $1,950
b. $1,800
c. $1,625
d. $1,560

99. Our depreciation cost as recorded for the current year amounted to $2,600. It was made up of 10 percent of $10,000 invested in plant when the price index stood at 80, plus 8 percent of $20,000 invested when the index stood at 100. Assume the index now stands at 150. Translate the $2,600 into current dollars.
a. $3,900
b. $4,275
c. $4,875

100. Our stockholders invested $1,000 in year 1 (when consumer price index was at 100) and $3,000 in year 8 (consumer price index was then at 150). Assume the current price index is 200. If the net assets of the company, when translated into current dollars, now total $5,500 (and no dividend has ever been paid), the accumulated results of operations to date reflect:
a. Net gain of $1,500
b. Net loss of $1,000
c. Net loss of $500

Name_____

Address_____

City_____ State____Zip_____

Final Examination Answer Sheet: The McGraw-Hill 36-Hour Accounting Course

See instructions on page 1 of the Final Examination.

1. _____	21. _____	41. _____	61. _____	81. _____
2. _____	22. _____	42. _____	62. _____	82. _____
3. _____	23. _____	43. _____	63. _____	83. _____
4. _____	24. _____	44. _____	64. _____	84. _____
5. _____	25. _____	45. _____	65. _____	85. _____
6. _____	26. _____	46. _____	66. _____	86. _____
7. _____	27. _____	47. _____	67. _____	87. _____
8. _____	28. _____	48. _____	68. _____	88. _____
9. _____	29. _____	49. _____	69. _____	89. _____
10. _____	30. _____	50. _____	70. _____	90. _____
11. _____	31. _____	51. _____	71. _____	91. _____
12. _____	32. _____	52. _____	72. _____	92. _____
13. _____	33. _____	53. _____	73. _____	93. _____
14. _____	34. _____	54. _____	74. _____	94. _____
15. _____	35. _____	55. _____	75. _____	95. _____
16. _____	36. _____	56. _____	76. _____	96. _____
17. _____	37. _____	57. _____	77. _____	97. _____
18. _____	38. _____	58. _____	78. _____	98. _____
19. _____	39. _____	59. _____	79. _____	99. _____
20. _____	40. _____	60. _____	80. _____	100. _____

About the Authors

Robert L. Dixon, Ph.D., CPA, is Professor Emeritus of Accounting, Graduate School of Business Administration, University of Michigan, where he taught from 1942 to 1974. Previously he taught at Yale and the University of Chicago and held the position of guest professor at MIT, the University of California, and North Texas University.

His nonteaching experience includes public accounting, consulting, and work on the principal committees of the American Accounting Association, American Institute of CPAs, and the National Association of Accountants. He has served as editor of the *Accounting Review,* president of the American Accounting Association, and AICPA Distinguished Visiting Professor. He is the author of two other books and numerous articles in professional publications.

Harold E. Arnett, Ph.D., CPA, CMA, is Professor of Accounting, School of Business Administration, University of Michigan, where he has taught since 1962. Previously he was a research associate at the American Institute of Certified Public Accountants.

He has authored many articles and seven books and monographs, served on numerous committees of a number of business and professional organizations, as well as consulted for businesses and business organizations.